The Mythic Meanings of the Second Amendment

DAVID C. WILLIAMS

The Mythic Meanings of the Second Amendment

TAMING POLITICAL VIOLENCE IN
A CONSTITUTIONAL REPUBLIC

Yale University Press
New Haven
& London

Earlier versions of some of the arguments in this book appeared in the following law journal articles, and they appear here with the following permissions: David C. Williams, *Civic Republicanism and the Citizen Militia: The Terrifying Second Amendment,* 101 Yale Law Journal 551–615 (1991), by permission of the Yale Law Journal Company and William S. Hein Company; David C. Williams, *The Unitary Second Amendment,* 73 N.Y.U. L.Rev. 822–30 (1998), by permission of the New York University Law Review; David C. Williams, *The Constitutional Right to "Conservative" Revolution,* 32 Harv. C.R.-C.L. L.Rev. 413–47 (1997), © (1997) by the President and Fellows of Harvard College and the Harvard Civil Rights-Civil Liberties Law Review; David C. Williams, *The Militia Movement and Second Amendment Revolution: Conjuring with the People,* 81 Cornell L. Rev. 879–952 (1996), by permission of the Cornell Law Review; David C. Williams, *Constitutional Tales of Violence: Populists, Outgroups, and the Multicultural Landscape of the Second Amendment,* 74 Tul. L.Rev. 387–494 (1999), by permission of the Tulane Law Review Association, which holds the copyright.

Set in Sabon type by Keystone Typesetting, Inc.
Printed in the United States of America by

Library of Congress Cataloging-in-Publication Data
Williams, David C., 1960–
The mythic meanings of the Second Amendment : taming political violence in a constitutional republic / David C. Williams.
p. cm.
Includes bibliographical references.
ISBN 0-300-09562-7 (alk. paper)
1. United States. Constitution. 2nd Amendment — History. 2. Firearms — Law and legislation — United States — History. 3. Political violence — United States — History. 4. Government, Resistance to — United States — History. 5. United States — Militia. I. Title.
KF4558 2nd .W55 2003
344.73'0533 — dc21
2002011549

A catalogue record for this book is available from the British Library.

The paper in this book meets the guidelines for permanence and durability of the Committee on Production Guidelines for Book Longevity of the Council on Library Resources.

10 9 8 7 6 5 4 3 2 1

For Susan, Benjamin, and Sarah

Contents

Acknowledgments

The right to bear arms is one of the most contentious subjects in modern America. Nonetheless, in writing on this topic for the past decade, I have been struck most not by the level of vitriol, but by the kindness, support, and generosity that many interlocutors have shown me, even across intellectual divides. Whenever I get discouraged, these colleagues remind me by example that informed, open-minded discussion is possible even on highly charged subjects. They renew my faith in the scholarly enterprise. They are too many to list, but I would like to mention Sanford Levinson, Akhil Amar, Frank Michelman, Steven Shiffrin, Glenn Harlan Reynolds, and Steven Heyman. They may not know how large a part they play in my own mythic landscape of the intellectual world, but I am deeply grateful.

For most of the period that I have been studying this subject, it has been my great pleasure to work at the Indiana University School of Law in Bloomington. After wandering far from the Hoosier State, I feel I have returned home to a true community of scholar-teachers. During this time, I have been blessed with a dean and an associate dean the likes of which I did not know the world could boast: Alfred C. Aman and Lauren Robel. Every day, Fred's enthusiasm, intellectualism, support, and example make me want to be a better scholar, and Lauren's sagacity, vision, idealism, and goodness make me want to be a better member of my community. I depend on the care that they have both shown me in such profligate measure.

At every level, I owe the most to my wife, Susan Hoffman Williams, and my children, Benjamin David and Sarah Jordan. For sixteen years, Susan has been my dearest friend and most cherished colleague. The elegance and power of her mind, the courage and compassion of her soul have given me endless inspiration and solace. At the age of eight, Ben has already become an intimate intellectual companion, with his own strong views on the constitutional organization of violence. And at five, Sarah makes the sun to shine merely by smiling.

Introduction

 This book is about the power of constitutional stories to tame the political violence that shapes our lives together. I begin with two very different stories familiar to almost all Americans. They mark out the poles of a continuum of attitudes: we trust the government to use violence against popular uprisings, yet we also distrust it; we trust the people to use violence against the government, yet we distrust them; in short, we believe in revolution, yet we also believe in order.

 Here is the first story: In 1776, the United States of America created itself in a great act of political violence against the British Empire, which was then its constituted government. Ever since, Americans have traced their existence and identity to this moment of bloody revolution. We believe that this origin reveals something fundamental about us. As a result, Americans have celebrated "freedom fighters" around the globe, and we have seen in those fighters an echo of our own birth story. We thus applaud political violence against government — under some circumstances.

 Here is the second story: In 1994, Timothy McVeigh blew up the Murrah Federal Building in Oklahoma City, committing the deadliest terrorist act ever on American soil. In his own mind, McVeigh was following in the footsteps of the Founding Fathers by resisting an oppressive central government. But far from applauding, Americans reacted with revulsion and horror. Today,

McVeigh is remembered not as a hero but as a convicted and executed murderer. He is not alone in this fate: over the decades, many Americans have engaged in violence against a government that they considered hostile, claiming the legacy of 1776. Yet not one of these movements received enough support to achieve its aims; all were eventually branded as criminal acts. Americans, then, fear and loathe political violence against government — under some circumstances.

America, in other words, holds a deeply ambivalent attitude about popular political violence: we approve of it except when we don't. That complicated mindset is built into the English language itself, constructing a conceptual world that shapes our thinking: *revolution* generally connotes legitimate resistance to an illegitimate government, but *rebellion* or *insurrection* connotes illegitimate resistance to a legitimate government. Across the decades, American constitutional and political thinkers have generally drawn this linguistic line: revolution is justifiable, but not rebellion. Yet that nomenclature merely pushes the inquiry back a stage: exactly what constitutes a revolution? and how is it distinguished from a rebellion?

The American constitutional tradition offers an answer to that question. In a nutshell, that answer can be reduced to two claims, which together constitute the thesis of this book. First, the Body of the People, to use the Framers' phrase, has a right to arms so as to make a revolution against a corrupt government. The *Body of the People* and *revolution* are terms of art rich in historical meaning. The Body of the People refers not to unaffiliated individuals but to the people as a whole, assembled in a universal militia and united by a common culture concerning the proper use of political violence. This universal body has the right to make a revolution, defined as a political uprising made by the people as a whole for the good of the whole. Second, Congress, as the ordinary representative of the Body of the People, has the right to maintain forces to suppress rebellions, defined as political uprisings made by a faction for the selfish good of that faction. In common understanding, George Washington made a revolution as the leader of a free and united people; Timothy McVeigh committed an act of rebellion by murdering fellow Americans.

Together, these two claims highlight two themes in the constitutional organization of violence: popular unity and checks and balances. First, the people must possess a high degree of unity on the appropriate use of political violence, and the goal of the Constitution is to allow them to express it. Any single mode of expression — directly in popular movements or indirectly in Congress — may, however, become corrupt. As a result, the Constitution allows the people to express their unity through multiple channels that check and balance each other. So when Congress is the best representative of the Body of the People, it has the right to suppress what it regards as rebellion. But when a popular uprising is the best representative, it has the right to overthrow what it considers to be a tyrannical government.

This constitutional tradition commends itself to our attention for a number of reasons. First, because our Constitution prescribes this answer to the problem of political violence, simple fidelity to that document requires us to grapple with it. Part 1 of this book will undertake that task by examining the Framers' views. Second, this tradition helps to illuminate the present cultural moment: the Constitution's treatment of political violence has become a high-profile item in an ongoing cultural war, and we can understand that war only if we understand the Constitution itself. Part 2 of this book will take up that task by examining the present dialogue on the meaning of the Second Amendment. Third, if wisely adapted to modern-day circumstances, our constitutional tradition may offer good answers to the problem of political violence in the twenty-first century. We need to find such answers now because talk of revolution, acts of rebellion, and the private ownership of firearms have become salient features of the cultural landscape. In the wake of recent harrowing incidents, America has had to confront its conflicted attitudes toward revolution. Part 3 of this book will suggest the concerns that should guide us in that task.

This book is thus about the way the American Constitution seeks to tame political violence. In other words, it addresses the way the Constitution distributes access to the means of violence, primarily firearms, to ensure that political violence is used for constitutional ends. In the modern debate, the principal text is the Second Amendment to the U.S. Constitution: "A well-regulated militia being necessary to the security of a free state, the right of the people to keep and bear arms shall not be infringed."[1] This book is therefore about the Second Amendment, its creation, and the way various people have interpreted it. Even though the Second Amendment has dominated discussion, however, it is not the only constitutional text relevant to the organization of violence. In Article I, the Constitution authorizes state and federal governments to manage a standing army and a militia and to suppress rebellion.[2] Any complete description of the constitutional organization of violence must heed both these sets of provisions.

No task is more fundamental to a constitutional order than the domestication of political violence. A constitution may prescribe a wonderful set of ideals for the conduct of government, one requiring democracy, liberty, equality, and justice. Those ideals will come to nothing, however, unless they rest on a set of supplemental norms designed to ensure that the ideals operate to govern a country in practice. Without these supplemental norms, the constitution will be only a paper wish for a better world, rather than the lived law of the land. Along with separation of powers, distribution of property, the jury system, and others, the constitutional organization of violence is central among these norms. To secure its own realization, a constitution should tell its citizens who gets to use political violence, under what conditions, how much, and to what ends.

Several elements of the claim that a constitution must endeavor to tame political violence bear emphasis. First, because it is so fundamental, the organization of political violence in a constitutional republic is commonly a task for the constitution, rather than for the government, at least in the first instance. The constitutional order may assign that task in whole or in part to a government, but it may also assign it in whole or in part to other groups, as (according to some) the Second Amendment does. Second, a constitutional order must organize and domesticate, rather than simply eliminate, political violence. With the exception of a tiny number of small, short-lived pacifist utopias, no constitution has sought to eradicate all political violence; at a minimum, constitutions give government some kind of police power to control insurrection. And it is important to remember that even this police power is still political violence — and so in need of constitutional justification and domestication. A good constitutional order may therefore minimize political violence, but complete abolition has never been a realistic goal.

Finally, although the constitution must seek to control both political and ordinary private violence, the domestication of political violence may, for two reasons, be the more fundamental task. First, insurrectionary violence may aspire to overthrow the constitutional order itself; only after the constitutional order has yoked in such challenges can it function at all. Second, in domesticating political violence, the constitution must organize the capacity of the government, and even of the constitution itself, for political violence. In other words, the domestication of political violence is part of the construction of the constitutional order itself. By contrast, the control of private violence is analytically a secondary step: once the constitution has organized itself (with its own mechanisms for violence) and reined in political challenges to that organization, it can then turn that organization to the suppression of quotidian criminality.

In organizing political violence, constitutions may deploy two styles of regulation. On the one hand, they may promulgate relatively specific rulelike prescriptions addressed primarily to governmental actors and courts and designed to be implemented like any other legal rule. On the other hand, they may promulgate large mythic stories addressed primarily to the citizenry as a whole and designed to explain to them their fundamental civic morality. In its organization of violence, the American Constitution contains some rulelike material, but in practice it has functioned largely through myth. Accordingly, this book is about the mythic landscape of the Second Amendment and related provisions, in the past, the present, and the future.

For some time, people have told two basic, conflicting myths about the Second Amendment, and these have given rise to the two main schools of thought on the provision's legal meaning: the individual rights school and the states' rights school (sometimes called the collective rights school). The states' rights school rests on a Weberian myth: with the sociologist Max Weber (although usually without referring to him) it holds that one of the defining characteristics of the state is its monopoly on the legitimate use of violence. The state enjoys this monopoly because it best represents the whole polity. Accordingly, private persons have no right to deploy political violence because they will act only in their own partial interests. Weberians recognize the inevitability of political violence, but they believe that humans can find redemption from their own aggression through state building.

When Weberians turn to the Second Amendment, they read it according to this myth. The provision contains two clauses: first, "A well-regulated militia being necessary to the security of a free state," which is sometimes called the purpose clause; and "the right of the people to keep and bear arms shall not be infringed," which is sometimes called the operative language. Each school of interpretation emphasizes a different clause. Weberians emphasize the purpose clause: in their view, this clause explains the whole reason for the provision, namely, to protect "a well-regulated militia." The amendment thus guarantees a right to arms only within the context of a militia, not an individual right to arms for self-defense or hunting. This school further argues that the amendment refers to a state militia, not a private one of the sort that has appeared on the American cultural landscape. They point out that eighteenth-century militias were creatures of the state, and they assert that the amendment's reference to a well-regulated militia suggests a militia regulated by the state. In short, then, this interpretation of the Second Amendment offers a Weberian view of the world: the provision protects only the right of the state to employ violence, and it delegitimates any rival power center that might hanker after armed might.

Such a view has obvious attractions to those in power. Although the Supreme Court has not offered a definitive interpretation of the amendment, the lower federal courts have generally adopted the states' rights view. Until recently, so did most establishment lawyers and legal academics. Yet the contrapuntal view, the individual rights school, has always sounded its discordant notes to a receptive popular audience, in the materials of the National Rifle Association (NRA), gun magazines, and op-ed articles in local newspapers. In the past decade, a large number of legal academics have joined the individual rights school, giving it greatly increased intellectual credibility.

In reading the Second Amendment, the individual rights school begins with the operative language: "The right of the people to keep and bear arms shall not be infringed." According to this view, the term *people* self-evidently refers to private individuals, so the Second Amendment protects a personal right to arms. When they turn to the purpose clause, these writers argue that eighteenth-century militias were universal, including every male citizen of arms-bearing age, and that these citizens were expected to bring their private arms to muster. When the Framers guaranteed a right to arms within the militia, therefore, they were ipso facto guaranteeing a universal right to private arms.

The organizing myths that undergird this interpretation are old and complex. Until recently, the individual rights school focused largely on the importance of private self-defense; the school paid scant attention to the issue of political violence. The focus on self-defense stems from a familiar story about the social contract: once upon a time, people existed in a state of nature. In this state, they could defend their natural rights as they saw fit, but, lacking a government, their condition was perilous. As a result, they entered the social contract to secure their own safety. Unfortunately, government cannot always protect its citizens, so people reserved from governmental powers the right of personal self-defense. Once again, this reading recognizes the inevitability of violence, but it promises redemption through personal defense: though there may be savages loose in the world, we each have the ability to hold off tragedy if we are alert and armed.

Anyone who has perused the pages of gun magazines will recognize the pervasiveness and power of this story. Yet this self-defense myth does not pose a fundamental challenge to government: it proposes that private persons should be allowed to resist only private attackers, not government agents. It portrays government not as oppressive but as incapable of being everywhere at once. Indeed, its internal logic suggests that more government might actually be better: if there really were a cop on every corner, we would be safer from criminals. As a result, although this story may have political implications, it is not about political violence, by or against government.

America has, however, also embraced another myth of popular arming, one that has everything to do with political violence. This populist myth may be even more central to our self-conception than the self-defense myth, and lately it has reemerged in the national consciousness with great potency. The NRA, many legal scholars, and the militia movement have contended that the Second Amendment guarantees a private right to arms so that the people can resist a corrupt government. In this familiar story, the people (imagined as an entity composed of individuals but somehow always acting with a single will) create government for certain ends; the government, however, sometimes becomes corrupt, serving its own interests rather than the public good; when the corruption becomes bad enough, the people have a right to revolt, overthrowing the current government and installing a more faithful one. For this reason, the people need to have private arms, and so the Second Amendment guarantees them that right.

Both of these myths, the populist and the Weberian, are powerful and venerable, and both illuminate important political truths. They are also, however, dangerously one-sided. Neither offers a balanced account of the Second Amendment or a satisfying approach to the problem of political violence. Put bluntly: in promising safety through a state monopoly on violence, the Weberian myth blinds itself to the atrocities that governments have visited on their citizens, especially in the twentieth century; correlatively, in promising safety through the private possession of guns, the populist myth blinds itself to the atrocities that private citizens have visited on other private citizens and government officials, especially in acts of rebellion and terrorism. The two myths advertise themselves as being hardheaded and realistic, and so they are — when specifying who should *not* possess the ultimate means of violence. The Weberian myth realizes that the people may not be the virtuous yeomanry of populist myth, and the populist myth realizes that the government may not be the impartial administration of Weberian myth. Yet when these accounts turn to considering who *should* possess the ultimate means of violence, they become oddly naive. The very populists who document government horrors in exacting detail seem to suffer from historical amnesia when they turn to the people. And the very Weberians who vividly portray the mass murders made possible by private gun ownership become unaccountably trusting when they reflect on governmental power.

Why are these myths so trusting in some ways and distrusting in others? Any Second Amendment myth confronts an unsettling truth: violence is an endemic part of human social organization. As a result, no country or citizen can ever rest secure that the future will be entirely under control — or even safe. Most Americans would prefer not to dwell too long on this truth. Comfortable in their powerful, stable country, many manage to convince themselves that Americans will never face revolution from within or oppression from above, as so many other countries have. But our Second Amendment myths force us to confront that stark possibility. The prospect can be terrifying, bringing on despair or cynicism: we may have a natural right to take up arms against a sea of troubles, but those with the most guns win. The alternative to despair is to try to domesticate violence through constitutional myths and structures. Yet given the facts of history, success seems fragile and uncertain. Given enough time, countries tend to break down, and so our comfortable lives could become chaotic and tragic. Desiring reassurance (even if it is illusory), we may reach for comforting but overeasy answers. Believing in a myth that promises safety, who would not be tempted to refrain from inquiring too closely into whether the myth can deliver on its promise?

And that is exactly what the Weberians and populists do. Facing full-on the terrible face of political violence, they look for someone to trust with the means of violence, a backstop to ensure that America will never become like Soviet Russia or the Balkans. In their view, if only we trust the state or the people with the means of violence, then all will be well. Like a child's magic blanket that will ward off the demons of the dark, this trust, if it can be sustained, will allow us to sleep at night. But it comes at an unacceptable cost: we must never examine too critically whether the people or the state really warrants that blind trust.

Any adequate account of the constitutional organization of violence must therefore not flinch from recognizing the dangers of political violence on all sides, from the state and from private people. This book offers such an account. It relies on a myth that once had currency in American constitutional thinking but has lost ground in the cultural battlefields of the past hundred years. In my view, this myth is more consistent with the history and language of the Constitution, and it better suits contemporary needs.

This account might be called the Framers' myth because its origin lies in the thinking of those who created our original constitutional scheme for taming violence. Rather than relying exclusively on the views of those who supported Article I (with its progovernment tilt) or those who supported the Second Amendment (with its promilitia tilt), it reads both together as part of a single document. It begins with the claim that a democratic polity can effectively domesticate violence only if the great bulk of the people—the Body of the People, as the Framers would have said—agree on a shared set of norms for the appropriate use of political violence and are prepared to defend those norms. If those conditions are not met, then it is unlikely that a democracy can long survive. The most important Second Amendment activity, therefore, is to secure those conditions. If those conditions are met, however, then the Body of the People has the right to exercise political violence in accord with those norms, that is, for what might be called the common good or the good of the whole. In accord with this myth, therefore, we should read the Second Amendment to guarantee arms neither to the state simpliciter nor to private individuals simpliciter but to this collective people. The first theme in this myth is therefore popular unity on the use of political violence.

The second theme, however, is checks and balances: the people should have multiple mechanisms through which to express their unity because every mechanism is potentially fallible. Most commonly, the people will speak through their elected representatives, especially Congress, which represents the whole. For that reason, Article I of the Constitution gives Congress (acting as an agent of the people) the right to suppress rebellions made by a faction against the good of the whole, especially local insurrections for local ends with the connivance of the local militia. Sometimes, however, governments become corrupt, acting in their own interests. For that reason, the Second Amendment recognizes the right of the people-in-militia to make a revolution for the good of the whole. Either way, the goal is the same: allowing the people to control the means of violence for the common good. Rebellion and tyranny are similar in that both pursue the good of the faction. For that reason, the people in their various manifestations should have the ability to suppress both.

The contrasts between the Framers' myth and the Weberian and populist myths are several.First, the latter two are institutionally simple: they insist that we should trust the state or private individuals as the ultimate bulwark of virtue. By contrast, the Framers' myth is institutionally complicated: recognizing that neither can be wholly trusted, it counterbalances the people-in-Congress and the people-in-militia in the taming of political violence. It maintains that revolutions against government are legitimate, but it also understands that rebels are inclined to think of themselves as revolutionaries and that governments are inclined to find revolutionaries rebellious. Accordingly, the Constitution does not grant government a monopoly on the use of force, but neither does it insist that the government let seditious movements flourish.

In addition, even the people-in-militia — the most populist element in this balance, the one celebrated by the Second Amendment, and in some ways the linchpin of the whole scheme — was itself a complex institution. Contra the Weberian and populist myths, the universal militia was not identical to either the state or the mass of private citizens but drew features from both. On the one hand, the militia had important connections to the government: the state raised it, so as to ensure that it would be universal (and not just a faction) and trained it to be virtuous (and not just self-interested). Existing for public purposes and in the public realm, the militia was very much a public institution. It cannot be reduced to the mass of private individuals, in all their self-serving multiplicity, with guns in their closets and suspicions about the government. On the other hand, the militia cannot be described as simply a servant of the legislature. Once the government erected the necessary scaffolding by which the militia could build itself, the militia had to exercise independent judgment. If the government should become corrupt, the Framers expected the militia to rise, acting on its conscience as a truer representative of the people than the government itself. Indeed, the Framers constantly contrasted a militia with a standing army, which would perform whatever odious task the government assigned it. Because it might have to create a revolution for the whole, the militia had to include the whole people-in-arms. In other words, it included the mass of private citizens; but those citizens existed in a common framework, and in the absence of that frame they became something else.

The second difference between the Framers' myth and the other Second Amendment myths involves the issue of shared norms. The Framers' story maintains that a polity can discipline political violence only if the citizenry generally shares a body of norms on its appropriate use. Indeed, this social covenant must be in place before any particular distribution of arms can do any good. From the Framers' perspective, therefore, it would be pointless to specify who gets to own guns if we are deeply fragmented on this subject. Instead, one must first heal the underlying division, so as to produce the appropriate social conditions for any distribution of arms.

The Framers recalled such common purpose in their own, recent revolution against Great Britain, and they anticipated that the militia, universal and trained to be virtuous, would show such unity. They did not deny that differences existed among Americans, and an emerging liberal ideology even celebrated those dissimilarities, within limits. But on the subject of the proper use of political violence, the Framers showed a distinct monoculturalist streak. Some yearned for a time when all citizens had a common, undifferentiated identity, but even those who welcomed modernization agreed that in this area Americans needed something like consensus. The alternatives were unthinkable: a fractious population kept in line by a domineering government or savage civil war.

That insight of the Framers' myth has much to offer the present debate. As the various sides have made clear, we will not find safety in trusting either the government or private individuals with the ultimate means of violence. Only broad-based support for a set of shared norms on political violence can reduce the danger of tyranny or chaos. The dialogue we need, therefore, is one that will search out and nurture such shared norms. Unfortunately, the debate over the Second Amendment exhibits the opposite characteristics: on both sides it is angry and fearful. Many of those in favor of gun control dislike and distrust ordinary gun owners; they want to control them, even to eliminate their "gun culture." Those in favor of gun rights often turn to talk of revolution because they believe the government no longer cares about them, dominated as it is by "special interests" rather than true-blue gun-owning Americans. Even some members of traditional outgroups like Jews, African Americans, and feminists have turned to self-arming as a way to break the power of anti-Semitism, white supremacy, and the patriarchy. Far from being a way to build consensus, discussion of the right to arms has become a means to express anger and despair over political solutions, limned by the prospect of violence. Indeed, in much right-to-arms rhetoric, one senses almost a yearning for violence as an alternative to the frustrating world of politics.

Because polities originate in and maintain themselves through violence, our Second Amendment stories go to the heart of our self-conception. The present mythic landscape of the Second Amendment reveals an American citizenry that despairs of finding unity. In many of its manifestations, the populist myth rests on a broad belief in redemptive violence. This belief, which underlies much of American culture, posits that chaos, usually in the form of an ethnic, racial, or political Other, constantly threatens to destroy civilization and that only violent resistance can save the world by securing order. When the Second Amendment is understood as the right of American citizens (representing civilization) to resist the forces of tyranny (the governmental Other), it takes its cultural power from this broader myth. That account, however, tends to become self-consuming. In arming to resist the forces of darkness, citizens often model themselves on those very forces. Revolutions that begin as a fight against oppression often become themselves oppressive once the genie of violence is out of the bottle. Thus, in imagining a threatening Other, the populist myth sows the seeds of distrust that will ultimately destroy the unity on which the Second Amendment depends. Populists may respond that we should simply trust the people, but revolutionary peoples have worked many of the great atrocities of the twentieth century.

On superficial inspection, the Weberian myth seems very different from the populist belief in redemptive violence. Whereas the populist myth celebrates resistance to an oppressive Other, the Weberian seeks to eliminate resistance through its state monopoly of violence. Most Weberians believe that in confining power to the government they are avoiding the dangerous American romance with redemptive violence. Instead, they hope for a European-style state, peaceful, well-ordered, and tolerant, that finds violence a distasteful necessity rather than an ennobling challenge.

In fact, however, the Weberian and populist myths have more in common than that characterization would allow. In the American climate, both accounts tell a story of a fragmented society in which one sector uses violence to control the other, "deviant" group. For modern Weberians, the government should vanquish and disarm dissident groups (imagined as culturally variant from Weberians themselves), through force if necessary. Rather than popular violence, the Weberians romanticize the strong arm of government that will discipline its rebellious children to make the world safe for its good, that is, Weberian, children. In much the same way, populists believe that citizens should vanquish and disarm dissident groups (a government that has lost connection to the people), through force if necessary. The myths disagree only on who will be disarmed and who will do the disarming. Thus, as divergent as the Weberian and populist readings are, they both take distrust and fragmentation as givens, and they both posit violence as a way to control that division. In other words, they imagine violence as the answer to a fractious population.

The Framers' myth, by contrast, starts at the other end of the problem: it imagines a harmonious population as the only possible answer to violence. And that point leads to the third difference between the Framers' myth and the other Second Amendment myths: the Framers' account necessarily aims to transform the world, so as to secure its own preconditions, while the others ratify reality as they find it. For the Framers' myth to work, Americans must share a social covenant on the use of political violence, and they must be able to express that covenant through the multiple channels of a system of checks and balances. There is reason to believe that those conditions do not hold today. The mythic landscape of the Second Amendment itself suggests that Americans do not share a body of norms on the appropriate use of political violence or on the right system of checks and balances to cabin that violence. More broadly, many commentators have noted the general absence of shared frameworks beyond individual preference.

We are, in other words, in something of a quiet crisis: our prevailing myths do not adequately domesticate political violence, and the Framers' myth no longer suits our lived social reality. We enjoy relatively low levels of political violence nowadays because most people feel relatively complacent. Political violence has, however, been an endemic part of the American landscape. Even today, alienated people vent their frustration through acts of terrorism, and if the reigning complacency vanishes, we may see a general turn to bloody direct action. We need, in short, to reconstruct the Framers' myth by adapting it to present realities. That reconstruction will involve developing myths and practices that will help us to generate shared norms and a system of checks and balances through which to express them. Although courts and legislatures can play important roles in facilitating and even guiding this reconstruction, it must ultimately belong to the citizenry because they bear the responsibility of making themselves over into a Body of the People. In other words, the Second

Amendment will function, as it always has, more as a regulative ideal, a grand myth for the citizens, than as a codelike legal provision for judges and lawyers.

Although I will suggest some general directions for this process, the real work can occur only in popular dialogue on the taming of violence. In that dialogue, Americans might rearrange the mythic landscape of the Second Amendment to make room for themselves as a people, rather than merely individuals submissive to or resentful of the rule of government. As a result, there is only so much that any commentator can say on this subject without presuming to substitute his judgment for the citizenry's. Nonetheless, I think this book can offer two caveats on reconstructing the constitutional organization of violence.

First, we cannot simply and passively apply the Framers' vision to modern circumstances; instead, it must be adapted and reconstructed. The Framers imagined the Body of the People expressing its norms through a universal militia and through Congress. Institutionally, today, we do not have a universal militia. Culturally, we do not now constitute a Body of the People with shared norms on the organization of violence. Indeed, commentators on the Second Amendment find the whole concept of the Body of the People so foreign that they imagine the Framers must have meant either private individuals or state governments. We live among the wreckage of this myth, and we cannot simply live it out today. We must therefore dispense with the game of Capture-the-Framers, in which each side insists that the Framers give clear instructions about modern social reality.

If we are to reconstruct the Framers' myth, then, we will have to begin by changing our reality to secure some of the preconditions under which it made sense. And in the modern world, those preconditions cannot be exactly the same as those the Framers imagined in the eighteenth century. For example, it is still true that we need a consensus culture on political violence, a culture that can shield the weak under its wings. Yet we have become much more individualistic, diverse, and multicultural than the America of the eighteenth century. Constitutional law has ratified that change, and most Americans celebrate it. Our unity cannot therefore be their unity; it must preserve the freedoms and difference that we have come to cherish, within an overarching commitment to taming violence together. Similarly, we will not likely revive a universal militia soon, and if we did we would not likely vest it with the power to overthrow governments. We could, however, incrementally diffuse partial responsibility for taming violence among a variety of responsible groups, rendering them the codefenders of their social covenant.

The second caveat to the popular dialogue on reconstructing the Second Amendment is that we need radically to shift the focus of the debate, by asking a radically different question. To date, we have been pondering how we might best distribute guns when Americans are deeply divided and intent on killing each other. There is, however, no good answer to that question: if we are deeply divided, governments will probably hurt us, and so will our fellow citizens. We must instead go back to a prior and more fundamental question: how do we secure the necessary normative consensus that will allow us to tame violence and to realize the Framers' myth to the extent possible under modern circumstances?

When we try to answer that question, the Second Amendment may take on a quite unfamiliar aspect. Instead of standing simply as a warning of the need for continual vigilance against the perfidy of others, it may also remind us of the importance and fragility of civic solidarity. The myth does not propose pacifism; it accepts that political violence will be with us always. And it does not propose a sentimental willingness to trust the untrustworthy; sometimes the people must suppress those who would hurt the common good. But this myth also recognizes that the seeds of danger lie as much within Us as within Them. Political violence by anyone can poison the wielders as easily as redeem. For safety from ourselves, then, we must look not to the reassuring feel of a gun but to our devotion to each other as coparticipants in a collective enterprise to make life worth living. Ideally, then, the Constitution should nourish that devotion among the people, a form of civic love, but the modern debate over the Second Amendment is characterized primarily by mutual suspicion and hostility.

Many Second Amendment mythographers may find the search for peoplehood naive and futile. They would urge us to accept human nature as they find it, fractious and unreliable, and find a structure to control it. The Framers' myth, however, finds that exhortation itself unrealistic: if the citizenry is deeply divided and violently inclined, tinkering with the allocation of guns will not save us from political dissolution. As frightening as that truth may be, we have no option but to work for solidarity on this subject. As a result, we are profoundly dependent on other people for our safety. In that sense, realism about the constitutional organization of violence actually demands hope: if political life comes down to force, we must hope that the people have the wisdom and love to use it for good ends. In the constitutional search to tame violence, perhaps the Second Amendment could serve most centrally as a symbol of that hope.

PART **I**

The Framers' Constitution

For some time, the bulk of commentary on the original meaning of the Second Amendment has been divided into two camps: the individual rights school, which reads the provision as a guarantee of an individual right to arms, and the states', or collective, rights school, which reads the provision as a protection for state-run militias. The division between the two camps has become stark, hostile, and creedal. Each side repeats its arguments and cites its proof texts with unfailing enthusiasm. Even though each school includes scholars of great stature, some in each camp claim that all their opponents lack intellectual credibility and have not a shred of evidence for their view. The very language of the amendment seems to encourage this dichotomous approach: to modern eyes, the purpose clause suggests that the amendment is about supporting a state militia, but the operative language suggests it is really about protecting a right of the people, meaning, according to some, private individuals.[1]

Is there any way to reconcile these dichotomous approaches, to move forward from this stalled trench warfare? In fact, there is: the Framers wrote the Second Amendment to protect the Body of the People, an entity reducible to neither the state nor private individuals but exhibiting qualities of both. Although raised by the state, the people-in-militia is not simply a servant of the government; instead, the Framers expected that if the state should become corrupt, the militia would rise against it. And although composed of private individuals, the Body of the People is not identical to them either: it is the people acting as a unified entity for the common good, not private persons acting on their own. My review of the historical material will therefore document two propositions about the Second Amendment: first, contra the states' rights theory, the Framers meant to recognize a right to arms for popular resistance to government; second, contra the individual rights theory, that right belonged not to individuals but to the people as a collective entity.

The Second Amendment, moreover, is not the only constitutional provision relevant to the constitutional organization of violence. If the Second Amendment gives the people the right to own arms so as to resist government, Article I gives Congress the right to raise armies and militias so as to resist insurrection. To modern eyes, these paired provisions seem to set up a profound tension: the people have the right to revolt, but Congress has the right to kill any revolt in the bud. In fact, when we examine these provisions in historical context, the tension is more apparent than real. Overall, the Constitution seeks to ensure that the people may make a revolution but that factions may not make rebellions. To that end, the Constitution offers the people two means of expression when it comes to using political violence: the first, through the militia, is direct and decentralized; the second, through Congress, is representative and centralized. Each has its advantages. Together, they offer a system of checks and balances to maximize the chance that revolutions will live and rebellions wither on the vine. The following historical account will therefore advance a third proposition, one that concerns not just the Second Amendment but the Constitution as a whole: this document does not commit ultimate control over political violence to any one entity; instead, it erects a system of checks and balances, the better to ensure the long-term safety of its citizens.

As background, I want first to explain what lawyers do, or should do, when they search historical records for legal meaning. This explanation is especially important because the debate over the historical meaning of the Second Amendment has become acrimonious. Such acrimony may grow out of the nature of the evidence: it is simultaneously too copious and too skimpy. On the one hand, there is too much evidence: people in the late eighteenth century had a lot to say about the right to arms, and a lot of it was contradictory. As a result, scholars can always find quotations from important men to support a position. On the other hand, there is too little evidence: the Framers offered surprisingly few direct expositions of the legal meaning of the Second Amendment, as opposed to their general musings on the abstract right to arms. As a result, relatively few authoritative pronouncements from the 1780s and 1790s exist, leaving modern commentators free to roam far afield in search of statements that reinforce their position.

In reviewing this material, therefore, I propose to observe four caveats that may help make the debate more balanced and productive. First, we must consider all the evidence, not merely the portions that support our preferred position. For example, as we shall see, the militia of the 1780s had a dual nature: it was raised and trained by the state to ensure its universality and its virtue, but it was also a popular body ready to resist government. Both of these facts are important, but each side in the current debate emphasizes only one. Many individual rights theorists emphasize the militia's universality to argue that it was really just another way of referring to private gun owners. By contrast, many states' rights theorists argue that because the state raised the militia it had to be merely a passive instrument of government. By emphasizing only part of the evidence, neither view accurately captures the complicated status of the eighteenth-century militia.[2]

Second, we must refrain from anachronistically assuming that the Framers worked within the same conceptual world as our own. For example, the modern policy issue that most animates the debate over the Second Amendment is gun control, and the question posed is whether the government may regulate private gun ownership. The contenders in this debate are individual gun owners, who would like to read the amendment as a protection for an individual right, and the government, which would like to read it as a protection for state power. Not surprisingly, therefore, the conceptual world of the modern debate rests on a simple opposition between government and individuals. As we shall see, however, the Framers did not see the social world in such simple terms: between the government and private individuals lay the Body of the People, which was collective but not strictly governmental, and the Second Amendment gave the right to arms to this entity.

Third, we must remember that the facts of history have relevance to the modern interpretation of the Second Amendment only as filtered through a legal screen. The task of the intellectual historian is to document in detail the thinking of an individual or generation. The task of the constitutional interpreter is to determine which, if any, of those details are relevant to the modern construal of the constitution. Some historical writing that may be peerless as history has trouble satisfying this test of legal relevance. For example, in one of the most noted articles in recent Second Amendment scholarship, the historian Michael Bellesiles has tried to prove that private gun ownership was uncommon until the late nineteenth century. He argues that this historical fact discredits the individual rights reading of the Second Amendment, as it explodes the idea that private gun ownership is a quintessentially American behavior.[3]

As a critique of historical myths, Bellesiles's work, if accurate, is interesting and important. As constitutional interpretation, however, it offers only half a story, for the question is not who owned guns but what significance the Framers attached to widespread gun ownership. If they in fact believed that a healthy republic rested on universal arms bearing, then the infrequency of gun ownership merely shows how far America departed from their constitutional ideals.

More broadly, some historians have emphasized that in the late eighteenth century Americans entertained multiple and contradictory views about the right to arms. As a result, for these historians it is not possible to speak of a "standard model" or a "single paradigm" of the Second Amendment.[4] This emphasis serves sound historical ends: it leads to a complex, nuanced, and complete picture. Legal analysis, however, cannot rest with all this multiplicity and contradiction because lawyers and judges are under an obligation to give operable meaning to the Constitution. If we adopt the historian's generous embrace of numberless voices, we will perforce conclude that the amendment cannot mean anything at all — at least as long as we use history to guide our interpretation. While constitutional interpreters must therefore begin with the historian's picture of variety and disagreement, they must find a way to transform it, through legal analysis, into an account that can provide the basis for deciding cases.

Writing history as history is one thing; writing history as an element of constitutional interpretation is another. Historians may revel in disorderliness, but lawyers look for order; historians may find virtue in dispensing with models, but lawyers must find them.[5] This difference arises not because one or the other group is perfidious or lazy but because historians deploy the facts of history for one goal, lawyers for another. It is regrettable that the two groups often condemn each other simply for being true to their worthwhile disciplinary norms. Historians commonly sneer at "law office history" as one-sided, simplistic, and polemical, when in fact judges and legal academics are trying to derive usable norms from a contradictory welter of views. And lawyers often scorn historians as irrelevant, obscure, and antiquarian, when in fact historians are trying to convey the richness of human life in the past.

Historians' appreciation of the complexity of history should remind constitutionalists that because the Framers' intent is never monolithic, it does not transparently yield legal norms. As a result, legal analysts cannot (though some try to) pose as passive oracles of the past, claiming incontestable authority from the sanction of history. Instead, lawyers must acknowledge that they are transforming the historical record into legal material, and they must accept their responsibility for that creative process. When constitutionalists obscure this responsibility, when they pretend to channel the Framers' spirits for us, they engage in an abuse, not because they have legally filtered the historical record but because they deny having done any filtering.

Historians, then, should create a luxuriant field of intellectual plants, and lawyers should prune it for legal relevance. In pruning, lawyers should not ignore evidence inconvenient to their preferred outcome, but rather apply standard legal guidelines designed to ensure that the history serves the goals of the legal system. First, material closer to the actual legislative history of the Second Amendment is more relevant than material farther away. Thus statements made by congressmen deliberating on the amendment's proposal are worth more than statements by sixteenth-century Florentine republicans. Second, statements made by ideological supporters of the amendment are more relevant than statements made by those who voted for it merely to placate its supporters. Third, views that are widely shared by those supporters are worth more than isolated examples of contrary views. Fourth, although the Constitution may historically be a product of jumbled and contradictory impulses, judges try to read it as a unified whole, resting on a consistent set of principles. As a result, when lawyers and judges survey the history of the Second Amendment, they look for a story that best brings principled coherence to as much of the Constitution as possible, and they discard the rest.[6]

Again, although the obligation of the historian may be to honor the unique particular of past life, the obligation of the court and its officers is to generate the shared normative framework that makes continued life possible. Historians may wince at the reductionism that seems implicit in this process, but the only alternative is to abandon history altogether as a source of legal meaning. In the long run, constitutional theory may decide in favor of that alternative, but for now consulting history remains an important part of American constitutional practice.

The fourth caveat, however, is that although constitutional interpretation generally begins with history, it does not end there. Even strict originalists, those who believe that constitutional interpretation consists exclusively in the determination of the Framers' intent, recognize that the Framers' principles must be applied to contemporary realities.[7] Strict originalism, moreover, has never been more than a minority position among judges and commentators; it has not commanded a majority on the Supreme Court at any time during the twentieth century. Instead, most constitutionalists have concluded that constitutional interpretation should have an evolutionary quality, although they might disagree about how exactly it evolves.[8] As a result, although I shall begin with a close examination of the history of the amendment, I'll not leave the examination there; rather, I will ultimately turn to the present and the future of the Second Amendment.

I offer here a historical account that strives to heed these four warnings: it weighs all the evidence, not merely the part that supports a preferred position; it enters into the Framers' conceptual universe rather than imposing ours on theirs; it prunes the historical material for legal relevance; and it offers this history as a starting point, not a terminus.

The Background of the Framers' Thinking

Over the past several decades, the historiography of late eighteenth-century intellectual life has undergone not one but a whole series of sea changes. First, following the work of Louis Hartz, scholars commonly opined that America was conceived in the womb of classical liberalism, with its emphasis on individual rights and self-determination; in this view, America has always been captive to a liberal orthodoxy that haunts us still. Then, with the work of Bernard Bailyn, Gordon Wood, and J. G. A. Pocock, came the "republican revolution" in the writing of American history: in this view, the categories of civic republican discourse, with its emphasis on virtue and the common good, so captured the late eighteenth century that it was difficult to think outside that frame. According to this account, liberalism came to dominate our national consciousness in the nineteenth century only slowly and after great struggle. Finally, scholars have begun to argue that both liberalism and republicanism played a critical part in the great debates of the last half of the century. These two strains swirled around each other and interacted in nuanced, variable ways in the minds of political thinkers. Some have even begun to write about a hybrid ideology called liberal republicanism, with an emphasis on both individual rights and the common good.[1]

In recognition of this complex inheritance, I address here the doctrine of revolution offered by each of these traditions, civic republicanism and classical liberalism. In chapter 3, I shall suggest that, whatever the general mix of ideas at the time, supporters of the Second Amendment tended to rely more on republican than liberal language when discussing this provision, as they put the republican fondness for the militia at the center of their thinking. In the end, however, it is not very important to decide which ideology enjoyed prominence in the amendment's history because the two strains of thought converge on the two propositions central to my thesis: first, the people enjoy a right to resist a corrupt government, but, second, the people enjoy that right as a collective entity, not as disconnected individuals.

Civic Republicanism

Historians like Bailyn and Pocock have traced the civic republican tradition from Aristotle, through Machiavelli and the Italian Renaissance, to the beginnings of the Commonwealth Party in seventeenth-century Great Britain and such figures as James Harrington and Algernon Sydney. This tradition influenced American writers of the eighteenth century, who commonly drew on it to explain their relation to Great Britain. Some historians have claimed that republicanism formed a virtual orthodoxy, a hegemonic discourse, for late eighteenth-century Americans. Others have denied that republicanism's influence was so vast, but no one has claimed it was absent. It was in this collection of ideas that the militia held central prominence. To understand why the Framers insisted in the Second Amendment that the militia was "necessary to the security of a free state," we must therefore turn to this tradition.

In brief, republicans held that the government and its citizens should pursue the common good rather than the selfish interest of a faction. They also believed, however, that governments and citizens are prone to corruption, to putting their own good first. When designing a constitutional organization of violence, therefore, civic republicans looked for a body that would most reliably pursue the common good. They thought they found it in the militia because it was universal, the people-under-arms. As a result, the militia's good was by definition the common good, as it embraced all of society. Republicans imagined the militia as a highly unified, organic entity, the institutional manifestation of the Body of the People. The militia thus straddled the divide between governments and individuals. The government raised it to ensure that it was universal. Under normal circumstances, the militia functioned as a state instrument, expected to suppress revolts. Yet the militia was ultimately a people's body, and if the government should become corrupt, the militia could suppress an insurrection against the common good by the government itself.

In either case, to deserve the trust entailed in bearing arms, the militia had to be universal and thus driven by a concern for the common good.

REPUBLICAN DANGERS

Eighteenth-century republicans shared certain views about the nature of human beings. First, they have public, political selves and for this reason can form cooperative ventures that will benefit all. The polity itself is a universal association "in which all types of men combine to pursue all human goods," and it can achieve a universal good that is more than the private interests of a few. At the same time, however, every individual has a private, particular self and self-interest, and his public and private selves can come into conflict. A good state is one in which citizens pursue the common good; a bad state is one that has been seized by a slice of society for its own narrow ends.[2]

Republicans therefore hoped to induce citizens to pursue the common good, but they faced a problem: the virtue of the state and that of its citizens are interdependent. To be virtuous, a citizen must live in a state that enshrines the common good; otherwise he can be no more than one bit of self-serving flotsam swirling around other bits, for there is no common good to serve. The state, however, will never enshrine the common good unless its citizens are virtuous; but, in turn, the only way they can become virtuous is for the state to enshrine the common good. Citizens make the state, and the state makes citizens; neither can be virtuous unless the other is.[3]

This closed circle created a republican paradox: citizens are simultaneously creatures of and creators of the state.[4] And this paradox raised for republicans the troubling question of how one creates a republic: the problem of origins. Virtuous citizens can create virtuous states, and virtuous states can create virtuous citizens, but how does one secure either of these in the first place without the other? In this paradoxical formulation, republics appear to have a self-levitating quality: they do somehow come into being, but only because historical conditions happen to be right, not because humans consciously create those conditions. As a result, a republican form of government might not be viable at all times and for all peoples.[5] Those hoping for a republic might simply have to wait for providence to deliver a virtuous people[6] or a virtuous government[7] to make it possible.

Even if the miracle did occur and a republican state came into being, it was always in danger of slipping into corruption: the problem of maintenance. Because state and society depended on each other, if either became corrupt it might contaminate the other. Because neither could serve as an anchor, republicans saw the path to perdition as short, smooth, and slippery. And the world contained many hostile forces: Fortuna, under various guises, always lurked to disrupt the best plans of men. At the first sign of corruption, then, there was only a limited time to save the republic before the Fall had become irreversible.[8]

This set of relations is connected to a third paradox: the complicated republican view on rights and autonomy.[9] In republican theory, citizens must be independent of the state in order to be able to critique it if it becomes corrupt: hence the republican denunciation of slavish subservience and praise of those brave enough to defy public ministers and even public opinion. In order to attain this independence, citizens must have rights that the political process may not touch, so that citizens will not feel threatened by reprisals from a corrupt government.[10] Only in this way will they feel free to pursue the promptings of their conscience in the political arena. This end of the paradox reflects one side of the interdependence between state and society: for a virtuous state to exist, there must be virtuous citizens.

Republicans also believed, however, that individuals are unable to be truly separate or fully independent because they are products of the state. Rather than presocial givens, the very values republican citizens hold are the product of politics — deliberative, healthy politics, one hopes, but politics in any event. Citizens, moreover, must not use their rights to pursue their self-interest in derogation of the common good. Thus the citizen cannot stand apart from the political process and use it as a mere instrument of his desires. This conviction reflects the other side of the state / society equation: for there to be virtuous citizens, there must be a virtuous politics. For republicans, then, rights are not only the precondition for good politics, but also the product of politics. As a result, citizens should not generally invoke their rights in such a way as to remove themselves from the decisions of the deliberative dialogue.[11]

Citizens must therefore have sufficient autonomy to stand against the state when it errs, but they must also be aware that their autonomy exists only for the common good. Republican virtue thus has two components: a good citizen must be self-abnegating enough to sacrifice his desires for the good of the whole, and he must also be independent enough to resist a corrupt state. There is no inherent contradiction in these dual duties because in both cases the citizen is pursuing the common good. When the state represents that good, the citizen must sacrifice his personal ends to the greater good of the state. In contrast, when the state is wandering, the citizen must resist. There is, however, a deep tension in the habits of mind required: republicans expected a citizen to be sometimes profoundly selfless and sometimes profoundly assertive. He must have the intelligence to know when to be which and the emotional agility to shift modes when appropriate.

SOURCES OF CORRUPTION

Because these paradoxes suggested that corruption could make a republic impossible at any time, republicans endlessly analyzed its causes and cures. By the eighteenth century, two main themes had emerged: the danger of an imbalance of estates, which concerned corruption in government, and the danger of professionalization, which concerned corruption in society.

Balance-of-estates theory presented society as naturally divided into three estates — the One, the Few, and the Many — each with distinctive political virtues and vices. Unchecked, any of these might misdirect the state to its own partial good, so a republican polity should balance the estates against one another, each walking a distinct path to the universal good. The classic example, praised by some as the most stable and perfect product of political art, was the British constitution, balancing power between the two houses of Parliament and the monarch.[12] Maintaining that balanced relation, however, was never easy.[13] In the eighteenth century, concern about imbalance in the estates focused on the Crown. As the empire grew by trade and arms, so did the power of the Crown, through new military organizations, especially the standing army, and through newly developed financial practices, notably taxes, credit, and banks. The core of the fear was executive dominance of Parliament: with its expanded resources, the Crown could buy the loyalty of members of Parliament by offering places and pensions in the royal service.[14]

During the imperial crisis, American colonials frequently expressed their grievances with Britain in similar terms: the tyrant George III had subverted Parliament, invaded historical colonial privilege, and appointed autocratic governors. Upon achieving independence, the new states reacted to this fear of the executive by drafting constitutions that curtailed executive power and expanded the power of the lower legislative house. In the process, they began to alter the meaning of mixed government by making it more democratic. They insisted that the Few and the One should not consist of hereditary estates, which tended to become overpowerful, throwing the balance into disarray.[15] Moreover, while most republicans believed that a natural aristocracy existed in America, they viewed this aristocracy as one of talent rather than of birth. Although the elements of government that reflected aristocratic virtues might be less populist than the others, all would be directly or indirectly elected by the people. In this manner, Americans developed a system of democratic republicanism in which the One, the Few, and the Many ceased to be separate estates and became distinct parts of a balanced government staffed by the people's representatives.[16]

In republican eyes, however, the threat of corruption also came from a second, newer source, imperiling not the balanced government but the citizenry itself. In the eighteenth century, as the economy and the empire modernized, the whole fabric of British society seemed in peril of being rent into partial interests. The new commercial society encouraged citizens to pursue selfish interests. Perhaps more important, it promoted specialization of economic function and so divided the citizenry into contending interests.[17] By contrast, English republican writers held up as an ideal the ancient republics in which each citizen fulfilled every function: working his land, voting his mind, and taking up arms to defend the polity.[18]

Many American writers shared these worries about Britain's social character. In their view, the English people had come to prefer luxury to liberty and so had come to peace with tyranny. More broadly, the degenerative effects of social development had fractured the English populace. Americans, by contrast, remained poised between rude barbarism and effete decay — sturdy but civilized farmers, independent and unspecialized.[19] Consequently, they retained a virtue Britons had lost. American concern over professionalization as a cause of corruption again reflected a democratic drift away from the ideal of mixed and balanced government. Although many republicans praised a deferential society, others cast themselves as champions of the Many against the One within balance-of-estates rhetoric. And in standing against specialization, some republicans went even further: they cast themselves not as the representatives of any particular estate but as those virtuous souls — the demos, the mass of the American people — who stood for an unspecialized republic against the corrupting tide of modernity.[20]

ARMS, ARMIES, AND MILITIAS

The danger of corruption in the government and in the citizenry prompted special anxieties for republicans in designing a constitutional organization of political violence. Republicans believed that the state must arm itself to resist foreign aggression and keep civil order. The distribution of arms, however, caused them great worry because whoever held the weapons and real property within a republic held ultimate control.[21] In arming itself, the state had two traditional options: a standing army or a popular militia. An army posed two great threats of corruption: first, it could become a tool of executive usurpation, subverting the balance of estates; second, it posed a risk of professionalization and factionalism.

Evidence of executive subversion was ample. Standing armies arose in England as a tool of the Stuart monarchs' ambitions for power, and memories of that period remained vivid for a long time in the minds of later republicans. Professional soldiers would follow the king's will rather than the common good because they depended on him for their livelihood; with the army at hand to enforce his will, therefore, the king would be tempted to adopt tyrannical policies. The army was, moreover, one of the chief avenues for subversion of Parliament, as many members held lucrative places in the king's service.[22]

American colonists were familiar with the consequences of executive control of the military. Throughout the eighteenth century, colonists experienced friction with contingents of British regulars stationed near them.[23] Following the Seven Years' War, this friction increased dramatically when Britain decided the colonists should pay for their own defense. For the first time, the imperial government levied a tax on the colonies for revenue purposes, and that revenue, ominously, went to the upkeep of the standing army, which in turn could be used to collect the tax. When the colonists refused to pay, famously claiming that taxation without representation was tyranny, the imperial government ordered the occupational military to enforce the policy.[24] Perhaps most alarmingly, the occupying army included not only British regulars but also Hessian mercenaries, foreigners who had no connection to the American common good at all. The colonists were experiencing a republican nightmare: an unrepresentative government was using a standing army to enforce an unjust policy against them.[25]

Like English radicals, many American republicans blamed George III for these abuses. Others maintained that Parliament, controlled by conspiratorial ministers and placemen, was at least as complicitous in the new policies.[26] It made little difference, however, whether Parliament or the king controlled the army because in either case it was not subject to the colonists' legislatures. After the Revolution, the framers of the new state constitutions took pains to ensure that the state military was under legislative, rather than executive, control. For some, this arrangement ameliorated their worst fears about the existence of a standing army.[27]

A standing army, however, posed a second threat: regardless of who controlled it, its very existence gave rise to social corruption through professionalization. The army was a symptom and product of the modern specialization of economic function because soldiers were trained to a particular trade, fighting, and so would seek to maintain their particular interests. Thus, the army desired foreign wars to justify its existence, ample taxes to support it, a strong executive to collect the taxes, and docile citizens to pay them.[28] The American Joel Barlow put the idea pithily: "Thus money is required to levy armies, and armies to levy money, and foreign wars are introduced as the pretended occupation for both."[29] Soldiers thus contributed to the breakdown of the common good in the same way any other professional group did, but with a special threat: it controlled the means of force. As society developed and diversified, many ignominiously chose to surrender the sword to a professional army. They thereby gained a luxurious way of life but lost their moral character and their only guarantee of liberty in the bargain.[30]

In republican theory, the citizen militia offered protection against all these dangers.[31] Republican thinkers imagined the militia as the universal people armed: the whole people, the *armato populato,* the very republic itself. To be sure, even as late as the end of the eighteenth century some hierarchical republicans believed the militia should reflect the underlying society, with social inferiors paying deference to social betters.[32] As I will elaborate in the next chapter, other republicans contemplated that the militia would be the most populist of political institutions. But either way, republicans imagined that the militia would not only mirror but actually consist of the whole of republican society: the people, however socially ranked and ordered. And that identification of the militia and the people made a militia incomparably more attractive than a standing army.

First, republicans thought the militia limited the dangers of executive usurpation. From the beginning of the republican tradition, theorists had associated the militia with the Many, rather than with the One. If the Many possessed the means of force, a despot could not wreak his tyrannical schemes without the support of the people: the militia could and should refuse to obey orders that, in its view, violated the common good. In other words, from an early date these thinkers vested a right of resistance in the citizen militia.[33]

In addition, reliance on a militia forestalled the dangers of professionalization. Unlike the standing army, the militia was not a separate order of society with separate interests; rather, it was society itself, in all its universality. Because it included all of the citizens of the republic, by definition it reflected the common good, not the good of a narrow segment of society. In addition, militia members were amateurs, not a professional caste of warriors. As a result, they waged war as full-time citizens and only part-time soldiers; unlike a standing army, they had no interest in fomenting wars to justify taxes to pay for their services. In that sense, republicans often envisioned the militia member as a quintessentially unspecialized citizen, Horatio at the Plough, whose own interests necessarily reflected the common good. At one moment, he controlled policy in his enfranchised role; at another, he controlled resources in his propertied role; and at a third, he controlled force in his armed role.[34] Indeed, for some republicans the citizen's status as militia member, because it represented a more direct form of democracy, may have been more significant than his role as voter.

As I explain in chapter 2, republican thinking about the militia lies at the center of the Framers' understanding of the Second Amendment. For now, let me merely reemphasize two themes: first, for critical ideological reasons, the militia had to be universal, not some random group of individuals less than the whole; and second, though a state body, it was expected to refuse unjust orders, so it was not merely an arm of the state. I shall develop these themes in greater detail in the next chapter, but first I shall examine the other great trunk of the Framers' intellectual inheritance, the tradition of classical liberalism.

Classical Liberalism

Like republicanism, liberalism permeated the discourse of the Framers in the 1780s. In its treatment of the constitutional organization of violence, however, liberal analysis generally addressed different concerns than did republican analysis. In considering resistance to government, the Framers found in republicanism a theory of processes and institutions: the danger of governmental corruption, the threat posed by a standing army, the hope offered by a militia. By contrast, liberalism, as exhibited in the work of its master expositor, John Locke, hardly discussed such concrete matters as how governments go corrupt and how the people can organize to resist. Instead, Locke offered a theoretical explanation of the legitimate origin of government and the reasons for dissolving it, with only limited explanation about how that was to be done. Nonetheless, close reading shows that, like the civic republicans, Locke reposed the right to make a revolution not in private individuals or state governments, but in a vaguely imagined Body of the People.

Locke's general theory of the social contract has exercised such an influence on the American political consciousness that it is broadly familiar in outline.[35] Humans first exist in the state of nature, in a "State of perfect Freedom to order their Actions . . . as they think fit, within the bounds of the law of Nature" (par. 4), which requires only that "no one ought to harm another in his Life, Health, Liberty, or Possessions" (par. 6). They are also in a state of "Equality, wherein all the Power and Jurisdiction is reciprocal, no one having more than another" (par. 4). As a result, if an individual violates the law of nature, every other individual has the right to "punish the Offender, and be executioner of the law of nature" (par. 8). The defining characteristic of the state of nature is therefore that "want of a common establish'd Law and Judicature to appeal to, with Authority to decide Controversies between them" (par. 87).

The state of nature is unsatisfactory because in the absence of a common judge, "however free, [it] is full of fears and continual dangers" (par. 123). As a result, individuals "put[] on the bonds of Civil Society" by "agreeing with other Men to joyn and unite into a Community, for their comfortable, safe, and peaceful living one amongst another" (par. 95). They create this community when every individual agrees to surrender the personal right to execute the law of nature, appointing the community as the common judge: "There and there only is Political Society, where every one of the Members hath quitted this natural Power. . . . And thus all private judgement of every particular Member being excluded, the Community comes to be umpire, by settled standing Rules, indifferent, and the same to all Parties" (par. 87). The advantages of civil society thus include a known judge, a known law, and the effective power to execute judgments (pars. 124–27).

This community then creates a government to administer the social contract. Locke does not argue that there is one best form of government; instead, he insists that the community may choose, "as they think good," from a wide range of governmental forms, including democracy, oligarchy, elective and hereditary monarchies, and "compounded and mixed Forms of Government" (par. 132). All legitimate governments are, however, subject to one vitally important limit: they must always serve the ends for which they were created, that is, the "preservation of [the citizens'] Property" (par. 222), meaning their life, liberty, and possessions. If governments ever cease serving those ends, the people may overthrow them and institute new ones: "Yet the legislative being only a Fiduciary Power to act for certain ends, there remains still in the People a Supream Power to remove or alter the Legislative, when they find the Legislative act contrary to the trust reposed in them" (par. 149). And Locke is quite blunt that revolution will usually involve force: "Whosoever uses force without Right [such as a tyrant] . . . puts himself into a state of War with those, against whom he so uses it, . . . and every one has a Right to defend himself, and to resist the Aggressor" (par. 232). Indeed, in response to Barclay's argument that subjects may resist a king only with reverence, Locke is scornful: "He that can Reconcile Blows and Reverence, may, for ought I know, deserve for his pains, a Civil Respectful Cudgeling where-ever he can meet with it" (par. 235).

Locke thus defends a right of revolution when the government ceases to serve the ends for which it was created; so much is clear and familiar. But who may make such a revolution and under what circumstances? The answers to these questions are much less well known, in part because Locke himself succumbs to some vagueness on these points. Many Second Amendment scholars of the individual rights school have argued that logically the right must belong to individuals: as individuals enter the social contract for their own reasons and by their own consent, so they must have the right to unmake the contract when, in their personal judgment, the government has become perfidious.[36]

These arguments are usually unaccompanied by textual citation, however, and in fact in the Second Treatise Locke says something quite different.

Locke describes not one but two contracts: the popular or social contract made between persons to form a society, and the rectoral or governmental contract made between that society and its government to authorize the government to act in the society's name and interests. At the very beginning of the last chapter of the treatise — "Of the Dissolution of Government" — Locke draws this critical distinction: "He that will with any clearness speak of the Dissolution of Government, ought, in the first place to distinguish between the Dissolution of the Society, and the Dissolution of the Government" (par. 211). The formation of society — Locke variously calls it the community, civil society, political society, the People, and the Body of the People — is historically prior to the formation of the government: "That which makes the Community, and brings Men out of the loose State of Nature, into one Politick Society, is the Agreement which every one has with the rest to incorporate, and act as one Body, and so be one distinct Commonwealth" (par. 211).

This popular agreement thus involves the decision of a group of individuals to make a future together, to become one people, and to abide by the will of the majority within the people so defined: "For when any number of Men have, by the consent of every individual, made a Community, they have thereby made that Community one Body, with a Power to Act as one Body, which is only the will and determination of the majority" (par. 96). The terms of this popular contract are thus fairly basic, and they do not specify the details of any particular governmental structure: "And this [popular contract] is done by barely agreeing to unite into one Political Society, which is all the Compact that is, or needs be, between the Individuals, that enter or make up a Common-wealth. And thus that, which begins and actually constitutes any Political Society, is nothing but the consent of any number of Freemen capable of a majority to unite and incorporate into such a Society" (par. 99).

After the formation of the community, the majority creates a government with a particular form in a second agreement, the rectoral contract: "The Majority having . . . the whole power of the Community, naturally in them, may imploy all that power in making laws for the Community . . . or else may put the power of making laws into the hands of a few select men . . . or else into the hands of one man" (par. 132). And the community grants that government a fiduciary trust to act for its good: "Government into whatsoever hands it is put . . . [is] intrusted with this condition, and for this end, that Men might have and secure their Properties" (par. 139) — again, meaning their lives, liberties, and possessions.

These two contracts, the popular and the rectoral, are dissolved in very different ways. The popular contract is extremely durable; once individuals have banded together to form a single people, little but outright annihilation can rend them apart: "The usual, and almost only way whereby this Union is dissolved, is the Inroad of Foreign Force making a Conquest upon them." And when society is so dissolved, the people return to a state of nature because it was the popular contract that brought them out of that state: "For in that Case, (not being able to maintain and support themselves as one intire and independent Body) the Union belonging to that Body which consisted therein, must necessarily cease, and so every one return to the state he was in before, with a liberty to shift for himself." Necessarily, when the community ceases, the government that it created must also cease: "Where the Society is dissolved, the Government cannot remain; that being as impossible, as for the Frame of an House to subsist when the Materials of it are scattered, and dissipated by a Whirl-wind, or jumbled into a confused heap by an Earthquake" (par. 211).

Dissolution of a government differs from dissolution of a society in two critical ways. First, governments may be dissolved not just when the society has been annihilated, but whenever the people become convinced that the government has misused them, even if the society is still intact: "There remains still in the People a Supream Power to remove or alter the Legislative, when they find the Legislative act contrary to the trust reposed in them" (par. 149). Second, when the government is dissolved in this way, power reverts to the community, bound by majority rule, not to individuals in a state of nature. The government is the creature of society and cannot exist without it; because the society is not the creature of government, the latter's disappearance leaves the former untouched. Locke returns to this theme again and again: "When the Government is dissolved, the People are at liberty to provide for themselves, by erecting a new Legislative. . . . For the Society can never, by the fault of another, lose the Native and Original Right it has to preserve itself" (par. 220); "And thus the Community perpetually retains a Supream Power of saving themselves from the attempts and designs of any Body, even of their Legislators, whenever they shall . . . carry on designs against the Liberties and Properties of the Subject. . . . And thus the Community may be said in this respect to be always the Supream Power, but not as considered under any Form of Government, because this Power of the People can never take place till the Government be dissolved" (par. 149).

Locke's terminology can be confusing in that he sometimes seems to suggest that on the dissolution of government, the people are plunged into a state of nature. In chapter 8, for example, he explains that once a person has by "express Declaration" agreed to become subject to a government, then he can never dissolve that connection "and can never be again in the state of Nature, unless by any Calamity, the Government he was under, comes to be dissolved" (par. 121). In chapter 18, he explains that even a king regarded as sacred may, "by actually putting himself into a State of War with his People, dissolve the government, and leave them to that defence, which belongs to every one in the State of Nature" (par. 205). On careful reading, however, these passages do not assert that on dissolution of the government the community is also dissolved and the people returned to a state of nature with respect to each other. Indeed, as we have seen, Locke repeatedly denies exactly that idea. Instead, Locke is here claiming that when the government is dissolved, the people are in a state of nature with respect to that government. Thereafter, they need feel no obligation to the officers or institutions of the government, and they may form a new one or choose new representatives.

In chapter 19, Locke offers this chain of analysis in clearer terms. Directly echoing his language from the previous chapter, he explains that when the legislature betrays its trust to the people, then "they put themselves into a state of War with the People, who are thereupon absolved from any farther Obedience, and are left to the common Refuge, which God hath provided for all Men, against Force and violence." Locke immediately goes on to explain, however, that although the people are absolved from obedience to the government, the preexisting community is not thereby dissolved. Indeed, that community then has the critical responsibility of forming a new government: "By this breach of Trust [the governors] forfeit the Power, the People had put into their hands, and it devolves to the People, who have a right to resume their original Liberty, and, by the Establishment of a new Legislative (such as they shall think fit) provide for their own Safety and Security, which is the end for which they are in Society" (par. 222).

Locke closes the Second Treatise with his most forceful and direct exposition of this relation between the rectoral and popular contracts. First, Locke asserts the great durability of the social contract: "To conclude, the Power that every individual gave the Society, when he entered into it, can never revert to the Individuals again, as long as the Society lasts, but will always remain in the Community." Next, he explains that the society creates the government in a second contract: "So also when the Society hath placed the Legislative in any Assembly of Men, . . . the Legislative can never revert to the People whilst that Government lasts." Third, he maintains that legislative bad faith can dissolve the rectoral contract and return power to the community, not to individuals: "When by the miscarriages of those in Authority, [power] is forfeited . . . it reverts to the Society." And finally, Locke closes his work by explaining that society may then make a new government: "The People have a Right to act as Supreme, and continue the Legislative in themselves, or erect a new Form, or under the old form place it in new hands, as they think good" (par. 243).

When the government is dissolved, then, power reverts not to individuals in a state of nature but to society. It necessarily follows that society, not individuals, must judge the necessity of a revolution and make it. Put simply, the right of revolution belongs to the Body of the People. This conclusion is implicit in Locke's whole analysis, but he also makes it express in several often-overlooked passages. In his view, when tyrants oppress individuals, those persons may have a limited right of civil disobedience, but not the right to unseat government. Only the community possesses that right, and for two kinds of reasons. First, as a practical matter, individuals cannot make a successful revolution without community support. Second, as a principled matter, an individual right of revolution would lead to countless baseless insurrections, and only societywide oppression can justify tearing down a government.

Locke was deeply sensitive to the charge that his doctrine of revolution would lead to anarchy, and he refutes the charge again and again by insisting that only the Body of the People may make a revolution. Thus, in chapter 14, he commands, "Nor let any one think, this [right of revolution] lays a perpetual foundation for disorder, for this operates not, till the Inconvenience is so great, that the Majority feel it, and are weary of it, and find a necessity to have it amended" (par. 168). Later, he insists, "Nor let any one say, that mischief can arise from hence, as often as it shall please a busie head, or turbulent spirit, to desire the alteration of the Government. 'Tis true, such men may stir, whenever they please, but it will only be to their own just ruine and perdition. For till the mischief be grown general, . . . the People . . . are not apt to stir. The examples of particular Injustice, or Oppression of here and there an unfortunate Man, moves them not" (par. 230).

Locke's contention here rests partly on the hardheaded observation that no revolution can succeed without majority support. Thus, he comments that individuals may have a theoretical right to resist the government, but in practice they will meet only with failure: "For if it reach no farther than some private Men's Cases, though they have a right to defend themselves . . . yet the Right to do so, will not easily ingage them in a Contest, wherein they are sure to perish; it being . . . impossible for one or a few oppressed Men to disturb the Government, where the Body of the People do not think themselves concerned in it" (par. 208).

Locke also believes, however, that as a matter of principle only the Body of the People can make a revolution. Throughout the Second Treatise, he worries about the charge of fomenting rebellion, and his requirement of broad support is his primary hedge against that danger. At one point, he elaborates the calculus that led him to this conclusion. In chapter 18, he praises those constitutions that hold the prince to be sacred by law, so that he cannot be held liable for any harm done in his person: "Than which there cannot be a wiser Constitution." In Locke's view, the reason for this princely immunity is that in his own person the prince can generally oppress only individuals: "For the harm he can do in his own Person, not being likely to happen often, nor to extend it self far; nor being able by his single strength to subvert the Laws, nor oppress the Body of the People." When only individual injustice is involved, individuals may still make "opposition . . . to the illegal acts of an inferiour Officer," but they may not try to unseat the head of government: "The Inconveniency of some particular mischiefs . . . are well recompenced, by the peace of the Publick, and security of the Government, in the person of the Chief Magistrate, thus set out of the reach of danger: It being safer for the Body, that some few private Men should be sometimes in danger to suffer, than that the head of the Republick should be easily, and upon slight occasions exposed" (par. 205). And in his last chapter, Locke quotes the royalist Barclay with approval, quibbling with him only on unrelated points: "This therefore is the Priviledge of the People in general, above what any private Person hath; That particular Men are allowed by our Adversaries themselves [that is, the anti-Royalists], . . . to have no other Remedy but Patience; but the Body of the People may . . . resist intolerable tyranny" (par. 233).

In short, then, when the government is dissolved, individuals do not revert to a state of nature, and they do not have a right of revolution separate from their community. They are still a part of political society, and they are bound by the majority decisions of that society. They may have individual rights to resist injustice, but they have no right in themselves to unseat the government. For Locke, an individual right of revolution would lead to endless insurrections and would be inconsistent with his conviction that peoplehood is perennial. Instead, the Body of the People, which includes every signatory to the social contract, must decide whether the government has breached the rectoral contract and, if so, what to do about it. On this score, Locke is very close to the civic republicans: he recognizes a right of revolution, but he vests it in the Body of the People.

So much is clear from a close reading of the Second Treatise; what is unclear is how Locke expected the community to organize itself in the absence of government. The point in democratic government, after all, is to offer the people a regular structure through which to express their will. In the absence of such a structure, the people may be little better than a mob. At one point, Locke himself seems to recognize this problem: "'Tis in their Legislative, that the Members of a Commonwealth are united, and combined together into one coherent living Body. This is the Soul that gives Form, Life, and Unity to the Commonwealth. . . . And therefore when the Legislative is broken, or dissolved, Dissolution and Death follows." And so it would appear that on the dissolution of government, the community is without "Form, Life, and Unity." Yet several sentences later, Locke explains that on the dissolution of the legislature the people must somehow act collectively to "constitute to themselves a new Legislative, as they think best" (par. 212).

This problem affects Locke's account not only of the dissolution of the government but of its formation as well: society must have some structure through which it can act to institute government. As he explains in the same passage, "The Constitution of the Legislative is the first and fundamental Act of Society, whereby provision is made for the Continuation of their Union, under the Direction of Persons, . . . by the Consent and Appointment of the People." In Locke's view, the "Essence and Union of the Society consist[s] in having one Will"; the legislature has "the declaring, and as it were the keeping of that Will," but only "when once established by the Majority" (par. 212). Before the legislature's establishment, the society itself has the declaring of its will, and it must have some process through which to declare it.

In other words, Locke presumes that the people have some kind of constitutional structure embedded in the social contract that is logically prior to the constitutional structure embedded in the rectoral contract—a sort of government before and behind the government. This structure applies before the government comes into being and after it dissolves; the people act through this structure to create a government in the first place and then to recreate it after a revolution. This pregovernment government is thus absolutely critical in Locke's analysis, yet he says remarkably little about how it operates other than explaining that it acts by majority rule.

Locke seems not to have regarded this silence as a deficiency; he never apologizes for it or even remarks on it. To some extent, his silence may grow out of the nature of his task: he means to define the relative rights and obligations of government, societies, and individuals rather than to detail the practical operations of political structures. As a result, once he has explained that the society has a right to make and unmake governments, his task is over; he does not need to explain how they can, should, or will organize themselves for the task.

Locke may also be silent about the exact structure of the community because he imagines that the individuals who make up the social contract have a great deal in common and thus do not need an elaborate formal structure through which to act. Locke is emphatic that human individuals have divergent interests; indeed, he writes the Second Treatise precisely to deal with that uncomfortable fact. Underneath that difference, however, lies a similarity: they are alike precisely in having different interests that they would like to pursue free of interference from each other. For that reason, they share at least four critically important features. First, they all have natural rights to life, liberty, and property. Second, they all possess the will and desire to pursue those rights, each as seems best to him. Third, they all have reason to allow them to pursue those rights: "The Freedom then of Man and Liberty of acting according to his own Will, is grounded on his having Reason" (par. 63). And fourth, because of these shared qualities, they enter the social contract for the same reason, to find a common judge.

Despite all their differences, these strong commonalities allow the people to congeal into one Body of the People, each individually consenting to the terms of political society: "If Man in the state of nature be so free, . . . why will he part with his Freedom? . . . To which 'tis obvious to Answer, that though in the state of Nature he hath such a right, yet the Enjoyment of it is very uncertain. . . . And 'tis not without reason, that he seeks out, and is willing to joyn in Society with others who are already united, or have a mind to unite for the mutual Preservation of their Lives, Liberties, and Estates, which I call by the general Name, Property" (par. 123). And so, if the people share so much that they can forge a social contract in the first place, presumably they share enough that they can forge a revolutionary movement when the government has violated its trust.

Locke thus leaves us with a difficulty: he plainly expects that the people will engage in collective action under extreme circumstances, but he gives little hint about how these loose individuals can congeal. And in this ambiguity lies the germ of a problem central to the modern interpretation of the Second Amendment: in a world of individuals, how is united revolutionary action possible? This problem will be one of the foci of parts 2 and 3 of this book. The problem is especially pressing because our political myths have become more and more individualistic. Locke's analysis of revolution rested on a tension: his fundamental unit of analysis was the individual, but those individuals somehow cohered into a collectivity. Today, some Lockean mythmakers have resolved that tension by suppressing its collective side: in place of the tightly integrated member of a revolutionary movement, our new stories involve solitary frontiersmen, cowboys, lonely lawmen, and brave individuals standing up to the power of Leviathan. As a result, modern individual rights theories of the amendment are strangely incomplete: they maintain that individuals have the right to own arms so as to make a revolution against government, but they never consider how such a revolution — by definition, a collective enterprise —

might actually take place. Apparently, when the time comes, these individuals will just know what to do. Locke's rich tension has become simple faith in the power of the individual to accomplish anything.

Locke himself, however, did not share such unmitigated faith in the individual. Instead, like the republicans, he vested the right of revolution in an entity, the community, the Body of the People, that was identical to neither individuals nor the government. On the one hand, the community is plainly not the government; instead, it is the government's creator, master, and judge. And when the time comes, the community might even have to take up arms against its own creature. On the other hand, the community is also not simply a random group of individuals; instead, it is a body, a people, bound together forever, with one will expressed through the decisions of the majority. This body is corporate and universal, but it is not the state. Today, we may have difficulty imagining such an entity, and indeed one may not exist. Locke and the civic republicans, however, placed that body at the center of their analysis of revolution.

The Framers thus received a dual intellectual legacy. The various strains of this legacy were at odds on many important matters, but they exhibited striking agreement on the constitutional organization of violence: the people as a collective entity, but not as individuals, have the right to resist a corrupt government. When it came time to design a constitutional organization of violence for America, the Framers modified their tradition in a number of ways, but they did not stray far from this core principle.

2

The History of the Second Amendment

Second Amendment scholars exhibit general agreement on the outlines of the historical process leading up to the adoption of the Second Amendment; they disagree primarily over the meaning of these events.[1] In 1776, the American colonies declared their independence from Great Britain, claiming a popular right to throw off the shackles of a corrupt government and constitute a better one. During the war, they exercised that right by fighting a revolution against the imperial government and by writing the Articles of Confederation, which instituted a weak federal government, subordinate in many ways to the will of the states. By the mid-1780s, however, many Americans believed they needed a stronger central government to institute good order. In particular, they hoped to create a federal government with sufficient armed might to suppress the backcountry rebellions, such as Shays' Rebellion, then flaring up. Over cries that they were betraying the revolutionary legacy of 1776, they wrote our present Constitution and presented it to the states for ratification.

The states summoned ratifying conventions, and for several months a vigorous debate raged between Federalist supporters of the Constitution and those Anti-Federalists who believed that the new federal government would be too strong, potentially becoming another imperial monster. Many Anti-Federalists particularly objected that the Constitution gave Congress broad power to raise a standing army and to regulate the state militias; they feared that these powers would allow the government to develop into a tyranny. Despite these concerns, some states ratified the Constitution without reservation. Others, however, voted to ratify but insisted on sending recommended amendments along with the ratification message. Typically, the conventions modeled these amendments on their own state bill of rights, protecting popular rights against the powers of government. Among these proposals were various clusters addressed to the organization of political violence — provisions that would limit Congress's power over the army and the militia and would guarantee the right to arms. The Second Amendment developed from these clusters. The origin of the amendment thus lies centrally with those Anti-Federalists concerned about excessive federal control of the state militias.

In 1792, James Madison, who had initially resisted the adoption of a Bill of Rights, changed direction, apparently to generate further support for the new regime among its recent opponents. He submitted to Congress a series of constitutional amendments drawn from the amendments proposed by the states. This list included a right-to-arms provision, which proved uncontroversial. Congress rewrote the language slightly and removed a clause providing that Congress could not make religious objectors bear arms. It then voted to submit the Bill of Rights to the states, and upon their ratification the first ten amendments to the Constitution became law.

That series of events is the skeleton, the bare bones, of the Second Amendment's history, and they are fairly clear. The reasons those events occurred and the intent of the actors involved, however, are much less clear, so that clothing the bones in the flesh of context has been a controversial process. At the center of this story is a fact that many modern commentators seek to obscure: the Constitution speaks in not one but two voices. The first voice is the largely Federalist voice of Article I of the original Constitution; it is a voice that worries principally about popular sedition and finds safety in congressional power. The second voice is the largely Anti-Federalist voice of the Second Amendment; it is a voice that worries principally about federal tyranny and finds safety in a popular militia.

The difference between these two voices should not be overstated: it is really one of emphasis rather than outright contradiction. The Federalists spoke principally in the tones of the first voice (and Article I), but they would not have denied that the people-in-militia have a right to arms for revolution. Similarly, the Anti-Federalists expressed their fear in the second voice (and the Second Amendment), but they never sought to eliminate Congress's ability to raise a standing army or supervise the militia. Relatively speaking, Federalists trusted Congress and a standing army more than the Anti-Federalists did, and the Anti-Federalists trusted the states and local militias more than the Federalists did, but neither group wholly trusted their preferred institutions nor wholly distrusted their dispreferred ones. And although Anti-Federalists may have been more inclined to republicanism and Federalists to liberalism, both borrowed freely from the two traditions. Relying on Locke, some republicans would trace the origin of government to the rectoral contract and its dissolution to government's violation of that contract. And some Federalists would adopt republican categories to argue that, if the government should become corrupt and use a standing army to suppress freedom, the state militias would be able successfully to resist.

Ultimately, therefore, these two voices can be rendered harmonious. Indeed, as our fundamental political morality, the Constitution should be interpreted as a consistent set of principles, rather than a document at war with itself. When we read the document in this way, however, we must not neglect the fact that it is composed of different pieces with different emphases; and it will as a result yield not a simple message but a complex and subtle one. It urges us to repose naive trust in neither the mass of private individuals nor the government but instead to reach for a more encompassing and realistic vision of the constitutional organization of violence.

The First Voice: Article I

Before it ever announces the necessity of a well-regulated militia in the Second Amendment, the Constitution intones the importance of congressional power over political violence in Article I. Congress has the power to raise and maintain a standing army and navy.[2] It also has the power "to provide for organizing, arming, and disciplining the militia, and for governing such part of them as may be employed in the service of the United States"; the states retain only "the appointment of the officers, and the authority of training the militia according to the discipline prescribed by Congress."[3] The Constitution, moreover, leaves no doubt that Congress should use these armed forces to suppress what it considers to be rebellion. Article III gives Congress the "power to declare punishment of treason";[4] Article I allows it "to provide for calling forth the militia to execute the laws of the Union, suppress insurrections, and repel invasions";[5] and Article IV mandates that the federal government "shall guarantee to every state in this Union a republican form of government, and shall protect each of them against invasion; and, on application of the Legislature, or of the Executive (when the Legislative cannot be convened), against domestic violence."[6]

The Constitution's first voice thus insists that Congress should have armed might to quell internal disturbances. Specific historical events contributed to the influence of this voice. The Articles of Confederation gave the central government very limited powers; in particular, Congress received no power to supervise the state militias. As the 1780s progressed, some Americans thought that the American social fabric was unraveling around them, and they looked to a stronger central government to restore the warp. Shays' Rebellion convinced these people that Congress needed greater control over the nation's men in arms. In 1786, several thousand men under the leadership of Captain Daniel Shays demanded tax reduction and debtor relief in the western counties of Massachusetts. Self-consciously emulating the direct action of 1774–75, the Shaysites closed down state courts to prevent the execution of debt judgments. Many local militia members cooperated with the insurgents or refused to take action against them. At the same time, other backcountry resistance movements were developing in many other states. Eventually, eastern militia units dispersed the Shays' rebels, who had never developed into a broad revolution, but the violence frightened the authors of the new Constitution.[7]

Virtually all historians agree that the Shays' Rebellion and similar unrest affected the drafting of the Constitution and led many to support its adoption. As the leading scholar of the rebellion explains, "The resulting union of American leaders originated at least in part from the domestic upheavals taking place in 1786 and 1787. To the nationalists, Shays' Rebellion reflected the overall inadequacy of a political system dominated by semisovereign states. . . . The New England rebellion also convinced some state-oriented leaders of the need for a more powerful national government. For many localists, Shaysite activity came as a shock."[8] The *Federalist Papers* refer repeatedly to Shays' Rebellion as a reason to support the new constitution, with its more centralized control over insurrection.[9]

The Framers responded to this fear by giving Congress an axial role in the organization of political violence. In their view, such delegation had many advantages. As leader of a unified nation, Congress could better protect its citizens against foreign aggression, and it could forestall domestic wars between the states.[10] In addition, Congress could more effectively control domestic insurrection within a given state. In *Federalist* number 9, Hamilton declares, "A firm union will be of the utmost moment to the peace and liberty of the States as a barrier against domestic faction and insurrection." Quoting Montesquieu, he explains that in a large republic, "should a popular insurrection happen in one of the confederate states, the others are able to quell it. Should abuses creep into one part, they are reformed by those that remain sound."[11] At the Philadelphia convention, Madison explained that because the states "neglect their militias now, the discipline of the militia is evidently a *National* concern and ought to be provided for in the *National* Constitution."[12]

In giving Congress this new role, the Framers relied on a conviction that Congress could domesticate political violence better than the local militias acting on their own. Congress's great advantage was that it represented the whole of the United States, not local interests, and thus could be trusted to act for the whole. Hamilton asks, "Who so likely to make suitable provision for the public defense as that body to which the guardianship of the public safety is confided; . . . as the representative of the WHOLE will feel itself most deeply interested in the preservation of every part; which, from the responsibility implied in the duty assigned to it, will be most sensibly impressed with the necessity of proper exertions; and which, by the extension of its authority throughout the States, can alone establish uniformity and concert in the plans and measures by which the common safety is to be secured?"[13] As a result, Congress could produce a uniform system of order that would forestall local insurrection: "One government . . . can harmonize, assimilate, and protect the several parts and members, and extend the benefits of its foresight and pre-cautions to each. . . . It can apply the resources and the power of the whole to the defence of any particular part. . . . It can place the militia under one plan of discipline."[14]

By contrast, the problem with decentralizing control of political violence was that individual states, individual militia units, even individual militia members, were free to make up their minds for themselves. That sort of piece-meal decision making portended simple havoc, not unified action of the sort that the Framers recalled (perhaps sentimentally) in the War for Independence. Grimly, the *Federalist Papers* map out a disastrous fate if the United States should not centralize control: states would likely go to war with each other; they would then develop standing armies, dangerous to their citizens' liberties; and, naively trusting their state governments, the people would not perceive the danger in these armies until too late.[15]

Furthermore, in the Federalists' view, instead of leading to broad popular control, the decentralization of political violence would create factional war-fare, in which a small part of the citizenry might come to dominate the rest. Madison warned that in the absence of a federal "power to suppress insurrec-tions, our liberties might be destroyed by domestic faction."[16] As Hamilton explained, "A turbulent faction in a State may easily suppose itself able to contend with the friends to the government in that state; but it can hardly be so infatuated as to imagine itself a match for the combined efforts of the Union."[17] And even if the local militia had the power to suppress faction, it might become infected with the virus itself. Ordinarily, if an insurrection "should be a slight commotion in a small part of a State, the militia of the residue would be adequate to its suppression; and the natural presumption is that they would be ready to do their duty." Hamilton, however, remembered too vividly the conduct of the militia during Shays' Rebellion. He warned that a federal standing army might be necessary to suppress broad-based insurrection: "If, on the contrary, the insurrection should pervade a whole State, or a principal part of it, the employment of a different kind of force [that is, regular troops] might become unavoidable. It appears that Massachusetts found it necessary to raise troops for suppressing the disorders within that State. . . . [W]hy should the possibility that the national government might be under a like necessity, in similar extremities, be made an objection to its existence? . . . Who would not prefer that possibility to the unceasing agitations and frequent revolutions which are the continual scourge of petty republics?"[18] And like its control of a standing army, Congress's regulation of the militia would secure the good of the whole against local factions: "The power of regulating the militia and of commanding its services in times of insurrection and invasion are natural incidents to the duties of superintending the common defense, and of watching over the internal peace of the Confederacy. . . . In times of insurrection, it would be natural and proper that the militia of a neighboring State should be marched into another, to resist a common enemy, or to guard the republic against the violence of faction or sedition . . . and this mutual succor is, indeed, a principal end of our political association."[19]

In trusting Congress with the dominant role in the organization of violence, the Framers departed from the old militia ideal in two significant ways. First, they were trusting a body composed of the people's delegates, rather than the people themselves, as in the militia. This departure seemed worthwhile to them for three reasons. First, Congress was a legislative body, and so under most circumstances it would act in a responsible way. Thus, Hamilton maintained of Congress's power to raise a standing army that "independent of all other reasonings upon the subject, it is a full answer to those who require a more peremptory provision against military establishments in time of peace to say that the whole power of the proposed government is to be in the hands of the representatives of the people."[20] Second, even if the people had only an indirect voice in Congress, at least Congress represented the whole of the people; as we have seen, the Federalists believed that local militias, by contrast, were given to faction. And third, if Congress ever did violate its trust, even the Federalists were certain that the Body of the People retained the right and the ability to overturn it by force.

The Framers' second major departure from the old militia ideal involved a reconceptualization of the nature of union: the *whole* for these Federalists was the United States of America, not some subunit like a state or a militia unit or a county. Only because they defined the whole in this way did Congress enjoy a natural advantage in perceiving the interests of the whole. If the Federalists had defined the whole in more local terms, then more local bodies would have had the advantage. Once the states were perceived as inextricably connected under one jurisdiction, then it was inevitable they would need a single national government with primary control over the means of violence to watch over their collective interests. Again, the Federalists believed that this reconceptualization was highly desirable for the reasons already outlined: as a firm union, the United States could better resist foreign aggression, keep peace between the states, and prevent rebellion within the states.

On both sides of the Atlantic, civic republicans had described the militia as an organic entity identical to the people itself; and Anti-Federalist supporters of the Second Amendment continued to do so even after Shays' Rebellion. Some Federalists, by contrast, saw in the militia for the first time a stew of atomism and diversity. Conceptually, then, both sides in this debate agreed on the importance of assigning the means of political violence to a stable, unified authority that could speak for the people. Institutionally, by contrast, they disagreed on who might best exhibit those qualities, Congress or the militia. Even Federalists did not believe that Congress should always be trusted; they reserved a right of popular insurrection under extraordinary circumstances. They did, however, believe that under normal circumstances the people as a whole could speak most effectively in Congress. Anti-Federalists believed, by contrast, that a distant and elitist Congress might speak poorly for the people as a whole; instead, they placed their faith in the militia, which at least included the entire citizenry.

The Second Voice: The Second Amendment

Although chronologically first, the first voice is still only half the story. As soon as this voice began to promise safety through central power, others offered a counterchorus in praise of another view, that of safety through popular arming. The Second Amendment grew out of this oppositional mind-set, a dissatisfaction with the Constitution as it then stood. Legally, the Bill of Rights (including the Second Amendment) is a series of amendments to the Constitution; legally, to amend the Constitution is to change it; one does not change a law unless one is unhappy with it; and, in fact, the people who initially proposed a Bill of Rights were unhappy with the Constitution, including its organization of political violence. In searching for the legal meaning of the Second Amendment, then, one must first ask why the provision's supporters were unhappy and what they wished to change, so as to understand what they managed ultimately to secure in the amendment.

The Anti-Federalists' opposition ran along several thematic axes. In place of a standing army and a select militia, they celebrated a people's militia; in place of federal preeminence in the organization of political violence, they embraced state power; in place of popular empowerment only by representation through Congress, they also espoused a right of popular resistance. To hear this different voice, one must understand the worldview from which it arose through a series of linked concepts: the citizen militia, the Body of the People, the right of resistance, the nature of revolution, and decentralization.

THE CITIZEN MILITIA: THE BODY OF THE PEOPLE

The Anti-Federalists proposed the amendment, in part, as an ode to that traditional republican paragon, the citizen militia. The amendment itself identifies its central conviction: "A well-regulated militia [is] necessary to the security of a free state." The Anti-Federalists originally agitated for the Second Amendment because they feared that Congress might abuse its powers of supervision over the militia. These objections took two basic forms. Many feared that a federalized militia might be little better than a standing army. Distant from the people, dependent on the central government, it would be a ready tool for the advancement of oppressive congressional designs. If faced with a refractory citizenry in one state, Congress could simply order militia from another state, distant from local concerns, to quell the rebellion. Thus, one Anti-Federalist warned his readers, perhaps a tad hysterically, that if any of them should resist Congress, it could "send the militia of Pennsylvania, Boston, or any other state or place, to cut your throats, ravage and destroy your plantations, drive away your cattle and horses, abuse your wives, kill your infants, and ravish your daughters, and live in free quarters, until you get into a good humour, and pay all that they may think proper to ask of you, and you become good and faithful servants and slaves."[21] Because of this fear, many argued for limiting Congress's power over the standing army and the militia, but these proposed structural amendments never became law.[22]

Others offered a different objection: Congress might simply neglect the militia and allow it to slide into ineffectiveness. A lifeless militia could not serve as a tool of federal tyranny, but neither could it serve any of its salutary purposes. And the easiest way for Congress to render the militia obsolescent would be to fail to keep it armed or, more directly, to disarm it. Patrick Henry asked, "Of what service would militia be to you when most probably you will not have a single musket in the State; for as arms are to be provided by Congress, they may or may not furnish them?"[23] Similarly, George Mason worried that Congress could render the militia "useless — by disarming them. . . . Congress may neglect to provide for arming and disciplining the militia; and the state governments cannot do it, for congress has an exclusive right to arm them."[24] Federalists responded that even under the unamended Constitution the states would have concurrent power to arm the militia, but Anti-Federalist suspicions were not so easily assuaged.[25]

Federalists further claimed that the two Anti-Federalist fears were contradictory: on the one hand, oppositionists feared that Congress would turn the militia into a powerful implement of federal wrath; on the other hand, they feared that Congress would turn it into a feeble shell of its former self.[26] In fact, however, the two fears were linked at a deeper level: either way, in the Anti-Federalists' view, the Constitution allowed Congress to destroy the independent puissance of the militia. And so these oppositionists agitated for amendments to protect the militia. This concern lies at the heart of the legal history of the Second Amendment.

Who was this militia, and why was its independence so important? By law, the state militias traditionally included every male citizen of arms-bearing capacity. As the Supreme Court summarized in one of its very few — and quite delphic — pronouncements on the meaning of the amendment, "The Militia comprised all males physically capable of acting in concert for the common defense." For example, in 1786, New York specified that the militia shall consist of "every able-bodied Male person, being a Citizen of this State, or of any of the United States, and residing in this State, . . . and who are of the Age of Sixteen, and under the Age of Forty-five Years." Similarly, in 1785, the Virginia legislature declared that its militia should include "all free male persons between the ages of eighteen and fifty years." In 1784, Massachusetts divided its militia into the Trained Band, which enrolled "all able bodied men, from sixteen to forty years," and the Alarm List, which included "all other men under sixty years of age."[27]

Advocates of the militia repeatedly stressed that it should include virtually every citizen. For example, the Federal Farmer explained, "A militia, when properly formed, are in fact the people themselves."[28] Mason asked, "Who are the militia? They consist now of the whole people, except a few public officers."[29] During the Revolutionary War, the New Castle County committee of safety in Delaware held that "a well regulated militia, composed of the gentlemen, freeholders, and other freemen, is the natural strength and stable security of a free government."[30] Similarly, in his plan for the Fairfax County militia, Mason called for a "well regulated militia, composed of the Gentlemen, Freeholders, and other Freemen."[31] Henry urged the Virginia convention to resolve that "a well regulated militia, composed of the gentlemen and yeomen, is the natural strength and only security of a free government."[32]

The language of the Second Amendment — "a well-regulated militia being necessary to the security of a free state" — grew out of this tradition. Its final version does not specify the militia's membership, but its history clearly indicates that it incorporates this universal definition. Many of the states' proposals for a Bill of Rights assert that the right to arms belongs to a militia composed not of random individuals or government employees, but of the Body of the People. In 1776, the Virginia Declaration of Rights maintained that "a well regulated militia, composed of the body of the people, trained to arms, is the proper, natural, and safe defense of a free state."[33] Following this language, the Virginia convention proposed that the federal constitution adopt a similar protection: "That the people have a right to keep and bear arms; that a well regulated militia, composed of the body of the people, trained to arms, is the proper, natural, and safe defence of a free state."[34] North Carolina's version followed Virginia's word-for-word, and New York's and Rhode Island's proposals differed only in specifying that the militia should include the Body of the People "capable of bearing arms."[35]

When Madison introduced his proposed version of the right to arms, he did not specify who should compose the membership of the militia: "The right of the people to keep and bear arms shall not be infringed; a well armed, and well regulated militia being the best security of a free country; but no person religiously scrupulous of bearing arms shall be compelled to render military service."[36] Given the tradition out of which this amendment grew, however, it plainly presupposes a militia composed of the Body of the People. Indeed, without any explanation for the change, the House Committee on Amendments revised Madison's language so that its version referred explicitly to a militia composed of the Body of the People.[37] Then, once more without explanation, the Senate's version referred to the militia without a specific membership criterion, and that formulation became the present Second Amendment.[38] In other words, the amendment dropped, restored, and dropped again a reference to the Body of the People, and no one thought the changes warranted a word of exposition — apparently because everyone understood that the militia implicitly included the Body of the People.

In short, the Framers would not have drawn a sharp distinction between the militia and the people because the militia was the people's military manifestation. This fact helps explain the language of the provision as well: the purpose clause, praising a "well-regulated militia," and the operative language, granting a right to the people, are not really in tension because both refer to the Body of the People, the whole of the citizenry arrayed in arms together.

To be sure, the Body of the People in militia did not include every adult. As the above provisions indicate, some people were considered too old or otherwise incapable of bearing arms in a military context. And the Body of the

People included only citizens, not all residents.[39] As a result, Blacks and Indians were typically excluded. Indeed, from early on, many colonies forbade the sale of firearms to Indians or other people of color, and a primary purpose of the militia was to control slaves.[40] Finally, as the century wore on, the militia laws came to be very laxly enforced and sometimes not enforced at all. Some state laws even allowed persons subject to militia duty to pay a substitute to take their place.[41] As a result, by the 1780s the concept of the old universal militia rarely came to realization in the world; it may have existed primarily as a paper concept, a legal ideal.

Nonetheless, the universal militia was the legal ideal, the ideal that became a part of the Constitution. The men who defined the militia as the Body of the People may have been aware that the militia had long since ceased to satisfy that definition, or they may have deluded themselves into thinking that the militia was something it was not. In either event, whatever the militia's real-world composition, promilitia forces believed it should include all capable citizens, and they presumed that definition in writing the Second Amendment. They had good reasons, within their frame of reference, for so insisting. This definition of the militia was not merely happenstance: it served deep ideological ends, connected to the right of resistance.

THE RIGHT OF RESISTANCE

For the civic republican tradition, as we have seen, it was critical that the militia be universal because the militia possessed the right to resist a corrupt government. To be legitimate, an armed uprising must be for the common good, rather than a factional interest. As a result, it must be made by the people as a whole, for the people as a whole. Inevitably, resistance by a segment of society would be made in its self-interest. Despite his individualism, Locke also assumed that the people would make a unified revolution; he rejected an individual right to insurrection as a reversion to the state of nature. In short, then, within the Framers' intellectual inheritance, the militia had to be universal because it had the right to resist — and vice-versa. In that sense, the militia was not a passive agency of the state but an entity with a mind of its own, using its independent judgment to decide when resistance had become appropriate.[42]

Given this inheritance, it is not surprising that the Framers generally believed that the militia had a right of resistance because, but only because, it was universal. Eighteenth-century Americans had firsthand experience of the benefits of the militia in opposing tyranny. Traditionally, to enforce their decisions, colonial governors had to rely on the posse comitatus and the militia. Colonial records are full of complaints that these popular bodies refused to enforce edicts perceived as unjust by the citizenry; sometimes, they even participated in popular opposition to such commands.[43] Colonial culture accepted some measure of violent resistance as a normal part of political life, although most in authority never accepted it. If the governors disregarded the people's wishes, the colonists thought it natural to go outside normal channels: to riot, burn royal ships, close down courthouses, assault royal officials and destroy their property, or pursue the many other courses of action that their disobedient minds could imagine.[44]

Most famously, Thomas Jefferson celebrated the right of the people to resist a corrupt government: "And what country can preserve its liberties, if its rulers are not warned from time to time, that this people preserve the spirit of resistance? Let them take arms. . . . The tree of liberty must be refreshed from time to time, with the blood of patriots and tyrants."[45] Less dramatically but more carefully, John Adams rejected a right to use arms "at individual discretion,"[46] but he celebrated broad popular arming and collective resistance. Quoting from Marchamont Nedham, he explained the practices of the classical world: "One consequence [of popular arming] was . . . 'that nothing could at any time be imposed upon the people but by their consent. . . . [T]he Grecian states ever had special care to place the use and exercise of arms in the people, because the commonwealth is theirs who hold the arms: the sword and sovereignty ever walk hand in hand together.' This is perfectly just." For that reason, as the ancients teach us, the militia should be universal: "Rome, and the territories about it, were trained up perpetually in arms, and the whole commonwealth, by this means, became one formal militia."[47]

During the ratification period, Anti-Federalists objected to the new constitution on the grounds that Congress might use its powers to subvert the militia's capacity to resist a corrupt central government. John DeWitt, for example, warned that congressmen "at their pleasure may arm or disarm all or any part of the freemen of the United States, so that when their army is sufficiently numerous, they may put it out of the power of the freemen militia of America to assert and defend their liberties."[48] A Federal Republican worried that Congress might use a standing army to "suppress those struggles which may sometimes happen among a free people, and which tyranny may impiously brand with the name of sedition."[49] The Federal Farmer maintained that to "preserve liberty, it is essential that the whole body of the people always possess arms, and be taught alike, especially when young, how to use them."[50] In the North Carolina ratifying convention, William Lenoir warned that Congress's new powers would allow it to "disarm the militia. If they were armed, they would be a resource against great oppressions. . . . If the laws of the Union were oppressive, they could not carry them into effect, if the people were possessed of proper means of defence."[51]

It was in Virginia, the crucible out of which Madison's draft for the Second Amendment emerged, that these fears were most articulately and forcefully expressed, by Henry and Mason, preeminent proponents of the need for a Bill of Rights. In famous words, Henry declaimed, "Guard with jealous attention the public liberty. Suspect everyone who approaches that jewel. Unfortunately, nothing will preserve it but downright force. Whenever you give up that force, you are ruined." He worried that Congress's power over the militia would subvert its ability to resist federal oppression: "Have we the means of resisting disciplined armies, when our only defence, the militia, is put into the hands of Congress?"[52] Mason reminded the convention that earlier tyrants sought "to disarm the people; . . . [I]t was the best and most effectual way to enslave them . . . by totally disusing and neglecting the militia."[53]

Federalists responded not that the militia had no right to resist, but that, as a practical matter, the Constitution, even without amendments, did not interfere with that right. Over and over, the *Federalist Papers* declare that an armed people would still be able to resist a tyrannical government. Thus, in number 46, Madison contends that if somehow the federal government managed to accumulate a standing army for tyrannical schemes, "it would not be going too far to say that the State governments with the people on their side would be able to repel the danger." Against any standing army "would be opposed a militia amounting to near half a million of citizens with arms in their hands, officered by men chosen from among themselves, fighting for their common liberties and united and conducted by governments possessing their affections and confidence."[54] Similarly, Hamilton insisted, "If the representatives of the people betray their constituents, there is then no resource left but in the exertion of that original right of self-defense which is paramount to all forms of government." And that right can best be executed in a large republic of the sort that the Constitution contemplated: "The natural strength of the people in a large community, in proportion to the artificial strength of the government, is greater than in a small, and of course more competent to a struggle with the attempts of the government to establish a tyranny."[55] Noah Webster similarly asserted, "The supreme power in America cannot enforce unjust laws by the sword; because the whole body of the people are armed, and constitute a force superior to any band of regular troops that can be, on any pretence, raised in the United States."[56] In short, then, virtually everyone in the constitutional generation, Federalist and Anti-Federalist alike, believed that the right of revolution would survive the adoption of the Constitution.

Where they disagreed was over the question of whether the new Constitution would frustrate the operation of that right. Federalists were sanguine about the document's operation. In response to the worry that Congress might raise a standing army, Hamilton responded that any such army would be small because of America's isolation. A small standing army would not interfere with the people's right of revolution: "The citizens, not habituated to look up to the military power for protection, or to submit to its oppressions, neither love nor fear the soldiery; they view them with a spirit of jealous acquiescence in a necessary evil and stand ready to resist a power which they suppose may be exerted to the prejudice of their rights."[57] In response to the worry that Congress might order one's state militia into another state to execute a tyrannous scheme, Hamilton protested that the militia would simply ignore the order and march on Washington instead: "Whither would the militia, irritated at being required to undertake a distant and distressing expedition for the purpose of riveting the chains of slavery upon a part of their countrymen, direct their course, but to the seat of tyrants, . . . and to make them an example of the just vengeance of an abused and incensed people?"[58] And in response to the concern that Congress might fail to arm the militia, Madison responded in the Virginia convention that states had concurrent power to arm them should Congress fail in its duties.[59]

Unconvinced that the federal government would be so harmless, Anti-Federalists agitated for a Bill of Rights. Their proposed amendments included limits on Congress's power to regulate the militia, prohibitions and restrictions on a standing army, and guarantees of the right to arms. In the end, Madison included only the third type of provision in his proposed set of amendments, which became the Bill of Rights. Unhappy with the absence of the other types, some Anti-Federalists actually campaigned against its adoption, in hopes of getting more.[60] Nonetheless, the origin of the Second Amendment lies with those Anti-Federalists who were dissatisfied with the Constitution's original organization of violence. They wrote the proposed right to arms provisions, they agitated for their adoption, and Madison introduced the amendments to ameliorate their objections. We should therefore look principally to their views in interpreting the right to arms. And so it bears repeating that these provisions were based on dissatisfaction with Congress's complete dominance of political violence under Article I; they were amendments to the Constitution designed to redistribute power away from the center.

In recent years, some commentators have rejected the idea that the Second Amendment reflects Anti-Federalist ideas. Garry Wills has emerged as the most forceful exponent of this group.[61] In his view, in interpreting the amendment we should look not to the Anti-Federalists but to certain Federalists who, he claims, rejected the militia's traditional right of resistance. He reaches this conclusion by two chains of reasoning. First, he observes that because the Anti-Federalists did not get a ban on a standing army, some ultimately resisted the adoption of the Bill of Rights: "Their main object had been defeated."[62] It is indeed true that the Anti-Federalists did not get all they wanted in the Bill of Rights. It is also true, however, that they got some of what they wanted, specifically the Second Amendment, and their desire for that provision grew out of their general thinking. As a result, while it is wildly implausible to read a standing army ban into the Constitution, we must still look to the Anti-Federalists' thinking in order to contextualize the meaning of the provision they did get.

Wills's second line of attack focuses on Madison's subjective motivations in introducing the Bill of Rights. In Wills's view, Madison introduced the amendment merely to placate Anti-Federalist opposition with flattering but empty talk about the militia. Madison did not really want to change anything in the Constitution: "If Madison had wanted to address the Antifederalists' real concerns, he would have done something about the four clauses [that is, Congress's military powers] on which the debates were obsessively focused. The fact that he did not do so means that . . . we must suspect beforehand that aggrandizement of the states was not a motive for drafting the Second Amendment." Instead, Madison's "actions were taken, in fact, to disarm opposition to the four military clauses in the Constitution."[63] Madison achieved this aim by mere empty rhetoric:

> Why then did Madison propose the Second Amendment? For the same reason that he proposed the Third, against quartering troops on the civilian population. That was a remnant of old royal attempts to create a standing army by requisition of civilian facilities. It had no real meaning in a government that is *authorized* to build barracks, forts, and camps. But it was part of the anti-royal rhetoric of freedom that had shown up, like the militia language, in state requests for amendments to the Constitution. . . . Sweet-talking the militia was a small price to pay for such a coup—and it had as much impact on real life as the anti-quartering provisions that arose from the same motive.[64]

So here is the meaning of the Second Amendment according to Wills: in his secret heart, Madison was merely planning a "coup," not a sincere effort at constitutional revision. He wrote a provision that had "no real meaning," no "impact on real life"; it was instead merely "sweet-talking," hollow "anti-royal rhetoric," a disingenuous ode to the virtues of a militia. In recent years, perhaps in the wake of severe criticism,[65] Wills has slightly changed his position. He now affirms that the Second Amendment does have one narrow stricture: on state request, the federal government must keep the state militias equipped for local service, even when not acting as federal instrumentalities.[66] Again, however, Wills reaches this conclusion by his reading of Madison's intent: Madison wrote the amendment merely as a clever ploy to "*protect* the powers of government" while appearing to grant concessions to the Anti-Federalists.[67]

The first problem with this argument is that, as we have seen, the Federalists' public statements were not so different from those of the Anti-Federalists: both assumed that the popular militias retained a right of resistance even after the Constitution. Although the Federalists did not want amendments, therefore, they would not generally have found it objectionable to recognize such a right. Let us assume, however, for the sake of argument that Wills is right: Madison and the other Federalists were proceeding entirely in bad faith. They offered their public statements as a smokescreen to buy support for the new regime. Their real intent, therefore, was to deceive their opponents with the appearance of change. And, Wills says, one should look to that "real intent" for our constitutional meaning.

By this line of reasoning, Wills proposes a startling technique for interpreting this amendment: we should look to the intent of those who did not want to change the document at all, rather than to the intent of those who did. That approach may help illumine the political climate of the times, but it is not the way that the law finds meaning in history. Even that most famous (or infamous) of originalists, Robert Bork, pulls back before the idea that constitutional interpretation should be reduced to psychoanalyzing the Framers:

> What the ratifiers understood themselves to be enacting must be taken to be what the public of that time would have understood the words to mean. It is important to be clear about this. The search is not for a subjective intention. If someone found a letter from George Washington to Martha telling her that what he meant by the power to lay taxes was not what other people meant, that would not change our reading of the Constitution in the slightest. Nor would the subjective intentions of all the members of a ratifying convention alter anything. When lawmakers use words, the law that results is what those words ordinarily mean.[68]

In introducing the Second Amendment, therefore, Madison should be understood to mean the words in their ordinary sense, the sense in which the Anti-Federalists would have understood them. Repeatedly and formally, Madison had endorsed a popular right of resistance; even if he had secretly (among friends and in his heart) outgrown that commitment, the Constitution will hold him to his words. And even if Madison had become less than enthusiastic about the Second Amendment, he still professed to be accommodating the Anti-Federalists' desires, so those desires should form the basis of our interpretation. The alternative is to allow constitutional drafters, with a nod and a wink to their colleagues, to fob off public demands for change with meaningless, cannily worded provisions. As a matter of constitutional law, that alternative is unthinkable because it would reward deception and manipulation rather than open, good faith dialogue.

In considering the meaning of the amendment, therefore, I begin with the Anti-Federalist objections to the Constitution because their proposals became the Bill of Rights. Then, during the later congressional debates on the amendments, only one person, the Anti-Federalist Elbridge Gerry, offered an extensive explanation of the Second Amendment's purpose. No Congressman contradicted Gerry or suggested a different purpose for the provision. Because the congressional debates are the most legally relevant background for the amendment, Gerry's remarks deserve careful analysis. Gerry rose to criticize Madison's draft for allowing Congress to exempt religious objectors from military service. (Ultimately, the Senate would delete this exemption but without explanation of its reasons). By way of context, he explained his understanding of the amendment's purpose: "This declaration of rights, I take it, is intended to secure the people against the mal-administration of the Government; if we could suppose that, in all cases, the rights of the people would be attended to, the occasion for guards of this kind would be removed. . . . What, sir, is the use of the militia? It is to prevent the establishment of a standing army, the bane of liberty."[69] Packed into this concise statement are the elements of the Anti-Federalists' vision: governments sometimes use standing armies to attack the people's liberty; the people therefore need to form a militia because with a militia in place the government might not rely on a standing army for security; and the militia would be infinitely preferable to a standing army because it will guard against governmental abuse rather than slavishly follow unjust orders.

Gerry then explained his objection to the religious exemption. He was concerned not that Congress might enlist conscientious objectors against their will, but that Congress might exempt so many people from service that the militia would become ineffective. In the course of this analysis, he overtly compares Congress to the British Empire, against whom the colonies had revolted only a few years before:

> Now, I am apprehensive, sir, that this clause would give an opportunity for the people in power to destroy the constitution itself. They can declare who are those religiously scrupulous, and prevent them from bearing arms. . . . Congress could take such measures with respect to a militia, as to make a standing army necessary. Whenever Government means to invade the rights

and liberties of the people, they always attempt to destroy the militia, in order to raise an army upon their ruins. This was actually done by Great Britain at the commencement of the late revolution. They used every means in their power to prevent the establishment of an effective militia to the eastward. The Assembly of Massachusetts, seeing the rapid progress that administration were making to divest them of their inherent privileges, endeavored to counteract them by the organization of the militia; but they were always defeated by the influence of the crown.[70]

In this passage, Gerry argues that the best paradigm for interpreting the Second Amendment is the American Revolution. According to Gerry, that model teaches the classic Anti-Federalist lessons: all governments, including the new Congress, have the potential to behave oppressively; to that end, they raise armies and destroy militias; the people must therefore keep the militia strong, organized, and broad, so as to protect their "ancient privileges" against the schemes of a corrupt government.

If the militia had the right to resist, however, the Framers were adamant that it had to be universal. Gerry hints at this point in the foregoing excerpt, but others made it overt. As the Body of the People, the militia could not act against the general good because the general good and its own good were one and the same. Samuel Adams, for example, argued, "The militia is composed of free Citizens. There is therefore no Danger of their making use of their power to the destruction of their own Rights, or suffering others to invade them."[71] Even some Federalists took that view. Tench Coxe, for example, believed that even without constitutional amendments the universal militia would block any federal oppression: "THE POWERS OF THE SWORD ARE IN THE HANDS OF THE YEOMANRY OF AMERICA FROM SIXTEEN TO SIXTY. . . . Who are the militia? *are they not ourselves.* Is it feared, then, that we shall turn our arms *each man against his bosom.*"[72]

For this reason, the Framers expressed deep suspicion of a standing army, which represented only a slice of society.[73] Many proposed amendments condemned reliance on a standing army: Virginia's proposal, for example, warned that "standing armies, in time of peace, are dangerous to liberty, and therefore ought to be avoided."[74] M. T. Cicero condemned reliance on a standing army in traditional republican terms: "Whenever, therefore, the profession of arms becomes a distinct order in the state . . . the end of the social compact is defeated."[75] The Federal Farmer also decried giving over control to "distinct bodies of military men, not having permanent interests and attachments in the community."[76] Gerry sounded the same note in the congressional debates on the amendment.

A less-than-universal militia was not much better than a standing army, and

Second Amendment proponents denounced it as a "select militia" that would pursue its own aims rather than the good of the whole.[77] In agitating for amendments to the Constitution, for example, the Federal Farmer wrote, "The constitution ought to secure a genuine and guard against a select militia, by providing that the militia shall always be kept well organized, armed, and disciplined, and include . . . all men capable of bearing arms."[78] John Smilie warned the Pennsylvania ratifying convention, "Congress may give us a select militia which will, in fact, be a standing army — or Congress, afraid of a general militia, may say there shall be no militia at all. When a select militia is formed; the people in general may be disarmed."[79]

These promilitia voices confidently predicted not only that a universal militia could resist a corrupt government, but also that in practice it might make the need for resistance very rare. Once the people as a whole had arms, potential tyrants would be loathe to trifle with their liberties.[80] Some militia proponents also believed that general arms possession made citizens more independent and less willing to tolerate an infraction of their rights. Resistance to despots may have been difficult and frightening, and acceptance of abuse may have seemed the easiest course. Not too far down that path, however, lay slavery.[81] A people armed and aware of its power would not start down that path, and so revolution might never be necessary.

REVOLUTION AND REBELLION

Second Amendment supporters thus endorsed a right of revolution as a key element in the constitutional organization of violence. Advocates of a militia, however, were not mindless purveyors of domestic unrest; they did not celebrate all acts of popular violence. As important as the Framers' support for some uprisings is their condemnation of others. Although the proponents of the Second Amendment argued that the Body of the People had a right of revolution, they were aware of the danger implicit in this right and so developed a number of limits on it. For example, a revolution must be a course of last resort, and its object must be a true tyrant, one committed to large-scale abuse, not merely randomly unjust or sinful in private life.[82]

The most important limit, however, was that only the Body of the People could make a revolution. When the Framers limited the right in this way, they correlatively were arguing that not all insurrections were legitimate. Instead, they carefully drew a distinction between resistance made by the people for the common good, which they called a revolution, and resistance made by a faction for a faction, which they called a rebellion or an insurrection. In the current debate over the Second Amendment, failure to observe this distinction has caused needless confusion: some states' rights theorists assume that because the Framers regarded some uprisings as illegitimate, they must have regarded them all that way; and some individual rights theorists assume that because the Framers praised some uprisings, they must have wanted to give private individuals the right to arms for their personal crusades. In fact, however, the Framers were more subtle than either of these camps.

The American revolutionaries believed that they had direct experience with the distinction between rebellion and revolution. No sooner had they completed a revolution against Great Britain than they proceeded to repress what they regarded as rebellions at home, such as Vermont's drive for independence, the Carolina Regulation, Shays' Rebellion, the New York tenant protests, the Whiskey Rebellion, and others.[83] The new rebels claimed the mantle of 1776; in their minds, they were holding to the faith of Washington and Jefferson by making a popular revolution against a distant, tyrannical government.[84] Following Shays' Rebellion, one royalist letter writer criticized the Massachusetts Supreme Court for hypocrisy in punishing the rebels: "You did formally commit many irregularities, in opposing the king and the ministry of the nation and wrongfully beguiled the people of this state and continent, with the desultory notion that they should not be commanded by any man whatsoever." He wonders, then, how the justices can justify themselves "in punishing any or more of your brethren for stopping, or endeavoring to stop any courts in this state?"[85]

The Framers of the Constitution had an answer: the War for Independence was a revolution in the common good, but the new uprisings were rebellions in the interests of a faction. Government had the right to repress rebellion but not revolution. Thus, Madison campaigned for federal control of the militia in order to suppress factional uprisings, not to quash a general revolution: "Without such a power to suppress insurrections, our liberties might be destroyed by domestic faction."[86] By contrast, Madison predicted that real federal tyranny would and should be met with resistance by the Body of the People: "A few representatives of the people would be opposed to the people themselves; or rather one set of representatives [the federal government] would be contending against thirteen sets of representatives [the state governments], with the whole body of their constituents on the side of the latter."[87] Similarly, in his proclamation condemning the Whiskey Rebellion, President Washington described it as a factional insurrection: "The contest [is] whether a small portion of the United States shall dictate to the whole Union, and, at the expense of those who desire peace, indulge a desperate ambition."[88] And Hamilton avowed that Congress could use the militia of one state "to guard the republic against faction or sedition" in another, rather than against a general revolution.[89] Indeed, Hamilton argued that the federal government should raise a small standing army because such a force could repress factional rebellion but not a true revolution: "The army under such circumstances may usefully aid the magistrate to suppress a small faction, or an occasional mob, or insurrection; but it will be unable to enforce encroachments against the united efforts of the great body of the people."[90]

In short, then, even that great Federalist triumvirate, Washington, Hamilton, and Madison, recognized a continuing right of revolution but not rebellion. And, strikingly, even the Shaysites themselves did not seem to disagree that the people had a right to make a revolution but not a rebellion. They merely claimed that their uprising was a revolution: by the time they took up arms, they had begun referring to themselves as the Body of the People, that legitimate author of revolutions.[91]

Those who condemned the backcountry rebellions generally pointed to two specific failings. First, some saw in them an assault on the right of property, which was a part of their vision of the common good. The insurrections were thus a factious, leveling attack by the have-nots on the haves. Hamilton, for example, described Shays' Rebellion: "If Shays had not been a *desperate debtor,* it is much to be doubted whether Massachusetts would have been plunged into a civil war."[92] Second, some saw in the uprisings a regional drive for secession, as Washington described the Whiskey Rebellion. The insurrections thus grew from an impulse to subdivide the nation, with the part rebelling against the whole.[93] But whether the rebellions were economic factionalism or regional factionalism, they were still rebellion in the eyes of their opponents — mere anarchy rather than a united revolution in the spirit of '76.

For the Framers, rebellions were akin to tyranny, inasmuch as both pursued a partial interest. Demagogues as well as despots could threaten the commonweal, and the universal militia should suppress insurrections by private groups as well as usurpations by public ministers.[94] In resisting a tyrant, the militia acted against the state apparatus, and in suppressing a rebellion, it acted for the same apparatus, but in either case its ultimate master was the same: the Body of the People and its general good.

The Second Amendment, then, reposes faith in the Body of the People in the hope that it will act for the good of the whole. For this reason, the Body of the People cannot be a collection of factions; if the people were that fragmented, popular uprisings could be only multiple rebellions. Instead, the people must have sufficient homogeneity to share a common good. Therefore, a people, in the sense used by the Second Amendment, is not a set of random individuals who happen to reside in the same territorial jurisdiction. Rather, it is an organic entity, with enough commonality and self-awareness to engage in united action. Second Amendment proponents therefore assumed that a revolutionary people should have a common culture on the use of violence.

A COMMON CULTURE

In the view of the Framers, because revolution had to be unified, only the Body of the People could make one. The institutional manifestation of the Body of the People was the citizen militia. For Second Amendment proponents, however, that institutional structure was not the only mechanism helping to make unified revolutionary action possible. In the Framers' rhetoric, the people also share a culture, animated by common views, values, and goals. Revolutions, in other words, are made by culturally united peoples, not by individuals.

The Framers seldom make explicit this assumption that the people will share a culture, but it is unmistakably implicit in their language. For example, the legal antecedents of the Second Amendment identify the militia not as "the mass of private individuals" but as the "Body of the People" — a phrase rich with meaning. The metaphor connotes organic connection; it suggests that the people will act as one body, with one will. Eighteenth-century writers understood the phrase in just that way. One leading scholar of colonial resistance explains: "Under the terms of England's revolutionary tradition resistance, like revolution, had to emerge from the 'Body of the People,' the whole of political society, involving all of its social or economic subdivisions. . . . This means that more modern conceptions of revolution as class movements are inadequate for understanding the colonists' particular political concerns. . . . [S]ince the people as a whole had to contract into government, similarly the dissolution of established authority — even in a limited sphere, such as pertained to the Stamp Act — had to be based upon a broad popular agreement."[95] The preeminent historian of American political violence elaborates:

> The close tie between the nascent idea of popular sovereignty and revolutionary events appears in Boston. G. B. Warden has written that "the growing unity" in revolutionary Boston "among . . . various groups" was connected to an "entity called the 'Body of the People.'" Patriots and their opponents all came to use the term "Body of the People" as a synonym for "a majority of the people" or "the greater part of the people." Soon the "Body of the People" referred to "the united will of the people" in symbolic substitution for "the Crown," and both legal and extralegal gatherings alike were characterized as the "Body of the People." In 1773 it was a meeting of the "Body" — justified as "representing all the people in the province" — that led to the Boston Tea Party.[96]

Examples of this usage could be endlessly multiplied. Jonathan Mayhew put the idea bluntly: the citizenry may make a revolution only when "the whole Body of the People . . . unite and determine as one Man."[97] Even the Declaration of Independence describes the American Revolution as an affair between peoples, not loose collections of individuals: "When in the course of human events it becomes necessary for one people to dissolve the political bands which have connected them with another, and to assume among the power of the earth the separate & equal station to which the laws of nature and of nature's God entitle them, a decent respect for the opinions of mankind requires that they should declare the causes which impel them to the separation."[98]

Similarly, promilitia writers argued that the militia was trustworthy because it comprised the people, which, as a corporate unity, could never turn against itself. As Samuel Adams explained, "The militia is composed of free citizens. There is therefore no Danger of their making use of their Power to the destruction of their own Rights."[99] Some writers used the first person plural to express the same idea: We could never hurt ourselves. Recall Coxe's questions: "Who are the militia? *are they not ourselves*. Is it feared, then, that we shall turn our arms *each man against his own bosom*."[100] This assumption of corporate identity is fundamental to the eighteenth-century defense of the militia: the reason the militia was so important was that it would not break down into factional squabbling.

This presumption of unity is especially striking because it was not unquestioned in the 1780s. As we have seen, many Federalists believed that local militias had become a seedbed of faction; in order to restore unity for the whole, they insisted that Congress receive ultimate command over them. So it was entirely possible to imagine that one part of the militia could turn against another. While we could not turn against ourselves, we could turn against them; and while there was no fear that each man would turn a sword "against his own bosom," he might turn a sword against another's. Yet the militia supporters unmistakably rejected this image of fragmentation: for them, in the militia there is no them separate from us, and the other's bosom is like unto our own.

Indeed, even the Federalists, who imagined the United States as divided into interest groups, nonetheless claimed that the citizenry would act as one in resisting federal tyranny. In *Federalist* 10, Madison famously advised that governments can never eliminate faction, and he argued that the existence of many factions in a large republic can even be useful because they will check each other.[101] In this growing acceptance of self-interest, Madison was a part of the liberalizing temper of his time. Yet in almost poetic terms, he also predicted sublime unity among the people in resisting federal oppression:

"One spirit would animate and conduct the whole. . . . A few representatives of the people would be opposed to the people themselves . . . [and to the state governments] with the whole body of their constituents."[102] Similarly, John Jay traced the country's origin to unity displayed in the American Revolution: "Providence has been pleased to give this one connected country to one united people — a people descended from the same ancestors, speaking the same language, professing the same religion, attached to the same principles of government, very similar in their manners and customs, and who, by their joint counsels, arms, and efforts, fighting side by side throughout a long and bloody war, have nobly established their general liberty and independence."[103]

Because he presumed the same unity, Hamilton believed that Americans had nothing to fear from a highly trained, select militia. Such a force would be able to resist a standing army, and it would release the rest of the citizenry from active service, though Hamilton also believed that "the people at large" should still be "properly armed and equipped" and assembled "once or twice in the course of a year." And, against the Anti-Federalists, Hamilton insisted that a select militia would not form a faction dangerous to the liberties of the people. Instead, because it was composed of citizens, the militia would be as one with the citizenry, so deep and familial was American unity: "There is something so far-fetched and so extravagant in the idea of danger to liberty from the militia. . . . Where on the name of common sense are our fears to end if we may not trust our sons, our brothers, our neighbors, our fellow-citizens. What shadow of danger can there be from men who are daily mingling with the rest of their countrymen and who participate with them in the same feelings, sentiments, habits, and interests?"[104]

In short, then, even those like the Federalists who had accepted diversity in most areas of civic life, nonetheless claimed that America possessed a core culture on the use of political violence. As striking as what is visible in the Framers' writing is what is not visible: the Framers never contemplate the possibility that a true revolution might lead to civil war. Instead, whenever they discuss such internecine conflict, they denounce it as rebellion. Although the War for Independence was itself a civil war, the Framers did not remember it that way. By the 1780s, the loyalists, perhaps one-third of the whole citizenry, had disappeared from Americans' historical memory, an amnesia that largely persists today. The Framers remembered their service as a time of ecstatic national unity, to be followed only later by a period of factional striving in the state legislatures.[105] The Framers' theory of revolution thus had only two ways to analyze disagreement among citizens during time of political unrest: either the uprising was not really a revolution or, if it was a revolution, then the dissenters must be a malignant cancer in the body politic. That tendency to ostracize dissenters began with the exile and suppression of loyalists at the nation's birth,[106] and it continued through the military response to back-country rebellions into the nineteenth century and beyond. Rebels, loyalists, and tyrants were all ex hypothesi aberrant groups, outsiders acting against the interests of the people, not fellow Americans with a different view of the world.

The Framers therefore hoped and believed that Americans possessed enough unity on the use of violence to constitute the kind of people that could make a revolution. But traditionally, civic republicans did more than idly hope for and believe in popular unity; they also required universal militia service because it would mold members to civic virtue. The militia was not just a mirror of society: it was a transformative experience. As we have observed, the republican citizen had twin duties: on the one hand, he should stand apart from the state to correct it when it fell into corruption; on the other hand, he should subordinate his interests to the state's demands as long as it stayed on the paths of virtue. The citizen thus had to judge when he could refuse the demands of the state, but he could not let his separate interests cloud his judgment. For many republicans, militia service helped train the citizen to the necessary habits of mind, the delicate balance between self-sacrifice and independence.

The self-sacrificial aspects of militia service were obvious. For the good of the state, citizens disrupted their chosen round of activities, often facing cold, disease, hunger, and danger.[107] The state expected the militiaman to bear these burdens in the knowledge he was keeping the republic safe. Militia service also required cooperation among citizens and subordination to orders, stimulated a commitment to comrades that could become a devotion to the public they represented, and exposed members to sermons and speeches exhorting them to virtue.[108] Many veterans of the Revolution recalled military service as the emotional high point of their lives; by the 1780s, they yearned for the *rage militaire* that had drawn them together in the war.[109]

Even as it encouraged self-sacrifice, militia service habituated members to independent self-government. In republican theory, arms were necessary to the autonomous selfhood of the citizen, making him dependent for his safety only on the body of his fellow citizens, not on the state apparatus or private individuals.[110] Conscious they held the reins of power, an armed people would never accept the idea that governors governed and citizens simply obeyed. As Joel Barlow explained, "A people that legislate for themselves ought to be in the habit of protecting themselves; or they will lose the spirit of both."[111] Thus, republican commentators denounced those supine peoples who, for comfort and convenience, surrendered their arms — along with their liberty — to a standing army; by contrast, they admired the independent, manly, civil but not servile citizen-soldier-freeholder committed to the common good but not enslaved to the state.[112] In the view of the promilitia activists, then, militia service could help Americans to become one people, united by a devotion to the good of the whole.

DECENTRALIZATION

Because they believed in a popular right of resistance, then, proponents of the Second Amendment wanted to keep the means of force close to the people, who were united by the militia structure and a common culture. For the same reason, they deeply objected to the Constitution's concentration of power in the new federal government. Traditionally, militia forces were local bodies, and supporters believed that this proximity to the people would prevent their capture by malignant governmental actors.[113] As we have seen, in the wake of Shays' Rebellion, the Constitution's first voice inverted this trust: it reposed confidence in a Congress that represented the whole rather than in local militia units, some of which had cooperated with the rebels. As Don Higginbotham puts the point mildly, "The militia provisions of the Constitution flew in the face of so much American thinking and experience and so became subject to Antifederalist attack."[114]

The debate over the Second Amendment was thus, in some measure, a debate about federalism, the appropriate division of power over the means of violence between the state and federal governments. Such worries supplied much of the impetus for its germination: faced with Congress's new Article I powers, Anti-Federalists sought to prohibit federal schemes to render the popular militia helpless. Indeed, the only point on which almost all modern commentators agree is that one purpose of the amendment was to ensure that state governments would have well-armed militias at their disposal.[115] At a minimum, then, the amendment forbids the federal government from unduly interfering with the state's ability to maintain this force.

To grasp the full meaning of the Second Amendment, however, we must remember why it was so important that the states be able to maintain such a body. Militias did not exist in a vacuum; states formed them to serve certain ends, and commentators wrote enconia to them for certain reasons. Of late, a number of commentators have argued that the primary reason states wanted some control over their militia was simply to keep local order. They wanted to ensure that they had an effective force to quell rebellions and, more disturbingly, to act as a slave patrol.[116] In fact, as noted earlier, the states did use their militias to these ends. The more important question, however, is whether these were the only reasons the states wanted to protect their militias.

Some have so argued, but only by ignoring an enormous amount of evidence.[117] In the debates over the Constitution and Bill of Rights, commentators primarily praised the militias as a way to combat federal tyranny. Federalists and Anti-Federalists alike agreed on the importance of this role. And the very reason Anti-Federalists worried about federal control of the militia was their fear that a corrupt Congress might disable the states' only protection against federal tyranny. At least in slave states, Anti-Federalists probably did wake up trembling with nightmares about slave uprisings, but they also woke in terror of congressional conspiracies. In fact, as we have seen, they saw the two as symptoms of the same problem: they hoped that the militia could protect the common good against threats from either factious rebels or factious tyrants. And Federalists sought to reassure those fears, not by denying the right to resist, but by affirming that the states would be able to resist even without amendments.

The Second Amendment thus protects a right of militias to keep arms so as to be ready to resist the federal government. The more difficult question is the exact role of the state governments in leading such resistance: specifically, does the amendment contemplate that resistance is legitimate only under the supervision of state governments? Or, contrariwise, does it contemplate that the militia may commence its own insurrection against federal tyranny if local governments fail to do so?

Federalists and Anti-Federalists alike imagined that because state governments could provide a rallying structure for resistance to federal tyranny, they would typically lead such uprisings. As we have seen, Anti-Federalists objected to the Constitution because they worried that Congress might interfere with the states' ability to maintain militias. By contrast, they never voiced a concern that the states might go corrupt. And the Federalists loudly proclaimed that if the federal government should lapse into tyranny, the state governments would be invaluable in organizing resistance. Madison effused, "Besides the advantage of being armed, which the Americans possess over the peoples of almost every other nation, the existence of subordinate governments, to which the people are attached and by which the militia officers are appointed, forms a barrier against the enterprises of ambition, more insurmountable than any which a simple government of any form can admit of."[118] And Hamilton predicted, "The state governments will, in all possible contingencies, afford complete security against invasions of the public liberty by the national authority. . . . They can discover the danger at a distance; and . . . they can at once adopt a regular plan of opposition, in which they can combine all the resources of the community."[119]

State governments, then, would ordinarily lead resistance because of their utility in organizing the people. Ultimately, however, the right of revolution belonged not to the state governments as such but to the Body of the People organized into universal militias. The Second Amendment itself insists that because militias are "necessary to the security of a free state, the right of the [Body of] the People to keep and bear arms shall not be infringed." And, although Hamilton recognized the advantages of state governments, he also recognized that the people had a right to resist even without them. In their absence, the problem in making a revolution was not legitimacy; it was merely finding a way to coordinate the activity of the people: "In a single State, if the persons intrusted with supreme power become usurpers, the different parcels, subdivisions, or districts of which it consists, having no distinct government in each, can take no regular measures for defense. The citizens must rush tumultuously to arms, without concert, without system, without resource; except in their courage and despair."[120]

The militia and the right of revolution became important legal concepts in the Anglo-American tradition long before federalism took center stage in American constitutional thinking. Through all those decades, champions of the militia regarded it as important because it allowed the people to resist government in general, not because it allowed the states to resist the federal government. Indeed, through most of this early period, the states and the federal government did not even exist. Then, after the Revolution, many states inscribed provisions protecting the right to arms into their state constitutions.[121] Those provisions could not have been about federalism. State constitutions govern the conduct of the state government, not the federal. State constitutions therefore could not have been designed to limit the power of Congress over the state governments. Instead, state bills of rights limit the power of the states with regard to their own citizens. Thus, these state provisions had to be a right of the people against the state governments, not a right of the states against the federal government. And, in context, that view makes perfect sense: the right to arms provisions grew up out of a belief in popular resistance, through the militia, against government in general. In all the many years since these provisions were put in place, no court has ever suggested that the right to arms in state constitutions is really a protection for state governments against federal tampering.

As we have seen, the proponents of the Second Amendment based its language on these right-to-arms provisions in the state constitutions,[122] so one should look to those provisions for insight into the meaning of the federal provision. In the debates over the Bill of Rights, no one suggested that the nature of the right to arms fundamentally changed when it became a federal guarantee. No one suggested that the people lost the right of resistance when the right to arms became federalized; no one suggested that the right to arms somehow became the property solely of the state governments. Those changes would have been such marked departures from the tradition that it seems incredible that no one would have remarked on them if they had been made.

Instead, the supporters of the Second Amendment argued only that in a federal system the Body of the People might have a new ally, a new tool: the state governments. Hamilton, for example, argues that a federal system actually helps the people resist government because "in a confederacy the people, without exaggeration, may be said to be entirely the masters of their own fate. Power being almost always the rival of power, the general government will at all times stand ready to check the usurpations of the state governments, and these will have the same disposition towards the general government. The people, by throwing themselves into either scale, will infallibly make it preponderate. If their rights are invaded by either, they can make use of the other as the instrument of redress."[123] Even for the arch-Federalist Hamilton, the state governments were not masters of popular resistance, but merely its coordinators.

The Second Amendment thus gives the right to arms to the Body of the People in militia. The state governments may legitimately help but not block a true revolution. If the state governments cooperate with a tyrannical federal government, the militia still has the right to conduct a revolution against the latter. That right, moreover, might in some circumstances include a right to resist the states themselves. Like all the provisions in the Bill of Rights, the Second Amendment creates rights against the federal government, not against the states. But if corrupt states are supporting the corrupt center, the people might have to conduct a revolution against them in order to effectuate their resistance to the center.

Remember, however, that the right to arms for revolution was subject to several critical constraints. First, the right of resistance belonged to the Body of the People, an entity that was (1) culturally united, (2) institutionally yoked into a universal militia by the state, and (3) subject to the state's orders except when the state had become demonstrably corrupt. Second, a revolution could occur only when the Body of the People had united behind resistance; any lesser movement constituted factional rebellion. Once the Framers had reconceptualized the whole as the United States, the Body of the People came to refer to the whole citizenry of the nation. And although the Anti-Federalists may have had mixed feelings about this reconceptualization, their amendments were attached to a document with a national reach. In particular, the Second Amendment created rights against the federal government, which by law governed all of America and whose Body of the People must therefore have included the whole of the American citizenry. In other words, any true

Second Amendment revolution would have to involve a massive rising of the entire American people, nothing smaller. As noted, the Framers were quick to condemn local uprisings as rebellions, not true revolutions. Third, although theoretically revolutions against the federal government might grow up in the absence of support from state governments, the Framers thought that possibility highly unlikely because the problems of coordination would be so profound.

In short, then, the supporters of the Second Amendment thought that revolution would be an extremely rare event because very few insurrectionary movements could meet the exacting criteria. If few uprisings could satisfy the criteria under eighteenth-century conditions, even fewer could do so today, as the citizenry has become steadily more diverse and as the universal militia has become only a dim memory. It is not a revolutionary act when a lone terrorist blows up a federal building or when local groups seek to secede from the Union or when eschatological prophetic movements stockpile weapons or when private, insular militias try to reclaim America for real Americans. When factions feel themselves aggrieved, they may have some natural right of disobedience — but they may not claim the right of revolution contemplated by the Constitution.

3

*The Original Legal Meaning of
the Second Amendment and the
Military Provisions of the Constitution*

The preceding two chapters examined the historical development of the Second Amendment and the military provisions of the Constitution, as background for their original legal meaning. This chapter will offer a formulation of that meaning, to the extent that the record allows. Here, then, is the original legal meaning of the Second Amendment: To ensure that the Body of the People is prepared to resist a corrupt central government, the Body of the People shall have the right to keep and bear arms. Here is the original meaning of Article I: To ensure that the People in Congress Assembled may resist a corrupt insurrection, Congress shall have the power to maintain and deploy military forces against domestic unrest. Finally, here is the meaning of the two read together: The people have two modes of expressing their will about the use of political violence — representatively in Congress and directly in the militia; either mode is subject to corruption, leading to tyranny on the one hand or insurrection on the other, and thus the Constitution empowers both so that they can check one another.

Original intent is not all there is to constitutional interpretation, and even if it were, conditions often change so drastically that constitutional provisions simply cannot bear their original meaning any longer. Still, we cannot know where we are unless we begin with where we have been. Moreover, most modern discussion of the amendment gives central significance to its original meaning; each side claims the Framers as devoted supporters of their view, as though Patrick Henry were a member of the NRA and James Madison a member of Handgun Control. Neither side can win this game because the amendment's original meaning does not speak in the same categories as the modern debate. To understand, therefore, what the original intent does not say, we must understand what it does say.

The Legal Meaning of the Second Amendment

THE OWNER OF THE RIGHT TO ARMS

The modern debate on the Second Amendment would force one to choose between only two options: the provision vests rights either in private individuals or in the government. In fact, the amendment's history indicates that the right to arms belong to the Body of the People, which is a sui generis element of eighteenth-century theory: the citizenry as a collectivity organized into a universal militia and unified by a common culture. This Body of the People is thus both supraindividual and nongovernmental, but the modern dichotomy between governments and individuals does not allow for such an entity. The insistence on that division causes needless confusion. Some individual rights theorists rightly observe that the Second Amendment empowers the people to resist a corrupt government, but they then conclude that the amendment must therefore give the right to arms to individuals, the only nongovernmental option in the modern dichotomy. The amendment does not, however, give a right to individuals because random clusters of individuals can perpetrate only rebellion and civil war; only a unified entity like the Body of the People can make a true revolution. Stressing this fear of rebellion, some states' rights theorists insist that the amendment must therefore give the right to arms to governments, the only supraindividual possibility in the modern dichotomy. But again, that can't be right because the people must sometimes resist government. . . . And so around and around the modern debate goes in a circle.

In fact, the modern world may have no good analogue for the Body of the People. As chapter 9 will explore, that fact may have significant implications for interpreting the amendment under current conditions. For now, it is sufficient to observe that neither the individual rights school nor the states' rights school has proposed a satisfying analogue. Therefore, despite both groups' protestations that they are only carrying out the original legal meaning of the amendment, they are really forcing that meaning into a modern frame that cannot hold it.

On the one hand, states' rights theorists generally argue that the Second Amendment protects only the states' right to maintain their National Guard units, which these writers identify as the modern equivalent of the old state militias.[1] The United States Code defines the National Guard as that part of the state militia that is federally recognized and funded and that is trained and has its officers appointed under Congress's militia powers.[2] The fact that the state supervises the guard does not prevent it from being a modern analogue for the Body of the People: as we have seen, the eighteenth-century militia generally was under state supervision. Instead, the problem with the guard as a modern surrogate is that it is not universal: the present authorized strength of the Army National Guard, for example, is six hundred thousand.[3] For some time, it has exhibited the behavior of a distinct interest group, lobbying for benefits and its own continued existence.[4] Indeed, the modern guard owes its existence in large measure to class warfare. During the great strikes of 1877, the militia sometimes refused to disperse strikers, so the business community urged a remodeling of the militia to make it more responsive to property rights.[5] Unlike the universal militia, then, the National Guard includes only a piece of the people. If it takes up arms for political ends, it will do so in its own interests and the interests of those like it.

By the same token, individual rights theorists err in equating the people's militia with private gun owners. For one thing, gun owners have experienced none of the training to mutual commitment that militia membership was supposed to induce. Indeed, people who own guns for self-defense typically associate firearms with fear of their fellow citizens, not solidarity.[6] Even more important, gun owners do not comprise a universal militia because gun ownership is itself not universal. Not all Americans own guns, and they probably never will. Today, although some people in every demographic category own guns, ownership is concentrated in certain groups. American gun owners are overwhelmingly male and married, more Protestant than Catholic, more white than black (in absolute numbers), and generally middle class. They reside primarily in rural areas, and many more people own guns in the South than elsewhere in the nation.[7]

In addition, as later chapters will elaborate, gun ownership currently functions as a central icon in a vicious cultural war between the "gun culture" and its "enemies." Rather than bringing Americans together, the very idea of owning guns divides people into hostile camps about the meaning of American life. We are, in other words, two Americas: gun owners and non–gun owners. The gun-owning part of America is merely one distinct subculture within the citizenry, not the citizenry as a whole, but if we have a popular revolution, it will be in its interest.

Individual rights theorists may respond that although de facto gun owner-ship may not be universal, their view would guarantee a de jure universal right to own guns. As a result, if some fail to own guns, they have only themselves to blame; their failure should not have fallout for others who have responsibly self-armed. This response, however, assumes that the point in the amendment is to guarantee a sphere of personal autonomy, so that the actions of one individual should not impair the rights of another. Many provisions in the Bill of Rights do work this way. But the Second Amendment is different. It is a fundamentally structural provision: it addresses the political relation between the state and the people as a whole. Its essential goal is not to provide liberal rights of individual autonomy, but to ensure that the power to resist remains with the universal militia. If the militia is less than universal—for whatever reason, including the "fault" of those who fail to self-arm—the means of political violence will then lie in the hands of a special interest, an unaccept-able situation for the amendment's Framers.[8]

In short, Second Amendment proponents believed that the militia had to be universal for all our sakes. And they did not intend to leave its universality to the chance decision of every citizen to arm himself: they insisted that the state should muster the militia, train it, and oblige every citizen to own a gun. To be sure, the proponents of the amendment never perfectly realized this ideal in practice, but it was still their ideal. Individual rights theorists sometimes blame others for not realizing the importance of universal arming in the Framers' thinking, but actually even these theorists fail to take it seriously enough. The vision of the amendment is not a nation in which all may own arms, but one in which all are in fact armed. If only a small portion own guns, the hope of the amendment will have failed as surely as if the government had prohibited arms altogether. Corruption—domination by narrow self-interests—can oc-cur through the machinations not only of the state but of armed private fac-tions as well.

As divergent as they are in some ways, then, both the individual rights and states' rights theories make the same mistake: they fail to recognize that the Body of the People in militia had to be universal. Indeed, the Body of the People does not even make an appearance in these theories. They assume a citizenry fragmented into subunits, and they then distribute guns among those units according to their respective rules. In short, what is missing from both is the Framers' hope of unity, their conviction that Americans can tame po-litical violence only as constituent parts of a community. These theories thus take for granted a world of hostility and division, one in which some segments of the population use their guns to control others. As I explain in part II, that vision has a certain power as modern mythography, but it is not the vision of the Framers.

THE UNIFIED LANGUAGE OF THE SECOND AMENDMENT

In the notion that the Second Amendment gives rights to the Body of the People rather than to individuals or states lies the best explanation of its language. As noted, the text of the amendment consists of the purpose clause — "A well-regulated militia being necessary to the security of a free state" — and the operative language — "the right of the People to keep and bear arms shall not be infringed." In the current debate, each school of thought essentially sacrifices the meaning of one clause to the other.

The individual rights school maintains that the term *people* refers unmistakably to the mass of private individuals, and therefore the operative language clearly creates a private, individual right to keep and bear arms. In this view, the purpose clause is merely philosophical rumination: it celebrates a universal militia but in no way limits the individual right contained in the second clause. The singling out of the militia thus offers only one purpose that a right to arms might serve, but it should not be regarded as the raison d'etre of the provision.[9] Notoriously, in its promotional material, the NRA quotes only the second clause of the amendment, omitting the irritating purpose clause.[10] Recently, Eugene Volokh has offered a sophisticated version of this argument. He acknowledges that the Framers may have written the Second Amendment largely to protect the militia, but he insists they deliberately decided to protect the militia through an individual right to arms. Thus, although they may have had a purpose in mind, they chose to specify how they wanted to further that purpose, and we are not now free to amend their choices. As a result, the operative language stands independent of its purpose clause: the Framers codified an individual right to arms and added the purpose clause as interesting surplusage that is irrelevant to its interpretation.[11]

But if preserving the militia is mere ballast, not the necessary intellectual context in which the amendment must be read, then why, one wonders, did its writers bother to single it out in the text of the Constitution?

In a similar way, the states' rights school sacrifices the operative language to the purpose clause. Writers in this camp maintain that the amendment specified its own and only purpose: the preservation of a "well-regulated militia." They further insist that this militia is simply a state agency like any other, with no element of popular independence. As a result, they read the operative language to mean that the people may keep and bear arms only when they are assembled in militia, under state control, to the extent that the state permits them to do so. And so in this reading "the right of the People to keep and bear arms shall not be infringed" becomes "the right of the states to arm the People in their militias" shall not be infringed.

But if the Framers of the amendment really wanted to grant the states powers, then why did they refer to the people, rather than to the states, in the operative language? These linguistic puzzles are the product of the modern debate's tendency to dichotomize the world into the state and private persons. If those are the choices, then the amendment can protect either a right of individuals or the power of the state, but nothing else. Each school of thought chooses one option and then ignores all inconsistent language. There is, however, a more satisfactory alternative, one that does not force a choice between these two poles but instead gives meaning to all of the amendment's text.

Specifically, the "People" and the "well-regulated militia" refer roughly to the same thing: the Body of the People, which is reducible to neither the mass of individuals nor the state. By referring to a "well-regulated militia" in the purpose clause, the amendment's writers revealed that the operative language refers to the "People" not as individuals, but as the kind of corporate body celebrated in Anglo-American revolutionary theory. And by referring to the "People" in the operative language, the writers indicated that the "well-regulated militia" in the purpose clause meant the kind of popular body, the universal militia, that the same revolutionary theory had long prized.

Reading the amendment as a consistent whole, without sacrificing one clause to the other, might be called unitary interpretation. It has several distinct advantages, some legal and some historical. Historically, it forces one to examine our modern preconceptions, and it is therefore likely to yield more sensitive interpretations. For example, if we approach the Second Amendment in this way, we might discern that in the Framers' minds, the sociopolitical world was not reducible to individuals and the state. Legally, basic canons of construction instruct us to read provisions in such a way as to make them internally consistent and not leave any part as empty surplusage.[12] Unitary interpretation respects these canons: reading the two clauses together renders the provision a coherent, meaningful whole.

Individual rights theorists object to this construction. (States' rights theorists might offer a parallel objection, but I have not discovered an example in the literature). Eugene Volokh, for example, argues that because other provisions of the Bill of Rights, like the Fourth Amendment, use the phrase *the people* to refer to individuals, the same phrase in the Second Amendment must mean the same thing.[13] Yet this contention fails to take historical changes seriously. In the eighteenth century, the Framers could use "the people" to refer indiscriminately to either individuals or the Body of the People because they saw no inherent contradiction between the two. Within their assumptions about the social world, people were simultaneously individuals and members of the people. As a result, the Framers would have seen no real difference between arming individuals and arming the people. As I explore in part II, by contrast, modern Americans tend to view individuals and an organic people as quite distinct things. American citizens are more individual than ever, but most have given up aspirations for peoplehood in the strong republican sense — perhaps rightly so. And when we allow modern individuals to arm themselves, we are not arming a people. Today, then, we must draw a distinction between the two uses of the term *people* and inquire which was primary in which amendment. Plainly, the Fourth Amendment emphasizes people as individuals, but the Second Amendment emphasizes them as members of an organic collectivity.

In short, at the highest level of generality, the Constitution uses "the people" to refer to "American human beings," but different provisions emphasize different attributes of those human beings. There is nothing anomalous about this sort of usage: the Constitution routinely uses a single phrase to refer to one general concept but with disparate emphases in the various provisions. Thus, the constitutional phrase *execute* and its various cognates all generally refer to "carrying out," but different provisions emphasize different elements of that concept, some of them in opposition to one another. For example, Article Two instructs the president to "take Care that the Laws be faithfully executed,"[14] meaning that he must enforce laws made by someone else. In this sense, the executive power is defined in opposition to the legislative power, which is the power to make laws. Yet Congress is also given the power to "make all Laws which shall be necessary and proper for carrying into Execution"[15] the powers listed in Article I, Section 8. This usage of *execute* refers to Congress making law, so as to carry out its legislative functions. It would clearly be improper to read these two usages to refer to exactly the same activity, and it would similarly be improper to read "the people" as always referring to exactly the same entity.

Trapped in a virtual orthodoxy of liberal individualism, many assume that the social world can be reduced to individuals (singly or as part of interest groups designed to serve aggregated individual ends) and the government that allows them to live together. When we contemplate the world in this impoverished way, we will labor to force the language of the Second Amendment into a framework that will not accommodate it. In fact, the social world is full of entities intermediate between the government and individuals, entities composed of persons connected through rich cultural and institutional commonalities. After decades of neglect, interest in these intermediate groups has begun to burgeon as some have found a fiercely individualistic world to be hollow and unhealthy. In part III, I will suggest that the Second Amendment, read in its original context, has something to contribute to this revival, and, correlatively, the revival may contribute to giving the amendment a modern meaning more congruent with its language.

THE SCOPE OF THE RIGHT TO ARMS

If the Body of the People is the entity that possesses the right to arms, it remains to define the nature of the right. Put simply, the right consists of a right "to keep and bear arms" so as to resist government should it become corrupt. Phrased thus, the right may seem startling, even terrifying, but it contains a number of important qualifications that bear emphasis.

No Mandate for the Body of the People

First, the right to keep and bear arms belongs only to the Body the People, an entity that is culturally united and institutionally bound into a universal militia. If the Body of the People or a close analogue does not exist today, the amendment simply cannot have its original meaning under modern circumstances. Parts II and III of this book will examine whether an analogue does exist and what the right might mean in its absence.

Although the Framers guaranteed that the Body of the People should have the right to arms, they did not constitutionally mandate that Americans must constitute a Body of the People. It probably never occurred to them to try to mandate cultural unity, as the law cannot realistically compel such a result. By contrast, they could realistically have tried to mandate a universal militia, and such a course would have been consistent with their belief in its necessity. Yet although the amendment contains precatory language praising a citizen militia, "a well-regulated militia being necessary to the security of a free state," it does not command one.

Even at the time, some condemned this failure to mandate a universal militia. Elbridge Gerry, for example, complained of the amendment's early phrasing: "A well regulated militia being the best security of a free State, admitted an idea that a standing army was a secondary one. It ought to read, 'a well regulated militia trained to arms;' in which case it would become the duty of the Government to provide this security, and furnish a greater certainty of its being done."[16] Similarly, Centinel declaimed, "It is remarkable that this article only makes the observation, 'that a well regulated militia, composed of the body of the people, is the best security of a free state;' it does not ordain, or constitutionally provide for, the establishment of such a one."[17]

No one offered a definitive explanation for the failure to constitutionalize a universal militia, but the most likely answer seems to be that the Framers simply assumed that the states would do the job without prodding. Remember that in proposing the Bill of Rights, the Anti-Federalists were concerned about the fearsome power of a new, distant, central government. At the moment, they did not worry about their local legislatures. Thus, some oppositionists proposed constitutional amendments to limit Congress's ability to supervise the militia and raise an army. Yet none of the conventions suggested that the states be constitutionally required to muster a militia of any sort.[18] As a result, all they tried to do in the Second Amendment was to ensure that Congress could not interfere with the maintenance of a universal militia.

In the event, the decision not to mandate a militia would be significant because the militia was fast falling into desuetude. Even in the 1780s Second Amendment proponents were experiencing a slippage between rhetoric and reality: they insisted that a militia was critical to the health of a free state, but they simultaneously let their militias slide into half-life. Although many states did require all citizens to own arms and serve in the militia,[19] in practice they departed from this ideal. As the frontier receded, serious military action moved away from the centers of population; states came to rely on expeditionary forces drawn from both volunteers and professional soldiers. The militia, by contrast, began to rust on the home front, turning out primarily as an occasional police force, often as a slave patrol. When it did turn out, it did not include all, or only, citizens. Rich men could purchase exemptions by paying poor men to go in their places, and sometimes even those who were not citizens could be subject to militia duty.[20] In short, the states' military forces had come less and less to resemble the military incarnation of the citizenry assembled.

During this time, many continued to insist that only a universal militia was appropriate for a republic, but they did not follow through on the commitment. The reason seems plain: on the one hand, they could not surrender the universal militia as a necessary concept, but on the other, they could not persuade themselves to undergo the sacrifices involved in universal service. As a result, they must have existed in a state of anxiety, insisting the militia must be the whole people, but knowing in fact it was not.[21] They thus left a dual legacy: to make sense, the Second Amendment requires a universal militia but does not assure its existence.

Over the decades, Americans have exacerbated that discrepancy. As it became plain that the *armato populato* would never become a reality, latter-day republicans began to express their sad disappointment in a population that shirked its civic duty to arm itself.[22] Today, only a small portion of the American citizenry is enrolled in the armed forces, the National Guard, and law enforcement agencies. Technically, all males aged seventeen to forty-five are members of the unorganized militia,[23] but that status has no practical legal significance. Such "militia members" are not required to own guns, to drill together, or to learn virtue. The statutory provision creating this "universal militia" is nothing more than a dim memory of a distant hope.

The Source of Arms: Private or Public

In short, then, the right created by the Second Amendment belongs only to the Body of the People, but the amendment does not guarantee that there shall be such a thing. The second limit on the right to arms is less a clear restriction than an ambiguity: the amendment does not specify *whose* arms the people may keep and bear — their own personal arms or the arms provided to them by the state for their militia service. This question goes to the heart of the modern debate on the meaning of the Second Amendment because gun control is the central policy issue. If the amendment protects the right of citizens to their private arms, then gun control may be unconstitutional; but if it protects only their right to state-issued arms, then regulation of private weapons would appear to pose no constitutional issue. If this issue is at the center of the modern debate, however, it was not so in the debate of the late eighteenth century. In point of fact, the Framers engaged in little discussion of this question.

In all likelihood, Second Amendment proponents did not dwell on the question because they did not care much where the militia arms came from, as long as they came from somewhere. Legally, it was common practice for the states to rely on the militia members' having private weapons. Legislatures customarily ordered militiamen to bring their own weapons to muster. As the Supreme Court emphasized in *Miller,* these regulations were often detailed and exhaustive. In 1786, New York required every militia member to provide himself with "a good Musket or firelock, a sufficient Bayonet and Belt, a Pouch with a Box therein to contain not less than Twenty-four cartridges suited to the Bore of his Musket or Firelock, each Cartridge containing a proper Quantity of Powder and Ball, two spare Flints." Massachusetts imposed similar requirements, and Virginia's provisions were even more complicated.[24] The Court summarized, "Ordinarily when called for service these men were expected to appear bearing arms supplied by themselves and of the kind in common use at the time."[25]

Similarly, Madison seemed to imagine that the amendment protected a right to private arms. Originally, he recommended that his amendments be incorporated into the body of the Constitution, in Article I, Section 9, between clauses 3 and 4, which deal with personal rights. He drew no distinction between the right to arms and the other amendments, and he did not propose inserting the right to arms into the part of Article I giving Congress the power over militias.[26] Others echoed that view: Tench Coxe explained that the amendment protected the right of the people to "keep and bear their private arms";[27] and Philodemos insisted, "Every freeman has *a right to the use of the press,* so he has to *the use of his arms.*"[28] Plainly, the Framers imagined that one way — perhaps the most familiar, normal way — to satisfy the amendment's requirements would be to allow private individuals to keep firearms that they could then bear in militia service.

At the same time, in all likelihood, Second Amendment proponents would have been just as happy for the state to supply arms to militia members, in lieu of their private arms — as long as the state really did supply them. The important point was simply that the militia be armed. Although many states forced militiamen to supply their own weapons, it was also common for states and colonies to maintain arsenals, most famously, the arsenal at Concord, captured by General Thomas Gage in an attempt to disarm the Massachusetts militia, an action that started the Revolutionary War.[29] As we have seen, the debate over the Second Amendment began in an argument over which government, state or federal, would and could arm the militias. The Anti-Federalists' great fear was that Congress might neglect to arm the militias and keep the states from arming them. In short, although people commonly assumed that militia weapons would rest over countless private hearths, they also assumed that they would come from public stores. The Framers apparently were quite indifferent to the source of militia weapons. Protecting private arms and protecting state-supplied arms would thus appear to be alternative, equally acceptable ways of satisfying the amendment's strictures. The one thing Congress could not do was to block militia members' free access to the weapons, wherever they came from, because the militia always had to be ready to resist the federal government by force of arms.

In the present debate on the meaning of the Second Amendment, the indifference about the source of militia weapons poses problems for both the individual rights and states' rights schools of thought. On the one hand, states' rights theorists may object to the notion that Congress may not prevent the Body of the People (if such a thing exists) from having free access to arms so as to resist a corrupt central government. On the other hand, individual rights theorists might object to the claim that once the universal militia has received military arms, from either the state or private sources, the Second Amendment has been satisfied. The amendment does not, in other words, command access to an unlimited variety of arms for an unlimited variety of purposes. If the state were to issue assault weapons to citizens to keep in their closets, rather as the government does in Switzerland,[30] then Congress might well be able to prohibit all other kinds of gun ownership: shotguns for hunting, handguns for self-defense, or multiple firearms of any kind. The amendment celebrates a citizen militia, not gun collecting.

Limits on the State Governments?

For decades the Supreme Court has held that the Bill of Rights limits the actions of the federal government only, not of the states. Congress may not invade the right to keep and bear arms, to free expression, or to a jury, but nothing in the first eight amendments prevents the states from doing so. In drafting the Bill of Rights, the Framers were fearful that the new central government might prove overpowerful and arbitrary. As a result, they wanted to limit *it,* but they did not worry much about the states at that particular moment.[31] As we have seen, the Second Amendment debates reveal just this set of attitudes: Anti-Federalists feared congressional tampering with the militia, but they were not concerned about state overreaching.

In its original conception, then, the Second Amendment limited only federal attempts to disarm the people. To be sure, the Framers would have been unhappy with comparable state schemes, but they did not look to the Second Amendment to block them. Instead, they hoped that because of their proximity to the people, the states would generally not attempt such a thing. And if some state legislature should try, then the right to arms provision in its own state constitution would stop it. In other words, the Framers did not unquestioningly trust the states, but they looked to limits other than the Second Amendment to control them.

In truth, the Second Amendment always depended on those state constitutional provisions for its real-world effectuation. If the states amended their constitutions to remove the right to arms, then state governments could disarm their citizens. If the federal government should ever become corrupt, the Body of the People would then be unable to resist it, and for practical purposes, the Second Amendment would have come to nought. Again, the Second Amendment does not mandate the conditions necessary to its own realization. The amendment, as noted, gives the right to arms to a universal militia, yet it does not command the states to maintain such a militia. Similarly, the amendment seeks to ensure that an armed populace can resist the federal government, yet it does not command the states to keep their citizens armed. For better or worse, the Anti-Federalists simply did not look to the amendment as their protection against the deeds of the states.

Since the Civil War, however, the legal situation has become much more complicated. After the war, the nation adopted the Fourteenth Amendment, which places substantial limits on state governments. Among other things, it provides that no state shall "deprive any person of life, liberty, or property, without due process of law."[32] In the twentieth century, the Supreme Court has held that this Due Process Clause forbids states from invading two groups of rights. First, states may not infringe rights that are part of "ordered liberty" — a vague and controversial concept that includes the right to reproductive and sexual autonomy.[33] Second, states may not invade certain of the rights specified in the Bill of Rights. The Fourteenth Amendment thus "incorporates" parts of the Bill of Rights against the state governments.[34]

This incorporation doctrine opens up the possibility that the Supreme Court should apply the Second Amendment to the states through the Due Process Clause. In the late nineteenth century, the Court twice refused to do so, holding that the federal right to arms limited only Congress.[35] These cases, however, are of limited precedential value because of their extreme age. The Court handed them down long before it had incorporated any of the Bill of Rights against the states; at the time, it would have denied that the First, Fourth, Fifth, and Sixth Amendments ran against the states. Now that the Court has changed its mind about those provisions, it may be ready to change its mind on this one as well.

This question, whether the Fourteenth Amendment should be read to incorporate the Second, is not a question of eighteenth-century attitudes. Instead, the question is about the appropriate legal relation between two provisions separated by almost eight decades. In the 1790s, the Framers would have agreed that the Second Amendment did not limit the states — period. But even if the Framers of the eighteenth century mostly trusted the states, the Framers of the nineteenth century — who had just survived a Civil War — did not. Even if the Bill of Rights does not apply on its own to the states, therefore, it may apply through the Due Process Clause. For that reason, an inquiry into the attitudes of the 1790s cannot, by itself, answer this question.

Yet the way one understands the original meaning of the Second Amendment may have a large impact on whether one thinks the right should be incorporated. States' rights theorists, for example, believe that the Second Amendment protects the power of the state to maintain its militia. But if the point of the provision is to *empower* the states, then it makes no sense to incorporate it as a *limit* on the state. Individual rights theorists, by contrast, read the amendment as an individual right, just like any of the other rights in the Bill of Rights. As the Supreme Court gave the Due Process Clause an increasingly libertarian gloss in the twentieth century, these theorists see no reason not to incorporate this right as well.[36]

If one reads the amendment to protect a right belonging to the Body of the People, the situation is more complicated. On the one hand, in passing this provision, the Anti-Federalist Framers plainly worried about Congress, not the states. They gave the right, moreover, to the Body of the People, not to loose individuals. And they plainly imagined that the state should have an important role in raising and training a universal militia to help constitute the People as a Body. In other words, the amendment does not contemplate a simple oppositional relation between government and individuals; fully to realize the right to arms, state governments and individuals must work together. Accordingly, the states must have freedom to fulfill their part of this alliance, namely, by raising and training the militia. In this way, the amendment should be read to empower the states to form the people into a militia. For that reason, it would be nonsensical to incorporate the Second Amendment as a simple individual right against state governments, especially state efforts to foster responsible gun use in the militia.

On the other hand, once the Body of the People has been formed, once the militia is up and running, it must then use its own judgment on whether the government has become corrupt. In order to perform this checking function, the militia must have routine access to arms. In the Second Amendment, the Framers sought to ensure that the federal government in particular would not disarm the militia. As we have seen, however, the Framers' worries about Congress were merely a reflection of their larger and older worries about government in general. The Second Amendment was hatched from state constitutional provisions placing the same limits on state governments: whatever the Second Amendment does to Congress, the Virginia Declaration of Rights did to the Virginia legislature.

At the time, the Framers may not have wanted to include limits on the states in the federal amendments because they trusted the state legislatures and state constitutions to do the job. With the advent of the incorporation doctrine, however, all that has changed: the Due Process Clause now includes some constraints on the states, drawing on limits that originally applied only against the central government. And part of the Second Amendment's original meaning makes it a natural candidate for incorporation: just as the Body of the People must be armed to resist a corrupt central government, so must it be armed to resist a corrupt state government. State disarmament schemes might therefore be unconstitutional under the Fourteenth Amendment for the same reason that federal schemes might be unconstitutional under the Second Amendment.

There is, then, a significant case for incorporating the right to arms against the states through the Due Process Clause. Two caveats are, however, in order. First, in its original meaning, the Second Amendment gave rights only to the Body of the People. Even if it were incorporated against the states, the Second Amendment would still necessarily refer to a national Body of the People: any smaller unit, such as the united citizenry of a particular state, would constitute a faction unless it were part of a solidaristic larger whole. After incorporation, state citizens might claim a right to resist their governments in alliance with the rest of the people. To claim a right in opposition to the rest of the citizenry, however, would involve the repudiation of the Second Amendment, not its incorporation. As a result, if the American citizenry does not constitute such a body today, then the amendment cannot mean what it once did. And if the amendment cannot bear its original meaning for federal actions, then that original meaning cannot be incorporated against the states. Before we consider the Fourteenth Amendment, therefore, we must consider the underlying meaning of the Second Amendment in the twenty-first century.

The second caveat is that we have so far been using a particular technique for analyzing incorporation: looking first to the original meanings of the Bill of Rights and then considering which provisions could sensibly be incorporated into the Due Process Clause. Following the Court's lead, most Second Amendment theorists use this technique. It is possible, however, to employ a different technique: one might look not to the meanings that the Bill of Rights bore in the 1780s but to the meanings that it bore in the 1860s. More specifically, one might consider how the Framers of the 1860s imagined the right to arms.

Akhil Amar has recently offered such an analysis. He has discovered that a great shift occurred in constitutional thinking during the nineteenth century. Although the eighteenth-century Framers may have understood the Bill of Rights as creating popular rights, the nineteenth-century Framers understood it in much more individualistic ways. In particular, Second Amendment proponents may have worried about popular resistance to a corrupt government through the militia, but Fourteenth Amendment proponents worried about the individual right to arms for self-defense. Their paradigm case shifted from Minutemen resisting the British army to freed slaves resisting the Klan. By the 1860s, the Framers had thus reimagined the right to arms, and they included this reimagined right—rather than the original—in the Fourteenth Amendment. In other words, the Reconstruction Congress did incorporate a right to arms against the states, but it was a private, civil right rather than a popular, political right to check the government.[37]

Amar's work suggests that the Fourteenth Amendment does include a right to arms, but this right has nothing to do with the constitutional organization of violence. Instead, it serves the functions that most modern commentators ascribe to it: because of inadequate policing, private persons may arm themselves against other private persons. Its goal is therefore not to control governments or rebellions or to distribute political power.

In Amar's rendition, then, the Fourteenth Amendment has no direct bearing on my subject because it does not address how political violence might be constitutionally organized. I will therefore not give it sustained attention, except to explain why it does not concern this book's thesis. If Amar is right and the Framers of the Fourteenth Amendment had a personal right in mind, that claim still goes to the original meaning only of that amendment, not of the Second Amendment itself. The Fourteenth Amendment may therefore protect a private right against the states, but the original meaning of the Second Amendment still refers to a popular right against the central government. In other words, whatever newer meanings they may also bear, the Second Amendment and Article I still provide the starting point for organizing political violence at the federal level.

In addition, even if its Framers referred to a personal right, one might still read the Fourteenth Amendment Due Process Clause also to include a popular right of arming against government, as part of the concept of "ordered liberty" defined by the living tradition of the American people.[38] In fact, one could imagine that both sorts of rights (personal and popular) apply against both governments (state and federal) through different interpretive techniques: against Congress, the Second Amendment protects a popular right under its original intent and a personal right under the living tradition enshrined in the Due Process Clause of the Fifth Amendment; and against the states, the Fourteenth Amendment protects a popular right under the living tradition enshrined in its Due Process Clause and a personal right under its original intent. I have now wandered far from the original meaning of the Second Amendment into modern thickets of constitutional interpretation—and that is precisely my point. Amar's analysis of the Fourteenth Amendment adds an important layer of new meaning to the constitutional right to arms, but it does not supercede the old one.

The Right to Arms and the Right to Revolt

The fourth limit on the right to arms involves another ambiguity in the historical record. To understand it, let us draw a distinction between two rights: the right to keep and bear arms for the purpose of revolution, and the right actually to make a revolution. Although related, these two are not conceptually identical. The former refers to the right to have in readiness the means of revolution, that is, guns, and the latter refers to the right to use those guns in resisting the government. Although the distinction may seem airy, it is important because although the constitution protects the first right, it is not clear whether it protects the second.

As I have discussed, Second Amendment proponents wanted to give constitutional protection to the people's right to keep arms for the purpose of revolution. By protecting a right to arms for revolution, these Framers necessarily indicated that it was sometimes legitimate to make a revolution. The right to arms must therefore presuppose an underlying right to revolution. What is not clear is the constitutional status of that right: the Framers might have meant to make it a constitutional right or they might have meant to leave it a natural right, lying behind the constitutional order but not of that order. Conceptually, then, we can imagine two constitutions: in the first, the Framers protected only the right to arms, in the expectation that the right to revolution would take care of itself as long as the people had guns in their hands; in the second, the Framers meant to bring the right to revolution itself into the constitutional system, so that when the people resisted government, they were engaging in an activity governed according to constitutional norms.

Like their ambiguity over the militia's source of arms, Second Amendment proponents did not much discuss this distinction between a natural and constitutional right of resistance. The reason seems inferentially clear: for most practical purposes, it did not matter. Supporters of the Second Amendment plainly did believe in a right of resistance. To make the right meaningful, they extended constitutional protection to the people's right to arms, so that they would always have the means to resist a corrupt government. But in extraordinary times, when the issue comes to push of pike, it does not much matter, for practical purposes, whether they can claim a constitutional right or only a natural one to revolt: either way, they have the right. All that really matters is that they already have arms in their hands, guaranteed by ordinary constitutional law, so as to make the right meaningful. As a result, the most that can reliably be said is that Second Amendment proponents presumed a right to revolution — whether natural or constitutional — by protecting a constitutional right to arms.

Recently, certain states' right theorists have argued that the Framers plainly did not believe in a constitutional right to revolution. The evidence for this claim, however, is tenuous. First, these theorists maintain that many writers, including many Second Amendment proponents, opposed particular insurrections after the Revolutionary War.[39] As we have seen, however, opposition to some uprisings does not mean opposition to all. The Framers of the amendment carefully distinguished between rebellions, which they opposed, and revolutions, which they supported. In condemning the Whiskey Rebellion or Shays' Rebellion, then, Second Amendment proponents were not necessarily denying a constitutional right of revolution. All they were really doing was denying that those rebellions were revolutions at all. Not surprisingly, then, the debate over those rebellions principally swirled around the merits of those particular insurrectionary movements.

To make their case, these theorists must show that the Framers generally condemned, in principle, any constitutional right of revolution, not that they condemned individual rebellions. So far, these writers have not carried that burden. A few isolated quotations, read out of context, appear to reject a constitutional right of revolution; on closer inspection, however, these passages turn out to be entirely ambiguous. For example, Michael Bellesiles points out that Samuel Adams, a hero of the Revolution, condemned the Shaysites: "The man who dares to rebel against the laws of a republic ought to die." When Bellesiles concludes, "Not a lot of support for the right of insurrection there,"[40] he apparently means that Adams rejected any constitutional right of revolution. In fact, however, the sentence bears closer scrutiny: Adams condemns those who rebel against the laws of a "republic"; as we have seen, for republicans like Adams, a republic denoted a government devoted to the common good. Read in context, then, Adams is saying only that rebellions — insurrections against a good government — are illegitimate. He says nothing about resistance to a corrupt government. Thus, he is really discussing only the merits of this particular rebellion and the government against which it was made, not an abstract right of revolution.

Similarly, Bellesiles maintains that Joseph Story, an influential early justice of the Supreme Court, though not a member of the founding generation, denied a constitutional right of revolution. Bellesiles first acknowledges that in his *Commentaries* Story connected the Second Amendment to a right of revolution, perhaps even a constitutional right of revolution (though again, his language is ambiguous; he could mean only that the amendment created a right to arms for the purpose of revolution): "The right of the citizen to keep and bear arms has justly been considered as the palladium of the liberties of a republic, since it offers a strong moral check against the usurpation and arbitrary power of rulers, and will generally, even if these are successful in the first instance, enable the people to resist and triumph over them." Bellesiles counters this famous passage with Story's less well known condemnation of the Dorr Rebellion in Rhode Island. Story branded as treason any action "to prevent the execution of any one or more general and public laws of the government, or to resist the exercise of any legitimate authority." Bellesiles concludes from this claim, "For Story the American Revolution put an end to the need for any more rebellions or uprisings; the country was now stable and secure, and the people should remain orderly."[41] In Bellesiles's view, then, Story was apparently a deeply contradictory figure: he praised resistance in his *Commentaries,* but he really despised it.

Read more carefully, however, Story is more consistent than Bellesiles would make him. In denouncing the Dorr Rebellion, Story does not condemn all uprisings. Instead, he chastises those who would rebel against "legitimate authority" and "general and public laws." In this condemnation, he tells us nothing about those who would rebel against a corrupt government making partial and self-interested laws. In fact, however, we already know what he thought about such revolutions, from his *Commentaries:* they offer a "strong moral check against the usurpation and arbitrary powers of rulers." Once again, Story is condemning rebellions, not all uprisings.

In short, then, I do not think we can know from historical evidence whether the Framers supported a constitutional right to revolution or only a natural one. States' rights theorists, however, have one last argument against a constitutional right to revolution, and this one is based not on historical evidence but on abstract logic. In their view, it is conceptually incoherent to claim that the Constitution could protect a right of revolution because by definition revolution involves an assault on the Constitution's own authority. In a revolution, the constitutional frame has been broken, the people have reverted to the state of nature, and they retain only their natural rights. While these historians therefore would agree that the Framers supported a right of revolution, they would insist that it can only have been a natural one.[42]

I will consider this claim at length in part II because it has little to do with historical evidence and much to do with the current mythic landscape. As I will argue, there is in fact nothing incoherent about a constitutional right of revolution. Revolution does not necessarily involve an assault on the Constitution; it involves merely an assault on the government. Even if a constitution cannot coherently sanction a revolt against its own authority, it certainly can sanction a revolt against government when the government itself is acting contraconstitutionally. A constitutional right to resist government is logically incoherent only if the government and the constitution are always one and the same thing. That claim, however, requires an unquestioning faith in government that was uncommon in the late eighteenth century; it has rather the quality of modern myth.

Instead, as we have seen, the Framers of the Second Amendment were more likely to find the ultimate basis for constitutional unity in the Body of the People. Civic republicans imagined that in a revolution, the people would act as an organic entity for the common good, the heart of their republican constitution. John Locke imagined that in a revolution, the people would sunder their contract with the government but not with each other; the community would overthrow the old government and then make a new one. And the Framers of the Second Amendment imagined that in a revolution, the people would act according to common norms, united by a common culture and the institutional structure of the militia. They did not believe that revolution would return them to a state of nature; indeed, they defined that kind of internecine conflict as rebellion or civil war, not true revolution at all. For the Framers, then, the social constitution making Americans a people was more fundamental, more perdurable, and more resilient than any contract with government. They assumed that it could continue into revolutionary conditions, and that only a constitutionally united people could make a revolution. The historical record may be too limited to conclude that the Framers specifically meant to constitutionalize the right of revolution, but doing so would have been perfectly consistent with the rest of their thinking.

For the purposes of argument, however, assume that it is conceptually incoherent to talk of a constitutional right to revolution. Assume that revolution must break the constitutional frame and deposit us in the state of nature. It still does not follow that the constitutional right to keep arms for revolution, as opposed to the constitutional right to revolution itself, is incoherent. Even if a revolution vaporizes the Constitution, that disruption occurs only with the onset of revolution. Before the revolution itself, the Constitution might guarantee to the people the right to arms, with the expectation that some day they might have to exercise their natural right to overturn settled governments, even the Constitution itself. There is nothing logically incoherent about this set of attitudes: it requires one to imagine only that Second Amendment proponents realized that the natural right of revolution sometimes trumped constitutional order, and they meant to build in some constitutional provision for that exigency. They expected that the Constitution would govern during ordinary times but also that the people might, from time to time, break out of that frame by force of arms, as they had during the Revolutionary War.

Even if "constitutional revolution" is oxymoronic, then, that incoherence means only that Americans cannot plead constitutional sanction for an armed assault on government. It does not mean that Americans cannot plead constitutional sanction for their ownership of guns, in preparation for a revolution sanctioned by natural law. Although it may not be clear whether the Constitution itself protects a right of revolution, it clearly does presuppose the legitimacy of revolution. To that end, it guarantees the Body of the People (or its modern analogue, if there is one) the means for its execution.

Reasonable Regulation

The fifth limit on the right to keep and bear arms is that it is subject to reasonable regulation, as are all other constitutional rights. This limit is not and cannot be based on the thinking of the Framers, who little considered the amendment's concrete meaning in specific cases. In this tendency, they resembled most of the framers of most of our constitutional provisions: they offered some lofty generalities and then left the precise application to later jurists. Those later courts, however, have not flinched from the task. Beginning with the original meaning of the amendments, judges have tried to reconcile the tradition of constitutional history with the current needs of organized society. As a result, though courts generally extend extraordinary protection to constitutional rights, that protection is never absolute. For each constitutional provision, judges have generated a slightly different doctrinal structure, in recognition that each right responds to divergent concerns.[43]

As I will explain in the next chapter, the Supreme Court has never offered a definitive interpretation of the Second Amendment, so it has never had occasion to develop an analogous body of doctrine. If it should ever do so, however, we should expect that the right, however defined, will be subject to some kind of reasonable regulation. It is beyond the scope of this book to speculate on the shape that doctrinal framework might take. It is important to remember, however, that even if the Court recognizes that the Body of the People has a right to arms, that right will not be absolute.

In the present climate, it would be easy to forget that fact. Some individual rights theorists, primarily in the political arena, object to any and all gun control legislation on the grounds that the Second Amendment right is absolute. Some states' rights theorists, again primarily in the political arena, object to giving the amendment any real content apparently because they fear that it would spell the death of reasonable regulation of guns. Both are mistaken, as responsible commentators have always insisted.[44]

A Private Right of Self-Defense?

Individual rights theorists generally maintain that in addition to protecting the militia, the amendment protects an individual right to own arms, for two purposes: first, resistance to government and, second, lawful private pursuits, such as hunting, target shooting, and self-defense. As to the former purpose, this book attempts to demonstrate that these theorists are mistaken: the proponents of the Second Amendment believed that only the Body of the People had a right of revolution, not individuals qua individuals. As to the second purpose, the subject is basically outside the scope of this book, as it is devoted to the constitutional organization of political violence. Nonetheless, there is a relation: analysis of the constitutional treatment of political violence may shed light on the claim that the amendment protects an individual right to arms for personal purposes.

Although many of the Framers probably did believe in an individual right to arms, there is very little evidence that they meant to protect it in the Second Amendment. As we have seen, the impetus for the amendment arose from worries about federal tyranny and regulation of the militia, not about honest citizens and crime. The language of the amendment itself suggests its concern with a "well-regulated militia" and the "security of a free state," rather than self-defense or hunting. In addition, early drafts referred to the Body of the People, rather than to individuals or persons. Finally, although the Framers voluminously discussed the organization of political violence in the debate over the amendment, no amount of diligent searching has revealed an unambiguous contemporary claim that the Second Amendment protected an individual right to arms for wholly private purposes.

As it is impossible to prove a negative, so it would be impossible to demonstrate conclusively that the amendment does not protect such a right. It is possible, however, to demonstrate that much of the evidence conventionally offered for this view does not really support it. For example, as I have discussed, Madison probably imagined that the amendment protected a personal right to arms,[45] but that fact says nothing about how those arms were to be used (individually or collectively in a militia) or to what ends (self-defense or resistance to tyranny). Similarly, individual rights theorists remind us that, in his draft for a Virginia constitution, Thomas Jefferson asserted, "No freeman shall be debarred the use of arms within his own lands or tenements."[46] This provision does sound like a protection for a wholly private right to arms, and it is good evidence that Jefferson believed in such a right. It has, however, little to do with the Second Amendment. Virginia did not, after all, adopt Jefferson's proposal; instead, it adopted a very different provision, the precursor of the Second Amendment: "That the people have a right to keep and bear arms; that a well regulated Militia composed of the body of the people trained to arms is the proper, natural, and safe defence of a free State."

Individual rights theorists have placed special reliance on events in Pennsylvania during the late eighteenth century.[47] The Pennsylvania Constitution of 1776 commands, "The people have a right to bear arms for the defense of themselves and the State."[48] Later, Pennsylvania ratified the U. S. Constitution without amendments, but Pennsylvania Anti-Federalists proposed a group of amendments, including a right to arms provision: "That the people have a right to bear arms for the defense of themselves and their own state, or the United States, or for the purpose of killing game; and no law shall be passed for disarming the people or any of them, unless for crimes committed, or real danger of public injury from individuals."[49] Individual rights theorists argue that these provisions protect a wholly private right to arms: they refer to a right of the people to defend "themselves," in contradistinction to "the state," and to kill game.

In the next chapter, I will discuss Saul Cornell's contention that in context the Pennsylvania material did not call for an individual right to arms. The more basic problem with reliance on this evidence, however, is its limited relevance to the Second Amendment. Whatever the Pennsylvania Constitution might have said, the Second Amendment does not say that the people have a right to defend themselves and to kill game — and no one ever offered that gloss. Instead, the Second Amendment belongs to a different family of provisions that concern the organization of political violence. In fact, to a lawyer's reading, the Pennsylvania Constitution might prove exactly the opposite of that proposed: when the Framers meant to protect a wholly private right, they knew how to say so. When they did not — as in the Second Amendment — that omission seems deliberate.

The Legal Meaning of the Military Provisions of the Constitution

I have dwelt at length on the original meaning of the Second Amendment because its historical context is now obscure to most Americans, and so it is often lost in modern polarized debate. By contrast, the ideas behind the military provisions of the Constitution are more familiar; only when read in conjunction with the Second Amendment do these clauses pose problems of interpretation. As a result, my treatment of these provisions can be more abbreviated.

The body of the Constitution gives Congress the power to suppress domestic insurrection and to define treason against the United States. To effectuate these ends, among others, the Constitution gives Congress extensive military power: to create and maintain the armed services and to organize and discipline the state militias. The practical meaning of these provisions is that Congress may use its armed might to crush what it considers to be uprisings against its constitutional authority. As we have seen, the historical reason for these provisions is that some felt that America needed a single overarching authority for the organization of political violence, so as to quell locally popular insurrections, even those supported by local militias.

The difficulty in this reading is that it creates an apparent tension between Article I and the Second Amendment. On the one hand, the Second Amendment gives the popular militia the right to resist Congress, even to make a revolution; on the other hand, Article I gives Congress the power to discipline the militia, even to suppress an insurrection. On the one hand, the Second Amendment grows out of a distrust of Congress and a trust of local militias; on the other hand, Article I grows out of a trust of Congress and a distrust of local militias. How, then, can we best read these two provisions together?

Historically, the two sets of provisions arise from two visions of America that were in some tension, at least in their emphasis and central concerns. The writers of Article I especially feared insurrection and wanted to give Congress the power to squelch it. Proponents of the Second Amendment intended the provision as a reaction against what they considered to be the excessive power of Congress created by Article I. Historians may therefore conclude that the Constitution simply contains disparate elements, inserted at different times by different people. Jurists, however, do not have the option of leaving things thus. The Constitution supplies the ultimate framework for resolving legal disputes, not only in court but also theoretically in Congress and among the citizenry. The law therefore finds constitutional inconsistency intolerable. We must therefore find a way to reconcile these two different visions.

One option would simply be to choose one vision over the other. In effect, both the Weberian and Populist myths pursue that option: populists stress the right of the people to revolt, while ignoring Congress's power to suppress insurrection; Weberians stress Congress's power to put down revolts while denying the ancient American belief in the right of revolution. The law, however, offers more subtle rules for reconciling disparate legal norms.

When there is an unavoidable contradiction between two constitutional provisions, the federal courts generally follow the latter of the two because it has repealed the former by implication.[50] Therefore, to the extent that Article I and the Second Amendment are in irremediable conflict, the Second Amendment wins, and the military provisions of Article I have become null. The courts prefer, however, not to find repeals by implication. They instruct us, when possible, to read constitutional provisions so as to render them consistent.[51]

Fortunately, such a reading exists for our material. The Second Amendment and the body of the Constitution are not in literal contradiction: even if the people are empowered to attack the government, and the government is empowered to attack the people, that situation does not involve contradiction, merely turbulence. While there is no literal contradiction, however, this arrangement appears to create an unlivable tension: it legitimizes armed conflict between the people and their government. In fact, though, that tension is only apparent. The Framers of the Constitution endorsed a right of revolution, made by the Body of the People for the good of the whole; they repudiated a right of rebellion, made by a faction for the good of a subgroup. The Second Amendment therefore recognizes the right of the people to make a revolution (but not a rebellion), and the body of the Constitution gives Congress the power to suppress a rebellion (but not a revolution).

In the abstract, this system is thus quite consistent. In practice, it still allows for a great deal of tension: what seems like a revolution to its makers may seem like a rebellion to Congress. When they come into conflict, therefore, each may believe that it is exercising its respective constitutional right. To some extent, this potential for conflict is simply endemic in the human condition; it is a fact of history that rightly or wrongly people rise in protest, and rightly or wrongly, governments try to put them down. In the end, with John Locke, all we can do is appeal to heaven for the just resolution of such conflicts. Yet the whole point in creating a constitutional organization of violence is to maximize the likelihood that political violence will be directed to good constitutional ends. As a result, we must consider how this apparent tension in the Constitution may actually help to alleviate the problems of political violence.

As we have seen, historically Article I and the Second Amendment represent different strategies for taming violence. The first would primarily trust Congress as a representative of the whole; the second would primarily trust the militia as the direct and local embodiment of the people. In isolation, either of these voices might have produced a simpler Constitution than the one we have. Yet this constitution, our Constitution, embraces both voices. Read as a whole, the Constitution thus offers the people two ways to express their will about the appropriate use of violence: directly, through the militia, and representatively, through Congress. These mechanisms have different strengths and weaknesses: the militia may be closer to the people, but it may also be seized by local, partial, and immoderate passions; Congress may be farther from the people, but it may also take a larger, more deliberate, and longer term view.

Those distinctions may seem familiar to students of the Constitution because they are the terms in which Americans have long argued about the respective merits of local or direct democracy and representative or central democracy. As with federalism, so with the organization of violence, the Constitution does not simply choose one over the other. Instead, it endorses both, yoking them as uneasy partners in a fraught balance. At its best, the Constitution prizes complexity over simplicity, and it recognizes the various truths of multiple perspectives.

In other words, for the organization of violence, Article I and the Second Amendment together create a system of checks and balances similar to the other constitutional structures of federalism and the separation of powers. Such systems represent a bet that the division of power among multiple actors will produce justice and safety for the people. The bet may not always pay off. When they do not work, these systems become stuck in gridlock or pointless conflict. When they do work, they create multiple, alternative layers of protection, rather than pinning all their hopes on one savior. Congress may therefore suppress rebellions, but if Congress itself ever becomes corrupt, the people may still make a revolution.

The Constitution contains many systems that deploy multiple and somewhat discordant routes to the same end. In *Federalist* number 10, for example, Madison offers two quite disparate defenses of the new central government. In his view, the great challenge for a republic is to control faction. No constitutional scheme can ever eliminate this vice because difference and self-interest inhere in human nature. Luckily, a strong central government offers two distinct advantages in blunting the effects of faction. First, he explains that in a large republic there are simply more public-spirited leaders, "proper guardians of the public weal."[52] As a result, the central government will likely contain more men of virtue than local governments. Madison also insisted, however, that it would be unwise to rely on such leaders as the only protection against faction: "It is vain to say that enlightened statesmen will be able to adjust these clashing interests and render them all subservient to the public good. Enlightened statesmen will not always be at the helm."[53] Happily, a central government offers a second hedge. Because they are small, local governments are subject to capture by a single faction. The central government, by contrast, contains so many factions that none can ever wreak its will unchecked: "Extend the sphere and you take in a greater variety of parties and interests; you make it less probable that a majority of the whole will have a common motive to invade the rights of other citizens; or if such a common motive exists, it will be more difficult for all who feel it to discover their own strength and to act in unison with each other."[54]

In other words, in Madison's view the new constitution offers a layered defense for the public good: with luck, virtuous leaders will control the government, but even if they do not, no single faction will be able to dominate. As do Article I and the Second Amendment, Madison's first and second routes to safety involve different actors with divergent characteristics, and they are in some tension. In addition, wholly apart from the first route, the second route by itself relies on the diffusion of power across multiple, contending actors: Madison hoped that factions would check each other in the national legislature. Similarly, the body of the Constitution and the Second Amendment rely on the tension-filled interaction of Congress and a popular militia to make room for revolution but not rebellion.

Federalism also functions in this way. For many, the main defense of the federal system is that it protects the citizenry by dividing power between contending levels of government. Among Supreme Court justices, Lewis Powell may have been the most articulate recent exponent of this view. He argued, for example, that the "Framers believed that the States would serve as an effective 'counterpoise' to the power of the Federal Government. The States would serve this essential role because they would attract and retain the loyalty of their citizens.... [Hamilton] maintained that the people would perceive the States as 'the immediate and most visible guardian of life and property,' a fact which 'contributes more than any other circumstance to impressing upon the minds of the people affection, esteem, and reverence towards the government.' "[55]

Similarly, the authors of the *Federalist Papers* defended the separation of powers on the grounds that it diffused power among contending parties. Madison, for example, insisted, "The accumulation of all powers, legislative, executive, and judiciary, in the same hands, whether of one, a few, or many, and whether hereditary, self-appointed, or elective, may justly be pronounced the very definition of tyranny."[56] Quoting from Jefferson's *Notes on the State of Virginia*, Madison argued that even though legislatures might be representative, they still should not be supreme: "An *elective despotism* was not the government we fought for; but one which should not only be defended on free principles, but in which the powers of government should be so divided and balanced among several bodies of magistracy as that no one could transcend their legal limits without being effectually checked and restrained by the others."[57] Indeed, not only should the legislature share power with the other branches, but it should be internally divided into two houses sharing power: "The remedy for this inconveniency is to divide the legislature into different branches; and to render them, by different modes of election and different principles of action, as little connected with each other as the nature of their common functions and their common dependence on the society will admit."[58] And to preserve their separation, these branches should sometimes be discordant, even conflictual: "The great security against a gradual concentration of the several powers in the same department consists in giving to those who administer each department the necessary constitutional means of personal motives to resist encroachments of the others. The provision for defense must in this, as in all other cases, be made commensurate to the danger of attack."[59]

The Framers thus celebrated both federalism and separation of powers because they both contributed to a system of checks and balances. Madison makes this shared origin explicit: "In the compound republic of America, the power surrendered by the people is first divided between two distinct governments, and then the portion allotted to each subdivided among distinct and separate departments. Hence a double security arises to the rights of the people. The different governments will control each other, at the same time that each will be controlled by itself."[60]

In short, this form of structural organization is very characteristic of our Constitution. It should therefore come as no surprise that the Constitution uses a similar system for organizing political violence, dividing it among different and potentially clashing actors, in an attempt to provide a "double security . . . to the rights of the people." Ideally, the various actors "will control each other, at the same time that each will be controlled by itself." This system is thus the original legal meaning of our constitutional organization of political violence.

In the twenty-first century, however, we face a puzzle in interpreting this scheme. If the Constitution created a complex balance between Congress and the people-in-militia, then if we mean to follow its historical meaning, we must try to preserve that balance. As the next part of this book will explore, however, that task has become quite difficult because of social changes. One side of the scales remains relatively unchanged: Congress may still have the power to suppress rebellions because it represents the people. The Body of the People, however, has changed dramatically. Institutionally, we are no longer assembled in universal militia. Culturally, not only have we become significantly more diverse, but celebration of that diversity has become a central pillar of American constitutional beliefs.

Indeed, the commitment to diversity has shaped most modern views of the Second Amendment itself. In the eighteenth century, Second Amendment proponents embraced a myth of unity: the people, existing and acting as a body, must be able to overthrow a corrupt government. Today, almost all interpreters of the Second Amendment embrace various myths of disunity. These stories borrow rhetoric from the old myth but give it a very different spin: in a world of dangerous fragmentation, the virtuous part of the citizenry must be able to use arms against the vicious part, so as to preserve itself. Virtuous homeowners must be allowed to arm themselves against vicious criminals; virtuous governmental bureaucrats must be allowed to disarm vicious gun owners; virtuous members of outgroups must be allowed to arm themselves against vicious bigots; and virtuous members of the militia movement must be allowed to arm themselves against the vicious interest groups that have captured Congress. In the midst of all these new myths, the Body of the People, safely bearing arms in deep consensus, has virtually disappeared.

When one part of the constitutional balance has dropped from sight in this way, fidelity to the historical meaning of the Constitution becomes difficult, even deeply problematic. Two things, however, are clear: we cannot safely blind ourselves to these historical changes, and if we do not constitute a Body of the People, we cannot simply recapitulate the original balance of power. We are, in short, at a moment of some crisis, and we need to examine how we got here and where we might go from here. Part II will begin that examination.

The Mythic Second Amendment Today

In the Constitution, the Framers left us a particular myth about the domestication of violence. By a myth, I refer to a thought structure, usually in story form, that organizes and inculcates part of a culture's belief system. In the Second Amendment and Article I, the Framers inscribed this legal myth: under ordinary circumstances, Congress should suppress rebellions in the name of the people; sometimes, however, the government becomes corrupt, and then the Body of the People should make a revolution. Fundamentally, this story is about unity under conditions of violence: acting for the people as a whole, Congress suppresses rebellions because such insurrections are factional; and when the people make a revolution, they are institutionally united in the militia and culturally united on the appropriate use of political violence. In other words, the Framers' answer to the problem of political violence was popular solidarity. The people will be safe from both tyranny and rebellion only if they have guns in their hands and shared beliefs in their hearts.

Since the adoption of the Constitution, Americans have become more diverse. Perhaps more important, they have come to celebrate their diversity. For many, unified peoplehood has ceased to be an attractive ideal; instead, individual rights have come to dominate constitutional discourse. Not surprisingly, myths of the Second Amendment have followed U.S. demographic and ideological changes. Where the Framers presumed substantial unity on political violence, our modern myths presume disunity as a fact of life. In these myths, the citizenry consists of individuals and groups that are armed and hostile toward each other, and the pursuit of commonality is never an option. In this world of mutual threat, the worry is that the bad guys will end up with all the guns, and so the point in the constitutional organization of violence is to allow some Americans to arm themselves against other Americans.

This point has always been apparent for individual rights theorists in their various paradigm cases: homeowners arm themselves against burglars, women arm themselves against misogynists, militia members arm themselves against everyone else. It is, however, no less true for states' right theorists: in their view, the Constitution allows the people running the state, as the only trustworthy group, to disarm by violence all who threaten them, including criminals and political dissidents. Citizens who are not in the government have the right to bear arms only as part of a militia that is firmly under state control. In these myths, then, we have a vision of threat and counterthreat, anxiety assuaged by the promise of dominion, mutual hostility resolved by victory for some and loss for others. In other words, the modern mythmakers' answer to the problem of political violence is not unity but subjugation: it's a war out there, and we'd better make sure that the good guys have the upper hand.

Part II of this book will trace the outlines of the modern mythic landscape of the Second Amendment. No book can completely document all the ways that people think about the constitutional organization of violence, but here I will describe enough of the main features to give the reader a clear sense of the overall topography. In offering this map, I will pursue four principal goals: first, to identify the deep myths that underlie the various modern theories of the Second Amendment; second, to demonstrate that these modern accounts are all myths of disunity, in contrast to the Framers' myth of unity; third, to argue that such myths of disunity will not fulfill their promise because they will not in fact tame political violence; fourth, on the other hand, to suggest that the Framers' myth of popular unity no longer squares with our lived social reality — as revealed by the very fact that all these myths presume disunity. As a result, neither the modern myths of disunity nor the Framers' myth of unity offers an adequate theory of the constitutional organization of violence.

In the last part, I examined the work of Second Amendment theorists to consider whether they accurately capture the provision's history. In this part, I examine the work of these theorists for a different reason: in their modern renderings of the Second Amendment, these writers offer important stories about the relation between violence, on the one hand, and democracy, identity, and freedom, on the other. In other words, I consider these writers not as historians but as mythographers, people who propose myths to describe how we should organize political violence. The goal will be to offer an account not of the Second Amendment's history, but of its powerful present, and the method will be to discern the organizing myths that lie behind these legal tales. I will therefore consider some of the same material (and some different), but from a new angle of vision.

Each chapter in this part will examine a different modern reading of the Second Amendment. Chapter 4, "Antirevolutionists," will consider a collection of theories that unite in one belief: the Second Amendment does not recognize a popular right to resist the government. As I will suggest, these theories rightly worry that if individuals have a personal right to insurrection, the most likely result will be terrorism and anarchy. These theories also insist, however, that the only way to domesticate that threat is to create a governmental monopoly of violence. In posing the alternatives thus starkly — either the government has a monopoly of violence or the republic will break down — and in choosing government as the only organ worthy of trust, these theories rest on a certain militarist myth: the citizenry is inherently violent and discordant; left to their own devices, they will kill each other; only the state (or, more accurately, the group of Americans running the state) can impose order and be trusted with control; and the world will ever be so. This myth thus assumes that the American citizenry will always be disunited, and the only hope is for some Americans — the responsible ones, those in the government — to dominate the others. In this myth, we hear nothing about the dangers of absolute governmental power or the importance of popular cohesion in avoiding civil war.

Chapter 5, "Libertarians and Populists," will look at two groups of writers who espouse the individual rights theory of the Second Amendment. First, it will examine the libertarians, a number of serious scholars and one federal appeals court, all of whom believe that the amendment recognizes an individual right to make war upon the government. As collective rights theorists would observe, this theory seems to invite anarchy, with every disgruntled individual shooting at government officers when he deems it appropriate. In fact, on closer inspection, these seeming individualists turn out to be populists: their rhetoric assumes that when individuals rise up, they will magically cohere into something called the people, which will oppose the government as a unit. These theorists rarely contemplate the possibility that, in the absence of a militia structure and a unified culture, the more likely result of insurrection by individuals is mutual slaughter. As a truly individualist theory, then, this view is untenable for practical reasons. As a populist theory, it raises the question whether the mass of Americans constitute a people capable of revolutionary action through the spontaneous coherence of individual wills.

The chapter will then consider that question by addressing the work of a group of writers who give the amendment an openly populist reading. Libertarians view the Second Amendment in abstract legal terms, and so they assign the right to arms to generic individuals, without regard to race, religion, or gender. By contrast, a certain slice of America, generally called the gun culture, has claimed the Second Amendment as its particular property. This culture has its roots in the seedbed of American populism: rural, white, Protestant, conservative, and southern males. Members of this culture generally believe that the Second Amendment represents the constitutionalization of their cherished values, expressed in mythic form. Like the libertarians, they claim that the amendment guarantees an individual right to own arms. Unlike the libertarians, however, they argue that only individuals from the gun culture really belong to the true American people. Correlatively, the gun culture's enemies, including the liberal elite and various outgroups, do not really belong. These populists thus claim for themselves the right to rebel against the federal government, which they perceive as being co-opted by their enemies. In other words, despite its populist rhetoric, this myth is one of disunity: although these populists claim to speak for the people, their people includes only a slice of the citizenry — those true American patriots who will stand against the internal enemies. And again, this myth is practically untenable, a flight from frustrating political loss into a fantasy of violent recompense.

Chapter 6, "The Militia Movement," analyzes the recent militia movement as an extreme example of this populist school of thought. The leaders of the movement have generated a surprisingly extensive literature detailing their theory of the Second Amendment. Like most populists, they claim that the amendment guarantees an individual right to arms for revolution, that only those individuals who belong to the people may make a revolution, and that the people includes only persons like themselves. Again, we witness the way that libertarian myths become populist myths and the way that old myths of unity become modern myths of disunity. The militia movement offers another lesson as well, about the difficulty of imagining a myth of unity under modern conditions of diversity. The movement offers a variety of ways to define the people: whites, Christians, libertarians, isolationists. In different ways, these definitions fail to encompass the whole American citizenry. By looking at these failures, we can survey the rich diversity in our cultural landscape and thereby gain a sense of just how unlikely it is that modern Americans will spontaneously congeal into a unified revolutionary movement.

Chapter 7 turns to a very different set of modern myths, myths woven by members of outgroups who believe in the use of arms to break the power of violent bigotry. Traditionally, many outgroups have found the Second Amendment to be culturally alien because they feared armed, populist movements like the Klan. More recently, however, some members of some outgroups have begun to claim the Second Amendment as their own. In their view, since the government will not protect them, they must seek to protect themselves. In so doing, they are engaged not only in personal self-protection but also in political action: they hope to defeat the forces of bigotry by taking up arms against them. And they offer a supporting myth about the Second Amendment: in their view, the provision belongs particularly to people like themselves — vulnerable groups ready to battle for justice, if only they have the means.

Once again, these outgroup myths are myths of disunity rather than unity: they presume that some Americans will kill others, and the only question is who will fit into each category. And once again, these myths are dysfunctional under modern conditions to the end of taming political violence. In some circumstances, it may make good policy sense for outgroups to arm themselves against hate violence. At a mythic level, however, it makes very bad sense to valorize this state of affairs as the Constitution's vision of American life. For outgroups especially, mutual self-arming will never secure a safe future; instead, only an inclusive culture, unified on the restraint of hate violence, could possibly achieve that end. In short, outgroups particularly need myths of unity, such as the Framers' actual myth of peoplehood, rather than the myth of perennial hatred that they ascribe to the Framers. In other words, the militia movement myth and the outgroup myth teach important, complementary lessons, though these lessons are the opposite of what their authors mean to teach us. On the one hand, the militia movement highlights how difficult it is to construct a modern people; on the other hand, the outgroups illustrate how important it is that we do so, lest the most vulnerable among us become subject to hatred and death.

The problem with all the myths in this part is not just that they do not square with the Framers' vision. The deeper problem is that they offer a false hope that we can tame violence by arming the right people against the wrong people. A nation deeply divided against itself on the use of political violence will ultimately collapse. Indeed, a nation that does not share a social contract on this subject could scarcely be called a nation at all. Those who would tame political violence, then, should worry less about who has the guns and more about how to create a political culture that binds us together. Paradoxically, these myths accomplish just the opposite: by emphasizing our endemic hostility, they encourage distrust and anger as constitutionally sanctioned attitudes. And, as we will see, many of these myths are very angry indeed.

4

Antirevolutionists

Until recently, most of the American legal and academic establishment believed that the Second Amendment was not a revolutionary text. These writers held (and hold) that the amendment does not recognize, explicitly or implicitly, a right to resist a corrupt government. Indeed, most of these anti-revolutionists argue that neither individuals nor even state governments have a right to arms for resistance. At most, the Second Amendment guaranteed the states, along with the federal government, a concurrent power to keep their militias well armed so that those militias could keep order. The amendment thus responded to only one concern: the states' worry that Congress might use its new powers to disarm the militias.

As we have seen, these theories ignore much of the intellectual context in which the Framers' worry about Congress's ability to disarm the militia occurred. They fail to explain why Second Amendment proponents deemed the militia "necessary to the security of a free state"; why they feared the federal government so much, particularly when it came to disarming the militias and the "People"; and what they expected this armed militia to do if the federal government ever became tyrannical. Instead, they offer a powerful myth based on a Weberian vision of the social world. First, they argue accurately that the Framers wanted to arm militias, rather than individuals as such. Second, however, they insist that militias must simply be instruments of the state, always and everywhere. This second step is crucial because it allows these theorists to conclude that the militia has no revolutionary capacity. Their identification of the militia and the state, however, comes from a selective review of the eighteenth-century evidence. As we have seen, militias enjoyed a complex status: sometimes they were instruments of the state, but sometimes they were independent, even revolutionary, actors. By contrast, these theories presuppose our modern conception of the social world as divided into only two entities: governments and individuals. In this dichotomy, if the amendment does not create an individual right, then it must guarantee a governmental power.

As a result, a Second Amendment right of revolution is nonsensical: governments must have a monopoly on the legitimate exercise of violence. These theories argue that an individual right to revolution is ludicrous because it would lead to anarchy. They then assert that because the Constitution grants individuals no such right, it must not grant the right to any body. In support, they point out that the Framers opposed many rebellions, and, based on this evidence, they conclude that the Framers must have opposed all revolutions in principle, at least after the adoption of the Constitution. For these theorists, all uprisings are alike because they share one characteristic: they all dare to take up arms against government, and for Weberians resistance to government — no matter how tyrannical it may be — is constitutionally impermissible.

Weberians offer an image of a very simple world: unless one wants to accept Timothy McVeigh's terrorism as constitutional, then one must give all power over violence to the government. The only alternative to anarchy is exclusive governmental authority. In fact, as we have seen, those are not our only options: one might deny both an individual right to political violence and also a governmental monopoly over it. Instead, one might acknowledge a power in the Body of the People to conduct revolutions for the good of the whole. Perhaps that old myth will not work well for us today. Despite the atrocities that governments have wreaked in the twentieth century, they may still be the most trustworthy bearers of the means of violence. If we are to make those judgments, however, we should make them self-consciously and pragmatically, as deliberate judgments about the viability of popular arming and governmental reliability.

These theories do not offer that sort of judgment. Instead, they invoke the authority of the Framers by reading them as modern Weberians. In their view, because the Framers did not endorse an individual right to arms, they must have believed that the state has a monopoly on legitimate violence — as do these theorists themselves. Because the Framers condemned some rebellions, they must have condemned all resistance to government — as do these theorists themselves. These claims, however, distort the thought world of the Framers.

Aside from the fact that they distort history, these myths do no good service in circumscribing thinking about the constitutional organization of violence today. Governmental authority, stability, and order are important, but so are popular engagement with the ordering of political violence and a healthy skepticism about governmental purity. It is too late in human history to repose perfect trust in any institution. Unhappily, these theories do just that. This trust is revealed most clearly in their treatment of the origin of the right of revolution.

Ultimately, most of these theorists concede that the Framers believed in a right of revolution, but in their view it was a natural right, not a constitutional one. They base this argument primarily on logical inference, rather than historical evidence: they claim that the Constitution could not sanction a right to resist the government because to resist the government is to resist the Constitution itself. That argument, however, presumes that only the government can ever truly protect the Constitution, and for that reason the Constitution must give a monopoly of violence to government. The options are stark: we can have constitution or revolution, but we cannot have constitutional revolution. If the government is true to the Constitution, then all resistance is treason to the Constitution itself. If the government is not faithful to the Constitution, then the Constitution has by definition been dissolved because it can never reside in the people. As a result, those who resist government can never claim to speak for the Constitution, only for themselves, whether as traitors (when the government is good) or revolutionaries in the state of nature (when the government is bad). Thus, although this myth invokes the virtues of collective action, it insists that constitutional unity can exist only through governmental power, and resisters are always auslanders in their own country. In short, this myth is not about popular unity, but about disunity contained through the strong arm of government.

The myth has attracted three sets of proponents. First, although the Supreme Court has not definitively interpreted the amendment, the federal appeals courts (with one exception, considered in the next chapter) have found in the provision only a protection for a state-controlled militia. Second, a group of lawyers have written law journal articles supporting the analysis of these courts. Third, more recently, a group of historians have written a series of articles and books attacking the work of individual rights theorists. This last group is generally unclear about what the Second Amendment demands; indeed, they often claim that one cannot construct a paradigmatic meaning for the amendment. They are clear, however, about what it does not mean: it does not protect a right to arms for revolution.

The Antirevolutionists' Second Amendment

JUDGES

One of the salient facts of Second Amendment scholarship is that the Supreme Court has never offered a definitive interpretation of the provision. For that reason, the field has been, as it were, without a center. In the nineteenth century, the Court handed down three Second Amendment opinions, but none addressed the substantive scope of the right to arms. The first held that the amendment does not limit private individuals: when one private person disarms another, that action cannot constitute an infringement of the right to arms.[1] The other two cases held that the Fourteenth Amendment does not incorporate the Second against the state governments.[2] Taken together, the three cases hold only that whatever rights it might protect, the amendment protects them only against the federal government.

In *United States v. Miller,*[3] decided in 1939, the Court finally said something about the right's substance. This case, however, offers little guidance about the modern Court's views because it is old and deeply ambiguous.[4] In *Miller,* the Court addressed a Second Amendment challenge to the National Firearms Act of 1934,[5] which prohibited, inter alia, possession of a sawed-off shotgun except under limited circumstances. The Court held that the amendment's "obvious purpose" was to "assure the continuation and render possible the effectiveness" of the militia. So clear was that purpose that the amendment "must be interpreted and applied with that end in view." The Court then held that because the parties had not offered "any evidence tending to show that possession or use of a [sawed-off shotgun] at this time has some reasonable relationship to the preservation or efficiency of a well regulated militia, we cannot say that the Second Amendment guarantees the right to keep and bear such an instrument."[6]

Miller's language is susceptible of at least two interpretations. First, the broad reading, offered by individual rights theorists,[7] argues that *Miller* rejected the Second Amendment claim because of the nature of the firearm: the parties had not shown that this gun was of the sort that militias might use. By denying the claim on this ground, the Court was correlatively saying that it would have upheld *Miller*'s right to the gun if he had shown that it was a militia-type weapon. Therefore, the Court implicitly held that the amendment protects a private right to certain sorts of firearms. The broad reading acknowledges that the *Miller* Court insisted that the amendment must be read to protect a militia, rather than individuals as such. In the view of these theorists, however, the *Miller* Court viewed militias as nothing more than the universe of private citizens. The Court explained that eighteenth-century militias "comprised all males capable of acting in concert for the common defense." Those private persons, moreover, were supposed to supply their own arms: "Ordinarily when called for service these men were expected to appear bearing arms supplied by themselves and of the kind in common use at the time."[8] For that reason, the Court would have found that private ownership of militia-style arms had a "reasonable relationship to the preservation or efficiency of a well-regulated militia."

By and large, the lower federal courts have rejected the broad reading. Instead of focusing on the particular type of gun, their narrow eading focuses on the particular use of a gun. In this view, the Court rejected the Second Amendment claim because the parties failed to show that Miller was going to use his shotgun while serving in a "well-regulated militia." The amendment therefore protects a right to arms only during actual militia service, not in private ownership. And these courts have a very specific definition of the militia in mind: in their view, it is a state instrumentality, entirely subordinate to state will, without independent judgment and without a popular character. For that reason, the people have the right to arms in the context of a militia only insofar as the state allows them that right. Thus portrayed, the militia acts merely as an agent of the state to keep order according to government fiat. It is not and was not supposed to be a communal form allowing the people to keep themselves organized for resistance to a corrupt government.

In 1942, the First Circuit inaugurated this line of decisions in *Cases v. United States*.[9] It held that *Miller* should not be read to protect private ownership of militia-style arms because "some sort of military use seems to have been found for almost any modern legal weapon." As a result, if *Miller* were read to protect private militia-type arms, Congress could regulate only "antiques or curiosities" and could not even control "distinctly military arms, such as machine guns, trench mortars, anti-tank, or anti-aircraft guns." Instead, *Cases* insisted that *Miller* did not attempt to "formulate a general rule applicable to all cases"; indeed, it seemed to the court "impossible to formulate a general test by which to determine the limits imposed by the Second Amendment." Each case, therefore, "must be decided on its own facts."[10] For the *Cases* court, however, one fact was dispositive in the case before it: there was no "evidence that the appellant was or ever had been a member of any military organization or that his use of the weapon under the circumstances disclosed was in preparation for a military career."[11] In short, then, the Second Amendment protects firearms use only within a formal "military organization," the sort of organization in which professionals hold "military career[s]."

In *United States v. Warin*,[12] decided in 1976, the Sixth Circuit explained more explicitly that the Second Amendment's "militia" refers only to a body that is wholly subservient to the state. The defendant claimed that he had a Second Amendment right to own a submachine gun, in violation of the National Firearms Act.[13] First, the court rejected any individual right to arms: "The Second Amendment guarantees a collective rather than an individual right." More particularly, the court explained that this collective right "applies only to the right of the State to maintain a militia,"[14] rather than to the right of the people, as a collectivity, to keep private arms.

In response, Warin argued that he was a member of the state's "sedentary militia," meaning all those subject to militia duty under Ohio law, and so had Second Amendment rights.[15] The court rejected this argument out of hand, on two grounds. First, Ohio law gave the right to own submachine guns only to the "organized militia." It is thus plain that, in the court's view, the amendment is a protection for state power to arm its militia as it sees fit, rather than for an individual right to arms. Second, the court held that wholly apart from state law, the Constitution itself refers only to an "organized militia." The court asserted, "There is absolutely no evidence that a submachine gun in the hands of an individual 'sedentary militia' member would have any, much less a 'reasonable relationship to the preservation or efficiency of a well regulated militia.' "[16] According to the *Warin* court, then, the Second Amendment protects arms bearing only by those subservient to the state in a formal military organization. Any more popular or independent entity does not belong in the amendment's ambit.

United States v. Oakes[17] similarly rejected membership in "alternative" militias as a basis for Second Amendment rights. The defendant argued that "even if the second amendment is construed to guarantee the right to bear arms only to an organized militia, he came within the scope of the amendment" because he was a member of two militia-like organizations. First, the defendant fit the membership definition of the militia contained in the Kansas Constitution: all "able-bodied male citizens between the ages of twenty-one and forty-five years." Second, he was "a member of 'Posse Comitatus, a militia-type organization registered with the state of Kansas.' " The court rejected both arguments with no hesitation and little explanation. As to the second claim, the court observed that the Posse Comitatus was "an apparently nongovernmental organization" and so could not be a militia. By contrast, the Kansas militia recognized by the state constitution was a governmental entity but, according to the Court, not the right sort. In the court's view, to allow the defendant to "keep an unregistered firearm which has not been shown to have any connection to the militia, merely because he is technically a member of the

Kansas militia, would be unjustifiable in terms of either logic or policy."[18] The court's language here is revealing. The defendant is only "technically" a member of the state militia, by virtue of the state constitution's designation of him as a member. Mere technical or descriptive membership, however, is not enough to bring the Second Amendment into play. Instead, one must apparently be in a formal organization under state supervision and training; only in such a body could keeping a firearm "have any connection to the [right kind of] militia." In the court's view, "logic" and "policy" so clearly command this state monopoly of violence that the Second Amendment should be read with that goal in mind.

All three of these cases hold that the militia has no will independent of the state; accordingly, it has no right to resist a corrupt state government. These cases do not directly address the relation of the militia to the federal government, but their view seems clear: just as the militia may not resist the state, so "logic" and "policy" dictate that the militia, even under the direction of the state, may not resist Congress. Surely, if the militia did have such a right, one would expect these cases to mention it.

In *United States v. Hale,*[19] the Eighth Circuit made that implicit view explicit. In fact, this case is generally more careful than the earlier ones, and it draws on recent scholarly work. Early in its discussion, the *Hale* court seems to hint that it might find some revolutionary potential in the amendment. Citing the work of Keith A. Ehrman and Dennis A. Henigan,[20] which I will explore in the next section, it held that when the Second Amendment was adopted, "the state militias functioned as both the principal units of military organization and as an implicit check on federal power."[21] The opinion does not explain how the militia might check federal power, but Ehrman and Henigan recognize that the states hoped their militias could resist federal tyranny by force of arms.[22] In addition, in the court's view, because militia members were expected to bring their own arms, the amendment originally "prevented federal laws that would infringe upon possession of arms by individuals and thus render the state militias impotent."[23] According to *Hale,* then, the Second Amendment protected the right of individuals to own arms so they could participate in their state militias and thus check federal power. To be sure, the court limits this right to state-supervised militias; it specifically denies that Second Amendment rights can grow out of membership in "sedentary" militias, "unorganized" state militias, or nongovernmental military organizations.[24] Still, the case seems to recognize that the amendment originally had a revolutionary quality, even if only of a federalist sort.

Shortly thereafter, however, the *Hale* court opines that this revolutionary quality is a thing of the past. In the two hundred years following the amendment's adoption, "state militias first faded out of existence and then later reemerged as more organized, semi-professional military units." Later, the militia became part of the "national guard structure," which is, for all intents and purposes, a federal agency: "The 'Federal Government provides virtually all of the funding, the materiel, and the leadership for the State Guard units.' " Given these changes, says the court, "we cannot conclude that the Second Amendment protects the individual possession of military weapons."[25] The court never explains why the National Guard, designed to be subservient to the federal government, can act as an acceptable analogue for the old state militias, designed to check the federal government. However the court reaches that conclusion, the result is clear: today, in our Weberian world, militias have no revolutionary function, neither toward the states nor toward the federal government, even under state direction.

What is noteworthy about these cases is not their insistence that the Second Amendment protects the right to arms only in a militia: the language of both *Miller* and the amendment itself are quite susceptible of that interpretation. Instead, what is remarkable is their casual assumption that the militia must refer to a pure state instrumentality, a simple servant of government. As a result, once these cases have concluded that the amendment reaches arms bearing only within a militia, they believe that the real analytical work is over because the nature of a militia is transparent. As we have seen, however, only at this point does the analytical work become interesting and difficult. The nature of an eighteenth-century militia was complex, but one fact is clear: if government had become corrupt, few people wanted the militia unquestioningly to follow its orders. A pure state instrumentality therefore cannot serve as a modern analogue. To be sure, sedentary or private militias cannot serve as good analogues either because they are not universal and have not been trained to virtue. These courts, however, reject such militias for a quite different reason: they are not wholly subservient state agencies.

The key analytical move in these cases is thus their complete identification of the militia and the state. This move grew not out of engagement with eighteenth-century sources, but from the courts' unreflective assumption that organizations like the militia — collective bodies bearing arms — must be state entities, pure and simple. In other words, the cases reflect the conventional modern view that the state has a monopoly on legitimate violence. The courts' thinking is thus heavily conditioned by a Weberian mythic structure. As a policy matter, it may be good to read the Second Amendment that way because that mythos may serve modern needs. If we are to reach that conclusion, however, we must openly consider which constitutional myth will best help us. We will not be aided in that task by claims that Patrick Henry and

Elbridge Gerry or even James Madison and Alexander Hamilton were really proto-Weberians.

LAWYERS

For decades before the explosion of writing on the Second Amendment in the 1990s, a group of lawyers and legal academics elaborated and documented the antirevolutionary theory of the Second Amendment that federal cases were then adopting. As these sources form the academic background for federal case law, they are an important part of the modern mythic landscape of the Second Amendment. A complete list of such articles would be quite long, but for illustrative purposes I have selected two for their influence, general sophistication, and relative recency.

As we have seen, Ehrman's and Henigan's *The Second Amendment in the Twentieth Century: Have You Seen Your Militia Lately?*[26] exercised considerable influence on the Eighth Circuit's *Hale* opinion. Ehrman and Henigan argue that the Framers of the amendment were concerned to "assure the states that, under the constitution, they would retain the right to maintain an effective, organized, citizen-based militia." They were not, by contrast, trying to protect an individual "right to be armed for purposes unrelated to militia service."[27] Ehrman and Henigan never suggest that the militia might rebel against the state governments; indeed, they insist that it was a "state-organized, state-run body" and that "the records reveal no discussion of a fear of state governments."[28] The authors do, however, explain that the states wanted the militias "for their own defense, as a means of fending off a dictatorial central government."[29]

Yet somehow with the passage of time, the amendment lost even this revolutionary quality. When the states neglected their militias, the federal government stepped in to keep them supplied and trained.[30] Over the years, the militia went through a "transformation from state to federal control"[31] and so became the "federal entity" called the National Guard. Because Congress keeps the guard armed and because no state requires its citizens to supply their own arms for guard service, "the guarantee encompassed in the second amendment imposes no restrictions on federal legislation seeking to regulate ownership or possession of arms by individuals." The linchpin of this argument is therefore the equation of the National Guard and the old state militias. Yet given Ehrman's and Henigan's own historical account, this identification is problematic. As they recognize, the old militias were to be "tools largely of the states, ready to fight the federal government," but today, "the federal government has ultimate authority and control over" the National Guard.[32] As a result, the guard entirely lacks the revolutionary potential so characteristic of the state militias.

Ehrman's and Henigan's only answer to this charge reveals the way their analysis is shaped by their Weberian commitments. They argue that the National Guard can substitute for the old revolutionary militias because the states consented to that transformation: "The second amendment was designed to assure the states and citizens that they could maintain effective state militias. However, the states and citizens demonstrated during the 1800s that they did not want to exercise that prerogative."[33] In other words, the states waived whatever revolutionary rights they and their citizens possessed by neglecting the militias during the nineteenth century. Since they would not maintain them, they were implicitly inviting Congress to take them over. Actually, it is not at all clear that the states were issuing such an invitation. Even though they neglected the militias, they might have seen no need for better ones at the moment. Or, more likely, they wanted Congress to arm and supply the militias but not to commandeer them, thus robbing them of their ability to resist federal tyranny.

More important, however, Ehrman and Henigan are assuming that state governments may waive their Second Amendment rights, turning over control of the militia to the federal government. Generally, the point in federalism is not to protect state governments in and of themselves; rather, the point is to protect the people by keeping control over some matters at a more local level. As the Supreme Court recently explained, "The Constitution does not protect the sovereignty of States for the benefit of the States or state governments as abstract political entities, or even for the benefit of the public officials governing the States.... 'Rather, federalism secures to citizens the liberties that derive from the diffusion of sovereign power.' "[34]

When federalism is so conceived, states are generally not allowed to waive their rights because they are not ultimately theirs to waive. Instead, they hold those powers in trust for their citizens. Again, the Supreme Court explains that the "constitutional authority of Congress cannot be expanded by the 'consent' of the governmental unit whose domain is thereby narrowed, whether that unit is the Executive Branch or the states."[35] As we have seen, the Anti-Federalists thought about the militia in just this way. The reason for giving the states control over their militias was not to augment state power for its own sake, but rather to allow the states to act as a counterbalance to federal power, so that their citizens' liberties would be safer. The states were the immediate beneficiaries, but the citizenry reaped the ultimate rewards.

By contrast, Ehrman and Henigan believe the states can waive these rights.

Therefore, they clearly believe that the ultimate beneficiaries of the amendment were the state governments, the citizens being merely onlookers. Here again we glimpse the Weberian roots of this mythmaking: control of violence belongs to governments as "abstract political entities," not as a way to "secure to citizens [their] liberties." Because government has a legitimate monopoly of violence, one set of governments may give some of its power to another set. The important thing is that only governments exercise this kind of power, not which government does so. In fact, Ehrman and Henigan plainly believe it a small point that state governments have given away their revolutionary potential, in clear contradiction to the views of the Anti-Federalists who agitated for the amendment.

In a separate article,[36] Dennis Henigan seeks to refute the view that the Second Amendment protects an individual right to revolution, which he calls the "insurrectionary theory."[37] He again argues that the point in the amendment was to protect the militia, which he describes, in good Weberian fashion, as "an instrument of governmental authority."[38] Quoting Roscoe Pound, he argues compellingly that an individual right to revolution might lead to anarchy: "In the urban industrial society of today a general right to bear efficient arms so as to be enabled to resist oppression by the government would mean that gangs could exercise an extra-legal rule which would defeat the whole Bill of Rights."[39] Henigan calls this disturbing portrait "the insurrectionist vision of America."[40] And he warns that the insurrectionist theory "represents a profoundly dangerous doctrine of unrestrained individual rights which, if adopted by the courts, would threaten the rule of law itself."[41]

On the other hand, Henigan recognizes that state governments relied on their militias to resist federal tyranny. He quotes Luther Martin's warning that in the event the states lost their militias, "if the general government should attempt to oppress and enslave them, they could not have any possible means of self-defense."[42] Similarly, he reminds us that Madison assured the Anti-Federalists that if the federal government should become tyrannical, "*the State governments with the people on their side would be able to repel the danger.*"[43] It would appear, then, that Henigan is arguing against only an individual "constitutional right to engage in armed insurrection against tyrannical authority, whether state or federal."[44] By contrast, he appears to believe that the amendment protects a right of the state, backed by its people, to resist federal tyranny. And although a government body, the militia is specifically "an instrument of *state* government."[45]

Yet this conclusion that the amendment protects a state right of resistance is still deeply threatening to Weberian sensibilities, with its yearning for order through rational government. An individual right of resistance might lead to worse anarchy than a state right, but a state right might nonetheless lead to great turbulence, even civil war of the sort the nation endured in the 1860s. And so not surprisingly Henigan apparently denies that the states retain a right of resistance, though he never explains how he reconciles this conclusion with his historical account. Early in his article, he endorses the view that the amendment currently protects only the National Guard, which is, as we have seen, a federal entity.[46] Yet if the guard now holds all the Second Amendment rights, then the states' own right of resistance has disappeared. Later, he relies on Congress's Article I powers to refute the individualist insurrectionary theory, but his argument seemingly eliminates a state right of resistance as well. He points out that Congress has the power to call out the militia so as "to suppress Insurrections." In Henigan's view, if Congress can suppress insurrections, then private individuals cannot possibly have the right to resist: "The Constitution cannot view the militia *both* as a means by which government can suppress insurrection *and* as an instrument for insurrection against the government."[47] Even within Henigan's own historical account, this argument proves too much: if Congress's power to suppress insurrections is inconsistent with an individual right to resist, then it should also be inconsistent with a state right to resist. Yet Henigan is sufficiently comfortable with federal preeminence that he is apparently undisturbed by this implication. It appears that his purpose throughout was simply to assert a federal power to quell any and all unrest.

We know, however — and in the early part of his article Henigan concedes — that the Framers saw no inconsistency between Congress's Article I powers and the states' use of their militia to resist federal tyranny. As noted, the consistency between these two provisions arises from the distinction between rebellions and revolutions: Article I allows Congress to suppress rebellions, and the Second Amendment recognizes a popular right to engage in revolutions. Owing to their mythic commitments, however, Weberians are unable to draw this distinction. All resistance to government—good or bad, just or unjust, vicious or virtuous, broad-based or factional—has the same constitutional status because it denies the government's monopoly on legitimate violence.

HISTORIANS

Before the 1990s, few legal academics argued that the Second Amendment protected an individual right to arms. But during that decade, everything changed: a large number of law professors, joined by some historians, began to advance the claim that the provision protected a personal right to arms so as to resist government. Some of these writers organized a group called Academics for the Second Amendment. They ran an advertisement in the *New*

York Times and submitted briefs in Second Amendment cases. Glenn Harlan Reynolds dubbed this theory the Standard Model of the Second Amendment, and the label gained wide use.[48]

In response, a number of historians began forcefully to critique the individual rights theory. Soon, they too organized and began to issue law review symposia. Although their main purpose is to refute the individual rights school in particular, they more broadly mean to deny the Second Amendment any revolutionary content. The chief theme of their work is that most people in the 1780s and 1790s were anti-insurrectionary, so the Second Amendment could not have been intended to sanction resistance to government.

For illustrative purposes, I will focus here on the work of Garry Wills, Michael Bellesiles, and Saul Cornell, who are among the most forceful, articulate, and prolific of the antirevolutionists.[49] Their writing is diverse, rich, and complicated, and no summary can exhaustively describe it. In chapter 3, I considered the substance of some of this work. In this chapter, by contrast, I will show how a Weberian myth underlies and conditions their approach to the historical materials. That myth reveals itself in a number of ways.

First, some of these historians use evidence selectively and so reveal a subtle Weberian bias. For example, Wills and Bellesiles give center stage to Federalists who (according to them) deceitfully sought to engineer a meaningless Second Amendment. Even if those Federalists existed, looking to their intent for the meaning of a provision they did not really support is a decidedly odd interpretive technique. Yet these commentators apparently wish to rely on this intent because they feel some affinity for the allegedly Weberian mythos of these Federalists. Similarly, although these historians argue that the point in the amendment was to protect the state militias, they virtually never recognize the revolutionary point in these militias. Instead, they insist that the states wanted to protect their militias for two reasons: to keep local order and to make it more likely that Congress would choose not to adopt a standing army.[50] Of late, many of these writers have emphasized that the militia's main purpose, as a local police force, was to act as a slave patrol.[51] These theories would substitute a proto-Klansman for the noble minuteman as the primary mythic icon of the militia member.

Beyond their selective use of evidence, the historians impose a Weberian frame of analysis on the Framers' non-Weberian thinking. Many of them, for example, insist that because most political leaders denounced particular rebellions, they must have rejected the legitimacy of all rebellion.[52] In fact, as we have seen, the Framers generally condemned those insurrections because they were unjust on the merits, not because Americans had no right of revolution in principle. Yet these antirevolutionists read a wholesale rejection of revolution into a retail rejection of specific rebellions: they assume that when people condemn uprisings, they must do so in the belief that the government has a monopoly on the legitimate use of political violence. Again, these writers are reading the Framers' writing in accord with their own Weberian convictions.

A close reading of two texts helps to illustrate this point. First, a recent law review article by Bellesiles asks probing questions of those who would "find in the Second Amendment a right to insurrection": "Who gets to decide? Who chooses when it is time for 'the people' to use their arms against the government? Does [militia leader] Linda Thompson get to decide? Timothy Mc-Veigh?"[53] The questions are good ones. They prompt us to ponder, as the Framers did, how the people can find unity in resisting a corrupt government. Bellesiles, however, intends these questions as rhetorical flourishes. In his view, if the government does not command a monopoly of violence, the only alternative is a Hobbesian war of all against all, and the Framers, being intelligent men, must have shared that view.

Thus, Bellesiles beats a tattoo for state control: "For [Justice] Story the American Revolution put an end to the need for any more rebellions or uprisings; the country was now stable and secure, and the people should remain orderly";[54] "The Framers knew what horrors faced them if they could not establish social and political order";[55] "The Framers' first concern was to create a country which would survive"; "Guns were to be used by those serving in the militia, as state laws made evident, and the militia's duty was to maintain order";[56] "An extension of violent opposition to authority as a regular component of government would have destabilized the nation from the beginning and guaranteed its failure. Fortunately the Framers were smarter than that."[57] Later in the same article, Bellesiles rebukes the individual rights theorists: "[Theirs] is a view which accepts and fosters the atomistic nature of society and can conceive of no communal strategy for collective security."[58] I believe that Bellesiles is correct in reaching this conclusion, but his Weberian position suffers from a similar blindness: he "can conceive of no communal strategy for collective security" other than absolute governmental authority because he believes that popular resistance to government can never be anything other than "atomistic" viciousness. It is certainly appropriate to worry that in some times and places — perhaps our own — unified revolution might not be possible. Bellesiles, however, has given that view the status of immutable myth and then ascribed it to the Framers.

In his article, Bellesiles is clear about what the amendment does not do: it does not sanction revolution. He says little, however, about what the amendment does do. Such reticence is in line with his Weberian convictions: he wants to assure that the provision does not allow infringement on the government's monopoly of violence, but he is not interested in giving it a positive meaning. In his book, he is a little more expansive: "The Second Amendment's purpose is fairly indicated by the ensuing debate and legislation. The House debate focused on two issues: the 'use of the militia' in preventing 'the establishment of a standing army,' and the wisdom of allowing religious exemptions for service in the militia."[59] Actually, his listing of these two issues does not "fairly indicate" the "Second Amendment's purpose"; it merely tells us the subject of the debates, not what the debates resolved to do about those subjects. To give the amendment meaning, one would need to answer the following questions: Why did the Framers want to prevent a standing army? Why did they prefer the militia? How did the Second Amendment protect the militia and forestall a standing army? And what, if anything, does religious exemption have to do with this cluster of ideas?

Instead of answering those questions, Bellesiles at this point returns to detailing what the amendment does not do: it does not interfere with the government's ability to control political violence. Thus, Bellesiles believes that the amendment's purpose is "fairly indicated" by legislation that "uniformly sought to regulate the militia, . . . while legislatures in every state further revealed their intentions in the limitations they imposed on gun ownership." In addition, the "leaders of the new nation followed Washington's lead in calling for a standing army backed by a smaller, more organized, and better-armed militia. The Constitution provided the framework for such a structure."[60] At the end of all this analysis, then, the reader still has no definite idea how the amendment actually limits the government. We know that it must; after all, that's the whole point of the Bill of Rights. Bellesiles's Weberianism runs so deep, however, that he simply declines to address the question at any length or with any specificity.

Saul Cornell's work on the Pennsylvania Anti-Federalists also relies on Weberian assumptions to read historical material.[61] Recall that the Pennsylvania Constitution of 1776 prescribes, "The people have a right to bear arms for the defense of themselves and the State."[62] And in the Dissent of the Minority, Pennsylvania Anti-Federalists recommended that the Constitution be amended to provide that "the people have a right to bear arms for the defense of themselves and their own state, or the United States, or for the purpose of killing game; and no law shall be passed for disarming the people or any of them, unless for crimes committed, or real danger of public injury from individuals."[63] Recall also that individual rights theorists have claimed this material reflects a desire to create an individual right to arms.

Cornell refutes this claim by reminding us of the civic republican thinking of these Anti-Federalists, with its emphasis on the sacrifice of individual rights to the common good. An influential Anti-Federalist, An Old Whig, reminded his readers that if "government were really strengthened by . . . surrender" of a private right, and if "the body of the people were made more secure, or more happy by the means, we ought to make the sacrifice."[64] And the Pennsylvania legislature apparently acted on this advice: shortly after adopting their constitution, "Pennsylvanians enacted a stringent loyalty oath. The Test Acts, as they were known to contemporaries, barred citizens who refused to take the oath from voting, holding public office, serving on juries, and transferring real estate. Individuals who refused the oath could be disarmed as 'persons disaffected to the liberty and independence of this state.' "[65] The language of the Dissent of the Minority, moreover, allows the state to disarm those individuals who might pose a "real danger of public injury."[66] In short, even if Pennsylvanians enjoyed an individual right to arms, it could easily be lost to the public good, so easily lost that it does not really resemble a modern individual right at all.[67]

Cornell, however, reads more into this evidence, rendering eighteenth-century republicans into proto-Weberians. According to Cornell, these Anti-Federalists not only denied an individual right to resist the government but also accorded the government a monopoly on political violence: "Gun ownership in Pennsylvania was based on the idea that one agreed to support the state and to defend it against those who might use arms against it. Only citizens who were willing to swear an oath to the state could claim the right to bear arms. Gun ownership in Pennsylvania was thus predicated on a rejection of the very right of armed resistance."[68] Here, however, Cornell has fallen into the modern dichotomized view of the world: if individuals do not own the means of political violence, then the only alternative is absolute state control. In other words, Cornell commits the same error of which he accuses individual rights theorists: "The effort to counterpose states' rights and individual rights is one of the most serious anachronisms in recent discussions of Anti-Federalism."[69]

As we have seen, for proponents of the Second Amendment, the alternative to an individual right of resistance was not a simple government monopoly on violence. Instead, they desired to give power to the Body of the People rather than to individuals as such, and they were quite comfortable disarming rebels. So it should come as no surprise that An Old Whig should urge readers to sacrifice for the "body of the people" or that Pennsylvanians should disarm people who pose a threat of "public injury." Under ordinary circumstances, a democratic legislature could be assumed to be acting as an agent of the people, so that sacrificing for the government was sacrificing for the people. During the Revolutionary War, in particular, American patriots concluded that the

Body of the People included only those devoted to independence. As a result, enemies of the new governments, "persons disaffected to the liberty and independence of this state,"[70] were by definition enemies of the people. When Pennsylvanians sought to disarm them, therefore, they acted in the belief that only the people should have arms, not that the government should monopolize violence.

For republicans, then, usually the state and the people were one. That general identity does not suggest, however, that the Body of the People had no right to resist if the state should turn against the common good. Indeed, as they were at that moment committing revolution, Pennsylvanians could not have believed that resistance to government was always illegitimate. Imagine that during the war, the Pennsylvania legislature decided to pull out of the revolutionary cause and make alliance with the British Empire against its sister colonies. It is inconceivable that An Old Whig would not have urged the people to resist. In fact, the language that Cornell himself quotes from An Old Whig directly suggests this conclusion: "Wherever the subject is convinced that nothing more is required from him, than what is necessary for the good of the community, he yields a cheerful obedience, which is more useful than the constrained service of slaves."[71] Citizens, then, should yield to state law when it serves the good of the community. But what if "more is required"? Obedience then would be "the constrained service of slaves."

Again, the historical Second Amendment requires a comfort with ambiguity that the modern debate will not allow. Sometimes the state serves the common good and sometimes not. Sometimes uprisings are revolutions and sometimes not. It would be analytically neater and perhaps more comforting simply to insist that the state or the mass of private individuals is always right. Modern analysts offer that neatness and comfort, but only by reading the historical record in accord with modern myths. To defend such a view, one must argue for its substantive merits, not claim the authority of its pedigree.

The Nonconstitutional Right of Revolution

Although this body of writing denies the Second Amendment any revolutionary quality, most antirevolutionists eventually and reluctantly concede that the Framers must have believed in some right of revolution because they had just created their nation through that right. These writers insist, however, that for the Framers the right of revolution could not have been a constitutional right; instead, it was a natural right, existing outside the constitutional order. As a result, although insurrectionists may have a right to resist the government, they may not claim the Second Amendment as warrant for that activity. In chapter 3, I briefly considered this argument as a claim about history. In this chapter, I will give it lengthier treatment to explore what it reveals about the mythic underpinnings of the antirevolutionists' view.

The antirevolutionists base their argument primarily on what they regard as an obvious logical inference: the Constitution could not grant a right of revolution without being conceptually incoherent, so the Framers, being intelligent men, could not have believed in such a right. The notion that a constitutional right of revolution is incoherent boils down to the idea that a revolution against government is always a revolution against the Constitution. Because a constitution must presume its own legitimacy, it could not coherently guarantee a right to undo itself, as that would deny its legitimacy. Therefore, because an attack on government is an attack on the constitution, the constitution could not vouchsafe a right to attack government.

That equation of constitution and government is not in fact conceptually required: when the government is attacking the constitution, then by attacking the government the people may actually be protecting the constitution. And the Framers undoubtedly understood that government and the constitution were not always identical: in making their revolution against Great Britain, many purported to be defending the British constitution. In other words, this argument grows out of an unexamined Weberian assumption: in the organization of violence, the government must be the ultimate constitutional authority. Because the antirevolutionists are deeply convinced of this truth, they are certain the Framers must have believed it as well.

Let us call this argument, that revolution and constitution are inconsistent, the inconsistency argument. The idea is not a new one in American legal mythography. Because of its centrality to the modern debate and its considerable pedigree, it deserves the kind of careful, sympathetic development that will reveal its structure, force, and implicit value commitments.

THE INCONSISTENCY ARGUMENT

Formally stated, the inconsistency argument has two primary elements. First, some have argued that by challenging government, revolutions seek to change the politico-legal order. The purpose of a constitution, by contrast, is to preserve that order. A constitutional right to revolution would therefore contradict the Constitution's raison d'etre — it would be a suicide note delivered by the Constitution even as it came into being. I will call this view the purpose-inconsistency argument. Second, some have argued that revolution and constitution have different methods. Constitutional government proceeds according to fixed rules within established institutions. By contrast, revolutions swirl out of control as the people take power into their own hands and throw everything up in the air. In a revolution, therefore, the constitutional frame cracks as citizens are plunged back into the state of nature. I will call this view the method-inconsistency argument.

Abraham Lincoln made the inconsistency argument the centerpiece of his first inaugural address, as he denied the Confederacy a constitutional right to revolution. He carefully distinguished between revolutionary and constitutional modes of change: "Whenever [the people] shall grow weary of the existing government, they can exercise their *constitutional* right of amending it, or their *revolutionary* right to dismember, or overthrow it."[72] Revolution could not be a constitutional right because the Constitution must presuppose its own perpetual legitimacy: "Perpetuity is implied, if not expressed, in the fundamental law of all national governments. It is safe to assert that no government proper, ever had a provision built into its organic law for its own termination."[73] In other words, the purpose of revolution, to overthrow government, contradicts the purpose of constitution, to ensure perpetual government: this claim is the purpose-inconsistency argument. In Lincoln's view, the methods of revolution and constitution were also contradictory. The constitutional method of change involves orderly elections: "By the frame of government under which we live, this same people have wisely given their public servants but little power for mischief; and have, with equal wisdom, provided for the return of that little to their own hands at very short intervals."[74] By contrast, revolution was a lawless activity: "Plainly, the central idea of secession, is the essence of anarchy. A majority, held in restraint by constitutional checks, and limitations, and always changing easily, with deliberate changes of popular opinions and sentiments, is the only true sovereign of a free people."[75]

After the Civil War, the Supreme Court embraced Lincoln's theory of revolution.[76] More recently, the Court reiterated this view when it upheld the Smith Act, which prohibited advocating the overthrow of government.[77] The Court found it self-evident that Congress must have the constitutional power to protect itself from uprising, apparently because the purpose of a constitution is to sustain government, not provide for its dissolution: "That it is within the *power* of the Congress to protect the Government of the United States from armed rebellion is a proposition which requires little discussion. . . . No one could conceive that it is not within the power of Congress to prohibit acts intended to overthrow the Government by force and violence." Furthermore, the methods of orderly constitutionalism and anarchical revolution are entirely at odds: "We reject any principle of governmental helplessness in the face of preparation for revolution, which principle, carried to its logical conclusion, must lead to anarchy."[78]

Modern antirevolutionist theorists of the Second Amendment are thus

carrying on a venerable tradition of thought. Garry Wills, for example, acknowledges that Americans have a natural "right of insurrection, which
plainly does exist whenever tyranny exists." He denies, however, that the right
comes from the Constitution because the purpose of revolution is to destroy
the Constitution: "The right to *overthrow* government is not given by government. . . . Modern militias say the government instructs them to overthrow
government — and wacky scholars endorse this view. They think the Constitution is so deranged a document that it brands as the greatest crime a war
against itself (in Article III: Treason against the United States shall consist only
in levying war against them . . . .) and then instructs its citizens to take this up."
In addition, the method of a revolution is to break the constitutional frame,
and it thereby plunges us into a world without settled authority: the right to
overthrow government "arises when government no longer has authority. One
cannot say one rebels by right of that nonexistent authority."[79]

Other antirevolutionists echo this claim in almost identical language. Cornell, for example, insists that the right to revolution "was not a constitutional
check, but a natural right that one could not exercise under a functional constitutional government. The people had a right to abolish their government
and resort to armed resistance in defense of their liberties *when* the constitutional structures of government ceased to function."[80] Bellesiles agrees: "Revolution, as Cornell reminds us, is a natural right, a last resort when the Constitution itself has been contravened; it is not itself a part of the Constitution."[81]
And Henigan observes that when raising questions about the right to revolution, "we must first understand that they are not questions of constitutional
law. Indeed, the questions themselves presuppose the end of constitutional
government. . . . [A]lthough a natural right to revolution may have been
necessary to achieve constitutional government, it cannot be a principle of
constitutional government."[82]

CONSISTENCY BETWEEN REVOLUTION AND CONSTITUTION

An impressive lineup of figures thus agrees that when armed resistance
to government comes in the door, the Constitution flies out the window. A
position characterized as self-evident by so significant an array must command attention. Nonetheless, the apparently commonsensical nature of this
argument is misleading because it paints with too broad a brush. Analytically,
resistance to government may occur in two situations: first, the government
may be acting in a constitutional way, and citizens rise up because they disagree with the Constitution; or, second, the government may be acting in
violation of the Constitution, and the people rise up to protect it. In the former
setting, the revolution is an assault against the Constitution. (Lincoln clearly

believed that the revolt of the Confederacy was this sort of uprising.) In the latter setting, however, the revolution actually preserves the Constitution against a corrupt government. One might call this species of revolution conservative revolution — in the sense that it conserves the Constitution, not in the sense that it adheres to right-wing political principles. Such a distinction corresponds to two usages of the term *revolution*. Originally and for many centuries, the concept of revolution referred to conservative revolution: the political wheel revolves back to its starting point, and the world witnesses a restoration of a prior order. Today, as a legacy of the French Revolution, the term is often used to refer to linear change, the substitution of a new order for an old, failed one.[83]

Consistent with a presupposition of its own legitimacy, the Constitution could guarantee revolutions made to preserve the Constitution and disallow revolutions made to overturn it. For this distinction to make sense, one must recognize that the government does not always represent the Constitution. The inconsistency argument fails to draw this distinction because it simply presumes that the sitting government and the Constitution are one and the same, always and everywhere. Wills's argument illustrates this failure to differentiate between the government and the Constitution. Wills uses the term *government* to refer indiscriminately to the Constitution and to federal officeholders. Thus, in his formulation, a revolt against officeholders is made to seem a revolt against the Constitution. If one substitutes more precise nouns, however, the apparent logic of the argument disappears. Recast in this way, Wills's claim, which seemed so self-evident, becomes obscure: "Yet the right to overthrow [federal officeholders] is not given by [the Constitution]. It arises when [federal officeholders] no longer ha[v]e authority. One cannot say one rebels by virtue of that nonexistent authority [of officeholders]. Modern militias say the [Constitution] itself instructs them to overthrow [federal officeholders] — and wacky scholars endorse this view."[84] None of this passage now makes sense. The right to overthrow the Constitution could not be given by the Constitution, but the right to overthrow officeholders could be. One cannot rebel by virtue of the nonexistent authority of officeholders, but one can make a revolution by virtue of the quite intact authority of the Constitution.

The inconsistency argument therefore presumes that the government is the only conceivable defender of the Constitution. In effect, it presumes that the Constitution must give government a monopoly on the legitimate use of force, as a matter of simple conceptual logic. That identity of constitution and government may be true for some constitutions, but it is not required by the concept of a constitution as such. Depending on the particular constitution's statist or populist underpinnings, the people may occupy a variety of roles in its interpretation and enforcement. To insist that all constitutions depend on a government monopoly of force is therefore not simple logical deduction: it is normative Weberian mythmaking.

More specifically, the distinction between a sitting government and the constitution refutes both the purpose–inconsistency argument and the method–inconsistency argument. The response to the former is straightforward: the purpose of a conservative revolution is to protect the Constitution, not to create a new legal order, so there is no inconsistency. The response to the second is slightly more complicated. The method–inconsistency argument supposes that when the people take up arms against government, the constitution is dissolved, and we revert to a state of atomism. Again, that formulation poses the options too starkly, as polar opposites: we are either in a regime of normal government or in the state of nature. In fact, there is a continuum between those two points, forms of association that are neither governmental nor atomistic. It is possible for a constitution to govern at least some of that continuum, even when conventional government no longer holds authority. For such a situation to hold, of course, the particular constitution would have to contain a set of implicit or explicit norms governing how such a revolution should be carried out. Many constitutions contain no such norms; they may assume that a revolution does initiate a state of nature. Particular societies may lack a vital social contract among the people, so that constitutional revolution may be a practical impossibility. But constitutional revolution is impossible only under such circumstances; it is not conceptually incoherent. Indeed, nothing prevents the framers of a constitution from specifying in detail the forms that patriots should follow in the event of a governmental assault on the constitution.

Antirevolutionists, however, argue that constitutional revolution is impossible for all people at all times, not just for some people at some times depending on their circumstances. This conviction cannot be based on mere logical inference. Instead, it must be based on a supplementary descriptive or normative assumption: as a matter of fact (not logic), when the government dissolves, people inevitably revert to a state of atomism. The middle ground between the individual and the state is barren. Once the government goes, no other social forms can provide any constitutional structure. Our only bulwark against savagery, therefore, is the government itself. As a result, anything is better than the dissolution of government. This supposition is by no means new. Indeed, in the eighteenth century, royalists used essentially the same argument to reject any doctrine of revolution: once one allows any resistance to formal government, Hobbesian chaos and anarchy inevitably follow because there is no middle ground.[85] That supposition may be descriptively accurate. It is not, however, what the Framers believed, and it is not logically necessary. It must therefore be defended, not merely invoked. And as I will later contend, there is a strong argument that this mythic premise is neither healthy nor necessary for modern Americans.

Alone among the antirevolutionists, Wills has sought to refute the claim, set out in my earlier work, that in defending the Constitution a conservative revolution does not dissolve the Constitution. He accurately paraphrases my argument: "If the government departs from the Constitution, then a revolution to restore the Constitution acts within the Constitution." He then offers two repudiations. First, within our system, the Supreme Court is the only authorized interpreter of the Constitution, so that the people cannot pretend to defend the Constitution on their own: "[T]he *constitutional* way to defend what is *un*-constitutional is through the document's own machinery of Supreme Court review (if elections and amendments fail). If that machinery is unworkable, then the Constitution is defunct and one cannot be working under its authority." Second, in U.S. tradition, Americans have always believed that a revolution necessarily dissolves the constitution: "Almost every revolution begins as the American one did, by saying that the social compact has broken down.... But when one replaces the defunct machinery, it is with a new regime, which must (and does) establish its own constitutional rules. This is what common sense calls a revolution — and it ... is what Sanford Levinson calls it, an appeal to heaven, a higher tribunal than the text of one document."[86]

Although Wills's argument in this passage is interesting, it must first be observed that he has actually abandoned the inconsistency argument. That argument maintains that in their nature, constitution and revolution are always incommensurable. Here, Wills argues that the U.S. Constitution happens to grant no right of revolution. The former is an argument from logical analysis, the latter an argument from the particular facts of American constitutional tradition. To defend the latter argument, therefore, one must adduce some evidence, rather than tease out the implications of concepts. Unfortunately, Wills does not attempt that documentation in this passage. Instead, consistent with his deep Weberian assumptions, he appears to assume that these truths are self-evident. In fact, in consulting the record one finds that his first claim (that the people have no role in constitutional interpretation) has always been highly controversial, and his second claim (that in the minds of the patriots, the Revolution necessarily began by dissolving the social compact) is plainly false.

As to Wills's first claim, it is true that the Supreme Court has always enjoyed a certain salience in the area of constitutional interpretation. Since *Marbury v. Madison*,[87] the Supreme Court has claimed the power of judicial review: when a case is properly before it, it can refuse to enforce governmental actions that it considers to be unconstitutional. That limited role, however, does not foreclose other Americans from taking a view on the meaning of the amendment and acting on it. Indeed, most American presidents, including Jefferson, Jackson, and Lincoln,[88] have claimed the right to disagree with the Court in the execution of their duties. Yet if other branches may disagree with the Court in carrying out their constitutional duties, it would follow that the people may also disagree in carrying out theirs — to the extent they have any such duties. Weberians might assert that constitutional interpretation is only for governmental actors, that the people should bow out. Again, however, that claim must rest on more than mere assertion: it must explain why the government is so trustworthy, the people not. And as we will see, it might be difficult to make that claim: Wills is contemplating a future for the people as constitutional spectators, increasingly detached from their country's fundamental civic morality.

Many have rightly observed that when people adopt different views of the Constitution, chaos might result. We therefore need an ultimate judge. The Supreme Court has sometimes claimed to be that judge. Going beyond *Marbury*'s claim that the Court may decide cases before it, it has sometimes argued that it may bind other actors in cases not then before it. It is, in this view, "supreme in the exposition of the law of the Constitution."[89] This view, again, has been highly controversial. As Lincoln explained the point in his first inaugural address: "Nor do I deny that such [Supreme Court] decisions must be binding in any case upon the parties to a suit as to the object of that suit. . . . At the same time, the candid citizen must confess that if the policy of the Government upon vital questions affecting the whole people is to be irrevocably fixed by decisions of the Supreme Court, the instant they are made in ordinary litigation between parties in personal actions the people will have ceased to be their own rulers."[90]

Even if we accept judicial supremacy in constitutional interpretation, however, it does not follow that the people may never be appropriate defenders of the Constitution. For one thing, the Court itself might join with the people in a revolution against the rest of the government; indeed, the Court could actually be the instigator of revolution. After all, the conception of courts "speaking truth to power" is deep in Anglo-American and other legal traditions.[91] Memorably, Edward Coke played an important part in the background for one revolution in England and provided much of the constitutional inspiration for another across the Atlantic.[92]

In addition, the Court has claimed to be constitutionally supreme only over those areas that are properly justiciable. On some questions, even though constitutional in nature, the Court simply will not pass judgment because it believes them unsuitable for judicial resolution. For example (and of special relevance to the issue discussed here), the Court has held that it will not enforce the Guaranty Clause, under which the federal government is required to guarantee to the states a republican form of government. In the Court's view, enforcing this clause would lead it into the sort of essentially political issues that it cannot fathom.[93] Yet if the Court cannot answer these sorts of questions, it seems even more unlikely that it could determine when the federal government has become so corrupt that the Body of the People has no choice but to rise. In the event of a true revolution, one with nationwide popular resistance against a deeply malignant government, it seems quite likely that the Supreme Court would declare the whole matter nonjusticiable.

In other words, Wills is simply mistaken, as a matter of constitutional law, that the only "*constitutional* way to decide what is *un*-constitutional is through the document's own machinery of Supreme Court review." More strikingly, however, even if his argument is somehow right, it is clearly not self-evidently right. The exact roles of the Court and others in constitutional interpretation present a difficult and vexed issue, one requiring careful consideration. Instead, Wills tries to resolve it by assertion and assumption: in his view, the people simply cannot have a role in deciding constitutional matters because it is obvious that only a governmental body can make those determinations. In Wills's mythic universe, Weberianism is so much a part of the fundament that he feels no need even to recognize there is a controversy.

Wills's second response to the idea that the people can sometimes be the constitution's defenders is that Americans have always denied that possibility. As noted earlier, I do not think the historical record is clear enough to reveal whether the Framers meant to constitutionalize a right of conservative revolution. What is clear is that they could have done so and been consistent with the rest of their thinking. The Anglo-American legal tradition has often endorsed the idea that the people, rather than the government, may best represent the constitution. As we have seen, John Locke believed that when government violates its trust, it becomes the true rebel: "For Rebellion being an Opposition, not to Persons, but Authority, which is founded only in the Constitutions and Laws of the Government; those, whoever they be, who by force break through and by force justifie their violation of them, are truly and properly Rebels. . . . [W]hen . . . the Legislators act contrary to the end for which they were constituted; those who are guilty are guilty of Rebellion."[94] Under these circumstances, the purpose of resistance to government is to suppress a rebellion against the constitution, not to undo the constitution. In addition, Locke believed that the methods of revolution and constitution were not antithetical. He argued that government perfidy undid the rectoral contract — the agreement between government and people — but it did not undo the social contract — the agreement among the citizens to form a people. As a result, even on the dissolution of government, the people were thrown back on the terms of the social contract, but not into a state of nature.

Later social contractarians continued to rely on this dual contract theory to explain revolutionary action in the absence of government. Radical pamphleteers, for example, analyzed the Convention Parliament of 1689 in these terms: the contract between James II and the people of Great Britain had been dissolved, but the people (or, more correctly, their representatives) continued to meet to forge a new contract with William and Mary. By the era of Walpole, this explanation of the Convention Parliament had become retrospectively orthodox.[95] In Hannah Arendt's view, the American colonies historically, not merely metaphorically, began in popular contracts, mutual promises more fundamental than the contract with government. Accordingly, when the revolutionaries severed the ties with Great Britain, they did not reenter the state of nature. Instead, power reverted to the local assemblies duly constituted by the original civil contracts, which in turn created a new American government. Further, because of this continuity in constituted order, the American Revolution never degenerated into lawlessness in the way the French Revolution did.[96]

Before the Revolution commenced, the Patriot John Adams and the Tory Thomas Hutchison may have agreed on very little, but they agreed that in resisting government the public may sometimes protect the constitution. As David Hackett Fischer explains, "John Adams in 1774 drew a distinction between 'public mobs' which defended law and the constitution, and 'private mobs' which took to the streets 'in resentment of private wrongs.' Adams believed that 'public mobs' were constitutional and even a necessary instrument of order. But he added that 'private mobs I do and will detest.' " Similarly, "the same conception of 'constitutional mobs' was also held by the Massachusetts Tory Thomas Hutchison, who observed that 'mobs, a sort of them at least, are constitutional,' even as he fell victim to their violence in Boston."[97]

Once the war commenced, the revolutionaries insisted that the established government was not the only possible defender of the constitution. Quite the contrary, they cast the British government as the aggressor against the social contract, and they saw themselves — committees of correspondence and inspection, ultra vires Continental Congresses — as the true protectors of the British imperial constitution.[98] Indeed, at least in its early stages, the American Revolution was largely a conservative revolution of the sort I am describing. To be sure, some revolutionaries maintained that they were exercising a natural right to revolution to protect other natural rights.[99] A large number, however,

saw themselves as constitutional conservatives reacting to the aggressive behavior of the British government.

Their constitutional grievances were of three sorts. First, they believed
that although they were entitled to the benefit of English law and the rights
of Englishmen, the British government was exercising arbitrary power over
them.[100] Second, they believed Parliament had no right to govern their internal
affairs or tax them.[101] Third, they believed the king was seeking to disrupt the
traditional balance of estates by bribing members of Parliament and colonial
legislators with places, pensions, and perquisites.[102] Eventually, the revolutionaries would declare independence and leave the empire altogether. Even
then, however, they would for a time seek to preserve what they believed to be
the essence of the British constitutional structure, now transposed to the other
side of the Atlantic: their new constitutions enshrined what the revolutionaries
took to be the traditional rights of Englishmen, and they created state governments modeled on the traditional balance of estates.[103]

I do not argue that the American revolutionaries never sought to change the
British constitution. Eventually, they self-consciously did so, in a variety of
ways. For example, they created new, more thoroughly republican legislatures,
and they sought to protect natural rights rather than the traditional rights of
Englishmen.[104] Neither do I argue that the Framers in fact sought to guarantee
a right of conservative revolution. But I do argue that they could have done so
without being inconsistent with their ideological heritage. They knew from
personal experience that government and constitution are not identical concepts, that government can wage war on the constitution, and that sometimes
the citizenry is the constitution's only hope. To argue that the Framers believed
government was the only conceivable defender of the constitution is to project
a Weberian mythology back onto a pre-Weberian worldview.

LIMITS ON A CONSTITUTIONAL RIGHT OF REVOLUTION

My primary purpose in this section has been twofold: to explain that
constitution and revolution are not mutually exclusive and to argue that in
supposing otherwise antirevolutionists are engaged in Weberian normative
argument, not logical analysis. As I have raised the possibility of constitutional
revolution, however, I feel it important to make an additional point not directly related to my primary purpose: any constitutional revolution would be
subject to rather severe limits. Taken together, these limits may be so significant that few real-world revolutions could satisfy them. In practice, armed
resistance may be so untamable that it always jumps the fence from settled
constitutional fields into the thickets of natural law.

First, particular constitutions might place particular limits on the right of revolution, including perhaps an outright denial of the right. In addition, two limits apply to every constitutional revolution because they conceptually arise from the purpose and method of such a revolution. First, the purpose must be to remedy a constitutional grievance by restoring the constitutional order rather than by substituting a new one. Second, the revolution must conduct itself according to norms prescribed by the constitution. Probably very few constitutions overtly detail how a revolution should be conducted, but one might draw analogies from explicit constitutional values and forms. For example, an American revolution would have to exhibit the elements central to our constitutional tradition: democracy, federalism, separation of powers, and individual liberty, rather than a revolutionary dictatorship. As revolutions create exigent times, the Constitution might not require a revolutionary movement to exhibit those elements to the same degree as government in settled times — just as the Constitution allows the government more flexibility during exigent, nonrevolutionary times.[105] But constitutional flexibility is not the same as constitutional desuetude.

Two issues problematize the exact scope of these limits: constitutional change and constitutional interpretation. Constitutions change in two ways: first, by internal processes, as by the amendment process set out in Article V, and second, by external force, as by suspension of the constitution by a military coup d'etat. In the former case, the change is constitutional because it takes place within the constitution's framework; in the latter, the change violates the constitution because it is forced on the constitution from without. Constitutional revolutions must seek to preserve the constitution, but they may also change it as long as they do so according to the constitution's own procedures. In fact, revolutions often occur during times of great constitutional change, and they may cause further change. As a result, the constitution may — with perfect constitutionality — be very different before and after the revolution. Furthermore, the constitution's rules for internal change during revolutionary times may be more permissive than its rules for change during settled times. As a result, constitutional change may occur thick and fast during a revolution, and it may seem that the constitution poses few real limits on a revolution. Indeed, the difference between the people creating new government under a natural right of revolution and the people pursuing constitutional change under a constitutional right of revolution may all but disappear from the perspective of those engaged in the process.

Similarly, issues of constitutional interpretation may render problematic the limits on constitutional revolution. In a diverse nation, disagreement over the constitution may be inevitable, both over its meaning and over the appropriate interpretive technique to divine that meaning. During settled times, the existence of a semiauthoritative interpreter like the Supreme Court might help to cabin that disagreement.[106] During revolutionary times, however, such an interpreter may be relatively less available, as the people have taken power back into their own hands. It is important not to overstate the differences between normal times and revolutionary ones on this score. Even during settled times, the existence of the Supreme Court does not forestall vigorous, even violent, disagreement on the Constitution's meaning. Indeed, as we have seen, people disagree even over whether the Constitution appoints the Supreme Court as its authoritative exponent. Furthermore, during revolutionary times, the Court might continue to sit as the people's constitutional court, or alternative tribunals like Continental Congresses or committees of correspondence might arise to cabin constitutional controversy.[107] As a result, revolutionary movement may be relatively unified on the meaning of the constitution.

Even so, disagreement on the constitution's meaning will typically be more severe during revolutionary times. Even if the revolutionary movement is itself unified, there are always two sides in a revolution, those allied with the government and those allied with the revolution. Both may see themselves as protectors of the constitution, but neither may recognize political relations with the other or with an overarching authority. As a result, resolution of the controversy by settled institutional mechanisms is not possible. Indeed, the American Revolution and the Civil War may both have become inevitable when one or both sides realized that agreement on a neutral tribunal or procedure was not possible.

The problems of constitutional change and interpretation are most acute when they go hand in hand. In such cases, people disagree over the interpretation of how constitutional change occurs and whether it has in fact occurred. This coincidence of the two problems was at the heart of the transatlantic dispute leading to American independence in the 1770s. The British imperial constitution was changing, and all sensed the drift. Disagreement occurred, however, over the nature of the change and how it could occur. Even in the twentieth century, people have not stopped disagreeing about who was right.[108]

At the most general level, Americans and Britons disagreed over whether parliamentary power was unlimited, so that even the constitution could not limit it. In the process, the colonists and the home country came to divergent definitions of constitution — for the former, a series of prescriptive "higher law" limits on government, for the latter a simple description of the structure of extant government. Both ideas were relatively new, but each side defended its favored theory as the current state of the British constitution.[109] From this basic division, opinion fractured into a variety of more subtle distinctions. Commentators have taken the following views on when, exactly, the American Revolution stopped being constitutional:

1. The American Revolution violated the British constitution as soon as it denied parliamentary supremacy because by 1770 the essence of the constitution had become Parliament's omnipotence.[110]
2. By 1776, the essence of the constitution was becoming legislative home rule for many units of the empire, united in allegiance to the Crown. The American Revolution therefore violated the constitution when it announced independence from the Crown in 1776.[111]
3. By 1776, the essence of the constitution was the local charters granting home rule to the individual colonies, which later became states. The American Revolution therefore violated the British constitution not when the colonies announced independence from the Crown, but when the American Constitution of 1787 claimed to derive its power from the people, rather than from the states.[112] In other words, the Americans violated the British constitution only long after the fighting stopped.
4. By 1776, the essence of the constitution was mixed government and the traditional rights of Englishmen. The Americans therefore violated the British constitution not when it derived power from the people, but when it embraced wholly democratic government and natural rights without regard to their traditional underpinnings.[113]

Doubtless there are many other possible views as well. Lacking an authoritative interpreter, we will probably never have an authoritative interpretation of the exact limits the British constitution placed on the Revolution of 1776.

In short, then, the claim that some revolutions might be constitutional would seem to have little significance in the real world. On the one hand, constitutional limits will be so difficult to satisfy in theory that few if any revolutions could qualify: constitutional revolutions must arise from a constitutional grievance, seek only restoration of the constitutional order, take only constitutional forms, and instigate change only according to constitutional rules interpreted according to constitutional techniques. On the other hand, those limits will be highly flexible, perhaps even illusory, in practice because of the problems of constitutional change and interpretation. And as I have noted, the historical record does not reveal even whether the Framers meant to constitutionalize a right to revolution itself, as opposed to the right to arms. If there is so little practical significance, why then is it so important to recognize that constitution and revolution are not conceptually opposed? The reason is that when we understand that the alleged opposition is not based on simple logic, we can come to see that it is instead really based on a Weberian myth. And only when we clearly see the outlines of that myth can we evaluate it as a basis for constitutionally taming political violence at the start of the third millennium.

Disciplining the Barbarians

The antirevolutionary theory of the Second Amendment ultimately rests not on historical evidence by itself but on a common myth through which these writers approach the evidence. The theory is not deficient for being based on a myth: probably all constitutional interpretations need myths to give them coherence and shape. Instead, the problem with this theory is twofold. First, its proponents seek to immunize it from discussion by ascribing it to the Framers: the antirevolutionists claim only to be passing on the founding wisdom, not pleading a case. In fact, as we have seen, the Framers embraced a quite different myth. If we move to a new story as more apposite to modern circumstances, we should do so through open discussion.

Second, if we did conduct that discussion, we might find that the Weberian myth does not serve well as a grand narrative for organizing constitutional violence. As the last chapter of this book will suggest, any acceptable interpretation of the Second Amendment will need to give the government an important role. In the antirevolutionary theory, however, governmental power is not merely one component but the whole story. For these writers, the answer to political violence is simply to assure that the government has supervision of all the guns. In the long run, that answer will not keep the genie of violence in the bottle because it places excessive trust in government and finds little hope for trust in anyone else. As a result, the theory is unbalanced. On the one hand, its faith in government tends to become unquestioning; on the other hand, it fatalistically accepts that private Americans will always be untrustworthy and mutually hostile.

The uncomfortable mythic truth that the Framers left us is that if we want to kill each other, we will. The government may try to stop us, but in the long run it cannot tame a hate-filled population without becoming oppressive. To tame political violence, therefore, we must look not only to the government but to the character of the citizenry. The Framers of the Second Amendment hoped that Americans would generally exhibit enough solidarity to be able to act in concert to control political violence. Antirevolutionists have abandoned that hope. Instead, they look to the strong arm of government to control us in our seething division. Indeed, many of them plainly regard those in the so-called gun culture as akin to barbarians in need of governmental discipline. In the face of their fear, they yearn for the promise of control, rather than the hope of redemption.

TRUST IN GOVERNMENT: REVOLUTION IN A DEMOCRACY

In the scheme of things, America has comparatively good government, government deserving of support and even affection. At some point, however, any government may become corrupt, even so corrupt that violent resistance to it becomes appropriate. In the twentieth century, governments killed their citizens on a massive scale, and although the American record may have been better than most, it has been far from perfect. In particular, as chapter 7 will explore, outgroups have always been vulnerable to governmental mistreatment or neglect, leaving them exposed to private hate violence.

Many have argued that in a democracy such as ours, the people do not need a right of revolution because they control the government at the polls. We can thus eschew the bullet box for the ballot box. For example, in rejecting a right to revolution, the Supreme Court observed, "Whatever theoretical merit there may be to the argument that there is a 'right' to rebellion against dictatorial governments is without force where the existing structure of the government provides for peaceful and orderly change."[114] In fact, however, one cannot devise, even in theory, a democratic system that will be immune from corruption and distortion. And once the system has been warped, it will have great difficulty reforming itself because the system will place in office those who want to retain the very system that gave them power.

This problem of democratic design is familiar to voting rights lawyers and other students of the political process. *Democracy* does not refer to a single, monolithic system. There are all sorts of democracies, and each sort serves some goals better than others. Over time, one's goals and needs may change, sometimes so much that a system that once seemed liberating may come to seem oppressive. For example, at America's birth, it broadly disenfranchised women, people of color, white men with little property, and others — the vast bulk of the population. Yet it considered itself a democracy, and most commentators still believe it was among the most democratic states of its time.[115] For all the disenfranchised groups, however, this system offered little or no opportunity for self-government. To suggest that they needed no right of revolution because they could control their government at the polls is, bluntly, a rude insult.

To be sure, these groups eventually secured the franchise, but only because enfranchised Americans changed their thinking and voted to open up the system. It did not happen because disenfranchised Americans flexed their (nonexistent) electoral muscle. In other countries, disenfranchised groups have had to take power for themselves. Even in this country, political violence may have played a necessary part in changing American culture to make possible the enfranchisement of outgroups. Before the Civil War, for example, almost no one seriously proposed that African Americans receive the vote; once the nation plunged into conflagration, however, the stakes were raised and the political situation became fluid. It suddenly became possible to imagine forcing African American enfranchisement on a reluctant South, a scenario that would have been inconceivable if the nation had stayed at peace. Indeed, African Americans helped to secure this transformation not by voting, which they could not do, but by fighting in the Union army.[116] In short, although these outgroups did gain the right to vote, the democratic system itself offered no guarantee of that result, such that revolution would necessarily be unwarranted.

The drawing of district lines offers another example of this phenomenon, that a democratic system, wonderful at its inception, can come to seem intolerable. Districting is a complicated business, but simplified hypotheticals can illustrate the essence of the problem. Imagine a country of one hundred voters divided into four districts of twenty-five voters each. Each district elects one representative to Congress (in the jargon, these are single-member districts), and whichever candidate receives the most votes wins (in the jargon, these districts run first-past-the-post elections). Imagine also that in each district, 45 percent of the voters are Reds and 55 percent are Greens. The Reds and the Greens have disparate values, programs, and visions for the future. Perhaps they are also largely of different races or ethnicities, or they speak different languages. Because of these differences, they usually vote as blocs.

In this scenario, the Greens will elect the representative from all four districts because they have 55 percent of the vote in each district. With 45 percent of the votes, the Reds will have 0 percent of the representation in Congress. From one point of view, this result is not a problem. Every individual's vote is counted equally, so all have an equal chance to affect the outcome. If the majority wins, there is nothing wrong with that outcome: majorities are supposed to control in a democracy. We can even imagine that this democratic scheme was designed with this philosophy in mind. Over time, however, the Reds have begun to sense the limits of this view in the face of entrenched political differences. They vote, and they vote, and they vote, and they try to persuade the intransigent Greens, but nothing ever changes. And because this system keeps the Greens in power, the Greens have little incentive to change anything. If the country has an inclusive political culture, the Reds might be able to persuade the Greens to change things. The structure of government, however, will not help; instead, it allows the Greens to keep power simply by retaining the status quo. What had once seemed a wonderfully democratic plan now seems like a method of systematic disempowerment for a substantial minority.

Like ideological change, social change can transform a fine democratic system into something like oppression. Imagine the same country: four single-member districts, first-past-the-post elections, twenty-five voters in each district, Reds and Greens, respectively, at 45 and 55 percent of the electorate. Imagine also that everyone in this country believes that distinct voting groups should receive roughly proportional voting power. They carefully draw district lines so that the Reds and the Greens each receive two districts, in rough proportion to their size. Then, however, things start to change: most of the Reds migrate from their own districts to one of the Green districts, eventually outnumbering the Green voters there. The new Red/Green district now has many more voters than the norm, and the two original Red districts have many fewer. The district lines, however, remain in place unless someone changes them, and so each district still elects one representative. Congress might correct this situation by redrawing district lines, but the system gives it little incentive to do so because by definition these legislators were elected by this districting scheme. As a result, the Reds now control their own two original (and now underpopulated) districts plus the overpopulated district that they have taken from the Greens. With a majority of the electorate, the Greens now have only 25 percent of the representatives. If the Reds and the Greens have different outlooks, the Greens will lose every important contest in the legislature. They will have no control at all.

Assume, if you like, that Congress is committed to the idea that every district ought to have the same number of voters, so they constantly revise the district lines to keep them equipopulational. People still migrate, and they still change their political stripes. After a few years, we have four districts, all with the same population but with this composition: in District One, twenty-five Green voters; in District Two, ten Green voters and fifteen Red voters; in District Three, ten Green voters and fifteen Red voters; in District Four, ten Green voters and fifteen Red voters. In this scenario, the Greens control only the first district. With 55 percent of the votes, they elect only 25 percent of the representatives. Again, they are left with no control.

Some may find all these scenarios far-fetched because they believe either that legislatures would not act in this shameless way or because the Supreme Court would not let them. Alas, the facts of history suggest otherwise. For many decades after the adoption of the Fifteenth Amendment, southern states adopted electoral schemes designed to disenfranchise African American voters. For many years, the Supreme Court ruled that, for technical reasons, it could not correct the situation.[117] Congress, in its turn, also refused to examine these voting schemes, claiming that aggrieved voters should go to court. Even after the Court began striking down discriminatory voting schemes, southern states simply kept passing new ones, in a protracted game of back-and-forth. Finally, Congress passed the Voting Rights Act of 1965 to help make African American enfranchisement a reality.[118] This process, however, took many years from the adoption of the Fifteenth Amendment — and it still goes on. During most of that time, self-government for African Americans in much of this country was a distant dream.

Even with full formal enfranchisement, the story of minority voting rights is not over. Because there are relatively few districts in which racial minorities are a voting majority, they have traditionally controlled very few elections, fewer than their ratio of the citizenry. Although they have the formal right to vote, therefore, they have had little real political power.[119] If they have distinctly different views and interests from the majority surrounding them, they may also feel they have little representation. In 1982, Congress amended the Voting Rights Act marginally to correct this situation. The act now requires states sometimes to draw district lines to create "majority minority" districts — districts in which minority racial groups form a majority, so that they can control the election.[120] It falls far short, however, of requiring that minorities form majorities in districts proportional to their numbers. The act itself specifically disclaims an intent to require proportional representation, and that language was an important part of the compromise necessary for the act's passage. Instead, the act mandates majority minority districts only under limited, hazily defined circumstances, now the subject of protracted litigation.[121] And apart from the law, the facts of residence patterns impose a limit on the number of majority minority districts: unless racial groups settle in compact areas, they cannot be grouped into a single district. The act itself, therefore, offers no guarantee that racial minorities will receive anything like proportional power.

It is, moreover, not at all certain the act will long survive. Politicians, lawyers, and judges have attacked it for creating a system of "political apartheid" in which voters are segregated into districts on the basis of their race.[122] Presently, a majority of the Supreme Court is prepared to strike down some majority minority districts as unconstitutional, and a minority would strike virtually all of them down.[123] In short order, we may return to an America in which racial minorities control almost no elections. And even if the act does survive, the future may not be very bright. If the critics of the act are right, this system of electoral "apartheid" encourages voters and politicians to conceive their interests in racial terms. In the long run, such thinking may split America into antagonistic racial blocs.[124] By definition, however, racial minorities do not comprise a majority. Even if they command proportional representation, they still will not be able to control the legislature. Instead, in the new world of identity politics, they will find themselves swamped in a fetid sea of racial animosity.

Whichever way we turn on racial issues, then, we face risks, and that point illustrates the general theme: no democratic system can offer assurance that it will always provide meaningful self-government. And if the future looks worrisome for racial minorities, other groups can expect little more protection from either Congress or the courts. For many years in this century, voters poured out of rural areas into the growing cities. Yet the state legislatures rarely redrew their district lines because they had been elected from those districts. Gradually, each rural voter came to have much more proportional power than each urban voter. Again, as with race, the Supreme Court refused to get involved for a long time.[125] Only in the 1960s did it rule, over intense opposition from politicians and dissenting justices, that the Constitution requires districts of equal population.[126]

Within the limits of equipopulationality, however, the states can gerrymander their districts pretty much as they like. In particular, when one political party seizes the statehouse, it can then redraw the district lines to ensure that it stays in office. A minority of the justices on the Supreme Court would hold such action entirely immune from judicial inspection.[127] The controlling center of the Court would strike down political gerrymandering only when it "will consistently degrade a voter's or a group of voters' influence on the political process as a whole."[128] The Court has never struck down a gerrymandering scheme under this standard, perhaps because in their view, "an individual or group of individuals who votes for a losing candidate is usually deemed to be adequately represented by the winning candidate and to have as much opportunity to influence that candidate as other voters in the district."[129] In other words, the fact that one party has rigged the system does not constitute an infraction because the winners are presumed to be equally concerned about everyone. Not surprisingly, politicians are not shy about taking this opportunity. As one Indiana legislator cheerfully confessed, "The name of the game is to keep us in power."[130]

In this discussion of democracy's ills, I have focused on districting, but the list could be greatly extended. Dominated by the two major parties, state legislatures routinely adopt measures to keep smaller parties off the ballot, so that they can never become serious contenders.[131] In the Supreme Court's view, most of these measures are perfectly constitutional because "the Constitution permits [state] [l]egislature[s] to decide that political stability is best served through a healthy two-party system."[132] Further, Congress has denied the people of various territories, such as Washington, D.C., and Puerto Rico, the right to vote for federal lawmakers. The courts have uniformly upheld these arrangements,[133] and Congress is unlikely to enfranchise these areas until it is in their political interest to do so.

In short, then, it is simply not true that democracy can or will always reform itself. It is not true that the ballot box will ensure meaningful self-government, when the ballot box has itself been rigged. And it is simply not true that the Supreme Court will or can fix all of the ills that plague American democracy; in this area, the Court has traditionally held a quite modest view of its role. To be sure, it is always better to reform the democratic system by use of that system. Revolutions and resistance to government typically become vicious and counterproductive. In my view, none of the ills that I have detailed comes close to warranting an armed uprising. The fact, however, that revolutions are usually unwise does not mean they are always illegitimate, even against a nominally democratic government.

Even during the American Revolution, the British government was, in a broad sense, democratic. In its view, the Americans were already adequately represented in Parliament, even though they did not vote in parliamentary elections. Because Britons everywhere shared the same general interests and views, Americans did not need separate representation of their own; they could count on Parliament to watch out for them. In that sense, the Americans were vicariously represented by members of Parliament elected by British voters. The American revolutionaries held to a different theory of democracy: in their view, because their interests were divergent from those of the residents of the home country, they needed to elect their own representatives.[134] Despite what we are taught in grade school, then, the War for Independence was not fought over whether America should have democracy. Everyone agreed that it should. Instead, the war was fought over what kind of democracy America should have. The British offered one form; the Americans wanted another. When the Americans found they could not secure change through the extant democratic system, they felt required to take up arms.

Because even the best democratic structures can turn malignant, unquestioning trust in those structures is not a balanced approach to the constitutional organization of violence. To its everlasting credit, the American democratic system has, over and over, reformed itself. Often those reforms brought real costs to those in power, as when men agreed to votes for women or whites agreed to votes for people of color. The democratic structure did not, however, force or even encourage these reforms: those in power could have gone right on enjoying their power while the system obediently kept down the powerless.

Instead, other forces must have brought on the change. Perhaps those in power feared armed uprisings, as individual rights theorists would doubtless suggest. In some cases, however — the enfranchisement of women, for example — armed revolt was obviously not in the offing. The more likely explanation is that the American political system has become ever more open because American political culture has become ever more open. To foster an open political system, then, we cannot simply trust government to do the job; we must seek ways to redeem the people themselves in their political culture.

In other words, the Second Amendment, the constitutional organization of violence, and internal democratic reform all come together on this critical idea: for a republic to work, the people must share a minimum of connection, trust, and mutual devotion. In the absence of this minimum, democracies will not peacefully open themselves to new groups, unified revolution will not be possible as an ultimate check on government, and the Second Amendment cannot bear any connection to its original meaning. Any adequate theory of the amendment must therefore not only be chary of excessive trust in government; it must also find a way to make the people trustworthy. Unhappily, the antirevolutionary theories show no interest in redeeming the people. Instead, they are content to let the government restrain the sinners among us.

CREATING A TRUSTWORTHY PEOPLE

The antirevolutionist theory of the Second Amendment relies on a control-and-command model of political violence: the government will discipline the populace through its monopoly on legitimate force. The citizenry may influence the government, but it has no direct role. This myth thus places its hope in a benign and well-ordered government, not in an involved and trustworthy populace. That hope represents a dangerous gamble: it predicts that even if we are divided, vicious, or inert, the government can keep us safe. As we have seen, one risk implied in that gamble is that the government may not prove so trustworthy. The more dangerous risk, however, is that it distracts us from the truth that the Second Amendment symbolizes: in organizing political violence, the only real hope lies in a citizenry full of people who do not want to hurt each other.

What we most need, therefore, are myths that emphasize the importance of civic connection. By contrast, the antirevolutionist theories encourage the view that the remedy for violent disunity is not popular unity, but governmental power, power sufficient to control a nation divided against itself. By insisting that the only hope is a strong government, these myths presuppose and to some extent encourage the view that Americans are and always will be divided. In short, per these myths, we need discipline, not love because love is not really possible.

Here are the elements of the mythic world that these theorists prescribe, elements I will explore in the pages that follow. First, the world is divided into government and individuals, and between the two the ground is barren, devoid of any supraindividual but nongovernmental solidarity. Government is therefore our only source of connection. Relatedly, the world is also divided into a realm of order, under the government, and a realm of disorder, during revolution. Because only government connects us, it alone keeps us from passing from one realm into the other. Second, social division is a given; these myths focus not on remedying that division but on controlling it through government. Indeed, by viewing the gun culture as the cause of America's problem with violence but making no real effort to understand that culture, these myths foment social division. Third, these myths insist that as part of the realm of disorder, resistance to government is incapable of being constitutionally disciplined. As a result, the myths do nothing to organize, tame, or shape the popular use of political violence. If it comes, it comes, and then we are all in hopeless trouble, so we can only hope the government keeps it at bay. Taken together, these elements project an almost despairing vision: wanting natural solidarity, we are a seething mass of turbulence held in check only by the force of governmental coercion; if we should ever erupt, all is lost.

Perhaps some of the antirevolutionist mythmakers do not personally subscribe to all of these elements. Some might, for example, believe that nongovernmental solidarity is possible and desirable. Nonetheless, whatever their private beliefs, the myth that they offer contains no hint of that possibility, presumably because they regard it as so ephemeral that it warrants no role in a constitutional account. The public story that they tell and ask us to accept is one in which the people are not redeemed, only controlled. Through these elements, these antirevolutionists conjure a world in which popular engagement with keeping domestic order has disappeared.

The Barren Ground and the Two Realms

Antirevolutionists argue that because the Second Amendment does not create a private right, it can create only a power of government. Because the militia does not refer to the mass of private individuals, it must refer to a state instrumentality, always under state control. Once the people have assaulted the government, they have returned to the state of nature, without any constitutional organization. In these myths, in short, the world is composed of individuals and governments, with only a barren ground between. Government is thus our only solidarity. Without it, we are random bits of flotsam on a sea of political unrest. More important, this portrait of the American populace is not merely a snapshot of its current composition. It is a constitutional vision: the Constitution gives government a monopoly on violence because it presumes the people to be without connection independent of the government. For all the hope that antirevolutionists express in government, they seem not very hopeful about human beings. In these myths rings an an echo of old Hobbesian premises: humans are essentially separate and pursue their own goods with scant regard for others; they do not exhibit spontaneous sociability; socialization into myths of solidarity cannot make them trusting or trustworthy; and only the strong arm of government can keep them from oppressing each other.

Similarly, the inconsistency argument sharply divides the political world into two realms: the sphere of order, maintained by the constitution, and the sphere of disorder, driven by revolution. Our only bulwark against disorder is the government because it and the constitution are one and the same. When government is functioning, however harshly or corruptly, at least we are still in the realm of order, however imperfect. When we take arms against government, we have willy-nilly plunged the country into the realm of disorder. The stakes could not be higher: in resisting the government, we have cried havoc, let slip the dogs of war, and invited all the evil spirits of the political underworld into our midst. By this mythic division of the world, therefore, the antirevolutionists cast their opponents as almost nihilistic: when people resist the government, they are sweeping away all that binds us together and keeps us safe. And when people defend a right to resist the government, they are proposing to plunge us all into darkness.

Again, the problem with this myth is its imbalance. It is true that many revolutions have ushered in vicious civil war. Violence tends to become, in the literal sense, un-ruly — though this truth holds for governmental violence as well as for popular. Revolutions often begin in high ideals but end in low brutality and revenge. And with our currently divided population, government may be the only thing that keeps us from each other's throats. If so, however, that fact should be bemoaned and changed, not ratified in constitutional myth.

There is, after all, another side of the balance. The antirevolutionists' myth ignores the tales of governmental oppression that are at the center of the individual rights myth. Similarly, they suppress the stories at the center of the Framers' myth, stories of relatively unified revolutions that brought political good into the world, though never unalloyed with atrocity. We know, in fact, that humans are capable of nongovernmental connection and trust.[135] And in recent years, as the social consequences of extreme individualism have generated concern, a veritable tidal wave of academic work has shown that reviving civil society — that sphere of social life intermediate between the state and individuals, such as the market, culture, and private associations — helps to create a more cohesive polity.[136] In addition, many constitutionalists of the eighteenth century placed great store in the ability of humans to create civil society.[137]

Although the antirevolutionists may be right that any uprising today would lead to vicious civil war, we must still consider whether a society without a lively social contract on the use of political violence can long survive. And we must determine whether, in the absence of such a contract, it is better simply to rely wholly on the government to save us from ourselves, or to try to redeem the people by forging a new contract. If the latter is the better path, then we need different myths, stories that do not simply ratify our present reality, stories that point to a better constitutional future.

Social Division

By invoking government to coerce us into order, these myths also presume social division as a constitutional given. It is because we have no solidarity outside of government that government must have a monopoly on violence. And again, the myths offer this vision not just as a contingent description of current reality but also as a permanent, constitutional state of affairs. The Framers, we are told, were too smart to trust the people with the right of revolution. Faced with a fissuring social landscape, they gave the government the power to keep the people in line. This image forms the heart of this constitutional myth, projected out indefinitely into the future as the basic truth of our collective life. To be sure, some antirevolutionists would likely welcome more social solidarity. In their minds, however, the hope for such connection is so naive it should not form a part of our basic myths. Instead, the Constitution tells a story of a fragmented populace and a strong government; the first is the problem and the second the solution, forever and ever, in our fundamental morality tale told across the generations.

In addition, though some might welcome more solidarity, some of these mythmakers encourage and participate in social division. As the next chapter will document, the Second Amendment is commonly perceived as an icon in a culture war between the gun culture and its enemy, the liberal elite. The antirevolutionists seem to view their own scholarship through this prism. They write as participants in the culture war, and they have identified their enemy: the gun culture and its intellectual apologists, whom they generally call insurrectionists.

Only if one understands the fervor of their crusade does the remarkable tone of much of this writing make sense. To put the matter bluntly, these writers do not adopt the dry, detached style typical of academic commentators in a debate over ideas. Instead, they engage in quite heated denunciations of their opponents, as though they believe themselves in a war to save the soul of America. For example, Cornell describes the individual rights theory as "the intellectual equivalent of a check kiting scheme."[138] Wills says of individual rights theorists, "The quality of their arguments makes it hard to take them seriously"; they argue "in dreary expectable ways" and "chase from one misquotation to another";[139] they are "wacky scholars,' who think the Constitution "so deranged a document";[140] "with scholars like these, the NRA hardly needs to hire its own propagandists";[141] "[it] sometimes seems as if our law journals were being composed by Lewis Carroll using various other pseudonyms"; "heraldry is mixed with haberdashery, humbug with history, and scholarly looking footnotes with simple-minded literalism."[142] Bellesiles insists that those who disagree with him "are political conservatives seeking to negate the government's authority to regulate firearms. . . . [I]t is a perspective which carries a heavy and violent price tag."[143] In point of fact, many individual rights theorists do not lean right but left, and they are not, as a policy matter, opposed to gun control.[144] Their scholarly research simply led them to their conclusions, which were not always welcome. Bellesiles, however, would prefer to rely on a stereotype of his opponents: they are all the same and all acting in scholarly bad faith.

The antirevolutionists' rancor is not limited to academic "insurrectionists;" it also extends to ordinary gun owners, whom they apparently perceive as members of an exotic and twisted caste. Bellesiles opens his book with an extended screed against the gun culture.[145] He asks, "How did we get here? How did the united States reach a point where children shoot and kill? How did we acquire a culture in which Santa Claus gives a six-year old boy a shotgun for Christmas? For Christmas!"[146] Plainly, Bellesiles believes the gun culture is responsible for America's violence. One might therefore expect that he would explore the inner workings of that culture, to understand why so many ordinary Americans have organized their lives around this symbol. Instead, he dedicates his book to showing that American gun ownership is largely the product of government encouragement. If true, that point is interesting as a matter of origins, but it tells us little about the nature of the culture itself and its implication (or not) in American violence. Bellesiles's entire research into the inside of the gun culture apparently consists of reading a few gun magazines, which are representative of only a slice of gun-owning Americans.[147]

Similarly, in her refutation of individual rights theory,[148] Wendy Brown gives central place to a personal story that reveals her attitudes toward members of the gun culture. Upon returning from a long hike in the mountains, she discovered her car would not start. Luckily, a man in a nearby Winnebago agreed to help her, and for two hours they worked on her car together. Yet

Brown felt profoundly uncomfortable with this man because of his membership in a culture very different from hers. She describes him as "a California sportsman making his way through a case of beer, flipping through the pages of a porn magazine, and preparing to survey the area for his hunting club." He was "wearing a cap with the words 'NRA freedom' inscribed on it." Brown initially concluded that she and he inhabited "opposite ends of the political and cultural universe." Having read Sanford Levinson's work, however, she wondered "whether, for all our differences, we may have shared a commitment to resisting illegitimate authority." She ultimately concluded, though, that she could not have shared "much of anything with this man. . . . [I]f I had run into him in those woods without my friends or a common project for us to work on, I would have been seized with one great and appropriate fear: rape. During the hours that I spent with him, I had no reason to conclude that his respect for women's personhood ran any deeper than his respect for the lives of Sierra deer."[149] In other words, although this particular man had spent two hours helping her out of the goodness of his heart, Brown is convinced he is a likely rapist because he is a member of the gun culture — and that is just how those people are.

In short, in their portrait of their opponents, the antirevolutionists are constructing a sinister and vicious Other that the government must control. Rather than trying to understand this Other, they rely on a superficial, highly stereotyped image. They then judge that image and find it savage. In fact, much of this work is overtly devoted to "myth busting," that is, to exposing as a pernicious fraud the idea that gun owning has ever added anything positive to the American character. Carl Bogus has argued that the armed militia functioned primarily to keep slaves in their place, not to fight for liberty against a corrupt government.[150] Wills devoted a book to condemning what be considers "a mythical history and jurisprudence" that sees "even in the organs of government itself only anti-governmental values."[151] And Bellesiles's book argues that until the nineteenth century Americans did not generally own guns and were not proficient in their use and that the militia was always incompetent and even risible. Instead, gun ownership became common only because the national government foisted it on the American people. In other words, American guns did not help create liberty against government; quite the contrary, gun owning was the product of governmental manipulation. Bellesiles is blunt about his reasons for writing this analysis: "There exists a fear of confronting the specifics of these cultural origins, for what has been made can be unmade."[152] And, quite obviously, Bellesiles wants to unmake the gun culture. These writers would therefore ask us to give up our myths that the gun culture is immutable and good; they would ask us instead to believe that it is shallow-rooted and bad. Once again, the antirevolutionists offer us a vision of profound disunity: they represent the civilized people squaring off against the gun culture. They seek not to heal a cultural war but to win it, through the power of government.

Finally, this ratification of social division also appears to underlie the conviction that the right to revolution can be only a natural right, rather than a constitutional one. In this scheme, revolutionaries (or even those who espouse a right of revolution) have placed themselves outside the constitutional scheme that binds us together. They become, in other words, strangers to America. This point helps to explain why antirevolutionists are adamant in insisting that the right can come only from natural law, not the Constitution. At first glance, it is not clear why the two sides in this debate care whether the right to revolution is only a natural one. After all, what difference does it make? If the people have the right to revolution, its origin is not important.

In fact, the origin of this right does matter. Practically, it matters for the constitutionality of gun control, which is the issue that drives much of this debate. If the right to revolution is only natural, then the right to arms for revolution might only be natural as well. As a result, if the government intrudes on either of those rights, it might be violating natural law, but not the Constitution. Ergo, gun control does not violate the Constitution. By contrast, if the right to revolution and its associated right to arms are constitutional, then judges should strike down gun control schemes in the here and now.

The origin of the right matters for another reason, subtler but perhaps more important in the long run. Since the Enlightenment, natural law has generally been understood as that law appropriate to human individuals by virtue of their moral status as human individuals. As a result, although often hazy, it is binding on all people in all places and times. Constitutional law, by contrast, is the constitution of a particular community. It is binding on its citizens by virtue of their membership in a specific, historically situated enterprise. Even when a constitution incorporates natural law, it adds an additional element of obligation, by making it part of the organic law for a particular community, rather than just the universal law for abstract individuals.

For that reason, the relationship among citizens during a constitutional revolution is different from their relationship during a revolution sanctioned only by natural law. Constitutional revolutionaries appeal to other Americans as Americans, citizens sharing a legal tradition and owing one another specific obligations. They may demand acquiescence in a revolution because of this set of shared norms, obligations, and histories. And they make their revolution as coparticipants in an ongoing cultural enterprise. By contrast, natural law revolutionaries must appeal to others as generic human beings who possess rights merely by virtue of being human.[153] Their revolution is potentially worldwide because political boundaries are simply arbitrary marks on a map. And so natural law revolution grows out of an appeal to natural right, rather than out of a shared identity as Americans. This kind of revolution therefore has a hazy, abstract, theoretical basis. It exists in a never-never land of ideal justice, and it cannot command the commitment from fellow citizens that the Constitution can.

Suppose for a moment the antirevolutionists are right. Suppose the right to revolution is and can be only a natural one, never a constitutional one. Suppose that only government can embody the Constitution. In this mythic world, revolutionaries cannot relate to other Americans through shared constitutional commitments. By preaching revolution, they have exiled themselves from the constitutional homeland. As a result, one need not respond to their arguments as constitutional claims, only as tendentious assertions of natural right. They are, in short, wild-eyed, un-American subversives. Several decades ago, communists bore the brunt of this charge; today, right-wing revolutionaries do. In both cases, the charge converted a whiff of revolutionary sympathy into an odor of constitutional heresy.

Through this antonymous rendering of *constitution* and *revolution,* therefore, antirevolutionists offer us the following portrait of this debate: the two sides are not one group of Americans disagreeing in good faith with another group of Americans; instead, they are the constitution's friends and its self-declared enemies—insiders and outsiders to the real American people. In fact, given how heavily the antirevolutionists rely on the Constitution's treason clause to reject a constitutional right of revolution, they plainly believe that insurrectionists are traitors to the people. And that view accords with the rest of their thinking: those who oppose government are destroying the only thing that holds us together; those who disagree must be deranged "gun nuts" who have odd Christmas customs and must be disciplined.

As so often happens, we find the poles in this debate meeting on a similar view of what is at stake. Each side believes that the other is outside the constitutional pale. The militia movement is convinced its enemies represent a dangerous conspiracy to subvert the Constitution, and the antirevolutionists feel the same way. The only difference is that the former associate the Constitution with the people, defined as people like themselves, and the latter associate it with the government, which is largely staffed by people like themselves. In both cases, the advocates are constructing an Other that does not really belong, that has exiled itself from our sympathies by its dangerous ideas.

Taming Popular Violence

Because antirevolutionists hold the realms of order and disorder as utterly separate, they have very little to say about disorder. By the time we take up arms, all bets are off, the bounds are burst, and the Constitution is dissolved. Revolution is a last desperate gambit, a place where nothing matters but who has the most guns. In this war of all against all, what is there to say? How can one even speak cogently when politics has been reduced to brute strength?

As always, phrasing the options in this polar way represents a dangerous gamble. If constitution and revolution have nothing to do with each other, then if revolution does arrive it is safe to bet that only anarchical warfare can result. If we have been raised on the idea that resistance to government bursts all the bounds, then we will likely act as though all the bounds have been burst during resistance. And if our constitutional tradition has never acculturated us into the responsible stewardship of political violence, then come the revolution we likely will act with scant regard for anything but personal power. If we have been entirely dependent on government for our safety, then we will be utterly lost if government disappears.

This gamble therefore does not make sense as a strategy for making revolution more orderly. Instead, it makes sense only as a strategy for making revolution so unattractive that no one would ever contemplate it. That attitude helps to explain the stance of these myths toward revolution. On the one hand, they deplore popular violence. But on the other hand, they proclaim that because revolution is strictly a matter of natural law, the constitution cannot regulate it so as to ameliorate its horrors. One would think that if these mythmakers fear revolution so much, they might try to devise ways to make it less horrible. Instead, they devote themselves entirely to explaining why government must have the power to keep it from ever happening. Plainly, in their view revolution is so awful that it is not even a thinkable option. If it comes, it comes, and we will all suffer — but our only hope is in the settled order. Telling romantic myths about revolution can only lead people away from the oases of governmental cultivation into the shifting sands of revolutionary wilderness.

In this myth, therefore, revolution is inherently incapable of discipline. Arendt powerfully expressed this distinction between violence of any sort and politics of any sort: "Where violence rules absolutely, as for instance in the concentration camps of totalitarian regimes, not only the laws . . . but everything and everybody must fall silent. It is because of this silence that violence is a marginal phenomenon in the political realm; for man, to the extent that he is a political being, is endowed with the power of speech."[154] Many Americans like to imagine that the Constitution provides some guarantee of justice, government by consent, and minimal political decency.[155] By contrast, many fear that in revolution there is no guarantee the just will win. Therefore, constitution and revolution must be contradictory because revolution stands for violence and constitution for reason. If these are our only choices, then it is best to gamble our all against revolution.

Yet sooner or later all countries face armed revolutions. We had therefore best hope that revolution is not inevitably fragmented and vicious, and we should seek to create a populace that could tame such violence through a deep social contract. By contrast, the antirevolutionists insist that we will always be divided, so we should accept that fact and place all our trust in government. Once again, then, these stories merely ratify current reality. They do nothing to transform it into a better world. In fact, the vision that these myths offer us is not inevitable. It is not necessary for *revolution* and *constitution* to be antonyms, and rendering them that way has pernicious consequences. Although the Constitution might rest in part on justice and consent, it has also rested in part on injustice and oppression. For example, the Constitution acquired jurisdiction over American Indians, African Americans, other involuntary immigrants, and women without their consent, and for many years it exercised that jurisdiction without allowing them representation.[156] And just as constitution can be less than wholly peaceful, revolution can be less than wholly violent. Again, Arendt expresses the point: "To be sure, not even wars, let alone revolutions, are ever completely determined by violence . . . . Because of [its] speechlessness political theory has little to say about the phenomenon of violence and must leave its discussion to the technicians . . . . A theory of war or a theory of revolution, therefore, can only deal with the justification of violence because this justification constitutes its political limitation."[157] In short, constitutionalism, like other political theory, can limit the justification of violence. Although there is no guarantee revolutions will heed that limit, there is no certainty they will not either. In any event, without an articulation of limits, revolutionary violence is more likely to become simply anarchic.

Recognizing that constitution and revolution are not opposites might have several beneficial consequences. First, constitutional discourse is theoretically tethered to a particular legal framework, which might supply some intellectual discipline for loose talk about revolution: to exercise a constitutional right to revolution, one must satisfy all the exacting limits we observed earlier. By comparison, discussion of revolution predicated on natural law can be highly unfocused and gauzy. For example, many writers vociferously argue for an individual right to revolution, but they are silent on when and how a revolution might legitimately occur. Apparently, the citizens will just know by consulting their sense of abstract right.[158]

Second, and relatedly, a constitutional right of revolution could provide a common frame of reference during revolutionary times, thus reducing schism and anarchy. At best, this common frame may help to preserve some connection between the contending sides. For example, during the American Revolution, moderates hoped to keep open the possibility of a formal alliance with Great Britain by asking only for a restoration of the status quo ante.[159] Similarly, the Civil War might have been delayed by the fact that both sides claimed to be acting within basic constitutional principles, however differently they may have understood them. After the war, that common framework may also have facilitated the reintegration of the Confederate states back into the Union. Even when government and revolutionaries are irreconcilably divided, preservation of a constitutional framework may promote unity within the revolutionary movement itself. Once the movement breaks that frame into the wilds of natural equity, everything is up for grabs, and submerged differences may become all too apparent.

This antonymous rendering of *constitution* and *revolution* thus leaves us with unsatisfactory options. If we embrace revolution, we must surrender constitutionalism, with its promise of stability and procedural regularity. We must decide to trust the revolutionary people under all circumstances, and so we must forget the revolutionary horrors of the past. If we embrace constitutionalism, we must surrender all possibility of popular revolution, with its promise of popular engagement in maintaining domestic order, even against government abuse. We must decide to trust the government under all circumstances, and we must forget the totalitarian horrors of the past. Either course is unbalanced.

Happily, the conceptual world is not so simple. We can seek to be both revolutionaries and constitutionalists at the same time. We can hope that government will be faithful to its mandate, but if it is not, we can hope that the people will force a restoration. We can seek to preserve constitutional structure while opening government to direct popular influence, and we can endorse revolutionary movements while seeking to limit them within constitutional norms. Combining all these desiderata in the real world would be hugely difficult, perhaps impossible, under present conditions. The task will be forever impossible, however, if we convince ourselves that revolution and constitution are inherently incompatible. Rejecting that false dichotomy might thus allow us to imagine a world in which we need not choose between our most deeply held political values.

When people contemplate the possibility of violent instability, they become afraid and seek certain safety. The antirevolutionists seek that certainty in government, but government cannot provide it, and neither can anything else. If we are so fractured that we cannot undergird our own stability, government may be able to hold us together for a short while. In the long run, however, if we lack a social contract, we have ceased to be a viable republic. If we wish to shore up our long-term safety, therefore, we must attend to that contract. Unfortunately, these myths encourage us to look in the wrong direction by urging us to depend on the government rather than on popular unity and engagement with the taming of political violence. These myths strive just to hold the line: in the face of social division, the government must restrain the savages — that is, the gun culture — among us. We need different myths, stories that open the possibility of transformation while remaining realistic about our current condition.

5

Libertarians and Populists

For decades, while established opinion held to the states' rights interpretation of the Second Amendment, many private Americans argued that it protected an individual right to arms. The NRA has most prominently espoused this view, but it has been joined by many citizens, including some serious scholars. Until recently, however, the individual rights theory had little to do with the constitutional organization of violence. Instead, these theorists argued primarily for a right to arms for private purposes, such as self-defense, and they mentioned revolution little or not at all. In the closing years of the millennium, however, that situation changed dramatically. In 1989, Sanford Levinson published *The Embarrassing Second Amendment* in the Yale Law Journal.[1] A figure of great stature in the field of constitutional law, Levinson suggested that the amendment might protect an individual right to arms, so that the populace might exercise a checking function on a tyrannical government. Suddenly, this view became respectable, and the law journals witnessed a flood of writing to confirm or contradict it. The Fifth Circuit Court of Appeals adopted this view of the amendment as the law for its circuit, becoming the first federal appeals court to break ranks with the states' right view and virtually inviting the Supreme Court to address the provision.

To assess the view that the Second Amendment protects an individual right to arms so that individuals may resist the government, I will examine the writing of four representative legal scholars—Sanford Levinson, Nelson Lund, Glenn Harlan Reynolds, and Don Kates—and the Fifth Circuit's opinion in *United States v. Emerson*.[2] An individual right to arms for resistance poses obvious concerns: it seems to imply that private citizens have an individual right to resist the government when they deem it appropriate. Under that implication, the individual rights theory becomes a charter for anarchy. Yet these writers are not anarchists, and they do not want their view to be used as a justification for antigovernmental terrorism. Accordingly, when they describe a Second Amendment revolution, their language shifts: rather than individuals resisting the government, they argue that the amendment gives the right to the people to make a revolution. Like the Framers, they imagine a united movement of the bulk of the citizenry rising up to do battle with a small minority that has captured the government. With few exceptions, they never discuss the possibility that an individual right to arms might give rise to vicious civil war.

In other words, the individual rights view has two parts, each with a distinctive rhetoric: it guarantees a right to individuals to own arms for the purpose of revolution; yet individuals qua individuals apparently do not have the right to make a revolution. Instead, that right belongs to a collective body, the people, that these writers rhetorically conjure but do not define. On the subject of arms ownership, then, these writers appear to be libertarians, but on the subject of revolution they veer in a populist direction.

Those libertarian and populist elements, however, sit together uneasily. If the Constitution provides for the arming of individuals, it is de facto individuals who will possess the ability to resist government. If those individuals comprise a unified people, they may make a unified revolution against government. If they instead comprise a great diversity of groups, some of them mutually hostile, then their resistance will reflect their division. When the revolution comes, America will witness not an organic uprising, but civil war, terrorism, and anarchy. In the Framers' language, individual arming may, if Americans are a people, lead to revolution, or, if they are not, to endless rebellion. It all depends on current social conditions. One cannot simply assume that an individual rights reading of the amendment will lead to popular revolution rather than to anarchy; one must instead argue for that conclusion on the basis of a realistic assessment of the modern world. Unfortunately, the individual rights theorists never make that argument. Instead, they conjure with the people: they rhetorically assume, without demonstration, that modern Americans somehow cohere into a single organic unit.

This chapter will therefore consider whether Americans constitute one people in the sense contemplated by the amendment. The prognosis is not encouraging. On many subjects, Americans are united. On the subject of guns and their legitimate uses, by contrast, America is deeply fissured into antagonistic cultural and identity groups. At its simplest, sociologists and others have described this division as one lying between the gun culture and its enemies. The gun culture has embraced guns not just as a tool but as a central symbol of its whole set of cultural values. The demographic heartland of the culture is white, rural, male, conservative, and predominantly southern—in other words, the general population out of which American populist movements have traditionally grown. Like other populisms, the gun culture has generally defined itself or been defined in opposition to two other sets of groups. First, it has opposed liberal, urban, educated, and cosmopolitan elites who would take away its guns. Second, a number of outgroups, such as Jews, feminists, and African Americans, have generally experienced the gun culture as deeply threatening and alien.

Many members of the gun culture embrace not only guns but also the Second Amendment as their particular cultural property. To them, this provision is the most important part of the Constitution, the part that pulls the rest together into a meaningful whole. In addition, in their view, the primary function of the amendment is to protect them and people like them because guns matter so much to them. And they have a mythic story to tell about guns, the government, and their culture: the Framers wrote the Second Amendment so that the people would always have the right to resist the government; in the years since, the rest of America has abandoned this priceless heritage, trusting government instead of their own arms. But the gun culture has held fast, and today it is the true inheritor of the Framers' mantle, the true people of the Second Amendment; when the time should come to make a revolution, the members of the gun culture will be its first, most important, and perhaps only participants. The Second Amendment is therefore the great manifesto of the gun culture: it affirms the culture's worth, protects its future, and guarantees its right to defend itself against the government and its lackeys. The Second Amendment, in short, assures the gun culture that it is central to the meaning of America.

In one sense, the gun culture's myth differs greatly from the other types of Second Amendment stories. For all their differences, the states' rights theorists and the individual rights theorists both approach the amendment as a formal and abstract rule of law applicable to all Americans alike. The former view it as protecting arms bearing only within a state militia, and the latter understand it as protecting a broad individual right to arms. Both schools of thought, however, share one conviction: the right to arms does not peculiarly belong to any subculture, any identity group, any race, religion, or gender. By contrast, the gun culture ultimately reads the amendment as a special recognition of its particular culture. In its view, the Constitution guarantees gun rights so as to protect its particular culture, rather than abstract personal autonomy. While members of the gun culture therefore adopt a rhetoric of liberal individualism, their fundamental commitments are populist: they claim to represent the true American people against threatening outsiders in Washington.

Because libertarians imagine an America full of generic individuals, they can imagine that those individuals might cohere into a single people: they are, after all, fundamentally alike in being generic. In the real world of American culture, by contrast, it becomes plain that people will respond to revolutionary conditions as situated selves: as members of racial, religious, ethnic, and cultural groups. What will result is not a single people organically rising against a corrupt government. Instead, what will most likely result is a hopeless confusion of contending, mutually hostile groups. In particular, liberal elites and many outgroups will reject participation in armed struggle for as long as possible, but parts of the gun culture will welcome the opportunity, viewing it as their prophecy fulfilled. As a result, the people most likely to claim the right of Second Amendment revolution for itself is not the united American citizenry sketched in the rhetoric of the individual rights theory. Instead, the most extreme elements of the gun culture will be at the vanguard of the revolution, claiming to speak for a true American people that is limited to people like them. In fact, as the next chapter will elaborate, the beginnings of this process are already visible in the violent activity of some parts of the militia movement.

The populist theory of the Second Amendment is therefore unsatisfactory for the same reason as the libertarian theory: it promises anarchy and terrorism. In the writings of these theorists, that promise may be obscured by predictions that the people will rise as a unit in the event of tyranny. In the end, however, that people is nothing more than the individuals and groups that comprise the American citizenry today—wonderfully and painfully diverse and dissentient. If the only choices were anarchy or tyranny, we might choose anarchy. And therefore if the only hedge against tyranny were an armed citizenry composed of mutually hostile individuals and groups, we might choose to repose ultimate power in those anarchical citizens. Before plunging into that dark night, however, we might try to discover whether there is a way to organize political violence that does not inevitably slide into either private or public oppression. That task of organization may be difficult, as part III of this book will explain, but it is the very point in constitutionally organizing violence. If we were prepared to accept no better, we would not even need to write a constitution: all by itself, the world reliably delivers untamed violence to our door. We write laws to try to improve that situation.

Libertarians

At the level of formal analysis, few modern commentators have overtly affirmed that in its revolutionary aspect the Second Amendment depends on the existence of a people. As we have seen, states' rights theorists deny that the amendment protects a right of revolution at all. By contrast, individual rights theorists argue that the people possess a right to own arms for resisting government.[3] They stress that the amendment refers to the "right of the *people* to keep and bear arms,"[4] language which they read as protecting the individual's right to own guns for revolution. They emphatically do not mean that Americans hold those guns only as a collective, organic whole; indeed, they are quick to deny that the amendment protects collective rights.[5] As a result, they never examine whether Americans constitute a unified people because that question is irrelevant to their interpretation.

Yet when one argues for an individual right to arms for revolution, it is difficult not to worry that individuals will abuse that right. Individual rights theorists developed their view by espousing a right to arms for personal purposes, such as self-defense. When they began to argue for a right to arms for revolution, they had to face new analytical and practical problems growing out of the inherently social nature of revolution. If individuals have the right to arms for revolution, do they also have an individual right to make a revolution? May the state then constitutionally prosecute them? If random individuals do not have the right to make a revolution, who does? When is a revolution warranted? Who should lead it? And how will we find agreement on those issues? Even if these theorists do not believe that the Second Amendment creates a right to revolution as such, they clearly believe that it mandates the conditions that would allow individuals to make a revolution. Yet must the state stand by until it is too late to block an insurrection by hate groups?

At the level of formal analysis, individual rights theorists largely ignore these questions. And yet they seem troubled by them because inspection of their writing reveals an implicit and very different attitude: when they imagine resistance to government sanctioned by the Second Amendment, they generally do not imagine a revolution made by individuals for individual purposes. Instead, they conjure with the people: they argue that as the people have the right to arms, the people will decide when and how to act. That argument, however, presupposes (and implicitly asserts by presupposing) that Americans constitute a people. It assumes that, revolting spontaneously and independently, individual Americans will meld into a body. When these theorists imagine otherwise, they look for ways to cabin the right, to bring it back under control.

The individual rights school has generated a rich, extensive literature. To illustrate my analysis, I will examine four prominent articles by four distinguished writers. I have chosen these articles because of their scholarly excellence, despite my disagreements with much of their analysis. These pieces, in other words, represent the individual rights theory at its best, yet they still fail to confront the significant problems in that theory.

For years before the recent surge in Second Amendment studies, Don B. Kates, Jr., was advancing the individual rights theory. At the time, few thought the amendment worth serious study, and, as we have seen, establishment opinion inclined to the states' rights view. For a long time, therefore, his was a voice crying in the wilderness. His most influential work, *Handgun Prohibition and the Original Meaning of the Second Amendment,* plays a seminal role in the development of the individual rights theory.[6] Until recently, it was the only Second Amendment article published in a "top ten" law review, and it has been widely cited.

Kates maintains that the amendment creates an individual right to arms for reasons that include resistance to government: "The second amendment's language and historical and philosophical background demonstrate that it was designed to guarantee individuals the possession of certain kinds of arms for three purposes: (1) crime prevention . . . (2) national defense . . . (3) preservation of individual liberty and popular institutions against domestic despotism."[7] Thus, for Kates, individuals may own arms for resistance in the same way they may own arms for self-defense. We would therefore expect Kates to describe resistance to government as an activity of those same individuals. Instead, in Kates's rhetoric, by the time individuals take up arms for revolution, they have lost their individuality and somehow become a united citizenry. Specifically, Kates insists that a united citizenry can successfully resist even a government armed with modern military weapons. He rejects the argument that "an armed citizenry cannot hope to overthrow a modern military machine" because it is wrong to assume that "a handgun-armed citizenry will eschew [effective] guerrilla tactics in favor of [ineffectively] throwing themselves headlong under the tracks of advancing tanks."[8] The people who had been "armed individuals" have somehow been transformed into "an armed citizenry."

Thus, when Kates discusses the right to own guns, he talks primarily about individuals, but when he discusses the right to use those guns in revolution, he talks primarily about the people as a collectivity. Sometimes, indeed, this ambiguity occurs even within his discussion of revolution, so it is difficult to tell whether Kates believes that loose individuals or a united citizenry is necessary to keep the government in line. He writes, "The issue is not really *overthrow-*

ing a tyranny but *deterring* its institution in the first place. To persuade his officers and men to support a coup, a potential military despot must convince them that his rule will succeed where our current civilian leadership and policies are failing. In a country whose widely divergent citizenry possesses upwards of 160 million firearms, however, the most likely outcome of usurpation (no matter how initially successful) is not benevolent dictatorship, but prolonged, internecine civil war."[9] In this passage, individualist and populist elements mix together uneasily. On the one hand, citizens are so "widely divergent" that no would-be despot could persuade them as a whole to accept his rule; the likely result would be "prolonged, internecine civil war." Kates thus paints a portrait of the citizenry as disunited in the face of usurpation. On the other hand, Kates seems to expect that most Americans will unite in "guerilla tactics" against the usurper, and he hopes the despot will entertain the same expectation. Indeed, his deterrence argument works only if the dictator fears that most of those Americans with "160 million firearms" will use them against him. Individuals and collective peoples thus walk in and out of this scenario with the shading of a phrase.

Whichever way one reads Kates's argument, however, problems arise. On the one hand, he may mean that the Second Amendment guarantees an individual right to arms so individuals may resist when they feel tyrannized. In that case, he must face the charge that his argument calmly contemplates individual insurrection as constitutionally warranted activity. Alternatively, he may mean that the Second Amendment guarantees an individual right to arms so that a united people may resist. In that case, he must consider how a "widely divergent citizenry" could ever coalesce into an organic people, especially since he has just predicted that usurpation will result in "internecine civil war."

Following Kates's article by several years, Nelson Lund published *The Second Amendment, Political Liberty, and the Right of Self-Preservation*.[10] Although Lund argues that the amendment protects an individual right, he generally imagines that the people will resist government as a unified mass. When he instead contemplates that Americans might resist the government as individuals, he so restricts the operation of the right as to render it almost nugatory. Like Kates, Lund begins by asserting that the right to bear arms belongs to individuals: "The language of the Second Amendment protects an individual's right to keep and bear arms."[11] But then he explains that individuals hold this right for collective safety: "The language also indicates, however, that this private right is protected for the sake of a public good. . . . The primary purpose of the people's right to keep and bear arms . . . is to allow them to act as a credible *counterweight* to the government's military forces."[12] Like Kates, Lund conjures with the people to explain how a revolution will work: in the first sentence, he insists that the right to arms belongs to individuals, but by the second sentence those individuals have congealed into a people (indeed, Lund calls them "*the* people") to counterweight the military. The mythic image contains two and only two simple elements: the government as a mass on one side and the people as a bloc on the other.

Yet Lund seems to question this myth even as he propounds it. Just at this point in his analysis, his attitude toward resistance suddenly becomes ambivalent, as he seems to sense that the American people do not constitute a bloc and civil war seems more likely than revolution. On the one hand, he argues that government oppression remains a live possibility in this country, so citizens must retain the right of resistance.[13] On the other hand, Lund would not allow private citizens to maintain "a stock of armaments and expertise sufficient to defeat either the armed forces of the United States, or even a state's National Guard, in battle." Allowing the citizenry to arm in such a manner would be "impossible" and "foolhardy," but, more important, the Constitution gives the federal government the power to "suppress Insurrections." In short, then, the Second Amendment does not actually guarantee American individuals the right to sufficient arms successfully to resist the government. In the end, for Lund the only point in the revolutionary Second Amendment is its psychological impact on the government: our governors will hesitate long before assaulting a (lightly) armed citizenry because "any use of military force depends upon a calculation of both the benefits and the costs of its use. . . . [A]ny factor increasing the anticipated cost of a military operation makes the conduct of that operation incrementally more unlikely."[14] Thus, having praised a popular right to revolution, Lund then drastically curtails it: the people may resist but not win, and the government may oppress but must pay the cost.

Lund might be driven to this equivocation because of his ambivalent attitudes toward the American citizenry. He is tempted to portray Americans as a single organic entity, but he also feels a sensible discomfort with that temptation. In defending the right to arms, he assumes that Americans are a united people that must have guns to resist the government. No sooner has he made that case, however, than he seems to realize that individuals might abuse the right to resist. As a result, he quickly affirms the government's right to suppress rebellions and dramatically limits the citizenry's right to arms. By the end, without the image of a united revolutionary people before him, Lund has virtually dismantled the right to revolution.

As noted, Levinson's *The Embarrassing Second Amendment* has had enormous influence.[15] Many credit it for launching the Second Amendment Renaissance, and it has affected political commentators, politicians, and even popular novelists.[16] Virtually all of these observers read Levinson's article as advocating the individual rights theory. Despite this widespread perception, however, Levinson's tone is careful, even tentative. Instead of advocating the individual rights theory himself, he often seems merely to be explaining the role of the right to arms in the Framers' thinking. In addition, he warns his readers that he means only to be exploring ideas, not offering definitive conclusions: "It is not my style to offer 'correct' or 'incorrect' interpretations of the Constitution. . . . [M]y general tendency to regard as wholly untenable any approach to the Constitution that describes itself as obviously correct and condemns its opposition as simply wrong holds for the Second Amendment as well."[17]

Amid this admirable circumspection, however, Levinson sketches the outlines of a possible argument: first, the amendment originally gave individuals the right to arms for resistance; second, those individuals would "presumptively" make a revolution as a united people; and third, that right to arms for resistance may still make sense. Levinson first suggests it may be wrong to hold that "the substantive right [to arms] is one pertaining to a collective body— 'the people'—rather than to individuals."[18] In the republican theory of the Framers, those armed individuals were a bulwark against state tyranny: "Just as ordinary citizens should participate actively in governmental decisionmaking through their own deliberative insights, . . . so should ordinary citizens participate in the process of law enforcement and defense of liberty rather than rely on professionalized peacekeepers." And Levinson describes "the Weberian definition of the state"—that is, the "repository of a monopoly of the legitimate means of violence"—as "a profoundly statist definition, the product of a specifically German tradition of the (strong) state rather than of a strikingly different American political tradition that is fundamentally mistrustful of state power and vigilant about maintaining ultimate power, including the power of arms, in the populace." Levinson summarizes this line of argument: "The strongest version of the republican argument would hold it to be a 'privilege and immunity of United States citizenship'—of membership in a liberty-enhancing political order—to keep arms that could be taken up against tyranny whenever found, including obviously, state government."[19]

Yet if the right to arms belongs to individuals, Levinson also stresses that in the Framers' view all those individuals would unite into a single virtuous people in opposition to tyranny. He introduces the importance of an armed citizenry thus: "Consider the possibility . . . that the ultimate 'checking value' in a republican polity is the ability of an armed populace, *presumptively motivated by a shared commitment to the common good,* to resist governmental tyranny."[20] Like other individual rights theorists, Levinson draws the sting from his argument by suggesting that in the Framers' view individuals will arise in shared devotion to shared ends. As a result, we need not worry too much about rebellion under an individualist reading of the Second Amendment.

Yet the Framers did not merely presume that the populace would be united in virtue. Instead, they held that an open question, and they believed that the right to revolution made sense only if they were so united. They had good reason for acknowledging that restriction: an individual right to resistance in the absence of such unity might lead to disastrous consequences. One must wonder, therefore, whether Levinson believes such conditions obtain today. Unfortunately, he does not answer directly, but at one point he seems to suggest they do. In response to those who argue that we need no longer fear government oppression, he warns that we still may need the right to arms: "I do not want to argue that the state is necessarily tyrannical; I am not an anarchist. But it seems foolhardy to assume that the armed state will necessarily be benevolent." Ordinary political safeguards will not necessarily protect us: "The development of widespread suffrage and greater majoritarianism in our polity is itself no sure protection, at least within republican theory. The republican theory is predicated on the stark contrast between mere democracy, where people are motivated by selfish personal interest, and a republic, where civic virtue, both in citizens and leadership, tames selfishness on behalf of the common good. In any event, it is hard for me to see how one can argue that circumstances have so changed as to make mass disarmament constitutionally unproblematic."[21] In other words, "mass disarmament" would be unconstitutional because, if our democratic process should ever come to be dominated by "selfish personal interest," the armed citizenry might have to "tame[] selfishness on behalf of the common good." This armed citizenry, therefore, must be a republican people, united in virtue, and if Levinson believes it can still serve this function, then he must still believe that Americans constitute such a people.

Regrettably, however, that belief is entirely implicit. Like other individual rights theorists, Levinson simply assumes that we are a people of sufficient unity to make a revolution; he never actually makes an argument to that effect. And so once again we see the drift from libertarianism to populism: the right to arms belongs to individuals, but somehow revolutions are always made by the people as a whole. As a result, Levinson never contemplates what a right to revolution in the hands of disunited individuals might entail. In light of his sensitive appreciation of republican theory, Levinson's assumption that the people will always be united is puzzling. As he details in the foregoing passage, Levinson recognizes that republicans worried that the American polity might disintegrate into "mere democracy," in which people pursued their selfish interests. But if the people have become so corrupt, it seems quite unlikely they would suddenly become "united by a shared commitment to the common good" in a revolution. Instead, revolution would be the continuation of politics by another means, with various groups pursuing their own selfish agendas against one another. To be sure, some revolutionaries have argued that the anarchic violence of insurrection can purify the people's souls, redeeming them from the pollution of mere politics, but as Levinson says of himself, "I am not an anarchist."

Glenn Harlan Reynolds's *A Critical Guide to the Second Amendment*[22] has also had a substantial impact on the debate over the Second Amendment. Reynolds wrote this piece as an introduction to a symposium issue of the Tennessee Law Review featuring a number of articles on the amendment, almost all from an individual rights perspective. Reynolds modestly describes his aims in this article: he hopes to "summarize and criticize" the corpus of existing scholarship.[23] In fact, however, Reynolds accomplished far more. First, he broke new ground in contemplating the implications of the individual rights theory for the right of resistance. Second, his article argued that scholars had come to agreement on the broad outlines of a single best interpretation of the amendment: "Indeed, there is sufficient consensus on many issues that one can properly speak of a 'Standard Model' in Second Amendment theory, much as physicists and cosmologists speak of a 'Standard Model' in terms of the creation and evolution of the Universe."[24] According to Reynolds, this Standard Model of the Second Amendment protects an individual right to arms for the purpose of resisting a tyrannical government. As we have seen, states' rights theorists viewed this claim as a gauntlet hurled down, and they responded with articles, books, and symposia. Reynolds's article thus served to galvanize the debate.

Of all the individual rights theorists, Reynolds may be the most reflective about the form that a Second Amendment revolution might take. Like the others, he argues that the right to keep and bear arms belongs to individuals: "The Second Amendment protects the same sort of individual right that other parts of the Bill of Rights provide."[25] And he also explains that the "ultimate purpose behind the right to keep and bear arms" is "protection against a tyrannical government."[26] Reynolds insists, however, that although the right to arms may be individual, the right to revolution is not. Drawing on some of my earlier work, he summarizes, "Thus, there can be no claim . . . that the Second Amendment guarantees a right for any individual to declare war against the federal government whenever he or she thinks the government is unjust."[27] Instead, the right belongs to the people: for the Framers, "the right of revolt could not be exercised by individual citizens or small groups, but only by the people as a whole."[28] Unless citizens act in concert, according to consensual standards, the risks are great and familiar: "Some citizens will think it is time to revolt when it is not, thus exposing the nation to enormous turmoil, loss of life, and economic damage where it is not justified—and perhaps creating a backlash against the right to keep and bear arms."[29]

Reynolds, therefore, must address whether Americans do constitute a people. To my reading, he makes two suggestions on this subject. First, he intimates that the state may have a role to play in constructing the people. Again relying on my earlier work, he writes, "Although the militia was a body that was, in a way, external to the state in the sense of being an institution of the people, the expectation was that the state, not private groups, would provide the foundation upon which the structure of the militia would be erected." For that reason, modern militia groups are wrong to argue that they "are the militia that the Constitution describes," and so they cannot claim the right of revolution.[30] And Reynolds suggests that state sponsorship of a universal militia might help to make the citizenry into a people: "If gun ownership is essential to give the Second Amendment meaning, then simply require everyone to own a gun. . . . [S]uch an approach is far more consistent with the Second Amendment than simply ignoring it would be. That we have fallen away from the Framers' ideals, after all, may be more of a reflection on us than on them. Furthermore, universal militia service might even help to reestablish the kind of civic virtue that all of us wish were present today."[31]

Reynolds thus suggests both that the state originally had an important role in constituting Americans a people and also that it might resume that role today. Yet the state does not currently serve that role: as Reynolds puts it, "We have fallen away from the Framers' ideals." Indeed, Reynolds is careful to insist that he is not proposing the re-creation of a universal state militia: "Please note that neither I, nor any Standard Model scholar of whom I am aware, argues that individual gun ownership *should* be made mandatory."[32] As a result, although the state might help to make us a people at some indeterminate point in the future, it does not serve that role today. We cannot rely on the old militia structure to give us the necessary unity.

Reynolds's other suggestion is that if law professors openly discussed the legitimate grounds for revolution, that discussion might provide the basis for popular unity necessary in times of revolution. He decries the failures of Second Amendment scholars to discuss this subject: "Standard Model scholars have paid almost no attention to the question of when such a revolt would be justified. . . . If we have the right to keep and bear arms in no small part so that, in the last resort, we can rise up and overthrow a tyrannical government, then one important aspect of the right would seem to be some basis for agreeing whether the government is tyrannical or not."[33] He observes that some Americans "are talking openly about armed rebellion," but the legal academy is providing them with no guidance: "Educating people not only about the right to keep and bear arms, but the circumstances in which the underlying reason for that right might emerge, could be essential. At the moment, the risk of a misguided revolt seems fairly remote, but that is the time to take steps."[34] Reynolds's own proposal is that no one has a right to revolution against democratic governments that adequately permit change by peaceful means. As a result, would-be modern revolutionaries are wrong to hatch plots against the federal government: "Our modern society, despite its ills, does not suffer from a lack of political participation; arguably, it suffers from too much."[35]

Reynolds's analysis is both reflective and bold. He directly acknowledges what other individual rights theorists generally ignore: if we are going to give individuals a right to arms for revolution, then we are going to have to arrive at some consensual standards for when a revolution might be warranted. In fact, such a discussion will probably be necessary (though perhaps not sufficient) to form Americans into a people on the use of political violence. As Reynolds would be the first to acknowledge, however, we have not yet had that discussion, and we have not yet produced that consensus. Indeed, Americans have very disparate views about when they might legitimately resist the government. In point of fact, Reynolds's proposal for discussion has not even been taken up by fellow academics. For the most part, Standard Modelers still rely on rhetoric to suggest that the people will revolt when the people think it time. So, like the state, dialogue may someday make us a people, but we are not there now.

In short, then, Reynolds makes explicit a claim implicit in other writers' work: although the right to keep and bear arms belongs to individuals, the right to revolution belongs to the people. The individual right to arms is therefore instrumental in nature: it serves to facilitate a populist right to resistance. Yet despite his thoughtfulness on this point, the two parts of Reynolds's theory fit together awkwardly. If the point in the individual right to arms is to facilitate the people's right to revolution, then the right to arms makes sense — in its own terms — only if Americans constitute a people. As we have seen, the Framers shared this view: they guaranteed the right to arms because they assumed that the people were so united — institutionally in the militia and culturally in a common worldview. Popular arming may be a good risk, but it must be calculated. It will not do to recommend an individual right to arms on the premise that the people will exercise that right in unity, unless we have reason for believing that the people will so act. Yet for all his thoughtfulness, Reynolds gives us no good reason for so believing.

The need for such a reason has become acute in light of the appeals court's decision in *United States v. Emerson*[36] because through this opinion the individual rights theory has, at a stroke, achieved judicial credibility and become law in the Fifth Circuit. In state court, Timothy Joe Emerson's wife secured a temporary injunction that restrained him from harming or threatening to harm her or their daughter.[37] Shortly thereafter, a federal grand jury indicted Emerson for possessing a gun in violation of a federal law—18 U.S.C. section 922(g)(8), which prohibits gun possession to anyone subject to a court order that restrains him from threatening an intimate partner and that "explicitly prohibits the use, attempted use, or threatened use of physical force against such intimate partner." The district court, however, dismissed the indictment. In the court's view, the Second Amendment protects an individual right, and application of this federal law to Emerson would therefore be unconstitutional.[38]

On appeal, the majority of a three-judge panel of the Fifth Circuit agreed that the amendment protects a personal right. The recent work of individual rights theorists directly laid the groundwork for this history-making opinion; in some ways, *Emerson* is the house that Kates and Levinson built. In introducing the individual rights model of the amendment, the circuit court itself commented that this theory "has enjoyed considerable academic endorsement, especially in the last two decades"[39]—citing to work by Levinson, Lund, Kates, and Reynolds, among many others.[40] The opinion itself reads more like a law journal article than a typical opinion: it is uncommonly long, dense with citation, and weighty with historical reference. The majority even reprimanded its sister circuits for adopting the states' rights view "without sufficient articulated examination of the history and text of the Second Amendment."[41] And concurring separately, Judge Parker plainly believed that the majority opinion should be understood as a response to recent Second Amendment scholarship: "No doubt the special interests and academics on both sides of this debate will take great interest in the fact that at long last some court has determined (albeit in dicta) that the Second Amendment bestows an individual right."[42]

Given this background, it is not surprising that the majority's opinion replicates the structure and primary arguments of a typical law journal article by an individual rights theorist. First, the opinion addresses precedent. Breaking with all other circuit courts but joining the individual rights theorists, the panel adopted the broad reading of *United States v. Miller*; in this view, the Supreme Court rejected Miller's claim because the amendment did not cover his type of gun, rather than because Miller was not a member of a state militia.[43] Second, the majority addressed the language of the amendment. In its view, the "people" refers to all individuals as individuals, and the "militia" of the preamble similarly referred to the whole of the private citizenry, ready for service.[44] Third, the court surveyed the history of the Second Amendment, arguing that although the Anti-Federalists wanted to protect both state power over the militias and the individual right to arms, the Second Amendment guaranteed only the latter.[45] And finally, the circuit reproduced a great deal of eighteenth- and nineteenth-century commentary that, in the view of individual rights theorists, describes the Second Amendment as a protection for the individual.[46]

The appeals court followed the work of individual rights theorists in another way as well: like them, the court first argues that individuals hold the right to arms, but then it maintains that come the revolution, a collectivity called the people will exercise those rights. As a result, the court implicitly asserts, we need not fear anarchy or civil war because in this rhetorical construct the people will act as one. Thus, the court bluntly holds that the right is individual and personal, not tied to the militia: "We hold . . . that [the Second Amendment] protects the right of individuals, including those not then actually a member of any militia or engaged in active military service or training, to privately possess and bear their own firearms." And as the opinion limits protection only to those arms that "are suitable as personal, individual weapons,"[47] the majority would appear to be asserting that the Second Amendment protects the right to arms primarily for personal uses like hunting and self-defense. In other words, would-be revolutionaries may not claim protection for their howitzers and stinger missiles so as to launch a revolution.

Thus, the panel keeps its focus on the use of arms in private contexts, rather than for revolution, a concept that the opinion generally keeps locked away in the attic. Even when discussing the militia, the circuit continues this focus. In its view, reading the amendment as an individual right does not render the preamble "marginal or lacking in true significance." Instead, an individual right to arms will serve the preamble's goals because it would "foster[] the development of a pool of firearms-familiar citizens that could be called upon to serve in the militia" and so "greatly reduce the need for a standing army."[48] Nowhere in this discussion does the panel hint that a militia might ever take up arms against the federal government. Instead, the point in the amendment was to protect private arms, which would make a militia possible, which would make an army less likely, which would then produce a central government less likely to trample its people's rights. Through this chain of causation, we secure freedom from federal oppression simply by owning our guns in a private setting, without ever invoking the right of resistance.

And yet, the idea that the Second Amendment contemplates armed resistance is present in the background throughout this opinion, if never explicitly confirmed in text. It makes its appearance most often in the historical materials on which the panel relies. They are too many to reproduce, but they include the passages most favored by individual rights theorists. For example, the opinion quotes Justice Story's claim that the Second Amendment "offers a strong moral check against the usurpation and arbitrary power of rulers; and will generally, even if these are successful in the first instance, enable the people to resist, and triumph over them."[49] Similarly, the court relies on Thomas Cooley's description of the amendment as "a necessary and efficient means of regaining rights when temporarily overturned by usurpation."[50]

At only one point does the panel assert in its own voice that the amendment protects a right to arms for the purpose of resistance. In footnote 53, the panel describes *Federalist* number 46, in which Madison promised that the new federal government could not become tyrannous because if it tried, then the people would simply rise up. In the circuit's view, therefore, "Federalist 46 clearly depends, in large part, on the people being armed. In this respect, Madison's rationale in Federalist 46 is substantially the same as that of the Second Amendment which he would craft over a year later." In other words, *Federalist* 46 and the Second Amendment have the same rationale: the people must be armed so that they may resist federal tyranny. And at just this point, the court's language profoundly changes. Instead of emphasizing the "individual, personal" nature of the right, the panel argues that the amendment enables the collective "American people" to resist: "Madison's message in Federalist 46 is clear: the Anti-Federalists were not to worry about federal tyranny because those who comprised the militia could resist tyranny since the American people were armed. Federalist 46 speaks about the significance of the government trusting the people with arms. . . . Federalist 46 clearly depends, in large part, on the American people being armed."[51]

As do the other libertarians, the panel thus veers toward populism when the subject becomes revolution: all those individuals, with all their particular aims and desires and values and beliefs, rhetorically and magically become a single entity. And all the worries about an individual right to arms for resistance — who can revolt? when? how? how will they coordinate? and what if there is disagreement? — disappear into the soothing embrace of an abstract noun: the people will act as a unit when the people think it time.

In the end, Timothy Joe Emerson lost before the circuit. Although the appeals court agreed that the Second Amendment protects an individual right, it reversed the district court on the grounds that the right is subject to appropriate regulation — as are all constitutional rights. According to the circuit, both Emerson and the district court would agree that the restraining order would have been consistent with the Second Amendment if it had "contained an express finding . . . that Emerson posed a credible threat to the safety of his wife."[52] According to the circuit, however, 18 U.S.C. section 922(g)(8) does not apply unless the state court issuing the restraining order finds that the party enjoined posed "a real threat or danger of injury to the protected party."[53] Further, the court found that Texas law would not allow the court to issue the order against Emerson without such a finding. Therefore, although Emerson enjoyed an individual right to his guns, that right was subject to regulation in order to protect the safety of his wife.[54]

Yet although Emerson may have lost the battle before the court of appeals, the individual rights theorists won the war. The Standard Model is now the law of the Fifth Circuit. The *Emerson* opinion, moreover, may force the Supreme Court finally to revisit *Miller* after all these years. As there is now a split in the circuits on the amendment's meaning, the Supreme Court may feel obliged to settle the issue, so as to provide the nation with some legal uniformity. And there is even some chance that the Supreme Court may adopt the Fifth Circuit's analysis. On the constitutional organization of violence, that analysis depends on an implicit but crucial premise: when it comes time to take up arms against government, all those individuals vested with the right to arms will become a people.

The principal failure of the individual rights theory is therefore its truncated analysis: it does not explain whether or how individual gun owners will become a people under revolutionary conditions. States' rights theorists often allege that individual rights theorists encourage anarchy and rebellion. In point of fact, these writers do not generally wish to give individuals or groups a right of resistance; they sensibly fear the consequences of any such course. Instead, they want to ensure that *the people* will have the right and the ability to revolt. Their failure is in simply assuming that individuals comprise such a people. The stakes are too great to rely on casual assumption: in pondering the constitutional organization of violence, we need to ponder openly and honestly whether we are a people, so that the amendment can still bear its original meaning.

Populists

When they discuss revolution, individual rights theorists thus usually become populists: the right to own arms for revolution may belong to individuals, but the right to use them in revolution belongs to the people. For either of those rights to make sense in its own terms, therefore, there must be something called the people to use the guns protected by the amendment. In fact, however, Americans have not comprised a united people on the use of guns for quite some time.

The theorists that I have discussed so far disagree on important substantive matters, often with rancor. They all agree, however, that the amendment should be approached as a formal rule of law applicable to all Americans rather than as the particular cultural property of some. They all therefore maintain that the amendment assigns rights to generic individuals, whether individual gun owners or militia members, not to groups or individuals defined by their race, religion, gender, or culture. Considered thus as a set of formal propositions, the Second Amendment should be understood not only for what it is but also for what it is not. It is not the special emblem of some particular group, and it envisions the social world as composed of abstract selves, not of a fractured collection of specific cultural identities.

If theorists have considered the amendment in this abstract way, however, many others have regarded it as a symbol in an ongoing *Kulturkampf*. So considered, the amendment is not a culturally neutral rule but the central constitutional icon for a special constituency: the gun culture. Thus, arguments about gun control and the Second Amendment are not just about guns; rather, they are about a whole collection of values, for which guns serve as a symbol. The national discussion about the Second Amendment and gun control is therefore marked by uncommon rancor because the participants are arguing about the worth of varying ways of life.

THE GUN CULTURE

The gun culture does not include all those who happen to own guns. Rather, it includes only those who find a special meaning in owning guns. This culture, like gun ownership in general, is concentrated in white rural males, especially in the South. Some years ago, B. Bruce-Briggs wrote what has become the classic exposition of this cultural battlefield:

> Underlying the gun control struggle is a fundamental division in our nation. The intensity of the passion on this issue suggests to me that we are experiencing a sort of low-grade war going on between two alternative views of what America is and ought to be. On the one side are those who take bourgeois Europe as a model of a civilized society: a society just, equitable, and democratic; but well ordered, with the lines of responsibility and authority clearly drawn, and with decisions made rationally and correctly by intelligent men for the entire nation. To such people, hunting is atavistic, personal violence is shameful, and uncontrolled gun ownership is a blot on civilization.
> On the other side is a group of people who do not tend to be especially

articulate or literate, and whose worldview is rarely expressed in print. Their model is that of the independent frontiersman who takes care of himself and his family with no interference from the state. They are "conservative" in the sense that they cling to America's unique pre-modern tradition—a neofeudal society with a sort of medieval liberty writ large for every man. To these people, "sociological" is an epithet. Life is tough and competitive. Manhood means responsibility and caring for your own.

This hard-core group is probably very small, not more than a few million people, but it is a dangerous group to cross. From the point of view of a right-wing threat to internal security, these are perhaps the people who should be disarmed first, but in practice they will be the last. . . . [T]hey consider themselves no threat to anyone; they are not criminals, not revolutionaries. But slowly, as they become politicized, they find an analysis that fits the phenomenon they experience: Someone fears their having guns, someone is afraid of their defending their families, property, and liberty. Nasty things may happen if these people begin to feel that they are cornered.[55]

The historians Lee Kennett and James LaVerne Anderson offer a similar analysis:

The gun, then, is part of a whole series of traditional attitudes about government, society, and the individual. They run, like so many threads, through the whole tapestry of the national past. In its essence, the gun controversy is a struggle between these attitudes and new ones. The city has spawned the new and negative view of the gun; rural and small town America tends to hold to the older, more positive view. There is also evidence of cleavage along class lines. . . . [T]he gun controversy [is] a skirmish in the larger battle over the nation's cultural values, a battle in which "cosmopolitan" America is pitted against "bedrock" America. . . . Cosmopolitan America foresees a new age when guns and the need for them will disappear; bedrock America conceives of it as 1984. Cosmopolitan America has always been concerned about its international image; bedrock America has always been nativist.[56]

After examining the writings of the gun press, another analyst summarizes the themes of the gun culture thus: "1. The gun owner is a patriot. . . . 2. The gun owner is social. . . . 3. The gun owner appreciates nature. . . . 4. The gun owner is able to survive through his weapons. . . . 5. The gun owner respects tradition and the teachings of his elders."[57] Finally, the sociologists James D. Wright, Peter H. Rossi, and Kathleen Daly provide a similar characterization: "The values of this [gun] culture are best typified as rural, rather than urban; they emphasize independence, self-sufficiency, mastery over nature, closeness to the land, and so on. Within this culture, the ownership and use of firearms are both normal and normatively prescribed, and training in the operation and use of small arms is very much a part of what fathers are expected to provide to their sons — in short, this training is part and parcel of coming of age."[58]

THE GUN CULTURE'S ENEMIES: THE LIBERAL ELITE

Both partisans and enemies of the gun culture in America thus agree on one point: a distinctive gun culture exists at the center of intense cultural division.[59] Perhaps the most patent contemporary enemy of the gun culture is the liberal elite that would take the culture's guns through gun control. The gun culture and the liberal elite are separated by several fault lines. The first is geographic: the gun culture is predominantly rural and small town, and its enemies are predominantly urban.[60] Moreover, the South is a special center of the gun culture.[61] The second fault line is ideological: cosmopolitan America believes in bureaucratic rationality and state authority, and bedrock America believes in armed self-reliance. The third fault line is class: the gun culture is predominantly working class, its enemies predominantly professional and upper middle class.[62] The fourth fault line involves internationalization: the gun culture tends to nativism, suspecting foreign ideas, while its enemies welcome them. The fifth fault line involves control of the production of knowledge: the gun culture believes that its enemies in the media and the academy have created a stereotyped image of gun owners. The sixth fault line is chronological: the gun culture sees itself as the preserver of traditional American values, its enemies as the proponents of new ideas, especially collectivism.

In short, in this description the cultural landscape of the Second Amendment is divided between bedrock and cosmopolitan America. In describing the landscape this way, many commentators emphasize the relative powerlessness of the gun culture: today, the culture feels embattled, distant from power, and disdained by an urban elite. Thus, Levinson writes, "For too long, most members of the legal academy have treated the Second Amendment as the equivalent of an embarrassing relative. . . . Those of us who agree with [an] emphasis on the desirability of encouraging different 'voices' in the legal conversation should be especially aware of the importance of recognizing the attempts of [gun culture members] to join the conversation. . . . [S]urely the call for sensitivity to different or excluded voices cannot extend only to those groups 'we' already, perhaps 'complacent[ly],' believe have a lot to tell 'us.' "[63] Wright, Rossi, and Daly hit the same note: "To members of the gun subculture, . . . the indictments of gun control advocates must appear to be incomprehensible, if not simply demeaning. We should not be surprised to learn that they may resent being depicted as irresponsible, nervous, potentially dangerous. . . . Indeed, one can only begin to understand the virulence with which gun control initiatives are opposed in these quarters when one realizes that what may be at stake is a way of life. . . . A critical issue in America is whether the doctrine of cultural pluralism should or should not be extended to cover members of the gun subculture."[64]

THE GUN CULTURE'S ENEMIES: OUTGROUPS

On this common map of the Second Amendment's cultural landscape, such traditional outgroups as Jews and African Americans do not appear. The gun culture's enemy is an urban elite that, on its face, is not associated with a particular race, religion, or gender. Indeed, to the extent that any bloc appears as an outgroup, it is the gun culture itself, powerless and reviled.

It is possible, however, to observe another division in the cultural landscape: as part of bedrock America, the gun culture has commonly proclaimed itself to be the voice of the true American people. In this self-image, far from being an embattled outgroup, the culture is the definition of 100 percent Americanism. Correlatively, the enemies of the gun culture include not merely urban elites but anyone who would contest that self-image. In this conception, the culture's enemies include outgroups like Jews, feminists, and African Americans, who have generally not felt themselves to be a part of the gun culture and who insist the gun culture is no more at the center of American peoplehood than they are.

Thus, I use the term *outgroup* in a special sense. I do not mean to define outgroups by their distance from political power or financial resources — although many suffer from that handicap. Instead, I define outgroups in cultural terms: when Americans have sought to define their peoplehood in strong cultural terms (as would the gun culture), certain groups have either been excluded or felt excluded from that imaginative construct. In my use of the term, outgroups are therefore those excluded from traditional notions of American peoplehood. To be sure, not all Americans would define their peoplehood in such a culturally restrictive way. But for those who have done so, Jews, African Americans, and feminists have generally fallen outside the bounds. These are the groups who have most to fear from an armed uprising of those who claim to represent the true American people.

If members of the gun culture feel embattled, they have not always felt so. Indeed, traditionally, these Americans have seen themselves as populist defenders of the establishment, the forces of law, order, and authority. As such, members of the gun culture were responsible for policing "deviant" elements within American society. Tracing the origin of the modern gun culture, Kennett and Anderson explain, "In the development of American society the enemy became internal. Society felt threatened by criminals, ethnic groups, racial groups, rioters, and malcontents. . . . Violence became more closely associated with the use of firearms. . . . [T]he Americans of the nineteenth century became armed individuals as a reaction to the increasing diversity and complexity of their society."[65] In that environment, "pervasive was the idea that the gun helped preserve the social fabric of the nation, 'the establishment.' Those who were not in that establishment, notably slaves and Indians, were the only people who had no business being armed. Even if they were, their cause was hopeless, for they would be outgunned. . . . Perhaps this was not the best solution, but it was a distinctly American one, incorporating the idea that the gun is its own antidote. . . . Elsewhere the armed masses remained a vision of revolutionaries. In America, by a curious inversion, they became a symbol of order and a conservative totem."[66] Richard Hofstadter similarly writes, "In the historic system of the South, having a gun was a white prerogative . . . [and] an important symbol of white male status."[67]

In his massive three-volume study of the myth of the frontier,[68] Richard Slotkin examines how myths of violence have supported dominant groups and subordinated outgroups. In particular, he argues that the myth of the frontier—that America takes its special character from its frontier origins— has been a central organizing story of American popular culture.[69] This myth's primary components are "regeneration through violence" and "savage war." In this story, Americans have achieved progress by separation from civilization on the frontier, regression to a more primitive state, and then redemption by means of violence. The most common form of such regeneration is the "savage war": "Ineluctable political and cultural differences—rooted in some combination of 'blood' and culture—make coexistence between primitive natives and civilized Europeans impossible on any basis other than that of subjugation. . . . [B]ecause of the 'savage' and bloodthirsty propensity of the natives, such struggles become 'wars of extermination.' "[70] This myth originated in the European experience with Indians, but later Americans used it as a favorite framework to explain the need to deal violently with resistance of any kind, such as labor strife and class warfare, African American unrest after the failure of Reconstruction and during the 1960s, antiwar protesting during the Vietnam War, and drug traffickers during the drug war.[71] In every case, this national mythology furnished a rationale for white male supremacy: "Even in its liberal form, the traditional Myth of the Frontier was exclusionist in its premises, idealizing the white male adventurer as the hero of national history."[72]

To this day, the gun culture often portrays itself not as one culture among many but as the true, authentic American culture. This self-portrait is especially vicious among some members of the militia movement. As I will explain in the next chapter, militia writers interpret the Second Amendment as conferring a right to revolution on a unified American people that excludes a wide range of Others: African Americans, Jews, secularists, internationalists, non-libertarians, and so forth. That self-portrait, moreover, is not limited to the militia fringe: even moderates in the gun culture describe it as the quintessence of the American experience. Eugene Balof writes, "Bearing arms is thus seen as not only a defense of the nation, but more importantly, the possession, use, and interest in arms is seen as a uniquely American . . . trait. The gun owner is an American just as the American is a gun owner."[73]

Even law review writers often identify the gun culture with a truer American culture. These commentators commonly argue that the gun culture is the authentic descendant of the Framers' worldview, and gun culture opponents are therefore cultural auslanders. Thus, in arguing that the right to arms should be protected through the Ninth Amendment, Nicholas Johnson writes, "By many accounts the framers envisioned a rural agrarian based America. . . . [W]e can usefully ask whether disarmament advocacy is driven by an urban vision that exalts luxury at the expense of individual liberty. To the degree that it is, it may be in conflict with our core constitutional values."[74] Then, after quoting Bruce-Briggs's description of the culture war reproduced above, Johnson opines, "An individual right to arms fits very comfortably within the vision of rural Americans. Because rural life is not glorified in our society, the rural vision may not be popular. Nonetheless, it remains reasonable to believe that vision of America is more in accordance with that of the framers than is the urban based view that may be the predominant influence on our popular culture."[75] Similarly, after quoting Bruce-Briggs, Don Kates writes, "If we assume that most modern scholars fall into the first of the modern value categories described above, it becomes understandable why they might find the views of the Founders so foreign, indeed repugnant. . . . For the second of the value categories described above accords perfectly with the views of the Founders, except that, as intellectuals themselves, its aura of anti-intellectualism would have struck no responsive chord in them."[76]

Even as sophisticated and culturally sensitive an analyst as David Kopel portrays the gun culture in the same general way. In his prize-winning work *The Samurai, the Mountie, and the Cowboy,* Kopel argues that different gun control schemes are appropriate for different countries because they have different cultures.[77] Countries like Japan and Great Britain, for example, can tolerate an invasive gun control scheme because their citizens trust the government, especially the police, and they may have good reasons for that trust.[78] Such a scheme would not work in this country, however, because guns and distrust of government are too central to the American cultural experience.[79] Thus, Kopel emphasizes the importance of paying careful attention to cultural variations when considering the role of guns and gun control in different countries.

Unfortunately, Kopel's nuanced appreciation of cultural difference falters when he comes to America's gun culture because he tends to portray it as the fundamental, enduring American culture, rather than merely one among many. He writes,

> Whether the framers chose wisely or not, their choice cannot be undone. Indeed, the Second Amendment simply reflected the social reality that Americans were already extremely well armed. Gun culture is too deeply embedded in the American soul to change now.... Foreign gun control ... postulates an authoritarian philosophy of government and society fundamentally at odds with the individualist and egalitarian American ethos.... Even if some Americans want their nation to be more like other countries, America cannot be more like them. There are too many guns in America, and too much of an individualist gun culture in the American psyche.... Instead of transplanting foreign gun control and culture to America, a realistic American gun policy must accept the permanence of guns in American life.[80]

In other words, for Kopel, guns reflect a central, ineradicable part of American culture; gun control, by contrast, represents a recent and hopeless attempt to graft elements of foreign culture onto America. For that reason, guns cannot be abandoned, but gun control can. Gun culture is the root of America, gun control culture a feeble and alien transplant.

In short, then, much of the gun culture sees no genuine cultural division among real Americans on the subject of guns; instead, they see America (represented by the gun culture) arrayed in battle against its enemies. In this map of the cultural landscape, the fault line lies not between bedrock and cosmopolitan Americans but between a true America and everyone else. In this alternative vision, gun owners are not a despised outgroup but the ultimate ingroup, responsible for controlling the margins. And they have a story to tell about themselves: once upon a time, they were America, justly glorified and dominant. In recent decades, their position has changed, as urban elites have come to control America, but the gun culture is still the true American way. Everyone else—not only the urban elite but outgroups who do not belong to the culture—should be seen as less central to the American experience.

Because stereotyping is so common in this culture war, I wish to be very clear about this claim. I am arguing neither that all or most gun owners are personally hostile to outgroups, nor that all or most members of the gun culture are personally hostile to outgroups, nor that proponents of the right to arms are personally hostile to outgroups. In the past, the gun culture has, on the whole, held regressive attitudes toward race, gender, and religion. Today, many, perhaps most, members of the culture may no longer hold those attitudes. For example, some proponents of the right to arms, David Kopel among them, are libertarians implacably hostile to bigotry as a restriction on liberty. In our new world, in which public revelation of bigotry is unacceptable, it is difficult to know how much the gun culture retains its old biases.

Personal bigotry, however, is not the point. The point is that the gun culture believes that it represents the true American people, and those who fall outside its bounds are correspondingly less central. And for one reason or another, the gun culture has a core constituency—white, rural males with conservative values, especially in the South. The NRA may launch membership drives for women, and some militia groups may point proudly to their few members of color. Those gestures, however, merely reinforce the point: African Americans, feminists, Jews, and members of similar outgroups are anomalies in the gun culture. Particular feminists, Jews, and African Americans may own guns; some may even view themselves as part of the gun culture. As a group, however, they fall outside the traditional gun-owning heartland. And in the gun culture's view, if they are not part of the gun culture, then they are also less American.

To some extent, outgroups are not part of the gun culture because they do not want to be: as I will detail in the next section, members of these groups see in the culture values antithetical to their own. But it must also be observed that even today outgroups are not part of the gun culture because that culture's milieu is not open to people from other backgrounds. For example, as observed above, the gun culture is "heavily masculine," centered on the father-son relationship and the male responsibility for protection.[81] Feminists who would problematize gender roles would not be welcome in such a patriarchal milieu. Similarly, per capita, Protestants are much more likely than other groups to own arms.[82] Revealing his own non-Protestant frame of reference, Bruce-Briggs explains, "The first gun at puberty is the *bar mitzvah* of the rural WASP."[83] Given the soil in which the gun culture has grown, this religious identification is not surprising: rural, conservative, nativist Americans have always been overwhelmingly Protestant, and they have identified Protestantism with the national character.[84] Indeed, when the gun culture describes its enemies as the urban, educated, professional, media-oriented liberal elite, it is difficult not to catch a whiff of anti-Semitism. As we will see, Jews for the Preservation of Firearms Ownership—a Jewish right-to-arms group—obviously senses this odor: in their view, when most gun owners imagine the hated "gun-grabbers," they have Jews in mind.

Similarly, as we have seen, the gun culture originated in the concerns of white citizens to control those of other races, especially African Americans and Native Americans. Today, the composition of the culture reveals its racial identification: rural, conservative, nativist Americans have always been white.[85]

Although African Americans own guns in roughly the same percentages as whites and arms bearing has been symbolically important to many African Americans,[86] still they are not part of the gun culture's bedrock America. As I will later elaborate, the gun culture has typically posed a threat, not a promise, to African Americans. Racial hierarchy and violence formed an important part of the gun culture in the South in the nineteenth and early twentieth centuries.[87] Even today, southerners own guns in much larger percentages than nonsoutherners, and white southern gun owners may display greater racial animus than white southern non–gun owners.[88] Moreover, racism has always blemished the tradition of rural radicalism that marks one extreme of the gun culture.[89]

Some members of the gun culture would surely resist this characterization. They would claim that perhaps once the culture excluded outgroups, but no longer. Such a claim, however, bears a heavy burden of persuasion. Populist movements of the common man have always grown from the rich soil of bedrock America. As I will detail in chapter 7, those movements have always imagined not one but two enemies — urban elites and outgroups — and populist violence has typically been directed not at elites but at despised outgroups. Things may have changed, but there is reason to hesitate before we casually accept that conclusion.

More important, it really does not matter why outgroups fall outside the gun culture, whether because the culture excludes them or because they have excluded themselves. The important point is that they do not in fact belong. Even today, the paradigmatic member of the gun culture is a white, Protestant, rural, conservative, nativist male. If the gun culture ever makes a revolution in the name of the people, it will largely be for the benefit of this sort of person. And therefore, populist readings of the Second Amendment cannot simply presume that the people will rise up in majestic unity. The myth of regenerative violence may no longer be bigoted (or it may), but it still pits a true American people against those who would corrupt the citizenry with their foreign ideas.

OUTGROUP ATTITUDES TOWARD THE GUN CULTURE

If the gun culture has exiled outgroups from its embrace, outgroups have also typically been voluntary exiles; the suspicion has always been mutual. Generally, outgroups have maintained that being a feminist or Jew or African American entails being in opposition to the gun culture. Sometimes these arguments verge on the essentialist claim that outgroups are inherently anti-gun, but more often they simply claim that outgroups have found the gun culture alien and threatening.

Thus, traditionally, guns have been culturally coded as male and antifemale. The status of guns as phallic symbols is a cliche in these post-Freudian days.[90]

As I will explore in chapter 7, many women learning to shoot guns find it difficult to overcome their socialization as women: their fear of guns, their aversion to violence, and their sense that guns are a part of male culture off-limits to them. Many feminists argue that women are either inherently or culturally nurturant and pacifistic, not militarist and violent. Thus, Ann Scales argues that the force inherent in militarism legitimates the silencing of women: "Militarism *normalizes* the oppression of women. It supplies the moral authority for relations of dominance and submission. . . . [T]he militaristic individual has been drilled in the necessity and legitimacy of the use of force. . . . This kind of force, hanging over our heads at every moment, has 'the ability to turn a human being into a thing while he is still alive.' . . . And that is a definition of women's otherness. Women have been imitating nothingness for a long time."[91] Sara Ruddick further argues that "maternal thinking" lends itself to a politics of peace.[92] Ruddick notes the typical belief that men make wars and women make peace,[93] but she rejects this absolute distinction because even mothers have warlike impulses to support soldiers and to fight for parochial interests.[94] Instead, she offers a more limited argument: under the right circumstances, maternal thinking can form a basis for a peace politics because it is rooted in caring labor, especially the care of bodies.[95] By contrast, she argues, militarist thinking abstracts away real human suffering and so makes violence easy.[96]

Wendy Brown, whom I have considered as a states' rights theorist, advances a feminist analysis of the Second Amendment that rests on this perceived antinomy between women and guns. First, she attacks a Second Amendment that takes no cognizance of gender, particularly "Levinson's vision of an armed citizenry, collectively resisting the excesses of state power on behalf of itself as a community." Brown argues that this superficially universalist vision ignores the lived experience of outgroups. She contends that Americans do not constitute a unified community and instead live under conditions of "thoroughly disintegrated public life and disintegrating social order, . . . of rampant violence within and against the urban poor and against women of all socio-economic classes." Under those conditions, a right to arms will largely hurt the "most routine victims of this 'right' ": "Black men between the ages of sixteen and thirty-four, for whom homicide is the leading cause of death, and women, one of whom is raped every six minutes, one out of three times at gunpoint or knifepoint."[97] Seeking to expose the bias of a purportedly universalist interpretation, she asks rhetorically, "Might there be something a bit 'gendered' about a formulation of freedom that depicts man, collectively or individually, securing his autonomy, his women, and his territory with a gun?"[98]

Having exposed the amendment as culturally biased, Brown then argues that women, feminists especially, fall outside this culture. She makes this argument by means of a personal story I have already reviewed: after a long hike, she discovers that her car will not start, but a man emerges from a nearby Winnebago and helps her start it. When she first sees him, her chief rescuer is wearing an NRA cap and perusing a pornographic magazine. Despite being helped by this man, Brown found herself reflecting that if she had met him alone, she would have feared rape, and "his guns could well have made the difference between an assault my hard-won skills in self-defense could have fended off and one against which they were useless." In other words, because of the "social positioning and experiences of men and women, in our culture," the right to arms primarily benefits men, as Brown observes by closing with rhetorical questions: "Who is the gun-carrying citizen-warrior whose power is tempered by a limit on the right to bear arms? Is he most importantly a republican citizen, or more significantly, a socially male one? Is his right my violation, and might his be precisely the illegitimate authority I am out to resist?"[99]

Similarly, many Jews have traditionally defined themselves as fundamentally nonviolent: gentle, weak, and rational.[100] In the face of long-term persecution, these Jews resolved to oppose violence with reason; indeed, some have argued that "speaking truth to power" is a central Jewish activity.[101] Perhaps the foremost scholarly exponent of this view is the anti-Zionist writer Michael Selzer, who maintains that "Jewish ethics and purpose derive from the rejection of power, from the actual *contempt of* power which pervades the Jewish ethos."[102] Some attribute theological significance to this ethical norm: God has commanded the Jews to adhere to the covenant, even in the face of persecution, by "representing God's ways in the world and by serving as God's spiritual agents in society."[103]

The identification of Judaism with nonviolence has also permeated popular Jewish culture. In their classic study of shtetl culture, Mark Zborowski and Elizabeth Herzog explain that the culture was "at one in regarding physical violence as 'un-Jewish'." In this view of the world, Jews emphasized "intellect, a sense of moderation, . . . and the cherishing of rational, goal-directed activities," and they rejected the un-Jewish "emphasis on the body, excess, blind instinct, sexual instinct and ruthless force."[104] In the 1940s, Jean-Paul Sartre famously celebrated this view of Judaism: "The Jews are the mildest of men, . . . passionately hostile to violence. That obstinate sweetness which they conserve in the midst of the most atrocious persecution, that sense of justice and of reason which they put up as their sole defense against a hostile, brutal, and unjust society, is perhaps the best part of the message they bring to us and the true mark of their greatness."[105] Finally, Paul Breines describes the continuation of this stereotype in the "Woody Allen figure, that is, the schlemiel: the pale, bespectacled, diminutive vessel of Jewish anxieties who cannot, indeed must not, hurt a flea and whose European forebears fell by the millions to Jew-hating savagery."[106]

Given this tradition, it is not surprising that Jews as Jews have generally located themselves outside the gun culture. Jews own guns in very low percentages compared to other groups.[107] All the leading mainstream Jewish organizations have taken strong positions in favor of gun control, and it may not be a coincidence that the leading advocate of gun control on Capitol Hill, Charles Schumer, is Jewish. Indeed, the central elements of the gun culture — violent self-reliance, toughness, a willingness to meet blow with blow — comprise a virtual definition of "un-Jewish" behavior in this view of Jewishness.

Similarly, African Americans have traditionally fallen outside the parameters of the gun culture. In fact, their relation to guns has been complicated and sometimes conflicted. On the one hand, there is no tradition of viewing guns as "un–African American" in the way that there is for viewing guns as un-Jewish or unfemale. Many southern Blacks participated in the outdoors hunting culture from which the gun culture grew.[108] In addition, as a result of the long tradition of disarming African Americans, many have seen self-arming as an important form of empowerment. Today, African Americans own guns in roughly the same percentages as others, and owning a handgun is a badge of manhood for some inner-city youths.[109] Indeed, some young urban black men romanticize revolutionary violence, especially as they perceive it in the figure of Malcolm X.[110]

Yet pacifism also has been a major part of Black culture as well, perhaps most notably in the work of Martin Luther King and the Southern Christian Leadership Council.[111] Most Blacks, moreover, are neither revolutionaries nor gang members; rather, they view guns in the hands of inner-city youth as a pestilence that is destroying their community. Not surprisingly, prominent African American intellectuals have generally condemned widespread gun ownership and called for tighter gun control. And as a group, African Americans are more in favor of gun control, especially handgun prohibition, than whites.[112]

However complicated the relation of African Americans to guns, their relation to the gun culture is much simpler: they have experienced its hostility. Even those African Americans fondest of guns do not commonly love the gun culture. African American revolutionaries have generally sought to break the white power structure. The first objects of an African American revolution would probably be urban, such as the police,[113] but rural, conservative, bedrock America would not be far behind. Indeed, Carl Rowan predicts that the next race war will come — and come soon — when Blacks take up arms to defend themselves from attack by the white racist members of the militia movement.[114] In fine, Black revolutionaries typically have shown no inclination to make common cause with the gun culture, to join with them in celebration of their shared devotion to self-arming. On the contrary, they have seen them as likely opponents.

Recently, Carl Bogus has argued that not only the gun culture in general but the Second Amendment in particular has threatened African Americans.[115] Bogus joins the states' rights theorists in maintaining that the amendment was designed to protect the state militias against federal disarmament. In Bogus's view, however, the concern to safeguard the militia grew from a desire to protect its function as slave patrol: "The Second Amendment may have been inspired as much by a desire to maintain a form of tyranny as to provide a means of resisting tyranny. . . . Why the fear about Congress disarming the militia? . . . Northern states would control Congress, and the North was finding slavery increasingly obnoxious. Intentionally or unintentionally, Congress might subvert the slave system by allowing the militia to decay. . . . [S]trong evidence suggests that the Southern states' concerns about maintaining the militias for slave control, and the Northern states' desires to relieve the Southern states' anxiety on the matter, were significant forces behind the Second Amendment."[116]

One could add many more examples of outgroups, including Asian-Americans and gays, lesbians, and bisexuals, who feel excluded from the gun culture, but the general point should be clear. As we will see in chapter 7, a dissenting chorus has recently arisen among some outgroups to problematize this simple division. Eloquent feminists, Jews, and African Americans have come to embrace the amendment. In their view, just as the gun culture has used firearms to control outgroups, those same outgroups can now use firearms to seek liberation. These dissenting voices, however, should not obscure the general map of the Second Amendment's cultural terrain: by and large, the gun culture, claiming to speak for the people, falls on one side of a deep divide; and outgroups and liberal urban elites fall on the other.

THE NATIONAL RIFLE ASSOCIATION

If the gun culture has an institutional home, it is the National Rifle Association. The NRA is a large, diverse organization whose members hold a range of views. The leadership, however, adduces a more unified message. Famously, one of its chief lobbyists explained, "You would get a far better understanding if you approached us as if you were approaching one of the great religions of the world."[117] These leaders consistently cast themselves as defenders of the people — by which they mean the gun culture — against its enemies, who would steal the people's guns, leaving it prey to enslavement. Perhaps the three most prominent personalities in the modern NRA have been Tanya Metaska, Wayne LaPierre, and Charlton Heston, all of whom have held various leadership positions in the organization.[118] The NRA's roots in the gun culture's view of the world are somewhat obscure in Metaska's writings, clearly implicit in LaPierre's, and pointedly overt in Heston's.

Metaska and LaPierre proffer a sustained analysis of the Second Amendment, and they exhibit the familiar slide from libertarianism to populism. Both assert that the amendment protects an individual right to own arms. Metaska explains, "The Second Amendment marks the property line between individual liberty and state sovereignty."[119] Similarly, La Pierre dismisses the view that "the Founding Fathers never meant that *individuals* should be armed."[120] Perhaps the most important function of this right is that it allows individuals to make a revolution against the government. Metaska ridicules the notion that the Founding Fathers wanted to "protect hunting" or "safeguard target shooting."[121] Instead, quoting Hubert Humphrey, she maintains, "The right of the citizen to bear arms is just one more safeguard against a tyranny which now appears remote in America, but which historically has proved to be always possible."[122] Similarly, LaPierre argues that the Second Amendment reflects George Mason's "deep-set belief that the individual armed citizen was the key to protection against government excesses and in defense of freedom."[123]

And yet, predictably, Metaska and LaPierre describe a revolution as an affair of the people, an entity that always acts in unity, rather than of individuals acting in their individual ways. Thus, Metaska asks her readership: if the courts should deny the right to arms, "care to side with the court? Or will you side with the Founding Fathers and the people as the final arbiters of our rights?" In protecting our collective security, the mass of individuals suddenly become a single entity: "Under the Second Amendment, we are not consigned the role of spectator in the struggle for freedom and safety. Under the Second Amendment, we are empowered to become what we should have been all along — an active participant with the state, a co-equal partner in the pursuit of personal and community safety."[124] Surveying the range of successful revolutions in the twentieth century, LaPierre proclaims, "Each of those triumphs tells a simple truth: a determined people who have the means to maintain prolonged war against a modern army can battle it to a standstill."[125] For that reason, he warns, "a people disarmed is a people in danger."[126] The active nouns in all these sentences are singular rather than plural — "a people," "the people," "an active participant," "a co-equal partner," or most simply, "we." And by that semantic choice, the sprawling array of Americans become a single organism, so that we need not worry about anarchy and civil war.

Who is this united people that will organically rise up against tyranny? Metaska and LaPierre agree that only those who protect the Framers' Second Amendment legacy are part of this true and organic American people. As does the gun culture generally, NRA leaders claim cultural primacy because of their perceived special connection to the Founding Fathers. As we have seen, Metaska asks, "Will you side with the Founding Fathers and the people as the final arbiters of our rights?" Later, she opines, "In the Second Amendment, they lit a fire of freedom. And we can read by the light of that fire the two lessons our Founding Fathers intended—power does not belong exclusively in the hands of the state and self-defense is indeed a *primary* civil right."[127] Similarly, LaPierre issues a call to arms: "Every American must leap to the defense of his or her liberties. We must answer, word for word, the vicious attacks that pour out from the TV screen and newspaper pages around the country. . . . We must not allow them to misinterpret our Founding Fathers' directives. Then, and only then, will freedom be safe for future generations."[128] Those who agree with the NRA are thus faithful children of the Fathers, truer sons and daughters than those who have left the ways of the people.

Which Americans have the courage to bear this crucial burden of fidelity? Metaska gives few clues. She repeatedly stresses that the Second Amendment, as she interprets it, benefits a huge range of people. She argues that Democrats, with their devotion to individual rights, should support the right to arms as much as Republicans. To illustrate the importance of a right to arms, she tells stories of a mother defending her child and African American civil rights workers driving off the Klan.[129] Her happy celebration of this diversity leaves the reader wondering why she believes that such a variable group could ever unite behind a single revolution. Metaska, then, appears to be a true individualist who deploys populist rhetoric only to assure us that a revolution need not be atomistic. In short, she conjures with the people.

By contrast, LaPierre deploys rhetoric that will alert members of the gun culture that he is talking about them. Most saliently, he condemns their traditional enemies. Repeatedly, he condemns gun control as a scheme by liberal elites who do not care about the needs of ordinary Americans, that is, the people. Quoting the columnist Charley Reese, he declaims, "The fact that gun control is an elitist effort at people control is easily verifiable."[130] Later, he insists, "Law enforcement's opposition to concealed carry . . . is political, ideological, and elitist. And it lays bare a basic distrust of the people they are sworn to serve."[131] Like others of the gun culture, he accuses the media of sharing this elitist bias, so that ordinary Americans cannot trust the media when they (slantedly) cover the issue of gun control.[132] He maintains, "Media bigwigs . . . set themselves above the average citizen feeding him or her a steady diet of distortion aimed at making everyone conform to their viewpoint."[133] According to LaPierre, on the subject of gun control and Second Amendment rights, the American people as a whole agree with the NRA rather than with the media and other liberal elites.[134] As a result, in his writing the NRA emerges as the people's advocate against a distant minority bent on subverting their fundamental freedoms.

More worrisomely and more subtly, LaPierre paints a portrait of the gun-loving American people in which feminists, Jews, and African Americans may feel distinctly out of place. For example, quoting a former legal director of the Anti-Defamation League, he blames "the American Jewish Community" for supporting gun control: "For years, much of the established Jewish leadership in the U.S. has been reflexively banging the drum for gun control." In his view, Israel survived only because its citizens embraced arms bearing, in contrast to the Jews who perished in the Holocaust: "The different fates of European and Israeli Jews in the past half century demonstrate the folly of a disarmed citizenry entrusting its rights and welfare to the supposed benevolence of its government. None should be more cognizant of this than the Jewish organizations so enamored of gun control."[135] LaPierre avoids open anti-Semitism by claiming that he has the best interests of Jews in mind: for their own good, Jews ought to oppose gun control. Nonetheless, he unmistakably suggests that "the American Jewish Community," as it is currently constituted, falls outside the gun culture. Whether he intends to or not, he reveals the gun culture's aversion to liberal, urban, media-connected "Jewish gun grabbers."

Similarly, his discussion of crime and race reveals to his readership that African Americans constitute an Other against which they define themselves. As in his discussion of Jews, he insists he has the best interests of minorities in mind: because crime disproportionately affects them, they should heed LaPierre's hardheaded advice.[136] In LaPierre's view, however, the cause of crime is society's failure to teach morality, especially the crucial lesson that individuals are responsible for their own actions, no matter how oppressive their backgrounds might be.[137] As LaPierre's discussion proceeds, it becomes clear — sometimes overtly, sometimes in code — that African Americans have failed more than others to heed this lesson.

Again, it is irrelevant to my point whether LaPierre is right in his diagnosis of the cause of crime. The crucial point is that he is speaking for a culture and an organization that apparently views African Americans more as a problem than as cultural brothers and sisters. Indeed, as LaPierre repeats stories of inner-city mayhem, it is difficult to avoid the impression that his readers are anticipating arming themselves *against* African Americans, rather than *with* them as part of the people: "Social factors obviously do play a role in crime, since young minority males from poor, broken homes are much more likely to commit violent crimes. But being poor or not having a pair of $100 tennis shoes should never excuse one person for attacking or killing another person"; "A Capitol Hill aide is murdered because the alleged killer wanted to murder a white"; "Overall crime rates have been stable or declining in recent years; however, . . . [t]he violent crime rate for blacks in 1992 is the highest ever recorded."[138] And so forth.

LaPierre is quick to explain that African Americans in general are not criminals: "Roughly 1.7 percent of black males account for *45 percent of all arrests.*"[139] In LaPierre's view, however, the fault lies not only with those criminals but with the African American community that produced them. To solve the problem of crime, we must teach morality, but, according to LaPierre, African Americans are distinctly failing in this task, through illegitimacy, reluctance to work, and welfare dependency. Thus, according to LaPierre, "the disintegration of the family has taken a frightening turn." This problem afflicts America in general, but it is plainly worse for African Americans: "Over the last thirty years the black illegitimacy rate has jumped from 25 percent to 68 percent generally, and 80 percent in the inner-city. Particularly grievous is the problem of children having children."[140] In LaPierre's view, moreover, illegitimacy brings on poverty, especially because single mothers do not want to work: "This lack of family formation, joined with a rise in family breakup, has also had severe economic and social consequences, especially *when combined with a lowered will to work.* As of 1990, the official poverty rate for two-parent households with one full-time worker was just 2 percent. For all two-parent households, it was 5.6 percent. For female-headed households, it was 32.2 percent, almost one in three. For single women who don't work, the rate was 67 percent."[141] Instead of working, single inner-city mothers go on welfare so as to continue their immoral ways: "Young women, that is, may in effect 'marry' welfare to set up their own households and have babies, no matter whether their fathers ever contribute to the children's upbringing. This is not to say that inner-city women are having children for the money; it is to say that federal funds enable them to escape the normal economic, social, and moral pressures against illegitimacy."[142] And so, according to LaPierre, the answer to crime is ending welfare subsidies, to "reconstruct the larger moral framework," by forcing poor single mothers to marry the fathers of their children or find a job.[143]

In sum, although LaPierre scrupulously avoids openly racist talk, he unequivocally believes that African Americans are failing in their obligations to raise good children — and they have only themselves to blame. Not surprisingly, then, LaPierre quotes with approval African American leaders who urge followers to look for the sources of their problems in themselves.[144] Once again, whether LaPierre's analysis should be thought racist is irrelevant; even whether it is accurate is irrelevant. What is relevant is that in LaPierre's view, African Americans have disproportionately failed in their basic obligations as American citizens; they have voluntarily exiled themselves from the respectable part of the American people — the part that the NRA represents and that embraces gun owning as symbolic of its traditional way of life.

Similarly, LaPierre maintains that feminist ideas have little place in the folkways of the people. For example, he insists that gun control will not help alleviate crime, but restoring the traditional family, which presumably means a family with a dominant father, might: "Changed hearts and the restoration of traditional and stable families . . . could, over time, bring safety back to our streets."[145] In resisting gun control for children, LaPierre celebrates the importance of strong fathers as the central transmitters of the gun culture's norms. He argues that adequately socialized children will not abuse guns: "Youngsters who have been taught safety and respect for guns are not the problem." Quoting from a government report, LaPierre reveals that fathers are the ones responsible for this socialization: "The socialization into gun ownership is also vastly different for legal and illegal gunowners. Those who own legal guns have fathers who own guns for sport and hunting."[146] As we have seen, the gun culture views inculcation into gun owning as part of the father-son relationship. There is little room in this vision for those who would upset traditional gender roles.

Sometimes, LaPierre reveals his androcentricity through coded language rather than overt statements. For example, LaPierre objects to legal rules requiring a defender to retreat — when this can be done safely — before using deadly force to repel an attack, especially when the attack is aimed only at property, rather than personal safety. Instead, LaPierre praises the "Castle Doctrine," "an ancient common law doctrine with origins going back at least to Roman law." This doctrine "proclaims that one's home is a castle and hence an inhabitant may use all manner of force, including deadly force, to protect it and its inhabitants from attack."[147] Although LaPierre states that the doctrine rests on the idea that "*one's* home is *a* castle," in fact the "ancient" saying is that "a *man's* home is *his* castle" — an idea deeply embedded in old patriarchal ideology. Despite LaPierre's rephrasing, the origin of the saying will likely be lost on few of his readers.

The same kind of coded language appears in LaPierre's discussion of

Attorney General Janet Reno's handling of the siege of the Branch Davidian compound in Waco, Texas. After the conflagration, many praised her for accepting responsibility. By contrast, LaPierre argues that accepting responsibility for an atrocity does not somehow absolve one from that responsibility. His language is extraordinary: "Some tried to make her a heroine for taking responsibility when, in fact, she could not escape it. But when Reno took responsibility she appeared to be saying, don't blame me, I stood up like a man and took charge."[148] Janet Reno is, of course, not a man; she was the first female attorney general. Yet in LaPierre's imagination, when she wants to claim credit for herself, she claims to be acting "like a man"—apparently because for LaPierre, acting courageously and taking charge are acting "like a man." In other words, the best that a female attorney general can do is to imitate a man—however poorly. In this context, it is relevant that many gun rights activists refer to Attorney General Reno as "Butcher Reno" for her role in the Waco siege.[149] That title, however, is often shortened to "Butch" Reno, with obvious double entendre: the problem with Reno is that she is a woman who has mannish ways, imagines herself a man, wants to do a man's job, and is trying to take men's guns.[150]

Such coded language may be subtle, but it is revealing, and the examples could be multiplied. So, pared to its essentials, LaPierre's analysis tells a powerful story. Once upon a time, there was a core American people, united by the Framers' principles. Some Americans are still true to those principles, but others have commenced a full-scale assault on the people. Those attackers include elitist supporters of gun control and media bigwigs, including the American Jewish Community, African American hoodlums and welfare mothers, and feminists who would disrupt settled gender roles. Such people are auslanders, threats to the people who hold fast to their guns and to the Framers' beliefs.

If Metaska is uncomfortable with gun culture populism and LaPierre refers to it in code, Charlton Heston openly celebrates it, offering fire and brimstone sermons to the faithful. Near the beginning of a speech that he made before the National Press Club, he encapsulates this theme: "Friends, let me tell you: we are again engaged in a great Civil War—a cultural war that's about to hijack you right out of your birthright."[151] That cultural war is not just about guns but also about a much broader collection of values: "As I have stood in the crosshairs of those who want to shoot down our Second Amendment freedoms, I've realized that firearms are not the only issue. . . . I am not the only target. It's much, much bigger than that." He then asks those who own guns to put up their hands. After a showing of hands, he queries, "How many of you own guns but chose not to raise your hands?" Those who were afraid to reveal their "conviction about a constitutional right" are "victim[s] of the cultural war." They have been "assaulted and robbed of the courage of [their] convictions." And Heston believes others have been similarly shamed into silence: "I could've asked for a show of hands of pentecostal Christians, or pro-lifers, or right-to-workers, or Promise Keepers, or school vouchers, and the result would have been the same." The war over guns is thus part of a broader war over traditional cultural values: "I've come to understand that a cultural war is indeed raging across our land, storming our values, assaulting our freedoms, killing our self-confidence in who we are and what we believe."[152]

This division thus lies between those who hold traditional values and those who do not. The division, however, also lies between demographic groups. On one side are the "self-styled elite,"[153] the "self-appointed social puppet masters,"[154] and the media who have used Heston as a "moving target."[155] On the other side lie those "rank-and-file Americans" being assaulted by the revisionists.[156] And the greatest victims of the culture war are the core constituents of the gun culture: "Heaven help the God-fearing, law-abiding, Caucasian, middle class, protestant, or even worse evangelical Christian, midwest or southern or even worse rural, apparently straight or even worse admitted heterosexual, gun-owning or even worse NRA-card-carrying, average working stiff, because then not only don't you count, you're a downright nuisance, an obstacle to social progress, pal."[157] Heston's prose brilliantly describes both the demographics of the gun culture and its sense of resentment at being moved from cultural dominance to cultural marginality.

Yet if the culture feels peripheralized, it nonetheless claims to be the true bearer of the meaning of America. For Heston, the culture war is not a skirmish over contending, legitimate visions of America. Instead, it is a Ragnarok between those who would preserve America and those who would destroy it. As do so many gun rights activists, Heston divides the citizenry between the true offspring of the Fathers and the bad seed. He asks, "So how do we get out of this mess? Moses led his people through the wilderness, but he never made it to the promised land — not even when I played him. But he did do his job — he pointed his people in the right direction."[158] Like Moses, a father figure who created a people through divine commandments, the American Founding Fathers birthed the American people through the Bill of Rights, which also has about it a divine quality: "Unlike the Ten Commandments, the Bill of Rights wasn't cut into stone tablets. But the text surely has that same righteous feel to it. It's as if you can sense the unseen hand of the almighty God guiding the sweep of a goose quill pen, while a bunch of rebellious old white guys sweated out the birth of a nation." Heston professes to "love this great nation, and the Constitution that defines it." But the revisionist "culture warriors" would assault both the Constitution and the nation: "They're revising and rewriting these truths, yanking the Bill of Rights out of our lives like a parking ticket stuck under your windshield wiper." In short, this "cultural war is not a clash over the facts, or even between philosophies. It's a clash between the principled and the unprincipled."[159]

Yet, fortunately, some Americans can still claim descent from these Founders: "No amount of oppression, no FBI, no IRS, no big government, no social engineers, no matter what and no matter who, they cannot cleave *the genes we share* with our founding fathers."[160] He urges his followers, in words that could have been copied from any ethnonationalist leader, to "trust the pulsing life blood inside you that made this country rise from mud and valor into the miracle that it still is."[161] And he promises them, "Our ancestors were armed with pride, and bequeathed it to us — I can prove it. If you want to feel the warm breath of freedom upon your neck . . . if you want to touch the proud pulse of liberty that beat in our founding fathers in its purest form, you can do so through the majesty of the Second Amendment right to keep and bear arms."[162]

It is impossible to tell whether Heston means us to read these passages metaphorically or literally. If we take them literally, Heston is arguing that only those who can trace their ancestry back to the Framers are true members of the people. As I will elaborate in chapter 6, that view is widely shared among leaders of the militia movement. Even if we take his claim only metaphorically, Heston insists that true Americans imagine themselves to have a genetic connection, a connection in "the blood," to those "rebellious old white guys" who are the only legitimate Fathers of any real American. Just as Reno must strive to be "like a man," all Americans must strive to be like those who can claim biological ancestors among the Framers. Apparently the following need not apply: feminists who see patriarchal attitudes among the Fathers and prefer to trace their ancestry to figures like Susan B. Anthony; Jews who perceive anti-Semitic attitudes among the Framers and prefer to trace theirs to figures like Louis Brandeis; and African Americans who discern racism among the Framers and prefer to trace theirs to figures like Frederick Douglass.

The stakes in this cultural war could hardly be higher: the life or death of the American people and that divine experiment, the American Constitution. As Heston explains, "There, in that wooden stock and blued steel [of a gun], is what gives the most common of men the most uncommon of freedoms. When ordinary hands are free to own this extraordinary, symbolic tool standing for the full measure of human dignity, that's as good as it gets."[163] Gun owners must therefore resist at all costs. Accordingly, Heston exhorts his followers in military metaphors so pervasive that a few examples cannot adequately convey his remarkable tone: "Do not yield, do not divide, do not call truce. It is your duty to muster with pride and win this cultural war";[164] "I promised to try to reconnect you with that sense of purpose, that compass for what's right, that already lives in you. To unleash its power, you need only unbridle your pride and re-arm yourself with the raw courage of your convictions"; "Americans shouldn't have to go to war every morning for their values. They already go to war for their families. . . . They prefer the America they built—where you could pray without feeling naive, love without being kinky, sing without profanity, be white without feeling guilty, own a gun without shame, and raise your hand without apology. They are the masses who find themselves under siege and long for you to get some guts, stand on principle, and lead them to victory in this cultural war."[165]

To emphasize the exigency of the circumstances, Heston also deploys another recurrent metaphor: he compares gun owners to Jews about to be killed in the Holocaust. He observes: "I remember when European Jews feared to admit their faith. The Nazis forced them to wear yellow stars as identity badges. It worked. So—what color star will they pin on gun owners' chests? How will the self-styled elite tag us? There may not be a gestapo officer on every street corner, but the influence on our culture is just as pervasive."[166] Later, he conjures an image of gun owners losing their guns that calls up images of Jews losing their lives: "Lines of submissive citizens, walking in lockstep, threatened with imprisonment, are bitterly surrendering family heirlooms, guns that won their freedom, to the blast furnace."[167] Some might think this metaphor anti-Semitic because the plight of gun owners today—no matter how bad it may be—cannot plausibly be compared to the plight of Jews killed in the Holocaust. To suggest otherwise trivializes the suffering of those Jews. But whatever its message about Jews in particular, the metaphor serves a generally polarizing function: it demonizes the gun-grabbers and strikes terror and hostility into the hearts of gun owners.

In these baleful warnings, the line between figurative and literal meanings once again becomes exceedingly obscure. Heston argues there is a metaphorical war going on and a metaphorical Holocaust in the offing. But he also urges his listeners to keep their very nonmetaphorical guns so as to resist very nonmetaphorical threats. His followers might imagine themselves going to the voting booth and town meeting to fight the metaphorical war, but they also imagine themselves grasping a "wooden stock and blued steel" to defend "the most uncommon of freedoms." The cultural war is only a metaphor now, but Heston urges true Americans to be well armed if it should ever become actual. And, as we have seen over and over, the gun culture believes that it knows how the battle lines will be drawn in that war.

In short, then, both libertarian and populist readings of the Second Amendment project that the American people will make a revolution as a united entity. Both depend on this projection so as to promise that political violence will not get out of hand when all are armed. Yet both fail to supply an adequate definition of that people. Libertarians simply fail to examine the subject at all: they rhetorically insist that all those individuals will just cohere at the appropriate time. Populists, by contrast, define the people in a way that is unacceptably limited. At best, they would include among the people only those citizens who share their basic political values. At worst, they place at the center of the people only a specific demographic class — white, rural, gun-owning males. In neither case does the populist reading project a truly unified uprising of the whole people against a few government miscreants.

The Militia Movement's Theory of
the Second Amendment

The militia movement's theory of the Second Amendment embodies the most extreme version of the populist interpretation. In this theory, elements only implicit in other populist readings become startlingly palpable. As do the NRA rank and file, members of the militia movement hold a variety of views. But the leaders, who are responsible for articulating the movement's official ideology, offer a theory of the amendment that is relatively uniform, internally consistent, dense with citation, and concerned with legality. In brief, these populists imagine a time when the right kind of people — people like them, however defined — will seize power, push the Others to the margin, and walk with the Framers again.

In the wake of the bombing in Oklahoma City, detractors have generally rejected the militia's constitutional analysis out of hand, without careful examination. Yet for several reasons I believe their ideas warrant sustained attention. First, militia groups have the capacity for violence, and so for practical reasons it is important to understand their animating ideology. Second, the militia's theory of the amendment allows us to glimpse mainstream populist theory in exaggerated form and so discern its central elements in starker outline. Third, the movement's attempts to define the American people are highly instructive for any reading of the amendment that would locate power in a united people. If Americans are to develop a healthy populist interpretation, we must avoid the errors the movement commits and surmount the problems it fails to surmount. Only once we catalogue these errors and problems will we have a realistic sense of the task. In the end, we may be less sanguine about success. At a minimum, we will lose the temptation simply to assume that American citizens comprise a single people capable of organic revolution.

The militia movement shares much with libertarians and more mainstream populists: all agree that the Second Amendment gives American citizens the right to arms for revolution; all fear corruption in the federal government; all perceive danger in disarmament; and all insist that the people will use their arms to make a revolution. Unlike the others, militia leaders place great emphasis on the importance of an organized militia for resisting the federal government. On inspection, however, the difference between militia leaders and other individual rights theorists turns out to be small: in the militia's view, the right to arms still belongs to individuals, but for practical reasons they should organize private associations with the aim of being prepared for revolution. These militias do not therefore transform the mass of individuals into a united people: the militias are themselves many, shifting, fractious, and partial, merely the resting ground of the individuals who comprise them.

As a result, militia leaders must explain how they can predict that the people as a whole will make a revolution. Their apparent answer is that the people will act in unity because the people include only a small slice of the actual citizenry. Militia leaders offer slightly varying definitions of the people, but they agree on one point: a grand conspiracy has captured the federal government, against which the people define themselves. In other words, the people are unified in opposition to the hypothesized Other that seeks to oppress the people. Even more distinctly than in mainstream populist theory, the myth of regenerative violence underlies this story. In this sense, the militia's paranoia is necessary, not incidental, to its Second Amendment theory: a revolution is possible only if a people exists, but for the militia a people exists primarily in being united to resist the federal conspiracy.

For heuristic purposes I divide militia thinking about conspiracies into four general themes, which identify four distinct Others. Most militia groups hold one or a combination of these beliefs. First, the overt racists maintain that the true American people includes only white Christians who share a particular conservative heritage; the "mud people," that is, everyone else, have conspired to rob this people of its birthright. This theory highlights the demographic problem in constructing a modern revolutionary people: it must include every demographic category of American citizens and yet still be united. Second, the internationalists believe that a foreign cabal led by the United Nations and including Russia, Israel, the Trilateral Commission, and third world countries has seized control of the federal government. These writers believe that Americans who do not share their belief in a conspiracy are deluded by the media or other elites. This theory highlights the epistemological problem in constituting a people: for Americans to make a revolution, they must perceive empirical reality in the same way. In particular, they must agree that the federal government has become so corrupt that revolution is the only answer.

Third, the antisocialists believe that a cadre of socialists has captured the federal government and is intent on destroying the constitutional liberties of American citizens. In their view, the income tax, land use regulation, and, above all, gun control violate the Constitution. Accordingly, the true American people includes only those who still protect the Constitution as the militia understands it. This theory highlights two problems in constituting a people. The first is the interpretive problem: even if the Constitution constitutes us as a people, we have not seen consensus on the meaning of that text for a long time, perhaps ever. It is difficult to see how the people can make a revolution as a body when they do not agree on the meaning of the document that makes of them a body. Second is the political problem in constituting a people: antisocialists are individualists who resent any intrusion on their freedom of action. Yet it is difficult to see how citizens can become a people if they are independent individuals with nothing in common but abstract freedom. These groups feel contempt for politics, but only by coming together in political space can citizens constitute themselves a people. Fleeing the political system into revolution does not actually free one from politics. If anything, it makes political problems even thornier because one must then construct a people without the benefit of a system. And this problem does not afflict just the militias: millions of Americans share their contempt for politics and so would have difficulty finding a forum for peoplehood.

Finally, the antisecular humanists believe that the government's conspiracy has targeted conservative Christianity, which is the inspiration and fundament of the Constitution. The views of this group raise most of the problems endemic to the other groups' theories. Constituting a people around conservative Christianity poses demographic problems (not all American citizens are conservative Christians), epistemological problems (in the minds of many, there is no conspiracy to de-Christianize America), and interpretive problems (by many accounts, the Constitution does not privilege conservative Christianity).

Any theory of Second Amendment revolution, then, must face demographic, epistemological, interpretive, and political problems. If the people included only a slice of the citizenry, as the militia leaders would have it, perhaps they could unite behind a common cause under revolutionary conditions. At this date, however, it is untenable to confine our definition of the people in this way. Yet if we cast the definition more broadly, we simply return to the prior problem: having a population so committed to individualism and so diverse, how can we credibly predict that these persons will congeal into a united people come the revolution?

The Revolutionary Second Amendment

Militia leaders have written an extensive pamphlet literature that contains a clear theory of the Second Amendment. Although some of their ideas are highly idiosyncratic, some of them mirror the thinking of more mainstream thinkers, even of the amendment's Framers themselves. In fact, the militias insist they have clung to the mental world of the Framers as the nation around them has fallen away. For example, the militia organizer M. Samuel Sherwood dedicated his book *The Guarantee of the Second Amendment* to Samuel Adams, John Hancock, George Washington, George Mason, and Nathanael Greene because of their dedication to organizing colonial militias against British tyranny.[1] Both the Militia of Montana (MOM) and Linda Thompson, self-appointed acting adjutant general of the Unorganized Militia of the USA, have issued declarations of independence from the federal government, documents self-consciously modeled on Jefferson's declaration.[2] MOM's version makes the analogy to the Founders explicit: "Just as our Founding Fathers of this country shook off their shackles of bondage, so must we."[3]

MOM markets a T-shirt that aptly summarizes the movement's theory of the amendment. It bears an image of an eighteenth-century militia member and the legend, "The Second Amendment isn't about hunting or target shooting. . . It's about FREEDOM!"[4] Although telegraphic, the slogan captures three ideas on which many theorists, including the Anti-Federalist proponents of the Second Amendment themselves, might agree: distrust of the central government, the right of the people to make a revolution, and the danger of disarmament.

DISTRUST OF THE FEDERAL GOVERNMENT

In language borrowed from the Framers, militia groups express their fear that the interests of those in government have dangerously diverged from the interests of the citizenry, so that officials are conspiring to empower themselves at the expense of the people. Thus, Thompson declaims, "The federal judicial offices and congress have set themselves wholly apart from and above the people, immune even from suit for their transgressions, answerable to none, and responsive to none except those who further their private interests."[5] MOM urges Americans not to "leave our fate in the hands of corrupted, self-serving foreign mercenaries [in the federal government]" or to "trust our fate to their decisions, which are fostered by agencies of our government and private corporations in it's [*sic*] employ."[6] Warning of martial law to come, Federal Lands Update explains, "Most of the citizens keep saying: 'Aren't those people we sent back to Washington representing our interests?' Frankly, no, they are not! Most have literally isolated themselves from their constituents."[7] In like manner, the Free Militia prophesies, "The fact that officials are infringing gun rights on every front is simply a manifestation of their inner tendency to empower themselves. Left unchecked, this tendency will lead to genuine tyranny."[8]

In this situation, militia groups fear that the federal government will use a standing army to execute its will against an unsuspecting citizenry. Again, these writers borrow heavily from the rhetoric of the Framers to express this fear. Thus, Thompson lists as one of the "Train of Abuses," "The federal government has kept among us, in Times of Peace, Standing Armies, without the consent of our [state] legislatures, or through the seduction and coercion of the state legislatures through the mechanism of 'federal tax monies.' "[9] Militia writers worry especially that the armed services would help to disarm the American public.[10]

The militias' fear focuses not only on the military but also on federal law enforcement agencies, above all, the Bureau of Alcohol, Tobacco, and Firearms (BATF). In the minds of many, the paramilitary equipment and training of federal agencies make them resemble more a standing army than conventional police: "Jack-booted, helmeted, armor-vested 'law enforcement' S.W.A.T. teams now conduct KGB-type raids by kicking down doors in the middle of the night."[11] Observers believe that two BATF actions, the assault on the Branch Davidian Compound and the siege of the white supremacist Randy Weaver at Ruby Ridge, contributed to a dramatic rise in militia membership.[12] Indeed, McVeigh's principal target in the Murrah Building may have been the BATF office. The bombing took place on April 19, 1995, two years to the day after the Waco assault, and militia members are very aware of that date.[13] MOM, for example, announced in its newsletter, "1. April 19, 1775: Lexington burned; 2. April 19, 1943: Warsaw burned; 3. April 19, 1992: The fed's [*sic*] attempted to raid Randy Weaver, but had their plans thwarted when concerned citizens arrived on the scene with supplies for the Weaver family totally unaware of what was to take place; 4. April 19, 1993: The Branch Davidians burned."[14] The warning concludes that Richard Snell, a convicted murderer with ties to the militia movement, would be executed on April 19, 1995, "UNLESS WE ACT NOW!!!"[15]

Also like the amendment's proponents, militia writers fear corruption more in the federal government than in local legislatures. To be sure, the militias do not trust any government, so they offer scant praise for the states. Sherwood reportedly instructed militia members to "go up and look [state] legislators in the face because some day you may be forced to blow it off."[16] As noted, Thompson believes state legislatures have already been corrupted by federal bribes.[17] One element of the militia movement, the Posse Comitatus, active in the 1980s but now reduced, maintains that government above the county level is illegitimate.[18] The overwhelming bulk of militia writing, worrying, and warning, however, involves the federal government, which militias believe is the locus of the conspiracy to destroy America. When revolution comes, it will involve a battle between federal forces and the citizenry. In this Manichean formulation, states, for good or ill, are not principal actors. Sherwood, for example, issued his threat against state legislators simply because he feared they would side with the central government in the coming civil war.[19]

THE SECOND AMENDMENT RIGHT TO REVOLUTION

Because government might become corrupt, in the view of militia leaders the Second Amendment guarantees a right to arms primarily for popular revolution, rather than for hunting or self-defense. The MOM T-shirt encapsulates this view. Thompson similarly argues, "The militia is what the Second Amendment is about, because it isn't about hunting ducks; it's about hunting politicians."[20] MOM further explains, "The majority of American's [*sic*] today, believe the reason that our fore fathers [*sic*] wanted the people to have the right to keep and bear arms was for the purpose of self defense against criminals, hunting, etc. This is *NOT* the primary reason for the enactment of the 2nd Amendment. Let's let Thomas Jefferson explain it for us: '*The strongest reason for the people to retain the right to keep and bear arms is, as a last resort, to protect themselves against tyranny in government.*' "[21]

Like libertarians and other populists, militia writers argue that the Second Amendment guarantees an individual right to arms so that the people may resist government. Once again, in this rhetoric, the right may belong to individuals, but these theorists assume that individuals will somehow cohere into a unity. Thus unified, the people can control government in two ways. First, by threatening revolution, an armed populace can discourage the central government from becoming oppressive in the first place. In this vision, the government should fear the wrath of its citizens. Thus, MOM attributes to Thomas Jefferson the statement, "When governments fear the people there is liberty. When the people fear the government there is tyranny."[22] At another point, MOM explains, "If the militia is independent and viable, then only laws which are right and just will come forth from the government."[23] Similarly, in issuing its "CALL TO ARMS!," the Free Militia exhorts, "Your right and duty is to arm yourself" because "the more citizens that own guns, the less willing the government will be to threaten us."[24]

Second, if the government should become oppressive, an armed and unified population can overthrow it. Federal Lands Update asserts, "IF THE GOVERNMENT USES ITS FORCE AGAINST THE CITIZENS, THE PEOPLE CAN RESPOND WITH A SUPERIOR AMOUNT OF ARMS, AND APPROPRIATELY DEFEND THEIR RIGHTS."[25] Many militia writers rely on the Framers for this proposition, Thomas Jefferson and Patrick Henry being favorites. Quoting the Declaration of Independence, the Free Militia instructs its members to "MEMORIZE": "That whenever any Form of Government becomes destructive of these ends, it is the Right of the People to alter or abolish it, and to institute a new government."[26] The Second Amendment Militia also quotes Jefferson in urging prospective members to join: "The Spirit of Resistance to Government is so valuable on certain occasions that I wish it to be always kept alive."[27] Henry's "liberty or death" speech makes regular appearances in the militia literature: "We are not weak if we make a proper use of those means which the God of nature has placed in our power. Millions of people armed in the holy cause of liberty, and in such a country as that which we possess, are invincible. . . . Is life so dear, or peace so sweet, as to be purchased at the price of chains and slavery? Forbid it, Almighty God! I know not what course others may take; but as for me, give me liberty or give me death!"[28]

DANGER OF DISARMAMENT

Finally, militia writers see a people disarmed as easy prey to federal oppression. Before a government attempts tyranny, it seeks to disarm the citizenry to make it helpless. The populace should therefore fear gun control as a sign of despotic designs afoot. In fact, many believe the conspiracy has already commenced. Federal Lands Update asks, "Why is the federal government in such a hurry to take away the guns of honest, law abiding citizens? Because once we are disarmed, we become as sheep. And the federal government, which has never been a friend of those who insist upon enforcing their Second Amendment rights, will come down hard upon it's [sic] people."[29] The Militia News clarifies the point: "The state must first try to break our will to resist, and then it must confiscate private firearms so that even with the desire and the will we will be unable to resist what is planned for us. This is what gun control is all about."[30] Another source speaks apocalyptically: "In the coming confrontation between the public and the government to disarm the citizenry, they may kill, arrest, imprison, and seize assets from tens or even thousands of

Americans; but they are unlikely to ever completely disarm the millions of Americans who understand the Second Amendment to the Constitution and the warnings of our founding fathers to never let the government disarm them."[31] MOM attributes the same view to Jefferson: "Thomas Jefferson also understood that those who would attempt to take away the liberty of the citizen's [*sic*] of this nation must first disarm them."[32]

According to militia writers, recent gun control statutes are part of a general conspiracy to oppress the American people. Many militia groups insist that when Sarah Brady testified in support of the Brady Bill, she proclaimed, "Our task of creating a socialist America can only succeed when those who resist us have been TOTALLY DISARMED!"[33] They argue that the same plot is behind the ban on assault weapons: "Assault rifles are the teeth of the Second Amendment. Without their bite, there is nothing to prevent a draconian state from devouring all of our precious liberties."[34] Indeed, "the really subversive thing about these two bills is that they are aimed at limiting militias more than at limiting crime."[35] MOM agrees: "The government by passing these Crime Bills and the Brady Bill have [*sic*] shown us that they are attempting to disarm the militias of the several states."[36] And militia writers fear that more persecution is in the works: "There are SEVEN (7) SEIZURE EXECUTIVE ORDERS which can be enacted with the stroke of a bureaucratic pen and the nation will be plunged into an absolute dictatorial, martial law mode of repression."[37]

In the militias' view, this moment in history is critical for the American people. If we proceed much further down the road of disarmament, we will have lost the ability to resist, and freedom will have flown this land forever. The comparison to Hitler's Germany is common. Federal Lands Update lists a series of analogies that begins, "1. In 1935, Adolph Hitler licensed all handguns. 2. In 1993, Bill Clinton licensed all handguns."[38] Similarly, the Free Militia asserts, "The U.S. 1968 Gun Control Act is a word-for-word translation of Adolf Hitler's German gun control laws of 1938 Nazi Germany."[39] A flyer distributed at militia meetings bears an image of Hitler in stiff-armed salute with the caption, "All in favor of 'gun control' raise your right hand."[40] More broadly, MOM argues that disarmament and suppression of the militia were responsible for oppression in East Timor, Poland, Czechoslovakia, Hungary, Romania, Yugoslavia, Italy, and Germany.[41]

Observers agree that along with the events at Waco and Ruby Ridge, gun control statutes are responsible for a rise in militia membership.[42] For militia groups, such statutes are not mere technical violations of the Constitution but direct attacks on the right relation between citizens and government. In this sense, militia groups maintain that the Second Amendment is the heart of the Constitution because when Second Amendment rights disappear, our other rights will quickly follow if there is no armed citizenry to defend them.[43] We have entered the hazardous times the Framers predicted: we can become like Stalinist Russia or Nazi Germany; or we can hold fast to our way of life — but only if we hold fast to our guns.

The Militia and the People

THE MILITIA

Beyond its tendency to exaggerate themes present in other accounts, the militia movement's theory of the amendment is unusual primarily in the role it ascribes to the militia. Like other individual rights theorists, militia writers argue that the eighteenth-century militia included the whole citizenry. From this observation, they conclude that the amendment gives rights to individual Americans rather than to a state militia. Yet unlike most individual rights theorists, these militia leaders stress that individuals must be organized into militias in order to realize the Second Amendment's goals.

To demonstrate that the revolutionary militia included the whole citizenry, these writers again rely on the Framers. Thus, the Militia News quotes George Mason, "I ask sir, what is the militia? It is the whole people, except for a few public officials."[44] Sherwood roughly quotes the Federal Farmer: "A militia, when properly formed, are in fact the people themselves. . . . [T]he constitution ought to secure a genuine force and guard against a select [that is, less than universal] militia, by providing that the militia shall always be kept well organized, armed, and disciplined, and include . . . all men capable of bearing arms."[45] More pithily, Federal Lands Update claims, "Our Founding Fathers defined WE THE PEOPLE as the militia."[46] Similarly, MOM maintains that it was not "the army, or the bureaucratic officials, members of parliament or Governors who made up the militia. . . . It was John Q. Public — the common man."[47] Militia writers further explain that under current law, U.S. armed forces are divided into the National Guard and the organized militia on the one hand and the unorganized militia on the other. According to these writers, the latter consists of the bulk of the citizenry and constitutes the militia contemplated by the Second Amendment.[48]

Like libertarians, then, militia writers identify the militia with the people as a whole unorganized by the government. Unlike libertarians and most other populists, however, they believe that, in the view of the Second Amendment, the people should organize into militias so as to combat government. Indeed, this aspect of militia thinking is what most attracts members[49] and what most alarms fellow citizens. Many Americans believe that the Second Amendment protects their private right to arms, but the militias are arming themselves as intentional political activity. Thus, MOM argues, "Many feel that it is too much to have a militia, that we need to just settle for the possession of arms. . . . [But] [t]he militia, under the second amendment, is to be able to bare [*sic*] arms, meaning to use them in a military confrontation. Not just pack them around the house, yard, or forest. To stand on the second amendment means that you are willing, able, and have desires of belonging to a militia, to whom the right of keeping and bearing arms is guaranteed."[50] Similarly, Federal Lands Update maintains, "The security of a free state is not found in the citizens having guns in the closet. It is found in the citizenry being trained, organized, equipped and led properly."[51] The Free Militia exhorts, "You need to be organized, equipped, trained, and coordinated with other like-minded men to effectively stand up to the growing arrogance of the federal government. It was said during the American Revolution that 'United we stand, divided we fall.' This is still true today."[52] The Second Amendment Committee explains the meaning of the provision: "By putting the militia at the forefront of the sentence which composes the Second Amendment of the Bill of Rights, they [the Framers] stressed the importance of the *collective* use of the right to arms."[53]

As the last quotation illustrates, there is a certain irony in the militia's focus on the collective aspect of the Second Amendment. Militia groups (who are even more progun and antigovernment than the NRA) agree with states rights' theorists (who are generally antigun and progovernment) that the militia clause is crucial to the provision's meaning. By contrast, some proponents of the individual rights view (who share with the militia an enthusiasm for gun rights) have sought to deemphasize the importance of the introductory clause of the amendment because they believe that the right belongs to the people, not to a formal militia. Notoriously, that clause does not even appear in most of the NRA's promotional material.[54]

The irony, however, is more apparent than real because states' rights theorists and militia groups mean very different things when they refer to the militia. The former believe the right to arms exists only in a state body under governmental control; the latter believe it belongs to voluntary militias created by private individuals. As one writer puts the idea, "At no time in our history since the colonies declared their independence from the train of abuses of King George, has our country more needed a network of active militias across America to protect us from the monster we have allowed our federal government to become."[55] For the militias, then, the right to arms is still essentially individual: private citizens with private arms should band together, pooling their resources in order to make them more effective.

THE AMERICAN PEOPLE

The militia theory of the amendment thus presents a tension: on the one hand, when the government becomes corrupt, the people will rise up as a united whole; on the other hand, the revolution will be conducted by militias that are only voluntary associations of private individuals. And so the militias face a familiar query: if the right to arms belongs only to individuals, in all their magnificent diversity, then how can the movement blithely assume that those individuals will make a revolution as a people? As we have seen, this tension infects all variants of the individual rights theory, and the militia leaders' stress on the importance of a militia does not save them from it, as their militias have no status beyond the individuals that make them up. A collection of private militias, therefore, comprises a people no more than does a collection of private gun owners.

In fact, the query is especially pressing for militia writers because even as they are arming in readiness for revolution, the bulk of the citizenry has disowned them. Indeed, as many observers have suggested, the militia draws its membership heavily from groups who feel unjustly disempowered by recent history: angry white males, conservative Christians, rural residents. They prepare for revolution when they feel neglected by the electoral process, and they dream of a time when people like them will again receive their rightful due. But that story is a fantasy of rebellion by a cultural faction, not of revolution by the people as a whole. If militia leaders launch a rebellion today, the bulk of the citizenry will not rise with them.

As do most populist theorists, militia leaders generally resolve this tension by a definitional trick: they assert that only those who enlist in the movement are truly part of the people. All others are traitors or auslanders. As a result, when the movement begins its uprising, they will have the people behind them because they have defined the people as those Americans who will stand behind them. Thus, the movement insists that it represents the American people in opposition to a tyrannical government. The Militia News summarizes this view: "THE U.S. GOVERNMENT HAS DECLARED OPEN WARFARE ON THE AMERICAN PEOPLE."[56] Federal Lands Update asks, "Who are the individuals and organizations that continually demand and insist that you do certain things which run contrary to; [sic] not only your beliefs and convictions, but to the convictions of *the vast majority of the citizens*. Our old friends; [sic] the federal government, of course." In time of crisis, "the militias will be the main defense against tyranny. At this present time, the people are warning federal government; [sic] let us alone or face the consequences."[57] Sherwood demands, "We must look at the reality of the situation and say, who is master, and who is the slave. Who is the servant, and who is the sovereign. In America, the people are the sovereign, then why are we subject to slave laws [that is, gun control laws] with which we do not agree."[58] MOM adds to the refrain: "When the codes and statutes are unjust for the majority of the people, the people will rightly revolt, and the government will have to acquiesce without a shot being fired, because the militia stands vigilant in carrying out the will of the people in defense of rights, liberty and freedom."[59]

These passages contain a powerful myth. In place of a nation of contentious individuals, most of whom disagree with the militia, we see the people, which includes only those who agree with the militia, arrayed in unity against the government. The apotheosis of this view is the condemnation of those who disagree as traitors. For example, the North American Volunteer Militia sent out letters that warn, "Each of you have [*sic*] taken an Oath to uphold the Constitution for the United States. The Oath is your contract with the people. When you violate your Oath of office you become renegade to the Constitution and guilty of treason. I am sure you know what the penalty is for treason."[60] Thompson issued an "Ultimatum" to each member of Congress demanding the repeal of the Brady Bill and of the Fourteenth, Sixteenth, and Seventeenth amendments as well as a declaration that Congress has no criminal jurisdiction on the "soil of any sovereign state." The document concludes, "If you do not personally and publically [*sic*] attend to these demands, you will be identified as a Traitor, and you will be brought up on charges for Treason before a Court of the Citizens of this Country."[61] Such talk of treason depends on the rhetorical supposition of a united people. America is not a place of discordant factions, each of which sends leaders to Congress, where the unseemly but legitimate squabbling continues. Instead, there is a single American people that embraces the views of the militia groups. Politicians who disagree are therefore not loyal Americans, representing other loyal Americans. They are traitors to the people, scheming Others in a land of consensus.

VISIONS OF THE PEOPLE

The militia can thus predict that the people will rise up as a unity because, in their view, only those who join the rising are actually part of the people. The people stalks through these theories as an actor with a discrete identity, full of resentment and purpose. As a result, militia leaders spend a great deal of time and attention considering who is (or can be) a part of the movement and, correlatively, a part of the people. Militia theories of the Second Amendment offer a variety of such visions of the people, but all concur on a central theme with three elements. First, there is an American people, unified in all important ways and represented by the militia movement. Second, federal officeholders that disagree with the movement are traitors to the people. Third, electoral politics will no longer serve to tame the federal beast because the traitors are not loyal Americans with different views; rather, they are plotting to harm the American people and the American way of life. Accordingly, resistance to government is legitimate revolution, not rebellion or civil war. In this sense, the militia theory of revolution depends on the creation of an Other: We may revolt against Them precisely because They are not Us. The myth of regenerative violence is alive and well in these accounts.

Although all militia groups construct an Other, they disagree on its precise identity. Correlatively, all militia groups assert there is an American people, but they disagree on its exact character. Militia writing advances four principal visions of the American people and the Other, all of which, I suggest, fail on moral or empirical grounds. Each vision illustrates a major difficulty in defining or constituting an American people under modern circumstances. Any theory that posits the existence of such a people must address these difficulties; in toto, they pose a mighty obstacle.

To facilitate the analysis, I have, as noted, divided militia thinking into four themes: overt racism, anti-internationalism, antisocialism, and antisecular humanism. These clusters of ideas are analytically distinguishable in the militia materials, and each suffers from characteristic failings. Yet most militia groups espouse more than one of these themes, and some espouse all, believing that an international conspiracy of socialistic secular humanists dominated by Jews and third world peoples in the United Nations is trying to disarm, secularize, and socialize the United States. Accordingly, while I distinguish the four visions for heuristic purposes, I do not mean to obscure their overlap in the real world.

The Overt Racists

Probably the best publicized and most malign militia theme is overt racism. In recent years, Christian Identity theology has propounded a shared set of core beliefs for many, from the Aryan Nations groups in Idaho, to the Covenant, the Sword, and the Arm of the Lord in Arkansas, to the Posse Comitatus in the plains states.[62] The most famous Christian Identity group is probably the Order, led by Robert Mathews, whose career of violence made headlines in the 1980s. The Order is not the only such band with a criminal history.[63] Indeed, there is some evidence that Timothy McVeigh had ties to Christian Identity groups.[64]

Christian Identity is a bizarre and byzantine thought system. The interested reader may find detailed expositions elsewhere;[65] I offer only the broad outlines. Some Christian Identity groups are not overt racists, but many are.[66]

Those who are offer a strange retelling of biblical history. In their account, the union of Adam and Eve produced Abel, and Abel's progeny gave rise to the nations of Israel, who were not, it turns out, Jews. Eve, however, also coupled with Satan to produce Cain. After fleeing Eden, Cain mated with animals to produce the mud people, that is, nonwhites. In 721 B.C., Sennacherib took the northern tribes of Israel (who were not Jews) as prisoners to Assyria, where they became lost to history. According to Christian Identity proponents, these lost tribes of Israel crossed the Caucasus into Europe and became the ancestors of modern Europeans. One tribe, Manasseh, eventually migrated to America to produce the Founding Fathers, who entered into a new covenant with God contained in the Declaration of Independence and the Constitution. Meanwhile, in 586 B.C., Nebuchadnezzar took the southern tribe of Judah into captivity to Babylonia. There, the tribe became debased: it converted to Satanism and bred with the children of Cain. The progeny of that union eventually became the people today known as Jews. The true Jews, however — the Chosen People, the Davidic line to whom God made his biblical promises — are Europeans and the descendants of Europeans in America. For centuries, the people called Jews have been trying to subvert Christianity and the American Way of Life. Lately, through the machinations of ZOG, or the Zionist Occupational Government, they have managed to take over the U.S. government.[67]

To date, Christian Identity and other white supremacist groups are fairly small, but they have been trying to co-opt the rest of the militia movement.[68] Some nonracist (or less racist) militia leaders are aware of this danger and have tried to combat it.[69] Yet while there may be few militia members who would espouse Christian Identity in its extreme form, anti-Semitic conspiracy theories are fairly common. In particular, a large number of militia groups believe that for a long time Jewish bankers have controlled the American government so as to line their own pockets.[70] Anti-Semitism sometimes combines with anti-internationalism and antisocialism, as when some assert that Jewish agents in the United Nations have taken over the federal government. For example, the Militia News explains that in the early years of the Republic, "with their rights and liberties insured [sic], and their opportunities almost unlimited, and with their Christian heritage, devotion to God, and splendid work ethic, the nation grew and prospered." Soon, however, the worm emerged in the apple: "Most honest historians now know that the Civil War was created in order to split and destroy the nation." This plot continues today: "Following the turn of the 20th century, Communism (the Judeo-Bolsheviks of Russia) and other diabolical movements and philosophies — Fabian socialism, materialism, atheism, and secular humanism — would, like malignant parasites, establish themselves in America. . . . The majority of the American people still have not awakened to the fact that every war in this century has been contrived and created, and the people have been deceived into providing the resources and children to fight these wars for the benefit of the international conspiracy which planned them."[71]

Gordon Kahl of the Posse Comitatus and Robert Mathews of the Order are martyrs for the racist militia. They were both killed in confrontations with federal law enforcement, and they both penned last letters as death approached. In wide circulation, these letters offer a valuable insight into their view of the people. Kahl explained that his troubles began

> after I discovered that our nation had fallen into the hands of alien people, who are referred to as a nation within the other nations. As one of our founding fathers stated, "They are vampires, and vampires cannot live on vampires, they must live on Christians." He tried to get a provision written into the U.S. Constitution that would have prevented Jews from living inside the U.S. He warned his brethren that if this was not done their children would curse them in their graves, and that within 200 years their people (the Jews) would be sitting in their counting houses rubbing their hands, while our people would be slaving in the fields to support them. This has happened exactly as was predicted. . . . We are a conquered and occupied nation, conquered and occupied by the Jews and their hundreds or maybe thousands of front organizations doing their ungodly work.[72]

Combining equal measures of white supremacy and anti-Semitism, Mathews recounts the same kind of awakening as Kahl:

> The stronger my love for my people grew, the deeper became my hatred for those who would destroy my race, my heritage and darken the future of my children. . . . By the time my son had arrived, I realized that white America, indeed my entire race, was headed for oblivion unless white men rose and turned the tide. . . . I came to learn that this was not by accident, that there is a small, cohesive alien group within this nation working day and night to make this happen. I learned that these culture disorders have an iron grip on both major political parties, on Congress, on the media, on the publishing houses, and on most of the major Christian denominations in this nation, even though these aliens subscribe to a religion which is diametrically opposed to Christianity. . . . [T]o be an FBI agent is nothing more than a mercenary for the ADL and Tel Aviv.[73]

An article in the Aryan Nations' publication *Calling Our Nation* encapsulates these themes of white supremacy, anti-Semitism, and militia resistance. The author warns that the federal government has become oppressive, as evidenced by Waco and Ruby Ridge.[74] The guiding strategy for this oppression is the destruction of race-identity: "Since the 1930s, govt. psychologists have attempted to alienate us from our [own] kind, to make us hate ourselves, and to foster the defeatist idea of Every Man for Himself."[75] To complete the enslavement, "our enemy has announced, via draconian new laws, that the 2d Amendment and therefore the entire Bill of Rights is dead." These nefarious schemes will not, however, succeed because "we are the militia and we are on the move," and "we will not be disarmed." Relying on the definition of the militia in the Militia Act of 1792, the author explains that the militia includes " 'all [w]hite men between the ages of 18 and 45.' Since we live longer today, this must be modified to include all white men who do not work for the government." This militia can handle any Zionist treachery the government can dish out: "We therefore are prepared for government to unleash its dogs of war against us for no lawful purpose — for no reason at all other than as an act of jewish [*sic*] terrorism designed to cow our fellow countrymen into submission."[76]

These militia groups thus hold a clear vision of the American people: only white conservative Christians need apply. In line with this vision, militia writers have developed a constitutional theory that limits full citizenship to such persons. The theory distinguishes between those groups made citizens by the original Constitution and the Bill of Rights (that is, white male Christians) and those made citizens by the Fourteenth Amendment (everyone else). The so-called Fourteenth Amendment citizens have a status inferior to the so-called sovereign or organic citizens. The exact details of this inferiority vary among the theorists. Some believe that all amendments after the Bill of Rights are currently void because they are the illegal products of a Jewish conspiracy;[77] accordingly, Fourteenth Amendment citizens are not really citizens at all. Others believe that the Constitution and the Bill of Rights are God's law and so may not be changed, but later amendments reflect only the will of men and so may be repealed. Accordingly, Fourteenth Amendment citizens could lose their citizenship and rights through constitutional amendment.[78] Still others believe that Fourteenth Amendment citizens "do not have unalienable rights, only limited statutory 'civil rights' that Congress has seen fit to grant them."[79] As a result, Congress could strip these citizens of their rights at any time.

To remove any doubt about the status of these inferior citizens, James Pace has proposed an amendment to the Constitution. The Pace Amendment has gathered many adherents, especially among Identity believers.[80] The amendment would first repeal the Fourteenth and Fifteenth amendments. In their place, the new provision would stipulate, "No person shall be a citizen of United States unless he is a non-Hispanic white of the European race, in whom there is no ascertainable trace of Negro blood, nor more than one-eighth Mongolian, Asian, Asia Minor, Middle Eastern, Semitic, Near Eastern, American Indian, Malay or other non-European or nonwhite blood, provided that

Hispanic whites, defined as anyone with an Hispanic ancestor, may be citizens if, in addition to meeting the aforesaid ascertainable trace and percentage tests, they are in appearance indistinguishable from Americans whose ancestral home is in the British Isles or Northwestern Europe. Only citizens shall have the right and privilege to reside permanently in the United States."[81]

The overt racists have thus adopted an incisive strategy for constituting a people in late twentieth-century America: because it is difficult to create a people from diverse citizens, the militia writers simply define the citizenry to include only those like them. That strategy has a certain historical resonance: eighteenth-century civic republicans could posit the existence of a common good because they restrictively defined the citizenry.[82] And if it were normatively defensible, that strategy might still work; white conservative Christians might, even today, have enough commonality to constitute a people and to act together in revolution.

The strategy, however, is not normatively defensible. The overt racists in the militia movement are ultimately recommending a species of fascism or at least ethnonationalism. In this view, Americans constitute a people because they share ethnic roots, and these ethnic roots produce in them a spirit of the *volk* that brings sublime unity.[83] Twentieth-century history chronicles in horrifying detail the moral bankruptcy of that point of view. The central proposition of modern democratic political philosophy is the equal worth of each individual regardless of race or religion.[84] Twentieth-century America portrays itself as a nation that values all races and cultures, rejecting ethnicity as a basis for nationhood.[85] Over the decades, white separatists have fought the growing pluralization of the American citizenry, but they have lost the demographic and moral race. To deal with this diversity, Americans have celebrated the importance of individual rights, allowing each to go her own way, even at the cost of unity.[86]

The overt racists among the militia groups thus illustrate the first problem in constituting a people: it is hard to create unity from demographic diversity. As would the overt racists in the militias, revolutionary movements have often found their unity in a shared sense of racial, religious, ethnic, or class identity. Modern Americans, however, share no such identity, and any defensible definition of the American people must include all its citizens. The racist route to peoplehood is therefore closed to us. As a result, the demographic problem is a formidable obstacle for any theory of the Second Amendment that relies on the existence of a people.

The Anti-Internationalists

A second group of militia leaders believes that the New World Order, which they variously identify with the United Nations, Jewish bankers, the

Trilateral Commission, and others, is subverting the American government. The details of the conspiracy are endless, variable, and notoriously subject to ridicule. Bill Clinton and George H. W. Bush are both members of this New World Order, as are many other government leaders.[87] The conspiracy began when the United States entered the United Nations in 1945 and thereby forfeited its sovereignty.[88] Since then, the United Nations has been seeking to disarm its member countries to pave the way for global domination.[89] Recently, the U.S. armed services have begun to train foreign troops on American soil in preparation for subjugating the population.[90] The signs of invasion are everywhere:[91] black helicopters have begun to appear;[92] money and even human beings have been implanted with computer chips to keep track of them;[93] the government is constructing holding pens for resisters;[94] road signs have been marked to guide the invading forces.[95] On an appointed day, the government will attack and disarm all of the militias.[96] Afterward, the real purpose of the Federal Emergency Management Agency will be revealed: to impose martial law after the suppression.[97] The government itself perpetrated the bombing in Oklahoma City in order to discredit the militia movement.[98] For these writers, the evidence is obvious for those with eyes to see and available on endless videotapes from militia catalogues.[99]

In these theories, militia writers have created a foreign, powerful Other in the New World Order, and they have correlatively constituted an embattled people. Indeed, if the theories were empirically accurate, the projected conspiracy might actually call forth an American people. The object of the alleged plot is nothing less than the violent destruction of the United States, and its American leaders are literally traitors, in league with foreign bodies. One publication explains, "No person can be loyal to the Constitution for the United States *and* uphold the Charter of the United Nations. They are as opposite as light and dark, good and evil, freedom and slavery, God and Satan. *No man can serve two masters.* Support of the United Nations by government officials and employees is a violation of their oath. Wittingly or unwittingly, it is treasonous."[100] Another writer asserts, "The time is at hand when men and women must decide whether they are on the side of freedom and justice, the American republic, and Almighty God; or if they are on the side of tyranny and oppression, the New World Order, and Satan."[101]

The problem with this vision of the people is that most Americans believe the conspiracy is a fantasy, a product of the overheated imaginations of right-wing paranoiacs. Militia writers have an answer to that charge: the New World Order has already taken over the establishment media and made it a propaganda machine. Most American citizens naively trust the media, but they have been made dupes.[102] Because the militias trust only information obtained through the militia network, they alone know the truth. They are a revolutionary vanguard, a twentieth-century Paul Revere calling the people to wake up before time runs out.[103]

In adopting this self-image, militia leaders draw on themes that form a genuine part of the historical Second Amendment. The Anglo-American revolutionary tradition is saturated with suspicion, even paranoia: the citizenry should always watch for signs of a governmental plot to subvert liberty.[104] The future leaders of the revolution will see those signs first, and they have an obligation to alert the rest of the citizenry. Indeed, the leaders of the American Revolution embraced exactly that self-image: they woke first to imperial corruption and then sought to open the eyes of others.[105] In Second Amendment theory, therefore, widespread disbelief in a conspiracy cannot disprove its reality. For Second Amendment theorists, there is no authoritative exponent of the truth: neither the king, nor Congress, nor the Supreme Court, nor the media can dictate to us. The people alone can decide the truth, but because the truth is often hidden, shadowy, and twisting, the people may need guidance from a small band of enlightened patriots.

The militia writers, however, ignore a critical constraint in the Framers' thinking: because only a people can make a revolution, the people must be convinced of the plot before the revolution can occur. Indeed, although the leaders of the American Revolution wished to convince the people, they also believed they could not act until the people became convinced.[106] It is important to understand that this limit is not merely prudential (it takes a lot of people to make a revolution) but moral (only a revolution made by the whole for the whole is legitimate). To be consistent with the Framers' prescriptions, then, the militias may not commence resistance unless and until they persuade the rest of us that a revolution is warranted.

That obligation of general persuasion highlights the next problem in constituting a modern and truly inclusive people: the epistemological difficulty. For a revolutionary people to exist, we must all see reality in the same way; we must perceive that the government has become so corrupt that only armed resistance will suffice. For such epistemological unity to exist, one of two conditions must obtain. First, we might all have undistorted and unmediated access to an objective reality that exists independent of our perceptions. Some traditional epistemology endorsed this view, but virtually all recent work in the field repudiates it, perhaps for the sciences but certainly for human affairs. Inevitably, we interpret our experiences through cultural frameworks of analysis, and if we have different frameworks, we will draw different conclusions.[107] Second, if we do not have unmediated access to an objective reality, we must all, despite our radical differences in situation, values, life history, and cognitive categories, share a universal perspective, so that we draw the same conclusions.[108] Yet a diverse, modern citizenry is much less likely to share such a unifying perspective than an eighteenth-century citizenry with more similar life circumstances, cultural inheritances, and mental landscapes.

The epistemology of the militia groups themselves illustrates this predicament. They reject the mainstream media; others accept the mainstream media. Whom are we to believe and why? According to the militias, we should believe them because they help make sense of recent history: the country has fallen into such a terrible state that there must be a conspiracy afoot. Thus, one group explains, "The obvious deterioration of the United States since the end of World War Two is really not a mystery, it is the result of a hidden agenda initiated by world socialists starting in the early part of this century."[109] As noted above, both Kahl and Mathews described their recognition of the conspiracy as an epiphanic experience, a clarification of conditions they had seen but not understood. According to one close observer, the Posse Comitatus followed a similar line of reasoning: farmers in the plains states were committed individualists, believing that individuals prospered or failed by their own work. By the mid-1980s, however, many farmers — good men, responsible citizens — were failing. How to explain this deplorable state? It must be the product of a conspiracy by international Jewish bankers to enslave true Americans.[110]

In short, according to the militia, we can know they are right because they can explain why the country has declined. There is, however, a problem with that epistemological argument: only those who believe the country has declined will find it convincing. Those whose condition has improved, for example, racial and religious minorities, autonomous women, and gays and lesbians, may disagree. We do not all perceive recent trends in the same way.

Outside observers offer varying explanations of the appeal of the militia's conspiracy theories, but all agree that militia thinking makes sense only to a limited slice of the citizenry. Some maintain that right-wing movements like the militia reflect a human proclivity to political paranoia, only barely contained in liberal democracies.[111] Militia groups have thus appealed in large measure to groups that feel unjustly disempowered.[112] Others contend that the militia gains members the same way other associations do: people make friends with current members in church, at gun shops, in community gatherings. They start to attend meetings and become drawn into the social world of the militia. Soon, they stop listening to the mainstream media and believe only what they have heard from their new friends. Before long, they are epistemologically isolated.[113] Whatever the correct explanation, all of these accounts agree on one point: conspiracy theories make sense to those with a particular background and a particular perspective — those who feel powerless, those

who frequent places where militia members gather. For these people, epistemology depends on ideology and biography.

Such dependence does not mean militia members are psychotic. Indeed,
observers agree that the militia movement is a genuine grassroots, broad-
based phenomenon. On the whole, militia members are ordinary people who
have come to believe in a conspiracy because that belief helps them make sense
of their world, given their values and personal histories.[114] In that sense, the
militia's epistemology is like much of the rest of America's political culture.
Liberals believe in right-wing conspiracies, conservatives in left-wing conspiracies, African Americans in white conspiracies, whites in African American
conspiracies, women in patriarchal conspiracies, and men in feminist conspiracies. This fracturing of American politics reflects, in part, the absence of a
shared epistemology. If we reach a crisis of armed resistance, our various
groups will see enemies everywhere, and we will enter not revolution but civil
war. With their restrictive definitions of the people, the militia may simply
exclude those who disagree with them. But other theorists, those who want to
defend a right of popular revolution by a people that really does include all
Americans, must find some way to overcome this epistemological difficulty.

The militia thus predict that the people will take up arms in unity, but their
epistemology actually highlights how unlikely it is that the American citizenry
possesses such unity. Popular unity depends on a consensual epistemology, but
the existence of the militia movement shows that we do not have such an
epistemology. We might be able to construct one through interaction, shared
institutions, and common life circumstances. Ironically, however, militia epistemology reduces the likelihood of such an achievement because of its inclination to paranoia. To construct a shared point of view, we must accept the
legitimacy of each other's perceptions and find a way to bridge them. Militia
leaders reject this course. In their view, if Paul Revere and Thomas Gage did
not see the world in the same way, the reason was deception, not good faith
disagreement, and the answer was revolution, not reconciliation. In a world of
plots and suspicions, we are driven ever farther apart, relying on our own
sources for information, seeing other groups as potential enemies. In short,
this mentality discourages the creation of a people where one does not already
exist. It thereby promises unified revolution and simultaneously precludes the
fulfillment of that promise.

The Antisocialists

Another strain in militia thinking asserts that socialists control the conspiracy in Washington. A socialist for these thinkers is anyone who wishes to
subvert American constitutional liberties, as the militias define those liberties.

A revolution against a socialist plot is therefore a revolution to protect the Constitution, as the revolutionaries understand it. In making war on the Constitution, federal officeholders have declared war on the American people because it is the Constitution that makes us a people.

This theme is common to many militia groups. For example, the Texas Constitutional Militia describes its "MISSION": "To defend the constitutions of the REPUBLIC OF TEXAS and of the UNITED STATES OF AMERICA. To uphold and to defend the Bill of Rights, seen as unalienable, given by God to free men that they may remain free." The Bill of Rights is under assault, so the people must respond: "It is to us, the inheritors of the task begun more than two centuries ago, to seek and to secure these same ideals in the face of the same threats expressed by Patrick Henry."[115] Similarly, the North American Militia warns treasonous officials, "We are prepared . . . to defend, with our life, our Rights to Life, Liberty, and the Pursuit of Happiness. We number in the thousands in your area and everywhere else. How many of your agents will be sent home in body bags before you hear the pleas of the people?"[116]

Federal Lands Update offers a similar warning: "They (the feds) are going to continue to chip away at our Constitutionally protected rights, until they wear us down, and we say, 'they've taken everything. I don't have anything left.' Which is what they are hoping for. Or we (you) can say 'HOLD! Enough! You have no Constitutional authority to do these things and if you insist, you will face armed and angry citizens.' Why do you think the militia are growing at such a rate? Because the people are mad."[117] As a final example, MOM gives the people a clear choice: "The purpose of the government is in the protection of the rights of the people, when it does not accomplish this, the militia is the crusader who steps forward, and upon it rests the mantle of defense of the rights of the people. . . . We can leave our government in the hands of corrupted, self serving foreign mercenaries . . . or we can return to the original intent of our founding fathers (who bled and died for this country), in the defense of our God given unalienable rights."[118] In these formulations, militia writers describe a group called us or the people in opposition to the governmental tyrants: "we" will make a revolution to defend "our" constitutional rights unless "they" stop their oppression. What makes us a people, then, is our possession of constitutional rights and a shared resolution to defend them.

Once again, however, this vision of popular unity is highly implausible. The militias offer an interpretation of the Constitution shared only by a slice of society, not by the citizenry as a whole. In point of fact, the people are more likely to go to war with the militia over the Constitution than to rise up in unity under its name. First, as already described, the militia see the Second Amendment as the cornerstone of their interpretation of the Constitution. In their view, the amendment gives private militias a right to revolt. Militia leaders condemn the Brady Bill and the assault rifle ban as not only unconstitutional, but also as part of a conspiracy to subvert the Second Amendment and thus all of American liberty. Similarly, the incidents at Waco and Ruby Ridge were not merely bungled attempts to serve arrest warrants; they were part of a conspiracy to disarm the public and eliminate those who stand in the government's way.

Second, many militia thinkers argue that the mandatory income tax is unconstitutional. Indeed, the tax resistance movement substantially overlaps the militia movement. Many tax resisters couch their positions in elaborate legal arguments, but to date, courts have accepted none of them.[119] For example, many tax resisters believe that the Sixteenth Amendment was never properly ratified. The Free Militia proclaims, "The 16th Amendment, which permits federal income taxes, WAS NOT ratified in the same language by three fourths of United States as required by Article V of the Constitution and is therefore invalid."[120] Others maintain that a citizen need not complete tax returns because the Fifth Amendment protects him from being compelled to surrender incriminating information.[121] Still others believe that the progressive income tax violates the Just Compensation Clause because "high wage earners are taxed to fund welfare and other entitlements."[122]

Third, antisocialists claim that much federal regulation of private and even federal land is unconstitutional. The so-called Wise Use movement also overlaps with the militia movement and has its own detailed ideology.[123] Wise Use supporters advance two main contentions. First, the Fifth Amendment prohibits the government from telling a citizen what to do with his own property. For some, this restriction would bar virtually all regulation. For example, the Free Militia decries, "The use of your property can be and is restricted by municipal zoning codes, state and federal environmental laws, and other governmental regulations for the 'public good', even if the use of the property that is forbidden does not harm the lives or property of others. All of these regulations somehow limit the personal use of the property and many limit or reduce the property's commercial productivity or value on the real estate market."[124] Second, the Constitution bars the government from limiting the access of private citizens to public lands and resources. According to some, the Equal Footing doctrine grants to every state all federal lands located within that state, so that the state but not the federal government may limit access.[125] According to others, however, even the state may not restrict access because public resources belong to the people.[126]

In short, according to militia writers, the Constitution mandates an extreme libertarian scheme. Anything more centrist is socialism, a term that militia writers use as an epithet to ostracize those who disagree with them. The prophecy attributed to Sarah Brady sums up this attitude: "Our task of creating a socialist America can only succeed when those who would resist us have been totally disarmed." One publication calls Clinton supporters "Clintonistas," apparently to associate them with South American communist movements.[127] Federal Lands Update warns, "The belief that private property makes us unequal still has millions of adherents here in America. These true believers normally do not use the S word (socialist) to describe themselves. They know well that most Americans are too politically illiterate to recognize socialism even as it bites them in the paycheck every Friday in the form of income taxes, FICA, et cetera."[128] Finally, in answer to the question "Does the USMA [U.S. Militia Association] have any political agenda?" the group answers, "No. We are not Democrats, Republicans, Independents, etc. Except that we are also not Socialists and Communists and allow none such to belong."[129] Socialists, in short, are beyond the pale, not a legitimate part of the militia or the American people.

There are two difficulties with constituting an American people in this way. First is the interpretive difficulty: the meaning of the Constitution is the subject of great controversy — witness the furor over busing, abortion, affirmative action, gay rights, women's rights, prayer in public schools, flag burning. For the Constitution to make us a people, we must have something approaching consensus on the meaning of that document, but in recent years the Constitution has generated as much dissension as agreement. An insurrection in the name of the Constitution would necessarily be a rebellion for a particular interpretation of the Constitution. The militias' own interpretation of the Constitution illustrates this danger. The militias claim to be speaking for the people, but they speak only for a minority. For example, according to one poll, only 33 percent of white males and 22 percent of all others believe that "citizens have the right to arm themselves in order to oppose the power of the Federal Government."[130]

Militia writers have an answer to this interpretive difficulty: if others would only use the right interpretive technique, there would be agreement on the Constitution's meaning. These writers insist we should passively heed the text of the Constitution and the original intent of the Framers. The Militia News, for example, asserts that the text is self-interpreting: "The vast majority of U.S. citizens are reasonably intelligent and can read, and the Constitution and Bill of Rights are written in plain language (the same English we read and write today) and are not difficult to understand. . . . The Second Amendment . . . consists of 27 plainly written words. . . . This declaration of the absolute, unequivocal, inalienable right of the people to be armed, needs no interpretation."[131] MOM emphasizes the importance of the Framers' intent, attributing to Madison the charge, "Do not separate text from historical background. If you do, you will have perverted and subverted the constitution, which can only end in a distorted, bastardized form of illegitimate government."[132]

These simple recommendations, however, underestimate the difficulty in reaching consensus on the meaning of the text. From the moment of its adoption, the Constitution has generated multiple schools of interpretation.[133] Constitutional scholars broadly agree that the abstract terms of the Constitution — due process, equal protection, privileges and immunities — are too open-ended to generate determinate, consensual results.[134] Indeed, much constitutional theory argues that language can have meaning only within an interpretive community that shares a framework of usage and analysis.[135] As the militias themselves demonstrate, we are not a unified interpretive community with reference to the Constitution. Even the justices of the Supreme Court, despite sharing a legal culture, often cannot agree. Many cases result in split decisions on matters of profound importance.[136]

In the face of such inevitable disagreement, militia writers reach for their trump card: those who disagree with them must be parties to or dupes of the conspiracy. Thus, the Militia News describes those who differ with the militia's reading of the Constitution: "The authors of those documents [the Bill of Rights and the Constitution] anticipated this very problem with those who would usurp the people's rights, and those weak and unprincipled souls who would foolishly compromise or surrender their rights."[137] To disagree with the militia, in other words, is to be outside of the volk. In fact, however, it is not traitorous to believe that the income tax and environmental protection are constitutional; it is merely to differ in good faith. Again, the mentality of suspicion subverts the possibility of a true revolution. If each group believes that disagreement can only be the product of treason and deceit, then Americans will never be a people sufficiently unified to make a revolution.

The second difficulty with the antisocialist position is the political problem: to become a people, individuals must find ways to interact. That process usually involves institutions and other forums that bring together people of differing backgrounds and allow or teach them to form a common venture. In early American history, as we have seen, the universal militia was supposed to serve that function. Because of their extreme libertarianism, however, antisocialist militias leave little space for such interactive, universal institutions. Militia writers are very suspicious of all governments, even democratic ones. In the view of many, individuals have not merely rights within a political system, but also the right to declare themselves outside all political systems, possessed of the powers normally associated with government. Thus, Thompson concludes her Declaration of Independence, "We, therefore the sovereign citizens of the several states of the united states . . . Declare that each of the sovereign citizens undersigned are, and of Right ought to be, Free and Independent Sovereign Citizens . . . each has the full Power to levy War, conclude Peace, contract Alliances, establish Commerce, and to do all other Acts and Things which an Independent Sovereign may do."[138] By contrast, Jefferson's declaration spoke not of individuals but of a people severing its bonds with another.

Even the militias themselves make no claim to bind the individual. The choice to join is voluntary, the product of spontaneous volition rather than of universal institutions. As the Texas Volunteer Militia puts it, "START YOUR MILITIA AND PATRIOTS WILL COME."[139] Militia internet sites are full of advice on how to attract members. The militias intentionally recruit from a relatively restricted pool of citizens. One posting advises, "Try to find like-minded persons in your area. Ask around. Try patriotic organizations, such as the VFW and the American Legion. Sound out people at gun shows and gun stores."[140] Within a militia, the majority has no authority to constrain a dissenting minority, which may always withdraw from the organization. Thus, MOM provides that it may "not be called into service without the sustaining vote of the Unit."[141] A sustaining vote requires unanimity: "At the time of the 'call to arms,' each man shall verbally sustain such call, to his immediate Officer, and in the roll call, 'all voices present' shall be presented to the Unit Commander as unanimous for the impending action and service." Come the revolution, militia members may depart at any time: "No member of the Unit shall be compelled to serve in a conflict which he can not morally support in his heart with all of his might and strength."[142] Similarly, "the Unit Commander shall be chosen by unanimous voice," but if unanimity is not possible, "dissatisfied members . . . may resign . . . for the purpose of forming a separate and independent Unit."[143]

The militia vision of the relation between individuals and government is thus almost a parody of classical liberalism. Individuals exist before governments, complete and whole in themselves. Each individual then makes the choice to enter a polity for his own reasons and may leave it at any time for his own reasons. Accordingly, everywhere and always, supraindividual organizations exist and take action only by the actual consent of each and every member. This theory of the social contract, moreover, is not just a metaphorical explanation for the origin of governmental authority; it is a prescription for the day-to-day conduct of actual governments and citizens. If individuals come together and find that they agree, well and good. If not, then they should simply go their separate ways.[144]

When applied to revolutionary militias, this propensity to schism virtually ensures that any armed resistance to government will be a civil war rather than a universal revolution. Absent from the antisocialist vision of human interaction are the political commitments that might make construction of a people possible: devotion to the citizenry as a whole and the nation as a structure; resolution to discuss differences, compromise, reconceptualize one's own interests, and enter into the perspective of others; recognition of the bonds that connect those in an ongoing political enterprise. In short, the antisocialist mentality leads toward fragmentation, not peoplehood. And that mentality is not just a problem of the militia. The bulk of the American public shares the militias' contempt for politics, although perhaps in a less extreme form; indeed, the most noticeable trend of the 1990s was widespread alienation from the political system.[145]

The Antisecular Humanists

Finally, many militia members believe that the conspiracy is trying to replace God with secular humanist dogma in the hearts of Americans. The Militia News recites a familiar litany: "We observe the systematic de-Christianization of the nation as the courts display an animosity towards every Christian symbol and every manifestation of Christian practice, teaching and belief. Bible distribution and even Bible reading is prohibited in government schools. Crosses, crucifixes and nativity scenes are banished from public property. Cross shaped gravestones are being removed from military cemeteries. Public prayer is prohibited at school sponsored events. Even the pledge of allegiance is now forbidden in many schools because of the phrase 'one nation under God.' "[146] Part of the alleged hidden agenda of the New World Order is to "destroy religious faith and moral standards. The government has taken God and his morality from us and in it's [sic] stead supports abortion, gay rights, schools dispensing contraceptives, and activities void of ethics."[147]

According to militia writers, such de-Christianization is especially shameful because Christianity is the fundament of American peoplehood. In this view, America has been great because it was founded on Christianity.[148] Indeed, Christian law is the basis of the U.S. legal system and the Constitution.[149] Therefore, to de-Christianize America is to violate the Constitution and traduce Americans' way of life as a people. Officials who seek to do so are oath breakers and traitors.[150] At this point in the analysis, antisecular humanism often merges with antisocialism: the government has begun a systematic assault on the liberties of American gun owners, property holders, and Christians.[151]

In this strain of militia thinking, the American people contains all and only those committed to God's law, as the militia understands it. Correlatively, the Other consists of those committed to taking God out of the godly republic. This vision illustrates most of the foregoing difficulties in constituting a people in late twentieth-century America. First, it faces the demographic difficulty: it facially excludes liberal Christians, Jews, Moslems, Buddhists, nonbelievers, and others.[152] According to the antisecular militia thinkers, these citizens at best deserve toleration because this country was not made for them. Second, this vision of the people encounters the interpretive dilemma: many Americans (including justices of the Supreme Court) do not believe the Constitution prohibits abortion, allows prayer in public schools, or codifies the Christian Bible.[153] Indeed, many Christians do not interpret the Bible to prohibit homosexuality or abortion or to encourage the commingling of church and state.[154] Finally, the antisecular account must confront the epistemological predicament: to militia writers, the de-Christianization of America is the product of a deliberate conspiracy to subvert America. Other Americans have a different view of reality: the Supreme Court banned prayer in public schools and restrictions on abortion because the justices were concerned about the rights of children and women; we have liberalized laws against homosexuality because many Americans do not regard gays as monsters; and in general, we have moved Christianity from its privileged legal position because of a conviction that the Constitution mandates equal treatment for all religions.

Armed resistance in the name of God's people, in short, would not be a revolution for the whole of the citizenry; it would be the start of a civil war along all too familiar cultural battle lines.[155] To date, with the exception of some killings at abortion clinics, some synagogue bombings, and some militia assassinations, we have waged this culture war primarily through political and judicial channels. Some of these militia writers hope to transform that metaphorical war into a real one, and they intend to be better armed and trained than their enemies. Like the other militia visions of the people, in other words, this one does not include all Americans in its revolutionary movement. Instead, the real function of the vision is to categorize some citizens as True Americans and to exclude others as traitors, based on differences in values and identities. The practical effect of the vision is plain: if the militia cannot win against these enemies through political or judicial means, its members have the right to shoot them.

The militia movement's theory of the Second Amendment is thus an exaggeration of themes present in more mainstream populism. Like Charlton Heston, various militia leaders claim a special connection to the Framers, assert that the Bill of Rights has the quality of divinely authored scripture, distrust the media and other elites, include in the people only those who agree with their political views, and insist that the core of the American people is god-fearing, gun-owning white, straight, male, conservative Christians.

I do not mean to suggest that Heston or the NRA would broadly endorse the militia movement's platform. Close examination of the militia movement's theory and its points of connection to other populist theories, however, offers important cautions to Second Amendment theorists. This country's dominant strain of populism has always been exclusivist. Populists have generally had a particular people in mind. This people includes much less than the whole of the American citizenry, but populists maintain that this group lies closer to the core of American identity. This vision of American democracy thus claims primacy for some parts of the population and condemns others to marginality. Disturbingly, much Second Amendment populism renders this vision through the prism of self-arming and civil war: come the revolution, the true people will again enjoy their rightful status because they have retained their guns.

This history of Second Amendment populism therefore offers two warnings to those who would give the amendment a populist gloss. First, given this country's traditions, Second Amendment populism tends to relapse into exclusivism. Populist theorists must therefore be painstakingly careful to produce a theory that will, in theory and practice, include the whole of the population. It will not do just to conjure with the people. Second, however, the militia movement's theories highlight just how difficult it will be to construct such a people, one capable of rising in unity to oppose federal tyranny. To construct such a people, one must overcome the demographic, interpretive, epistemological, and political difficulties. In toto, those problems pose an enormous obstacle.

And yet, as the next chapter will explore, we may have no choice in the matter. We must try to construct a people on the constitutional use of political violence because the alternative of decentralized violence is unthinkable for those most vulnerable to it.

7

Outgroups and the Second Amendment

The situation of cultural outgroups, that is, those who fall outside traditionally restrictive visions of the American people, also offers cautions to modern theorists of the Second Amendment. On the one hand, these groups have the most to fear from a theory of the amendment that narrowly defines the people. As a result, they reinforce the warning against exclusivist populist theories. On the other hand, these groups have the most to gain from a broadly inclusive populist theory because in the long run the only solution to violence against outgroups is popular unity on the appropriate use of force. As cloudy as the horizon may seem, the condition of outgroups provides the most compelling reason not to surrender the hope for peoplehood expansively defined. And this peoplehood might form a critical component of a Second Amendment for the new century.

I examine here a new group of theories about the Second Amendment offered by members of some outgroups. As we have seen, Jews, African Americans, and feminists have generally found the Second Amendment to be culturally alien territory, the homeland of a gun culture that has never welcomed them. In recent years, however, certain Jews, feminists, and African Americans have begun to argue that outgroups should embrace the Second Amendment as a personal right to arms.[1] In brief, these theorists argue, "If you can't join 'em, then fight 'em." Because part of America will always be armed and hostile toward outgroups, then outgroups, too, should become armed and hostile, using the master's tools to dismantle the master's house. In short, the Second Amendment has become multicultural: populists claim it for themselves, but so do some outgroup members.

Although new and few, the outgroup theorists pose a question of great significance to a constitutional republic. In theory, the Constitution promises a scheme of law that is protective of all its citizens. In practice, however, whether America delivers on those promises depends on the constitutional organization of force: if the means of violence resides in the wrong hands, then the promises will come to nothing. These outgroup theories maintain that America will most likely fulfill its constitutional promises if the means of violence is diffused through the population. For that reason, one should read the Second Amendment to protect an individual right to arms.

The outgroup theories share two features. First, they use an avowedly perspectival approach to interpretation of the amendment: they argue that, from the perspective of their various groups, the Second Amendment should be interpreted as a personal right, so that group members can arm themselves against hate violence. Second, they argue that the Second Amendment projects a social world fragmented into hostile identity groups; hence outgroup members need a personal right to arms. As a result, although these theories seek to guarantee an individual right to arms, they hope individuals will use their arms in highly political ways. As members of identity groups, they will severally and collectively resist attacks by members of other identity groups. In the long run, such self-defense efforts will not just protect individuals; they will also help break the power of anti-Semitism, misogyny, and racism.

These theories tell a powerful tale of state indifference to hate violence against outgroups. They effectively argue that under some circumstances, at some places and times, outgroups might be wise to arm themselves as a matter of prudence. Yet the theories go farther than such contingent and prudential claims. Fundamentally, they argue that the Constitution requires us to accept a particular vision of the social world: America is and always will be composed of identity groups so mutually hostile that the only protection is self-arming against one's blood enemies.

In response to state indifference or hostility, the outgroup theories argue for a scheme of decentralized violence, in which outgroups may defend themselves. In fact, however, in a regime of decentralized violence, outgroups usually suffer, as such conditions generally benefit angry populist movements. In the short term, outgroup self-arming may provide some safety. In the long run, however, as long as the culture remains filled with hate, decentralized violence will hurt the most vulnerable elements of the citizenry. When the state is untrustworthy and the population is hostile, the only course of any safety is changing the culture so it will not be filled with hate. In the absence of such a culture, outgroups will suffer, no matter who has the guns.

Unhappily, the outgroup theories try to buy some short-term gains at the expense of long-term ones: they allow outgroups to arm themselves, but they frustrate the creation of a protective consensus culture. The theories are constitutional tales about the ineradicability of hate violence. Ultimately, they leave outgroups in a hopeless situation: they must choose between decentralized violence, with its threat of private oppression, and centralized violence, with its threat of public oppression. Instead, outgroups need to strive for a more hopeful third option: a consensus culture not filled with hatred. The outgroup theories of the Second Amendment, however, frustrate the nurturance of such a culture. They do not merely urge outgroups to take up arms against a world presently filled with hatred; they also argue that the Constitution itself assumes the world will always be filled with hatred. For that reason, the Second Amendment guarantees outgroups a permanent right to arms — their ultimate hope for safety in an unsafe world.

We define our hopes and dreams, in part, through the constitutional tales we tell. The outgroup constitutional tales of violence grant no possibility of redemption; they tell us we can realistically hope for no more than what we have at present. In so doing, they deny the Constitution one of its most important functions, that of positing an ideal of social justice which we may never perfectly realize but to which we are commanded to aspire. Outgroups have always needed the Constitution to fill that role, and they still do. Angry populists may rest content with a fragmented social world because it favors their dominance. Outgroups, by contrast, may prudently arm themselves against a present threat, but if they wish for safety, they can never stop dreaming of a better day.

Jews for the Preservation of Firearms Ownership

The tradition of Jewish meekness explored in chapter 5 is only one strand in a rich historical experience. Collectively and individually, from biblical days to the present, Jews have always exercised power.[2] There have been Jewish soldiers, gangsters, and even shtetl thugs, the *ba'al-guf*. Through the ages, many Jews armed themselves to resist persecution.[3] In the nineteenth century, Zionism arose as an alternative to assimilation, seeking to replace accommodation with militant nationalism.[4] After World War II and the Holocaust, many Jewish emigrants began to celebrate the martial virtues as they struggled for a homeland in Palestine. With Zionism's efflorescence in the state of Israel, armed might again became a culturally respectable Jewish option.[5] Among American Jews, Israel's victory in the Six-Day War brought great pride and a new appreciation for the uses of violence.[6] For many, the image of the enfeebled shtetl Jew took a back seat to that of the bronzed sabra warrior or the merciless Mossad agent. For such Jews, the Holocaust has become a testament to the folly of Jewish passivity; the Warsaw uprising and Masada have become central stories;[7] and the fundamental pledge has become "Never again."

Jews for the Preservation of Firearms Ownership (JPFO) appears to be a fringe by-product of this cultural movement. JPFO, a Milwaukee-based organization headed by Aaron Zelman, Jay Simkin, and Alan Rice, claims to have four thousand members.[8] Its mission is to alert the public to what it believes are the dangers of gun control. Its major works are *Lethal Laws* and *"Gun Control": Gateway to Tyranny.*[9] These works have received generally favorable reviews by Second Amendment theorists of the individual rights school. Moreover, despite its small numbers, JPFO has received a great deal of media attention because of its strong views.[10]

GUN CONTROL AND GENOCIDE

According to JPFO, gun control "has a down-side. A very nasty one. . . . the down-side of 'gun control' is genocide. There have been at least seven major genocides in this century. . . . In every case, a 'gun control' law was in force before the genocide began."[11] If there is no gun control, genocide cannot happen: "In the 20th century 'gun control' is a necessary precondition for genocide. Until and unless a hate-driven group gets control of the government mechanism and disarms its intended targets, genocide simply cannot and does not occur."[12] JPFO thus believes that gun control proponents have blood on their hands: "Those seeking more 'gun control' — or who accept existing 'gun control' laws — need to consider whether or not they still can support a *policy that promotes genocide*. . . . [T]hose who back 'gun control'. . . *must be recognized as supporting genocide*."[13]

The claim that gun control leads to genocide grows out of JPFO's basic political philosophy. In its view, the "formula for genocide has three parts: *Hatred; *Government . . . ; *'Gun Control'." Unless all three are present, "genocide does not occur" because genocide happens only when a hate-driven group seizes control of the government and disarms the people. Unfortunately, because it is a "basic human emotion," hatred "cannot be 'banned.'" Similarly, although government has "an inherent capacity to do great evil," it is, "in some form, a necessity for civilization." Therefore, "'gun control' is the only part of this formula that need not be present." Because hatred and government cannot be eliminated, the only way to prevent genocide is to ensure that the "people are on guard and armed."[14]

JPFO adduces many examples of modern genocides made possible by gun control,[15] but their central example — indeed, the story that drives their analysis — is the Holocaust. In 1928, the Weimar Republic enacted a permit and registration system, and in 1931 it prohibited the public carrying of arms.[16] With the passage of these laws, "the fate of Jews in Europe was sealed."[17] In 1933, when Hitler came to power, he inherited the Weimar gun control scheme, allowing the Nazis to achieve "an iron grip on Germany."[18] In 1938, the Nazis wrote their own gun control law forbidding Jews from owning any weapons but exempting themselves. Shortly thereafter followed the stages of the Holocaust: the Kristallnacht pogrom, "Mass Murder by Shooting" in Russia, and ultimately "Mass Murder by Gassing." Only the Warsaw ghetto resisted by force of arms, and it ultimately lost because it was "woefully underequipped."[19]

According to JPFO, the risk that gun control will lead to genocide exists everywhere, even in America. Indeed, JPFO suggests that a genocidal conspiracy may already be afoot. They argue that the Gun Control Act of 1968 was "likely based on the Nazi Weapons Law of 18 March 1938."[20] In their view, the Library of Congress translated the Nazi law for Sen. Christopher Dodd four months before the American law was passed, so the Gun Control Act "is identical, word for word, in tone and in content, as that passed by Adolf Hitler in 1938."[21] For JPFO, gun control is a "Nazi cancer" "implanted" in America,[22] in order to "soften the underbelly of the USA for the slice of the global government knife."[23]

JPFO's rhetoric dwells on this theme at great length. On billboards, bumper stickers, and other materials, the organization has used an image of Hitler in stiff-arm salute next to the words, "All in favor of gun control raise your right hand."[24] In opposition to candidates who favor gun control, they have distributed pamphlets bearing a swastika and the slogan, "Stop Hitlerism in America."[25] They compare Sarah Brady to Hitler: "Hitler knew that a lie — endlessly repeated — can win acceptance. So does Sarah Brady";[26] "Brady's use of Hitler's tactics leads to a 'Final Solution' for law abiding gun owners."[27] And they compare Waco to Warsaw: "We saw the government go into Waco, Texas, pretty much as the Nazis went into Warsaw. As it was in Warsaw, so it was in Waco."[28] One member of JPFO summarized, "Vote only for politicians who trust the people to own all types of firearms and who have strong pro–Second Amendment voting records. . . . I see creeping fascism in America, just as in Germany, a drip at a time; a law here, a law there . . . soon you have total enslavement."[29]

Because the risk of another Holocaust is real, JPFO criticizes Jewish organizations and leaders that support gun control. A central goal of JPFO is "to expose the propaganda and myths used by all anti-gunners, but particularly by some Jewish anti-gunners."[30] Such Jews have failed utterly to learn from history: "The hardest lesson of the Holocaust . . . is that 'gun control' is a lethal policy. Jews have been a major victim of this policy. Yet 'leaders' of several Jewish communal groups—e.g., the American Jewish Congress, the B'nai Brith among others—still support 'gun control.'"[31] Such Jews mistakenly promote subservience as a survival strategy: "Jews have always tried too much to ingratiate themselves to government. But let's face it, when there's too much government it's not good for Jews. It's just not in the best interest of Jews to be disarmed."[32] According to JPFO, these Jews are also stirring anti-Semitism: "[Congressman Charles] Schumer and other Jewish gun-grabbers . . . cannot see that their gun control activities fuel the fires of real anti-Semitism, as . . . gun owners of all races and creeds increasingly find their civil rights to own guns reduced by these pro-criminal Jews."[33] In short, procontrol Jews, like all "those who back 'gun control' . . . must be recognized as supporting genocide"—perhaps the worst charge that one modern Jew can hurl against another.[34]

JPFO'S INTERPRETATION OF THE SECOND AMENDMENT

From this analysis, JPFO concludes that Americans should arm themselves and resist gun control as a way of preventing genocide. They further contend that the connection between gun control and genocide furnishes a basis for interpreting the Second Amendment. According to JPFO, "government can do good only slowly, but can do great harm [such as genocide] quickly." For that reason, "the Framers of the Constitution . . . designed a system based on limiting government's power; created a civil right of the law-abiding to be armed; did not impose on the government the duty to protect the average person."[35] In other words, according to JPFO, the Framers adhered to JPFO's political philosophy: because they knew gun control leads to genocide, the Framers banned gun control.

In JPFO's view, although many commentators stress the importance of guns for "self-defense against criminals, or for hunting," those "uses cannot be the main reasons that the private ownership of firearms was mentioned in the U.S. Constitution." Because the Framers did "not deal with trivial matters," the Second Amendment really "was written . . . to protect individual freedoms from encroachment by government." In short, despite the "way in which the private ownership of firearms is discussed" in the Second Amendment debate, JPFO urges us not to "miss[] the point—that 'gun control' is the key to genocide."[36]

JPFO's interpretive approach to the Second Amendment is thus perspectival, derived from their perspective as late twentieth-century Jews. Their reason for supporting the amendment is that it may forestall the sort of genocide wrought by the Nazis. Moreover, the political philosophy they ascribe to the amendment is one that they have derived from reflecting on the experience of those threatened with genocide. In short, they offer a Second Amendment understood through the lense of the Holocaust. Similarly, the world of JPFO's Second Amendment is populated not by abstract individuals but by situated selves possessed of ethnicity, group loyalty, and cultural agendas. In some respects, JPFO's message appears highly assimilationist by urging Jews to join the gun culture. More fundamentally, however, JPFO's argument rests on a vision of the inevitability of ethnic balkanization, since hatred is perennial.

On the one hand, JPFO intends its interpretation of the amendment to apply to all people, regardless of religion or ethnicity. Because hatred is universal, all need to be armed to resist genocide. The lesson of the Holocaust is thus a lesson "for Jews and Gentiles alike."[37] Indeed, JPFO plainly desires that gun-owning Jews should gain admission to the gun culture. Some have argued that both assimilation and Zionism were attempts to "normalize" the Jews: assimilation, because it was normal to be a full citizen of a nation-state, and Zionism, because it was normal to have a nation-state of one's own.[38] Comparably, JPFO's work attempts to normalize the Jewish experience in America, by gaining acceptance from true, gun-owning Americans.[39] Notably, JPFO does not discuss Israel's importance in securing the safety of Jews; instead, it emphasizes the importance of Jews arming themselves in America.

In fact, JPFO finds that it has more in common with the gun culture than with other Jewish organizations. In an interview, Zelman explained that "two factors inspired him to found JPFO: studying the Holocaust, and growing up in Tucson, Arizona."[40] As we have seen, JPFO accuses "Jewish gun-grabbers" of stirring anti-Semitism in the gun culture. Instead of blaming the gun culture for its anti-Semitism, JPFO blames other Jews for creating this hatred. Plainly, they identify more with other gun owners than with other Jews.[41] And JPFO even shares some common ground with the militia movement itself. Both distrust the media and the government, believe that a conspiracy is afoot to deprive Americans of their liberties, and argue that the purpose of the Second Amendment was to prevent tyranny. In fact, the militia movement has sometimes relied on JPFO material and arguments.[42]

In sum, then, JPFO tends to find commonality with other gun owners. At the same time and more fundamentally, however, JPFO imagines American culture to be riven by ethnic animosity. Indeed, the inevitability of that hatred is the reason for the rights granted by the Second Amendment. In JPFO's vision, the amendment's prime function is to allow ethnic and religious groups to defend themselves against genocide by other groups: "Hatred between groups of people is the root cause of genocide. Such hatreds are commonplace. But such hatreds do not usually lead to genocide. A genocide becomes possible when hatred between groups of people reaches a point where one or more parties seek a 'final solution' to the problem, a 'final solution' that involves murdering other party or parties."[43] If there were no such threat, the reason for JPFO's version of the amendment would disappear.

These two elements of JPFO's thinking—its drive to build bridges to other groups and its deep suspicion of other groups—are in some tension. That tension is especially apparent when JPFO extends the hand of peace to groups that are anti-Semitic, such as elements of the militia movement. JPFO's underlying philosophy helps to explain this tension. In JPFO's view, genocide is possible only when a hate group seizes control of the government: "Until and unless a hate-driven group gets control of the government mechanism and disarms its intended targets, genocide simply cannot and does not occur."[44] Thus, JPFO conjures a world in which only government can threaten armed citizens because only government can disarm them. This focus on public violence has two important consequences. First, it allows JPFO to build bridges to other groups without particular worry. Unless those groups seize government, they cannot perpetrate genocide; until then, they are in the same position as JPFO, that is, fearful of a government that wants to disarm them. Second, it makes more plausible JPFO's claim that self-arming can prevent genocide because citizens need fear only the government, not each other. After all, "ordinary civilians outnumber government armed forces—military and police—by about 100-to-1."[45] As a result, "genocides can be prevented if civilians worldwide own military-type rifles and plenty of ammunition."[46]

JPFO has thus simplified the social world into a single duality: average citizens against the government. That division, however, dangerously oversimplifies, as JPFO of all groups should know. As I will explain later, private violence has always been a threat to American outgroups, thanks in part to the gun culture's proclivity to take up arms to further its political goals. Moreover, the line between private and public violence is very fluid. As we will see, the government can allow, even encourage, private pogroms by strategic inactivity, and private hatred can become public hatred as a result of elections or coups. Finally, private people often cooperate with public hate violence. Some have argued, for example, that most ordinary Germans were willing participants in Hitler's final solution.[47]

In other words, a different vision of the social world is more plausible but more threatening to JPFO's project: rather than the people versus the government, we see a variety of groups, showing some love and some hatred toward one another. Some have power in the government, and some own private fertilizer bombs. Some of the latter are anti-Semitic, and, in troubled times, more may join them, blaming their woes on the Western world's traditional scapegoats. JPFO must know how plausible this vision is because they insist that the Jews in Nazi Germany stood alone, receiving no aid from their neighbors or even from Jews in other countries.[48] Today, it seems much more likely that the militia movement will commit mass murder against American Jews than that the government will do so. This vision of balkanized ethnic groups is actually the world that JPFO itself imagines, except that it steadfastly refuses to recognize the danger of nongovernmental violence. If JPFO took that danger seriously, it would be much more difficult for it to sustain the claim that universal arming is the answer to hatred.

Women and Guns

The relation of women to guns has always been more complicated than one of simple opposition. Frontier women used guns to defend their families, and today many women in the gun culture find no tension between women and guns. Though guns may be culturally coded as male, these women are comfortable handling and using them. To them, guns seem an unremarkable part of life, and they own guns in significant numbers.[49]

In recent years, however, a new feature has appeared in the cultural landscape of the Second Amendment: according to some, urban women have begun to purchase sidearms for self-defense in record numbers, out of fear rather than culture.[50] In point of fact, this trend may have been greatly exaggerated. Faced with slumping membership, the NRA began a public relations program aimed at women.[51] At about the same time, faced with slumping sales, some major gun manufacturers began similar advertising campaigns.[52] Smith and Wesson then commissioned a Gallup poll, which concluded that the rates had skyrocketed.[53] Other studies have found, by contrast, that the percentage of women who own guns has not increased[54] and that the typical female gun owner remains a married resident of a rural, relatively safe, hunting household — in other words, a member of the traditional gun culture, not a frightened urban professional.[55]

Whether more women actually own guns, however, may not be as significant as the perception that they do. The press has issued a blizzard of stories announcing the trend, reporting the results of the Smith and Wesson poll without much scrutiny.[56] Most important, some women gun owners have drawn a connection between their gender and their guns. Women in the gun culture are gun owners who happen to be women. By contrast, the new gun owners view their ownership as a political act, a defiance of gender structures. Unlike earlier women owners, the new ones tend to be politically liberal and to identify themselves as feminists.

Women gun owners' new self-consciousness is fairly broad-based. The movement has a house journal, Women & Guns magazine, which has had a readership of twenty-five thousand.[57] Across the country, firearms training seminars for women have appeared, to help them overcome their aversion to guns.[58] In a number of states, women have formed lobbying groups to fight gun control, claiming that the right to arms is a women's safety issue.[59]

Perhaps the two most prominent figures in this movement are Paxton Quigley and Naomi Wolf, although they have achieved prominence in quite different ways. Quigley was once a gun control activist, but when a friend was raped, her views underwent a sea change.[60] She wrote a best-selling book, *Armed & Female,* to argue that guns are an effective and constitutionally sanctioned form of self-defense for women.[61] Today, Quigley is a spokeswoman for the movement and leads self-defense seminars for women.[62] In sum, she is the guru of the women and guns movement, the very model of a modern, armed, self-reliant woman.

By contrast, it is not clear that Naomi Wolf has ever touched a gun, and she is certainly not an expert on women's self-defense. Rather, Wolf is a best-selling feminist author who celebrates women's self-arming as part of a new trend in feminism.[63] In *Fire with Fire,* she urges women to abandon what she calls "victim feminism" and embrace "power feminism": "What is power feminism? It means taking practical giant steps instead of ideologically pure baby steps; practicing tolerance rather than self-righteousness. Power feminism encourages us to identify with one another primarily through the shared pleasures and strengths of femaleness, rather than through our shared vulnerability and pain."[64] Rather than remaining pure in their powerlessness, therefore, feminists should fight "fire with fire": they should take up "the master's tools" — such as "the electoral process, the press, and money" — because "it is only the master's tools that can dismantle the master's house."[65]

Guns are among those tools. Wolf celebrates the women and guns movement: "As violence against women reached epidemic proportions, women were not just sitting around. Quietly, carefully, with thorough training and in unprecedented numbers, while they looked after their families and tended their marriages, they were also teaching themselves to blow away potential assailants."[66] Women & Guns magazine "addresses the unlabeled power feminism of women in the American mainstream"; in letters to the magazine, "one can hear the pioneer feminism of women who know that no one will take care of them but themselves."[67] For these women, "victim feminism's worldview is far from accurate, and less than useless. The fact is that women are psychologically burning the clothing of victimization."[68]

POWER FEMINISM AND GUNS

Following Wolf's analysis, one could say that the women and guns movement is made up of women who generally consider themselves to be power feminists, who reject "victim" feminism's association of women with nonviolence. Their argument draws on three feminist themes: empowering women; gendering the subject; and maintaining that the personal is political.

Empowering Women

For these women, self-arming is a logical extension of feminism's drive to empower women.[69] In their view, guns can empower women to lead full lives, feel less fear for their safety, and enjoy fewer restrictions on their movements. By using a gun, women can take responsibility for their own protection. As one woman summarized, "In many ways, it's an extension of the women's movement. The same way we've decided we're perfectly capable of taking care of our economic well-being . . . we're also capable of taking care of our personal and physical well-being."[70] Julianne Versnel Gottlieb writes a column for Women & Guns entitled "Dear Self-Reliant Reader." In it, she argues that guns empower: "We must realize that we, and only we can — and will — be responsible for our personal safety. I do not choose to be a victim. I choose to be a woman with power and I will use whatever means I need to attain this goal. I choose to carry a firearm in certain situations. . . . It is my choice."[71] Quigley calls her self-defense course "Women's Empowerment."[72] She argues, "Women have finally decided to protect themselves. It's the last avenue to independence and liberation."[73]

For the women and guns movement, then, the central reason for arms ownership is self-defense.[74] Guns allow mothers to protect children, and they facilitate employment and travel by allowing women to be safer in public.[75] Most centrally, guns empower women to resist rape, domestic abuse, and sexual harassment. Wolf writes, "Women's relationship to violence is changing. Ordinary women are at a turning point. The fury generated by sexual abuse, which has traditionally been turned inward, is beginning to be directed outward."[76] And self-arming allows women to rely on themselves, rather than on the men in their lives or the state, which cannot or will not adequately protect them. As one woman explained, "A big part of learning how to use a gun is self-reliance. The police aren't psychic. They come when they are called. We're socialized to think that some man on a white horse is going to come and rescue us. That's a fairy tale."[77]

For that reason, women in the movement have harsh words for "victim" feminists who support gun control—rather as JPFO denounced "Jewish gun-grabbers." Karen McNutt declaims, "What is truly amazing is the large number of otherwise intelligent, so-called 'liberated' women who blandly accept and even promote the idea that women are incapable of defending themselves with these devices."[78] And Peggy Tartaro accuses feminist gun control advocates of elitist paternalism: "This particular self-described liberalish feminist still thinks women can make up their own minds, thank you very much. And she thinks that while not every woman may want to include a firearm in her own self-defense options, that those who do shouldn't be subject to ridicule."[79]

Gendering the Subject

As do so-called establishment feminists,[80] the women and guns movement argues that too often the law views matters from either a masculine or a gender-neutral perspective. Instead, the law should "gender the subject": in analyzing the right to arms, it should take both a woman's and a man's perspective because the right might mean different things to different genders. And reversing the traditional wisdom, the movement argues that the right to arms is more important to women than to men.

One of the earliest essays to discuss women and guns, by Ruth Silver and Don Kates, protests the failure of both sides in the gun control debate to consider directly "the viability of women's self-defense."[81] By contrast, the authors argue that women have greater need of guns than do men because of their relative physical weakness: "[Women's] freedom is made possible by the opportunity to possess a handgun. To paraphrase a saying from the Old West: God didn't make men and women equal. Colonel Colt did."[82] This notion that guns are a gender-equalizer has become a slogan in the movement. One woman put the idea colorfully: "That's my equalizer with a man that's going to do me bodily harm. . . . I'd just aim for the crotch and hit the heart."[83]

Similarly, in the movement's view, gun control falls especially heavily on women. This criticism applies to all gun control because "women are more vulnerable to attack, and have more at stake in battling new controls than men do."[84] Particular forms of gun control also have particular problems. Tartaro condemns waiting periods because women are more likely than men "to be first time purchasers of guns": "Waiting periods . . . kill women."[85] One lobbying group condemns discretionary licensing statutes because police tend to grant licenses primarily to men: "This discrimination against Colorado's women is deeply violent."[86]

The Personal Is Political

The women and guns movement also echoes the feminist conviction that the personal sphere always has political implications.[87] On the one hand, the movement defends a personal right to arms, but, on the other hand, it hopes this self-arming will have two consequential effects in the public realm. First, buying a gun will wean women of reliance on men and upset conventional gender roles. As Quigley explains,

> Socialization processes that connect femininity to many styles of weakness and helplessness may paralyze many women, teaching them the fear that restricts their ability to defend themselves. . . . Sometimes it takes weeks or even months before these women begin to realize that they are physically and mentally capable of successfully defending themselves against an aggressor. . . . Moreover, a great many women also dislike and fear guns and consider it normal female behavior to react in that manner. These emotions may be a consequence of a myth that perpetuates the idea that guns belong to men as if they were some sort of cultural prerogative. Some women . . . perceive guns as an extension of a man's masculinity, giving him perhaps an undeserved power.[88]

McNutt proudly proclaims that society would consider her a "very bad girl" because "I carry a gun. I have no faith in the protective shield of some Victorian sense of innocence. . . . [If] my .38 is too small, I'm sure my .45 will do the job."[89]

Second, although the right to arms is an individual one, the movement hopes that general self-arming by women will help to break the general power of misogyny. Proponents and opponents of the movement agree that it grows out of a deep well of anger about women's oppression. Ms. Magazine explains that women possess "a certain off-the-record vein of vengefulness, a mother lode of anger, a vast buildup of unrequited insults and injuries. . . . Sweet revenge. Women's interest in guns — such as it is — isn't just about fear. It's about fighting back."[90] One gun dealer made the point in similar terms: "Women have suffered from purse snatchings, rapes, and all kinds of humiliations. They're absolutely disgusted with government's feeble attempts to do anything for them. And they're getting pissed off."[91]

Supporters of the movement believe this anger can be channeled into a large-scale resistance movement. Quigley explains: "If a number of women say 'enough is enough,' we're going to see a real 'take back the night' movement."[92] Even Letty Cottin Pogrebin, founding editor of Ms. and a critic of the movement, sees the appeal in this hope: "My reaction surprised me. I'm for gun control and nonviolent conflict resolution, yet suddenly I imagined every woman armed, powerful and instantly equalized — not as an aggressor but as a confident defender of her safety and physical integrity. Wait until some guy attacks us on an empty street: POW — one less pervert; BANG — another rapist blown away. . . . [P]istol-packing mamas will fight back: ZAP — victims no more."[93]

In this way, the movement blends individual and collective aspects of the right to arms. On the one hand, each woman possesses an individual right to arms; she alone has the choice to buy a gun; and she alone must pull the trigger. On the other hand, these individual exercises of the right are part of a general movement that has, in the movement's view, immense political significance. When a woman fights off an attacker, she is also fighting the forces of misogyny. When she overcomes her fear of violence, she contributes to a shift in the cultural attitudes that consign women to victimhood. And when she joins with other women in gun training classes or in reading Women & Guns magazine, she is affirming that there is strength in armed sisterhood.

The apotheosis of this line of thinking is the common claim that the solution to *political* violence against women in Bosnia and other countries is women's *personal* self-arming — echoing JPFO's claim that the solution to the Holocaust was Jewish self-arming. After recounting the atrocities in Bosnia-Herzegovina, Gottlieb protests, "I have never read or heard one reporter — male or female — who has decried the fact that these women have no way to defend themselves. They never comment on, refer to, allude to, or allow that any woman — every woman — should have the right to choose not to be a victim."[94] In a later column, Gottlieb supplies the same prescription for other countries: "The same horrendous practices are taking place in Haiti and Rwanda. With each new revelation, the United Nations continues to pass economic sanctions and demand the restoration of the 'rightful' governments. It's not working. It's time to do something so that the victims can protect themselves."[95] Even Wolf has warm words for women's self-arming in the Balkans: "In the Balkans, women have begun to take part in the violence that has engulfed the region, and to reject their submissive roles in the patriarchal culture. 'Women have changed since the beginning of the war,' Sarajevan Jasna Delalic said. 'Women have banded together. . . . I will never slave for anybody anymore.' . . Balkan women are reacting to their victimization with a matter-of-fact military vengefulness. . . . [A Sarajevan doctor explained,] 'I've treated eighteen raped women. . . About a third wanted to have their gynecological problems resolved and then went out and picked up a gun.' "[96]

THE SECOND AMENDMENT AS AN EQUAL RIGHTS AMENDMENT

The interpretation of the Second Amendment offered by the women and guns movement grows directly out of its analysis of the importance of self-arming to women. In this sense, the interpretation is perspectival: it is the Second Amendment as understood through the lens of power feminism. And it rests on a vision of the social world as deeply divided by gender animus: the reason for the right to arms is that women need to defend themselves against misogynist men, not so that abstract individuals can defend themselves against other abstract individuals. For the movement, the Second Amendment is a kind of Equal Rights Amendment: like Colonel Colt, it equalizes the difference in physical strength between men and women and so gives women freedom of movement and physical integrity.

The editors of Women & Guns directly connect their interpretation of the amendment to perspectivalism and the vision of a divided social world. The magazine describes itself as "a publication primarily for women, primarily by women and presenting a strong proactive stand on the right to keep and bear arms for women."[97] For better or worse, the state has no constitutional obligation to protect women: "Many courts have held that police have no obligation to protect individual citizens."[98] For this reason, we should read the Second Amendment to allow women to protect themselves. Gottlieb, for example, denounces Hillary Rodham Clinton for believing that "government is the only entity able to make choices for you and me." By contrast, "I, Julianne Versnel Gottlieb, believe that the individual can make the best choices for the individual." In so doing, she follows in the footsteps of Dolley Madison, wife of "James Madison, the author of the Second Amendment," and "a woman who time and again in her long life made the choice not to be a victim." Similarly, Gottlieb feels a close connection to Eleanor Roosevelt, who "carried a small handgun in her purse. She made a choice not to be a victim."[99]

After claiming these women, along with Molly Pitcher, Martha Washington, and Abigail Adams, as Founding Mothers, Gottlieb tenders an interpretation of the amendment as viewed through the lens of power feminism: "If the U.S. Constitution gives me the right of privacy — the right to control the destiny of what occurs to my body — it gives me the same right of privacy to choose to protect myself from assault, rape or worse. . . . I believe that the Second Amendment of the Bill of Rights gives me the individual right to make a choice if, and/or how, I am going to do so. . . I believe that as a mother, I have the same rights when it comes to the protection of my children. I believe that as a wife, I have the same rights for the protection of my husband."[100] In another column, she writes that the Second Amendment "was included in the Bill of Rights over 200 years ago to protect us from tyranny from within, as well as from without. It is what I fight for so that you and I do not become victims like those tortured women in Bosnia-Herzegovina today and who knows where tomorrow."[101] The staff of Women & Guns draw the conclusion: "If we allow the gun-control lobby to chip away at our constitutional rights in the name of crime control we will be taking the first step in guaranteeing that we are victims."[102]

Quigley also extends a perspectival interpretation of the amendment, though her perspectivalism is more subtle. Her formal analysis of the amendment is quite gender-neutral, relying heavily on the work of the individual rights theorist Kates. She begins with a number of quotations from early American thinkers on the importance of the right to arms. She then argues, following Kates, that the militia to which the amendment refers is the unorganized militia, composed of every private householder. And she concludes by arguing that the threat of tyranny is still real, so we should continue to embrace the Second Amendment.[103] None of these arguments is overtly perspectival. Quigley's interpretation of the amendment, however, occurs in a book devoted to the idea that women need guns to be free. Her analysis of the amendment contains no discussion of the importance of the Framers' intent or a written constitution. Instead, she values the amendment, as she interprets it, because it promises to help women in a divided social world, and she argues that we should value the amendment for the same reason: "The real issue is not the polemics of guns versus no guns; rather, for some women it is the choice of being victor or victim."[104]

This view of the amendment has also made its way from the popular press to the law journals. In the University of Illinois Law Review, Inga Anne Larish condemns "the exclusion of women's concerns in the gun control debate" because "women are most in need of guns for self-defense. All else being held equal, women are physically weaker than men and will continue to be victimized by men whether or not men have guns."[105] Moreover, the police have been especially deficient in "preventing the crimes which greatly and disproportionately affect women, such as sexual assault and domestic violence."[106] As a result, gun control falls especially heavily on women. In practice, laws requiring carry permits discriminate against women, who generally cannot demonstrate need because they do not carry large amounts of cash.[107] In addition, a complete gun ban would help "men who perpetrate violent crime against women" because "for most women, men's fists are lethal force."[108]

Unfortunately, the current discussion of the meaning of the Second Amendment ignores these women's concerns. The Framers wrote the amendment "in gender-neutral language," but the "problem with gender-neutral law is its assumption that such laws concern themselves with women's interests, when a close examination reveals that the interpretation, discussion and application of the law often ignores women."[109] Thus, states' rights theorists completely ignore women's need for self-defense, reading the amendment instead to protect only "states' right to maintain militias." Even those in the individual rights school "speak in terms of a male fight, generally agreeing that one of the primary purposes of the [Second Amendment] was to guarantee an individual's right to defend 'himself.' "[110] Larish never describes how she would interpret the amendment in detail, but it is possible to infer her reading from her analysis. If we read the amendment with women's needs in mind, we would presumably endorse a strong personal right to arms for self-defense, and we would find most gun control unconstitutional. Like Quigley and Gottlieb, then, Larish offers a perspectival Second Amendment (indeed, she subtitles her article "A Feminist Perspective on the Second Amendment"), understood through the lens of women's concerns and resting on the vision of a world saturated with misogynist crime.

An Afro-Americanist Reconsideration

Although African Americans have never been part of the gun culture proper, African American culture has often produced and celebrated courageous acts of armed resistance. Before the Civil War, slave states kept African Americans disarmed, but they still rose repeatedly in revolt.[111] After the Civil War, southern Blacks formed private militias to resist attacks from white supremacist groups, and northern Blacks did the same to resist white urban mobs — in both cases with little success.[112] During the civil rights movement, Robert Williams pioneered collective self-defense strategies in resisting the Klan, and he authored the classic tract on the subject, *Negroes with Guns*.[113] Across the South, Blacks organized local chapters of the Deacons for Defense and Justice to similar ends.[114] As the sixties proceeded, African American violence became more widespread and less organized: in the face of racial injustice and the assassination of Martin Luther King, rioting erupted in many of the nation's large cities.[115] Capping a decade of growing militancy, the Black Panther militia put the Second Amendment at the heart of its political platform: "*We want an immediate end to* POLICE BRUTALITY and MURDER of black people. . . . We believe we can end police brutality in our black community by organizing black self-defense groups that are dedicated to defending our black community from racist police oppression and brutality. The Second Amendment to the Constitution of the United States gives a right to bear arms. We therefore believe that all black people should arm themselves for self-defense."[116]

In recent years, some Second Amendment theorists of the individual rights school have crafted an interpretation of the Second Amendment that puts African American resistance at the center of focus. In this view, the right to arms is especially important to despised groups, like African Americans, who have good reason to distrust the state. Some came to this view because of their experience in the civil rights years. Kates, for example, explains, "As a civil rights worker in a Southern state during the early 1960s, I found that the possession of firearms for self-defense was almost universally endorsed by the black community, for it could not depend on police protection from the

KKK."[117] Such theorists argue that the purpose of much gun control has been to disarm African Americans. In the post-Reconstruction South, some states passed laws banning ownership of cheap handguns, so that only those (overwhelmingly white) people of ample means could own a handgun. In other southern states, sheriffs simply confiscated the weapons of African Americans, even in the absence of laws banning ownership but with the assistance of registration laws. Still other states imposed heavy taxes on handgun sales, comparable in effect to poll taxes. And yet others enacted discretionary licensing laws, under which the police could deny permits to "undesirables" like African Americans.[118]

Some theorists further maintain that even more recent gun control is motivated by a desire to keep guns out of the hands of African Americans and the poor. In this view, for example, the principal effect of the Gun Control Act of 1968 is merely to make guns more expensive by restricting the import of cheap foreign arms. For that reason, the act functions as a "poll tax" on Second Amendment rights.[119] Similarly, many believe the agitation for a ban on Saturday Night specials proceeds from a fear of Blacks with guns: "It is difficult to escape the conclusion that the 'Saturday Night Special' is emphasized because it is cheap and is being sold to a particular class of people. The name is sufficient evidence—the reference is to 'niggertown Saturday night.' "[120] According to this argument, the sorry history of racist gun control indicates that one cannot trust the state with a monopoly of force. Hence, the African American experience argues in favor of an individual rights interpretation of the amendment.

Although many have contributed to this interpretation, its master expositors are two gifted scholars, Robert Cottrol and Raymond Diamond.[121] The impact of their work has already been significant: their writings have been frequently reprinted, and they have been cited favorably by a Supreme Court justice.[122] Their work contains two main themes, one historical and the other theoretical. First, they detail the historical relation between American race relations, on the one hand, and the right to arms, on the other. In this exposition, they emphasize that gun control has often hurt African Americans and self-arming has helped them. From this evidence, they develop their second theme: the Second Amendment should receive an individual rights reading because gun ownership is an important safeguard for African Americans and other despised groups in a country plagued by bigotry. They explain, "This article explores Second Amendment issues in light of the Afro-American experience, concluding that the individual rights theory comports better with the history of the right to bear arms in England and Colonial and post-Revolutionary America. The article also suggests that Second Amendment issues need to be explored, not only with respect to how the right to keep and bear arms has affected America as a whole, but also with an eye toward subcultures in American society who have been less able to rely on state protection."[123]

Cottrol and Diamond begin their historical sketch with the colonial background of the right to arms. They demonstrate that by the eighteenth century, English law had come to recognize a right to keep and bear arms, but that right was highly qualified along class and religious lines. American law eliminated those distinctions and substituted racial ones: white citizens, whatever their class or religion, had a right and a duty to be armed, but African Americans enjoyed only limited arms rights. As America became a society divided by race, white Americans felt threatened by Native Americans on their borders and slaves in their midst. As a result, they wanted both to arm themselves and disarm people of color.[124]

Next, Cottrol and Diamond summarize the ideology of the Second Amendment: "If necessity forced the early colonists to arm, the Revolution and the friction with Britain's standing army that preceded it—and in many ways precipitated it—served to revitalize Whiggish notions that standing armies were dangerous to liberty, and that militias, composed of the whole of the people, best protected both liberty and security."[125] When the new federal constitution gave Congress the power to organize, arm, and discipline the militia, many feared that Congress would use its new powers "to both destroy state power over the militia and to disarm the people."[126] As a result, state legislatures proposed a constitutional amendment to protect the right of the population to keep and bear arms: "It is against this background that the meaning of the Second Amendment must be considered. For the revolutionary generation, the idea of the militia and an armed population were related. The principal reason for preferring a militia of the whole over either a standing army or a select militia was rooted in the idea that, whatever the inefficiency of the militia of the whole, the institution would better protect the newly won freedoms than a reliance on security provided by some more select body."[127]

At this juncture, however, the Afro-Americanist reconsideration hits a serious snag: this militia of the whole did not ostensibly include African Americans. Shortly after Congress proposed the Second Amendment, it adopted the Uniform Militia Act, which "called for the enrollment of every free, able-bodied white male citizen between the ages of eighteen and forty-five into the militia."[128] For Cottrol and Diamond, it is critical that many white Americans were racists before and after the founding generation because the whole reason for reading the amendment as an individual right is to allow African Americans to resist white violence. The presence of racism in the founding generation, however, is a problem for Cottrol and Diamond: if the Framers were violent white racists, then their Second Amendment itself would be infected with racism as well. In fact, Carl Bogus has argued that the amendment was really designed to guarantee the right of whites to own arms so as to subjugate Native American and African American people. As a result, instead of embracing the amendment, Bogus's Afro-Americanist reconsideration would reject it as a vestige of an oppressive and archaic worldview.[129]

Cottrol and Diamond avoid this problem by arguing that "while [the Uniform Militia Act] specifically included only this limited portion of the population, *the statute excluded no one from militia service.*"[130] In other words, the statute only seems to be racially exclusive: it required that white men enroll but allowed the states to enroll others as well. Cottrol and Diamond advance three bits of evidence to support this reading. First, in the antebellum period, states both North and South sometimes enrolled Blacks, especially during times of invasion. Second, northern (but not southern) states generally allowed Blacks to own guns.[131] Third, "the authors of the statute had experience, in the Revolution, with a militia and Continental Army considerably broad in membership," in that African American men and even some women had served, though with controversy. As a result, "it is likely that the framers of the 1792 statute envisioned a militia broader than the one they specified." Cottrol and Diamond use this analysis of the Uniform Militia Act to give the Second Amendment a nonracist reading. If the Framers imagined an inclusive militia in the statute, it stands to reason that they intended the same sort of militia in the amendment: "The widespread use of blacks as soldiers in time of crisis and the absence of restrictions concerning the arming of blacks in the northern states provide another clue concerning how to read the Second Amendment. . . . [The broad militia envisioned by the 1792 statute] suggest[s] to us how broad the term 'people' in the Second Amendment was meant to be."[132]

In short, because of the demands of their theory, Cottrol and Diamond must portray American culture as violently racist before and after but not during the founding generation. This portion of their historical account seems the least plausible. They give no causal explanation for this break in the pattern of racism, nor any written evidence that the Framers intended a multiracial militia. Instead, the best contemporaneous evidence, the Uniform Militia Act, specified a monochrome body. Cottrol and Diamond argue that the act implicitly allowed but did not require a multiracial militia, but they suggest no explanation of why the Framers might concoct such a scheme. The most obvious reason for requiring whites but not Blacks to enroll is that the Framers distrusted Blacks; but that reason would lead to excluding Blacks altogether.

Cottrol and Diamond argue that we can infer that the act would allow a multiracial militia from the fact that militias sometimes included Blacks. As Cottrol and Diamond admit, however, that inclusion was controversial and occurred only as a concession to necessity in times of dire need. Moreover, the militia sometimes included women, but even Cottrol and Diamond do not argue that the Uniform Militia Act permitted a multigender militia. There is a different, more plausible explanation of the act's language: in wartime, the militia had included Blacks, but that experience had been so controversial that Congress decided to exclude them in peacetime. Should the need arise again, Congress could adopt a more expansive definition.

After this implausible rendering of the founding period, however, Cottrol and Diamond resume their historical account with their customary care. Their work is long, careful, and detailed, so a summary can give only a flavor. Their theses are clear and constant: gun control hurts African Americans, and self-arming can help. In the North, for example, Blacks formed militias to resist white mobs. The central example is the Cincinnati riot of September 1841: on the first night, an African American militia beat off a white mob; the second night, a white militia disarmed the African Americans, and the mob then returned to wreak havoc.[133] Cottrol and Diamond draw the lesson: "The 1841 Cincinnati riot represents the tragic, misguided irony of the city's authorities who, concerned with the safety of the black population, chose to disarm and imprison them."[134] In the South, both before and after the Civil War, the states enacted gun control to disarm Blacks.[135] Nevertheless, southern Blacks resisted white violence by force of arms, and Cottrol and Diamond observe, "This right [to arms], seen in the eighteenth century as a mechanism that enabled a majority to check the excesses of a potentially tyrannical national government, would for many blacks in the twentieth century become a means of survival in the face of private violence and state indifference."[136] The civil rights years also bear out this lesson: "Blacks in the South found the Deacons [for Defense and Justice] helpful because they were unable to rely upon police or other entities. This provided a practical reason for a right to bear arms."[137] Even today, the state does a poor job of protecting African Americans. Although the threat of white violence might seem to be waning, "many fear a decline in the quality of that atmosphere."[138]

The primary threat to Blacks today, however, is no longer "the horrors of white lynch mobs" but "the tragic black-on-black violence that plagues the mean streets of our inner cities."[139] To this point, Cottrol and Diamond have built their case on the specter of collective white violence, so this shift to individual African American crime seems an important break. Indeed, Cottrol and Diamond acknowledge that "a case can be made that greater firearms restrictions might alleviate this tragedy." Nonetheless, they believe the recent past gives no reason for abandoning the individual rights interpretation of the Second Amendment. Whether the threat comes from African American or white violence, American governments have never protected African American citizens: "A society with a dismal record of protecting a people has a dubious claim on the right to disarm them. Perhaps a re-examination of this history can lead us to a modern realization of what the framers of the Second Amendment understood: that it is unwise to place the means of protection totally in the hands of the state, and that self-defense is also a civil right."[140]

In conclusion, Cottrol and Diamond analogize the fate of the Second Amendment and African Americans: both have traditionally been marginalized by courts, policymakers, and scholars. That parallel treatment may not be a coincidence: "Throughout American history, black and white Americans have had radically different experiences with respect to violence and state protection. Perhaps another reason the Second Amendment has not been taken very seriously by the courts and the academy is that for many of those who shape or critique constitutional policy, the state's power and inclination to protect them is a given. But for all too many black Americans, that protection historically has not been available."[141]

Cottrol and Diamond present an interpretation of the Second Amendment that is vastly more sophisticated and nuanced than those offered by JPFO and the women and guns movement. Nonetheless, their interpretation shares two features with those. First, it is perspectival: from the perspective of African American history, they argue for an individual rights reading because Blacks have not been able to rely on the state for protection. Second, this theory of the amendment rests on a vision of the social world fractured along lines of bigotry. In this view, Blacks have traditionally needed personal firearms because of white violence. Recently, the primary threat may have shifted to "black-on-black" violence, but the reason that Blacks need guns to defend against this intraracial violence is still interracial animus: the state, indifferent to the fate of its African American citizens, has always failed to protect them. At its worst, white America has turned a violent hand against its African American citizens; at its best, the white citizenry will be quiescent and the state indifferent while Blacks kill one another. The message to African Americans is clear: in matters of violence, you can rely on no one but yourselves.

Outgroups and Political Violence

These outgroup theories of the Second Amendment all rest on a perception of the state as indifferent or hostile to outsiders. For that reason, the amendment should protect a regime of decentralized violence: because the state will not protect outgroups, it should allow them to protect themselves. Yet as powerfully as these theories document the danger in a state monopoly of force, they pay strikingly little attention to the dangers inherent in decentralized violence. In point of fact, private ordering of violence usually favors self-styled populists with hostile intent to outgroups. Even if these outgroup theorists are right in their conviction that the state cannot be trusted, they prescribe an equally hopeless alternative. This choice is not really a choice at all: in a scheme of decentralized violence, outgroups will be oppressed by private groups; in a scheme of centralized violence, they will be oppressed by the state. Either way, they will be oppressed. We must ask for a third option.

The only hope for better treatment of outgroups is a consensus culture more protective of these groups; only in such a culture would the threat from private *or* public violence abate. In other words, if the problem is hate violence, the only answer is less hatred. Outgroup theories of the Second Amendment, however, actively frustrate the creation of such a culture. Perhaps the theorists are right that sometimes outgroups would do well to arm themselves. As a matter of prudence, outgroups might buy guns, and as a matter of policy, the state might let them. These theories, however, do not merely counsel outgroups to take up arms against the present reality of hate violence. Instead, they extrapolate from that present reality to a prescriptive constitutional story. In this view, the Constitution requires us to assume, not as a matter of current prudence but as fundamental law, that Americans will always be divided by hatred. For that reason, they must always prepare for war against one another. Telling such stories can only help them come true, and outgroups will be left to choose between hopeless options. Ironically, then, as constitutional myths, these stories defeat the very goal they were written to secure.

DECENTRALIZED VIOLENCE

In the face of public and private hostility, the new outgroup theories propose a scheme of decentralized political violence so that outgroups may defend themselves. For these theorists, the Second Amendment thus guarantees a right both individual and political/collective. It is individual in the sense that each individual has a right to arms; it is political/collective in the sense that these individuals use their arms as members of collectivities: people attack them as women or Jews or African Americans, and they resist as such. In resisting, whether in groups or as individuals, they are not only defending themselves, but also seeking to make political change. JPFO's analysis is the most collective: the group paradigmatically imagines Jews as a group resisting a tyrannical government. The women and guns movement is the most individual: it paradigmatically imagines a lone woman resisting a lone attacker. And the Afro-Americanist reconsideration lies in between: Cottrol and Diamond focus on private associations of African Americans resisting private associations of white attackers. Yet all three interpretations argue that individuals have rights to arms so that they may pursue political ends.

In projecting a socially divided world, these theories are more realistic than theories that conjure with the people, imagining a false unity. Unhappily, in proffering a realistic vision of the social world, the theories also create new problems. These theorists interpret the Second Amendment to guarantee a general right to arms, not just a right for Jews or African Americans or women. As a result, everyone, including racists, misogynists, and anti-Semites, may possess the means of violence. To be sure, these outgroup theorists would emphasize that they endorse the use of arms only for self-defense, not hate-filled aggression. The genie of decentralized violence may not, however, be stuffed back into the bottle so easily once it is released. General arming may help virtuous resistance, but it also helps vicious attacks. And in effect, these theories mandate or presume a state that is not strong enough to block hate violence. If the state were strong enough to suppress bigoted violence in advance, it would also be strong enough to quash outgroup resistance. And the whole point in these theories is that the state is either so corrupt or incompetent that citizens must take up the burden of self-defense. In this view, outgroups must choke down the knowledge that the state cannot or will not protect them; they are on their own. That, however, is a state of affairs that outgroups should fear, not welcome — for three reasons.

Outgroups and Guns

First, outgroups should fear a regime of decentralized violence because they simply do not have as many guns as their enemies. Saul Alinsky provocatively described the Black Panther militia: "They haven't got the numbers and they know nothing about revolutionary tactics. What kind of revolutionary is it who shouts that all power comes out of the muzzle of a gun when he knows damn well the other side's got all the guns?"[142] Alinsky's comment is equally applicable to the outgroup theories of the Second Amendment. African Americans and Jews are a small fraction of the population. Women actually constitute a majority, but as a group — and the same could be said for Jews — they own fewer guns, are less comfortable with them, and are more reluctant to use them than others. The women and guns movement is seeking to change that state of affairs, but despite publicity of an alleged trend, the numbers have probably not changed much.

By contrast, decentralization of violence will likely favor those groups with roots in the gun culture. It is no coincidence that the gun culture has traditionally seen in the Second Amendment a constitutional symbol of its right to primacy. Today, the element of the gun culture most likely to exploit a regime of decentralized violence is the militia movement, a development unlikely to promote the health and safety of African Americans and Jews. To be sure, JPFO has made common cause with the militia movement, and some militias even have Jewish and African American members.[143] For such people, the fear of government bulks so large that it blinds them to the danger of private violence. It is not true that the enemy of my enemy is necessarily my friend.

Violence in Revolutionary Conditions

Second, beyond being outnumbered, outgroups should fear decentralized violence because it tends to increase bigotry among the general population, especially when it is accompanied by attack on the legitimacy of the state. Essentially, the outgroup theories prescribe a state of permanent, incipiently revolutionary conditions. For these theorists, the state can claim no monopoly of force, and its legitimacy is always suspect. Indeed, the theories presuppose the state's illegitimacy vis-à-vis outgroups, as they presume that the state will not provide even the most basic security for them. For that reason, the Constitution positively empowers private groups to use violence in order to secure political change.

In the absence of a presumptively legitimate state, identity affiliation has typically stepped in to fill the need for order. Recent events in Europe graphically exemplify this tendency. To the surprise of many, the breakup of autocratic states often gave rise to a revival of ethnic hatred, previously held in check by a strong government. Michael Walzer writes, "Ethnic and religious differences survived, and wherever they were territorially based, local agencies, which were more or less representative, retained some minimal functions and some symbolic authority. These they were able to convert very quickly, once the empires fell, into a kind of state machine driven by nationalist ideology and aimed at sovereign power—and opposed, often enough, by established local minorities, the great beneficiaries of the imperial regime and its last and most stalwart defenders."[144] In Russia, hard right nationalist sentiment existed under the Soviet regime, but in the chaotic conditions after that regime's fall, it became a vigorous force.[145] Similarly, Josip Tito's strong central regime managed to hold the various nationalisms of Yugoslavia together; with its demise, the Balkans have again become balkanized, and the phrase *ethnic cleansing* has entered the popular vocabulary.[146] Other contemporary examples could be listed in great number.[147] As between totalitarianism and decentralized violence, outgroups have no good choice.

Even the history of genocide, on which JPFO relies so heavily, illustrates the tendency of revolutionary change to increase hate violence. *Lethal Laws* opens with a revealing discussion of *Revolution and Genocide,* a comparative study of twentieth-century genocide by the late Robert Melson of Purdue University. Zelman et al. quote Melson to the effect that domestic genocide has killed more people in the twentieth century than international war. *Lethal Laws* then faults Melson, however, for failing to explain that gun control causes genocide.[148] In so arguing, JPFO ignores Melson's central thesis about what does cause genocide. This failure is not surprising because Melson's thesis directly undermines JPFO's key contention that decentralized violence is good for Jews.

Melson's thesis is that the genocides he examined—including the Holocaust, the Armenian genocide, the destruction of the Russian kulaks, and the Cambodian autogenocide—were all products of political revolution.[149] Melson forcefully explains the link between revolution and genocide: "Every revolution results in not only the collapse of a state's political institutions but also the loss of its legitimacy and the destruction of the political myth that links rulers to ruled." Upon the demise of those old myths, the revolutionary movement must create new ones: "Political myths are basic to revolutions because, in a compelling manner, they tell the tale of the revolutionary state's origins; they identify and define the new state's true citizens, 'the people'; they target its enemies; and they formulate its goals."[150]

This process of revolutionary mythmaking is dangerous for outgroups because in defining the true people, the myths must also define a contrasting class—the enemies of the state. Melson's explanation is directly relevant to modern Second Amendment theory:

> Revolutionary myths and ideologies have implications for genocide in that every revolutionary vanguard that has achieved state power seeks to restructure the state and give it a new basis of support. . . . Having come to power in a revolutionary situation, a new regime is presented with the opportunity to shape society in its own image and to construct and define who is this "people" from whom the revolutionary state will seek its legitimacy. . . . The impulse to reconstruct and redefine the political community and to exclude from it whole categories derives in part from the exigencies of the postrevolutionary situation. This is always characterized by domestic disorder, a lack of legitimate authority, and often war. . . . [R]ecasting the political community according to a revolutionary vision implies that groups and classes, whole

categories of human beings, will not fit into the postrevolutionary society. These will have to be reshaped, reeducated, reformed, or permanently excluded from the new order.[151]

In short, then, Melson never comments explicitly on whether gun control is good for Jews, but he argues powerfully that decentralized violence and the failure of state legitimacy is bad for them.

In this country as well, political violence has usually taken a racial and ethnic form in the absence of effective government. Indeed, it seems to be a distinctive aspect of American culture that political violence takes this guise, rather than a class-based form. Ted Robert Gurr, perhaps the most distinguished student of American political violence, explains: "One distinctive feature of the American experience is the relative unimportance of conflict defined in class terms compared with conflict along lines of ethnic, religious, and national cleavage. . . . [T]he participants in episodes of ethnic and racial rioting saw themselves and their opponents through the lense of communal identification, not class ones. Communal loyalties and antagonisms were a consequence of ethnic and national diversity in a society established and dominated by English settlers. The dominant Anglo-Americans defined Indians, blacks, Irish, Jews, and Italians as separate and to varying degrees inferior people. Little wonder, then, that if and when the latter groups mobilized in conflict, they did so as communal or identity groups rather than making class alliances across ethnic lines."[152] Another student of the field presents a similar summary: "Unlike Europe, so little of the violence in the United States ha[s] been insurrectionary. Most ha[s] involved one group of citizens against another, rather than citizens against the state. Class conflict ha[s] been overshadowed to an extraordinary degree by ethnic, religious, and racial conflict."[153]

Populist Power in Decentralized Violence

The third reason that outgroups should fear decentralized violence grows out of the first two. Because outgroups are small and decentralized violence promotes bigotry, reactionary movements can sometimes succeed at using violence for political ends, but movements for inclusion generally fail. Gurr summarizes: "The use and threat of violence on behalf of social reform usually has stimulated a backlash of defensive violence. Campaigns of violence to reverse threatening social and political change, however, succeeded in those times and places where their purposes were widely supported. The use of intimidation and violence by the Ku Klux Klan, by lynch mobs, and by vigilantes are cases in point."[154]

The evolution of the conflict dynamic in the civil rights movement is a familiar example of this theme. In the early years of the movement, demonstrators sought in nonviolent but provocative ways to cause southern racists to attack them; appalled at images of such violence, whites elsewhere came to endorse the cause of civil rights. As a result, the movement secured impressive advances, including landmark civil rights legislation.[155] As the decade of the sixties wore on, however, the movement's conflict dynamic shifted from non-violent provocation to violent assault, especially in the form of urban rioting. This shift stirred a white backlash that led to waning support for measures to improve the condition of African Americans.[156] The lesson is clear: outgroups cannot achieve their ends by violence on their own. They need the support of others, and the use of widespread violence usually causes them to lose that support.

As a result, it is not surprising that as a cultural icon the Second Amendment has had a populist cast. As we have seen, while Europeans were coming to disregard the right to arms, Americans came to cherish it because of their fear of the outsider. As a result, they organized the Body of the People into a universal militia, and the Framers celebrated this ideal in the Second Amendment. Later, populist Americans embraced gun ownership as a way to keep "deviant" elements, such as new immigrants and the labor movement, in line.[157] And today, the primary constituency for the Second Amendment is the gun culture, which claims to represent the true American people, as opposed to arriviste interlopers with European ideas about the role of government. At its most extreme, the gun culture shades into the militia movement, which claims to be protecting the people against those who do not belong.

As a populist text, the Second Amendment shares the advantages and disadvantages of populism in general. On the one hand, populism has a democratic and egalitarian face: members of the people should all enjoy the same basic rights and status. In this aspect, populism has opposed self-styled elites, and it has served as a force for the liberation of the common man and even sometimes the common woman.[158] On the other hand, populism has also had a more sinister, racist, nativist, sexist, and anti-Semitic side. Although some populists sought to extend rights to women, Jews, and Blacks, others sought to keep those groups in thrall.[159] Thus, American history has witnessed the spectacle of Jacksonian democrats seeking universal suffrage for white men and simultaneously insisting on the subjugation of women, Blacks, and Indians.[160] Similarly, at the end of the nineteenth century, populists attacked the power of urban wealth while simultaneously defending white supremacy in the South.[161] More recently, George Wallace and Pat Buchanan have built populist movements by tapping a vein of anger among "average" Americans (meaning white, Christian, and working class — in other words, the gun culture) at immigrants, Blacks, and others.[162]

These egalitarian and hierarchical strains in American populism are not actually in contradiction because populists believe in equal rights, but only for members of the people. Others cannot enjoy equal rights because they are inferior or "unassimilable" or both.[163] This affection for the people as a political concept is the great promise and threat of populism.[164] The promise has been self-rule through egalitarian democracy—for members of the people. Even the insistence on exiling unassimilable elements grows out of this commitment because populists insist that democracies depend on a shared civic culture.[165] If democracy is populism's promise, however, oppression of outgroups is its threat. For outgroups, populism is a dangerous game to play, one that can always turn ugly. If some are inside the people, some must be outside. For that reason, it is no coincidence that outgroups have shied away from populism, preferring instead discourses that stress the rights of individuals against the legislative majority.[166]

When it turns violent, populism has generally shown its ugly, exclusive side. The examples are many and the reasons easy to surmise. As we have seen, in a regime of decentralized violence, citizens need a source of order and a basis for legitimacy other than the state, and they often find it in affiliation with identity groups. Private violence succeeds primarily when used to defend the conservative order against threatening changes—such as the movement of Blacks, women, and Jews into positions of respect, autonomy, and power. Finally, populists generally turn to the gun after becoming convinced that the political process has been captured by enemies of the people.[167] And for populists, the best evidence of that capture is that the system no longer values them the way it once did; instead, it showers traditional outgroups with "special" favor.[168]

In short, then, the traditional cultural landscape of the Second Amendment actually makes good sense. The absence of state legitimacy and decentralized violence are conditions prone to produce an exclusive and belligerent populism. The gun culture might welcome that situation, but for outgroups it represents danger. Populism has attractive aspects, but its great downside is precisely its ambiguous attitude toward outgroups. In other words, it makes best sense for outgroup theorists to issue warnings about decentralized violence, rather than to embrace it.

CONSTITUTIONAL TALES OF VIOLENCE

Outgroup interpretations of the Second Amendment leave outgroups with only two choices. First, they could commit to a state monopoly of violence, only to face the state indifference or hostility documented in these stories. Second, they could commit to decentralized violence, only to face the private hate violence I have described. Neither path is acceptable. The only viable future is one these theories never mention: the creation of a consensus culture that welcomes outgroups and pervades the way that both state and private sector use violence. It is not particularly useful to consider whether a hate-filled state with a monopoly of violence is worse than a hate-filled society composed of armed groups. Instead, we should be asking how to reduce the general level of hatred. Reducing that level would make both state and private sectors more trustworthy, and the debate over their relative trustworthiness would become less burning.

In arguing the necessity of such a consensus culture, I do not mean to propose that the culture need be placid, monolithic, or immutable. In fact, such a culture need serve only one end: it must provide a common account of the way that violence should be used to resolve differences, especially those between identity groups, and it must include only enough of the citizenry effectively to tame hate violence. Hope for such a consensus need not be predicated on the belief that America can ever eliminate such violence, or that the struggle against bigotry can ever cease.[169] Instead, it is predicated on two more modest beliefs: (1) only cultural change (as opposed to private arming) can significantly control hate violence; and (2) such cultural change is possible. Those assumptions are borne out by history: the level of hate violence in this country has diminished over time because of the delegitimation of racism, anti-Semitism, and misogyny.

Ironically, the general adoption of these outgroup theories would frustrate the creation of such a culture. These theories function at two levels. First, they prudentially counsel outgroups that, in the face of hostility, they should overcome their aversion to guns and to fighting back. Criminologists and sociologists disagree on whether this counsel is well advised, and the question is outside the scope of this work.[170] Second, however, these theories make a different and more far-reaching claim: in their view the Constitution itself presumes, and requires that we presume, a world in which hatred is so endemic that decentralized violence is the only hope. As constitutional stories, these tales of violence do not simply protect outgroup gun ownership until we arrive at a less hate-filled culture; rather, they actively block the creation of such a culture. They may help in the short term but only with unacceptable long-term damage.

As we have seen, every theory of the Second Amendment rests on and prescribes a myth about the nature of American society. To create a consensus culture protective of outgroups, we need stories of unification based on justice, but these outgroup theorists offer us stories of violent division rooted in mistrust. These stories share six constituent elements. Taken together as constitutional storytelling, these elements would sharply circumscribe the possibilities of our common political life. They hold out no possibility of redemption.

Perspectival Interpretation

First, these stories adopt a perspectival interpretation of the Second Amendment, rooted in the particularities of their group experiences. In doing so, they seem to embrace a central element of postmodernism: truth is inevitably a matter of perspective, produced and determined by the background of the truth seeker.[171] Also like postmodern multiculturalism,[172] these theories maintain that society is fractured into contending identity groups, so that consensus is virtually impossible. The best we can hope for is the uneasy coexistence of the various cultures, living next to one another but each perceiving the world in its own way. Correlatively, we cannot hope for a constitutional culture that would hold across society in delimiting violence.

Yet lacking that hope, outgroups will inevitably suffer. If multiculturalism is to be more than an apology for the dominance of the strong over the weak, it must aim for the peaceful coexistence of disparate groups. But to have peace, we must also have shared norms governing the interaction of groups and specifying when violence might be justified. In other words, to some degree, we must all be uniculturalists on the subject of the constitutional organization of violence: We need such a common culture so as to mark off a safe field within which America's many subcultures can contend in peaceful ways. Indeed, if there is no agreement on the use of violence, peaceful disagreement and multiculturalism itself become impossible.[173] Similarly, at some level we must all be proceduralists: insofar as we celebrate diversity, we need agreement on procedures that will allow us to cope with its existence. This insight is at the heart of classical liberalism,[174] and it retains its force in the face of modern social fragmentation. In short, then, a purely perspectival approach may be appropriate for some constitutional provisions, but not for the Second Amendment.

The outgroup theorists might argue that I have exaggerated their position. They might contend that although they approach the Second Amendment from a specific perspective, they do not deny the possibility of a societywide reading cobbled together from a variety of perspectives. The nature of their argument, however, denies that possibility. Because the perspectives of various groups differ on whether the amendment should be read to protect a right to arms, it would not be possible simply to agglomerate them. We must therefore privilege some interpretations over others, and these theorists forcefully argue that we should choose theirs. They would vigorously dispute the idea that if other perspectives (those of bureaucrats, would-be tyrants, or people who are afraid of guns) counsel a contrary interpretation of the amendment, then we should read the amendment not to protect a personal right to arms.[175]

Alternatively, the outgroup theorists might argue that insights derived from *their* perspectives should appeal to groups from *all* perspectives. As we all might someday be at the mercy of a tyrannical or indifferent government, so we all should support a universal right to arms. The problem with this contention is that the very history of racism, misogyny, and anti-Semitism compiled by these outgroup theorists belies the hope that such an appeal will reach potential oppressors. As Cottrol and Diamond so effectively document, southern white supremacists enacted legislation to disarm African Americans, never considering that someday the government might try to disarm them. Similarly, as JPFO details, the Nazis sought to disarm Jews and other "enemies of the state" without any flicker of concern that they might someday be branded enemies of the state themselves. Blinded by hate, oppressors do not usually realize that they might someday become the victims of hate.

In other words, we will not have a unified constitutional culture on the organization of violence so long as we consult only the perspectives of identity groups as they are presently constituted. A consensus culture can result only from prolonged political interaction in which groups come to accept the necessity of a shared vision and so redefine their own identity as including the viewpoints of others.[176] These stories, with their unrelieved insistence on a single perspective, give no hope for such an enlarged sense of perspective. Neither, as the next several sections explain, do they assert a vision of the political process through which we might accomplish that task.

Hatred and Suspicion

In these theories, the social world is and always will be composed of hostile, violent groups. Hate violence is the whole predicate of these theories. If the state could and would control private violence or if the general culture were safe, then outgroups would have no need of the right to arms. To remain viable, then, the theories must presuppose that hatred is a permanent element of the social world. As we have seen, JPFO overtly asserts that the Constitution guarantees a right to arms because such hatred is inevitable. Although they concede that racism waxes and wanes, Cottrol and Diamond, too, argue that African Americans will always need a right to arms because violent racism will always be an important force in America. I have been unable to find any discussion by the women and guns movement on whether misogyny is ineradicable, but a positive answer seems implicit in their claim that the right to arms must be constitutional—and so permanent. Even if these theorists might acknowledge that a unified social world is conceivable, moreover, they would argue that we should always act as if that world does not exist and is not possible. The point in constitutionalizing these stories is that the storm of hatred can always appear, suddenly and violently, even amidst sunny skies. The people—meaning, for these theories, all the discordant groups in society—

have a right to arms because they must keep on their guard. In short, suspicion is the fundamental relation among each identity group, other identity groups, and the state.

The result of this suspicion is a profound circumscription of our political life together. As I will elaborate in chapter 9, we know that a well-functioning democracy depends on a measure of civic trust among its citizens.[177] For the outgroup theories, however, it is only good sense to distrust the motives and perspectives of those from other groups. In fact, the theories require us never to trust each other so far as to attempt a collective organization of violence. Instead, each individual must decide when and whom to resist, and the Constitution ensures that he will have the means to do so. As a result, some groups will inevitably attack other groups, setting up a round of reprisals that will keep hatred on the boil. In the stories told by these theories, the right to arms has benign consequences: women fight off rapists, African Americans fight off the Klan, Jews stop the Holocaust. But in a fractured world, other real-life stories feature the right to arms in a less savory light. In Northern Ireland and the former Yugoslavia, conditions of decentralized violence have resulted in wounds so deep that a consensus culture may never be possible.[178] Closer to home, violence between African Americans and Jews has further poisoned already strained relations between these once allied groups.[179] This tension is especially relevant because the outgroup theorists include both African Americans and Jews. The former tell stories of resisting the Klan, and the latter tell stories of resisting the Nazis, but it is equally likely that some members of each group will use their personal arms to kill members of the other group.

The Functional Equivalence of All Constitutional Visions

In these outgroup theories, all groups retain the right to arms alike, regardless of the malignancy of their constitutional visions. Further, these groups hold the right to arms so that they may resist the state or other groups if, in their perspectival opinion, such resistance is warranted. The Deacons for Defense and Justice stand on the same footing as the Klan before this Second Amendment. Thus, on the issue of self-arming, the state will treat all constitutional visions as if they were morally equivalent. To be sure, some may believe that hate groups have an inferior constitutional vision, but no group has the right to insist that the state disarm another group, no matter how threatening that group may be. As a result, in practice all have a right to maintain their point of view by force of arms, and each group has no choice but to meet opposing groups on the field of battle.

This functional moral equivalence grows out of the suspicion considered in the last section: no one is in a position to decide who should be armed and who not, because no one is trustworthy enough. We must keep the means of violence decentralized because no one, including the state, holds a privileged position in determining when violence should be deployed for political ends. The result is that the decision to use violence has an irreducibly subjective quality: as we cannot trust the state or some other putatively authoritative body to make such determinations for us, we must each decide, and those decisions, inevitably, will differ.

In analyzing the actions of the Black Panthers, Cottrol and Diamond seek to repudiate this subjectivity: "The Deacons for Defense and Justice are to be contrasted with the Black Panther Party for Self-Defense. The Black Panther Program included [an assertion of Second Amendment rights]. . . . Yet, the Black Panthers deteriorated into an ineffective group of revolutionaries, at times using arguably criminal means of effectuating their agenda."[180] In other words, the Panthers, unlike the Deacons, violated the criminal law and so were objectively in the wrong, whatever their subjective views. Yet this repudiation of subjectivity is inconsistent with the premises of Cottrol's and Diamond's approach. They cannot mean that groups should never exercise their Second Amendment rights in such a way as to violate current law; the whole point of their historical exploration is that the state cannot always be trusted to pass just or constitutional laws. If the state of North Carolina had criminalized the use of guns for self-defense, the Deacons would have become criminals just like the Panthers, yet their cause would have been no less worthy than before. But if the state cannot be trusted to judge the justice of violent action, who can? In the view of Cottrol and Diamond, only individuals can decide when to take up arms. In assassinating police officers, the Panthers were doing exactly that, because from their perspective they were defending themselves against the white power structure. Such extreme fragmentation would make the creation of a unified, protective culture supremely difficult.

The Rejection of Political Structures

The outgroup theories assert that the solution to the *political* problem of hate violence is *personal* self-arming by outgroup members. Of necessity, individuals may sometimes organize for collective resistance, as when women enter self-defense classes or African Americans form private militias. These associative efforts, however, are only — and, by the premises of these theories, can only be — the product of individual wills spontaneously deciding to enlist. Like eddies in the ocean, they form when individuals swirl toward one another, and then they disappear when the perceived need for collective self-defense is past. Organizations thus derive their legitimacy entirely from the will of their members. As a result, these theories harbor deep suspicion for formal institutions such as the state, the army, and the United Nations. At best, these bodies will be ineffectual, at worst tyrannical. By contrast, true Second Amendment associations follow the model of private voluntarist groups; they resemble mutual aid societies, religious denominations, and reform movements.[181]

The theories dramatically assert the effectiveness of private armed associations and the ineffectiveness of political structures in solving political problems. Thus, JPFO maintains that Jews perished while the United States and international society dithered or intentionally ignored the Holocaust; the better course would have been to arm European Jews. Women & Guns magazine asserts that international peacekeeping would not solve misogynist violence in Bosnia; the better course would have been to arm Bosnian women. Even Cottrol and Diamond ignore the fact that only the Union army was effective in suppressing white supremacist violence during Reconstruction;[182] instead, they praise African American self-arming after withdrawal of the troops.

These accounts, then, offer no theory of the collective organization of violence beyond the claim that individuals should act as seems best to them. Because they trust only individuals, the theories explicitly condemn state attempts to control the means of violence, but they also implicitly condemn any association, public or private, that attempts to control violence except through the spontaneous agreement of individuals. In other words, the theories reject the use of authoritative political structures as a means of organizing political violence.

Earlier, I argued that the women and guns movement echoes the feminist claim that the personal is political: giving women a personal right to arms can have great political significance. In fact, however, the echo is terribly distorted. Like all of these theories, by insisting that the only effective solution to hate violence is individual self-defense, the movement in reality reduces the political to the personal. Mainstream feminism takes exactly the opposite approach. For most feminists, the point in claiming that the personal is political is to seek political solutions to problems traditionally dubbed private and thus ignored in the public sphere.[183] Indeed, those feminists may believe the women and guns movement actually denies that the personal is political because the movement seems to reject the idea that there *is* a political. In the view of the movement, if police cannot protect women, then women should stop whining and protect themselves. At that point, however, misogynist violence ceases to be a public concern and disappears again into the hidden world of private relations.

In short, the outgroup theories are so sensitive to the concern that state power corrupts that they will instead tolerate a regime of private ordering in the realm of armed power. As I have argued, however, decentralized violence usually leads to hatred and bigotry. When it does, these theories allow no way of collectively correcting the situation because they have rejected political structures as a way of organizing political violence.

Relating Through Arms

These theories also maintain that violence is more basic than peaceful politics to the life of the state, and, concomitantly, that citizens relate to one another more fundamentally through arms than through political participation. All of the theories assume the perennial existence of hatred and celebrate outgroup self-arming in response. By contrast, they never mention the possibility of changing the political culture so as to make it more protective of outgroups. Instead, the theories condemn the state and, implicitly, the political process behind it as unreliable or perfidious or both. For that reason, the theories insist that outgroup members would be foolish to depend on the state for protection; instead, they should depend on themselves and their identity group. Similarly, the theories sometimes repeat an argument central to the individual rights theory of the Second Amendment: the right to arms is our most important right because it is the practical guarantor of all other rights. If we give up our guns, we lose control over government, which may then run roughshod over the Constitution.[184]

This constitutional vision is stark: underneath the veneer of peaceful politics lurks a more essential world of primordial hatred, waiting to boil over. We may relate to fellow citizens through politics, but we should remember that in an instant they could become our oppressors. Politics is no more than a precarious holding action against the forces of hatred; our ultimate bulwark of safety is our personal capacity for violence.

The Constitutional Mandate

The constitutional mandate element of the stories is implicit in the foregoing five themes, but it is so important it bears separate mention. The social world described in these stories, full of division and violence, may be an accurate portrait of the world in which we now live. These stories, however, argue that the Second Amendment requires us to act as if the social world will always be divided and violent. Indeed, the theories maintain that this mandate of eternal vigilance is the great insight of the amendment: the world may look safe now, but it could change in a moment. Whatever cultural progress might be made is untrustworthy; only a good gun is real protection.

The Constitution, in this view, is a realist document: it requires us to take people at their worst, to guard against their proclivity to do evil. These tales help us to deal with a fallen world; they offer no vision of a better one. Thus, this vision rejects a different model of the Constitution, one that sees it as a redemptive force, a bridge to a better future.[185] Outgroups, however, cannot afford to abjure redemptive constitutionalism because the present and the past are too bleak. Regardless of who controls the guns, outgroups will not be safe in a hate-filled culture, so the only hope is to reduce the hatred. That path may seem idealistic, but there is no alternative. In that sense, redemptive constitutionalism may be much more realistic than urging outgroups to celebrate the private ordering of violence.

In short, telling these constitutional tales of violence creates costs for outgroups. Moreover, the stories will likely create very few gains, for similar reasons. In a protective culture, outgroups would not need the Second Amendment because the state would voluntarily protect them or guarantee them a right to arms. A constitutional right to arms is thus important only when the culture is deeply hostile. But in such a culture, it seems wildly implausible that the state would ever create and protect a constitutional right to arms for outgroups. It defies common sense to believe that a state would allow the killing of outgroups but simultaneously protect their Second Amendment rights. In positing a world filled with hatred and violence, these stories virtually preclude a world scrupulous about fidelity to the Constitution. In short, these tales make sense as accounts of guerrilla resistance, not as constitutional myths. The work of Cottrol and Diamond illustrates this problem. In scrupulous detail, they document the way gun control statutes have been used to disarm African Americans, in violation of the Second Amendment as they understand it. They conclude from this survey that gun control statutes do not help Blacks. Their work, however, also leads to another conclusion: in the face of widespread racism, the Second Amendment has not helped Blacks either.

On balance, then, this style of constitutional storytelling grants little hope to outgroups. Such stories undercut the only long-term hope, that is, the creation of a protective, consensual culture on the organization of violence. Correlatively, the stories offer little short-term hope to outgroups because a constitutional right to arms will be relatively useless to them in the absence of such a protective culture. For outgroups, fighting hatred with guns may be a necessary stopgap in a dangerous world; it cannot be an ultimate solution.

Culturally, Second Amendment dreams have traditionally been populist dreams. They yearn for the people, democratic, militant, and united, rising up against its enemies. Like much of populism, those dreams can be noble. They have inspired campaigns for social justice, resistance to unjust authority, and at least one revolution — our founding myth, the War for Independence. They hold before us a particular constitutional ideal: the people in its most democratic and unstructured guise, taking power into its own hands when the government fails to honor its obligations. Such dreams, however, can also become nightmares. Direct democracy always runs the risk of becoming majoritarian tyranny. The people may be wise, just, and tolerant, but they may also be angry, bitter, and intolerant. Generally, when the people feel betrayed by government and compelled to take up arms, they look for the cause of their felt disempowerment. In an old American tradition, rather than finding the cause of their distress in an increasingly complex world, they seek out the enemies of the people that have betrayed them. Too often, they find these enemies in outgroups who in fact have even less power than they.

Under such conditions, outgroups may have no choice but to arm themselves, and if the state cannot or will not protect them, it may have an obligation to let them protect themselves. Such self-defense efforts, like populist dreams, can be noble. They represent an ideal of courageous self-reliance in the face of hatred. But however noble it might be, this ideal is still only an adaptation to an unacceptable reality: a world poisoned with bigotry. While it may be important to retain armed self-reliance as one cultural ideal, it is vitally important that we not transform it into an ultimate constitutional vision. The temptation to do so is great, as the ideal rests on values we deeply cherish. A people that finds its origin in resistance to tyranny may, perhaps must, find these tales of violence enormously resonant: after centuries of oppression, a group declares that it will suffer no more, resolved to die free men and women rather than to live slaves. But like all values, these are only partial, and they must be balanced by a dream even more dear: the search for a society that is peaceful, harmonious, and protective of all its citizens.

PART III

*Reconstructing a Constitutional
Organization of Violence*

8

The Silent Crisis

My discussion has traveled far across the mythic landscape of the Second Amendment, from past to present. Now at the end, the journey has brought us to a point of silent crisis. Every constitutional order must seek to tame political violence. The Framers bequeathed a particular mythic structure for that task: the people acting directly through the universal militia, checked and balanced by the people acting indirectly through the legislature. As my review of the modern mythic landscape has shown, however, Americans today do not generally embrace that myth, and, given the changes in U.S. demographics and values, it would be surprising if they did. Yet, having abandoned that original myth, we have replaced it with myths that do not adequately serve the purpose of taming violence. In every case, these stories fruitlessly pit one segment of the population against another in hopes that if the right people have the guns all will be well. But if the population is fragmented and filled with hate, no amount of tinkering with the distribution of guns will solve the problem. Only something more radical will serve. The present crisis, then, is that our original myth no longer fits our situation or commands our allegiance, and our current myths fail to perform the tasks entrusted to them. We have no effective account of the constitutional organization of violence; we are in a mythic vacuum.

The term *crisis* seems appropriate because the task of taming political violence raises the deepest issues and emotions. Lying beneath discussion of the Second Amendment is a profound, and profoundly uncomfortable, spiritual truth: we do not control our own destinies and hence are not proof against threat. This truth is a fact that much of American culture seeks to suppress. Medical science has reached such an advanced stage that many assume they and their loved ones will live their lives in perfect health and die at an advanced age. When death comes, it generally occurs offstage, hidden from public view in hospitals and clinics. And in an age of supposed compassionate conservatism, America is snipping away at the welfare safety net in the belief that people can control their own destinies without public assistance. "We" the policymakers are confident we will never fall so low or need such help.

Such denial notwithstanding, misfortune, suffering, and death are still a part of the human condition, and we will not eliminate them by ignoring them. At the political level, we can never ensure that we will remain safe from public or private violence. The secret police or a populist mob might arrive on our front porch in the middle of the night. And so we depend thoroughly on the contingencies of history. We may live out our lives in peace and stability, sampling the good things that life offers — or we may not. And when we contemplate that truth, we may experience deep fear, for we must face our vulnerability and acknowledge our dependence on social structures, the political culture, and the good will of others for our safety.

The Framers seem to have understood this truth. In resisting the British Empire, they had launched themselves on a perilous course. Against all odds, they achieved independence, only to have their new nation erupt in backcountry rebellion. They must have sensed time and again that their country and their futures were teetering on the brink of dissolution. And as a result, they understood there was no guarantee of safety, no structure of government or distribution of arms that could assure the triumph of the virtuous. This awareness did not make them despair, but it did cause them to plan with the truth of perennial uncertainty ever before them. As we have seen, they trusted both the people-in-the-legislature and the people-in-militia, but they also understood that neither offered perfect reliability. As a result, they created a system of checks and balances in organizing constitutional violence: the legislature could suppress what it saw as rebellion, but the militia could make what it regarded as revolution. In addition, the Framers understood that the people could make a revolution only if they were united. They assumed that Americans did constitute such a unity, but there was no guarantee they always would. And if they did not, then revolution was not possible; and if revolution was not possible, neither was ultimate popular control of the government. In the Framers' view, therefore, we are all dependent on our fellow citizens for our public safety.

By contrast, our modern myths, reflecting the trend of modern American culture, seek to deny the truth of our ultimate dependency and vulnerability. The antirevolutionists imagine a world in which the government controls all the guns and thus all dissident elements. In this world, we can be safe, but only if we trust the government with the means of force. This account omits any hint that the government might itself abuse its power, such that an external check might be appropriate. The populists and the libertarians-cum-populists imagine a world in which the people, however defined, somehow cohere into a united whole, possessed of the force to overawe a perfidious government. This story omits any recognition that the people will more likely break down into vicious civil war or anarchy, such that governmental authority may be necessary to forestall insurrection. Only the outgroup theorists, as would be expected, contend that there is no truly safe course as between a hostile government and a hostile population. Even these writers, however, minimize the risk in a scheme of decentralized violence as the lesser of two evils.

Perhaps modern mythmakers promise safety because the field of Second Amendment studies is so angrily divided, and one thus feels required to promise more than one can deliver. Perhaps, however, a different explanation is closer to the bone. If we imagine we can fix the problem of political violence through a proper distribution of arms, then we may feel in control of our destinies. If, by contrast, we acknowledge that no distribution of arms can protect us, we are left feeling out of control. And if the Framers were right that only popular unity can pose any real bulwark against political violence, the problem becomes even worse. Generating solidarity among Americans seems a daunting, perhaps insuperable task: the steps that we might take to that end are vague, amorphous, and of uncertain utility. We are left doing what we can and hoping it will be enough. Hoping, however, can be difficult. It seems neither so concrete nor reassuring as the cold steel of a gun in the hands of the right person.

Many Americans are confident that revolution or tyranny happens only somewhere else, in unstable new republics or old authoritarian states. And indeed, the United States is not currently erupting into large-scale political violence. For that reason, our crisis is silent because even though we lack a viable myth for taming violence, we face no imminent upheaval. Nonetheless, to believe that the silent crisis can never become vocal is naive and inconsistent with our constitutional tradition. As long as the citizenry is happy, it may not revolt; and as long as the government is just, it may not need to. In its organization of violence, however, the Constitution must address bad times as well as good. If conditions should turn bad — if the economy took a sharp downturn or if the United States should lose its global preeminence — Americans' relative complacency might face serious challenges.

In fact, political violence or the threat of violence has never been absent from U.S. history. Although large-scale resistance has been rare, low-level unrest has been virtually endemic. And even though large-scale tyranny has been unusual, focused oppression of specific groups has been virtually the norm. Indeed, today, the riven mythic landscape of the Second Amendment is vivid testimony to a tension that threatens to erupt into violence. Increasingly, members of some groups are expressing their attitudes toward members of other groups through the rhetoric of self-arming, rather than through politics: "we" had better keep our guns close so we can resist "them." Indeed, Second Amendment fantasies are staple fare on the modern American menu. When people become frustrated with politics, they sometimes come to believe that only force will serve to cut whatever Gordian knot is keeping them from securing what they want. Even if they never actually shoot anyone, they are imagining they might, preparing themselves, perhaps relishing the satisfaction that vanquishing one's enemies might bring. And as they start to interpret their experience through the prism of whatever Second Amendment myth they have adopted, popular division limned in violence comes to seem natural, inevitable, and constitutionally sanctioned.

The emotions evoked by the amendment may help explain the inclination to render it into myth, rather than into precise legal rules. The problem of political violence is so threatening that narrow doctrinal propositions seem an insufficient response; instead, we seek an explanation in the viscerally compelling material of myth. In contemplating the reality of political violence, we do not want merely a line of court cases setting out the rights of the relevant parties. Instead, we look for an account of how violence comes into our lives, what it means, and how we can constrain it to good ends. It is therefore not surprising that Americans have been disinclined to analyze the Second Amendment purely as a matter of prudence and policy, in the way they might determine an appropriate speed limit. Instead, this provision seems inextricably connected to larger questions, such as the nature of American democracy and citizenship. One cannot reduce the amendment to a matter of technique or technology.

Today, however, we no longer share a common Second Amendment myth to help us tame political violence. In fact, while promising more safety than any scheme could deliver, the myths that we do have are more likely to contribute to our disintegration. And so one of the ironies of this mythic landscape is that in asking for what we cannot have, we give up what we might be able to have. In seeking after security in an armed government or people or identity group, we surrender any possibility of more general solidarity, which can never be ensured and which can never even ensure our safety but which might at least help to tame the demons loose among us. And that situation is our crisis: looking for safety, we have brought ourselves to a perilous position. As long as the American citizenry is basically content with its lot, we may witness neither revolution nor tyranny. But if times should turn bad, we have no common constitutional framework for taming the violence that might erupt.

At the start of a new millennium, therefore, we must turn to the writing of new myths that suit our present circumstances, make no promises they cannot keep, but nonetheless might ameliorate this silent crisis. To formulate such myths, we must first discern the nature of the need that they must fill. We must understand, in other words, how we traveled from a world in which the Framers' myth made sense to a world in which none of our Second Amendment myths answers the problem that called it into being.

The Exotic Landscape of the Eighteenth Century

Despite their differences, all the many current myths about the Second Amendment presume that the citizenry is hostile and disunited and that the amendment deals with that fact not by fostering unity but by allowing the trustworthy to threaten the untrustworthy. As we have become more diverse and individualistic, we have generally abandoned hope for a common culture on the use of political violence. The Framers' myth of unity seems exotic at best, threatening at worst. Indeed, it may have seemed so even at the time the Framers were inscribing it, a memory of an old dream of popular organicity. In other words, the Framers' myth, as powerful and hallowed as it may be, no longer suits present circumstances.

To be sure, the Framers recognized some of the disunity present in the American landscape; they were not seized by a romantic fantasy of national oneness. In areas other than political violence, some of the Framers even celebrated difference. In economic and religious life, many took it as a given that people would hold divergent interests and opinions. And even within the domain of political violence, the Framers of the Second Amendment itself insisted that complete unity could never be taken for granted. Indeed, the fact of division was the reason for their effort to tame violence: precisely because they recognized the danger of tyranny and rebellion, they sought a framework to control it. And in recognition that no one can be wholly trusted, the framework created a system of checks and balances. In their hardheaded way, then, the Framers left us no vision of ecstatic merger with an armed volk who will always act for the good of the mystical nation. Instead, in seeking to yoke constitutional force to the service of constitutional ideals, they saw that people will disagree over the merits of a particular resistance movement. As a result, they produced an institutional structure with multiple guardians of the public weal. That system gives no guarantee that justice will prevail, but then there is never any guarantee: the best we can do is to arrange things to maximize our chances.

Yet if the Framers were not German romantics, neither were they modern pluralists or individualists. Even though they recognized that it might be difficult to discern who spoke for the people, they nonetheless sought a system in which the people's voice could be heard. Even though they created a complicated structure balancing force against force, their goal was to increase the chance that force would ultimately favor the interests of the whole. Even though they recognized that some uprisings were illegitimate, they defined them precisely by their departure from the common good. And even though they recognized there were false revolutions in the world, they celebrated true revolutions, in song, story, and legal encomia, as the hopeful expression of a united people. For all that they acknowledged that some degree of disunity was inevitable, then, the Framers hoped and expected that the people would exhibit a core of unity for taming political violence. If the government should become tyrannical, there was only one way to redeem the system: the people would make a revolution. If the citizenry of America was deeply discordant, government perfidy was virtually irremediable. On taking up arms, such a citizenry could create only civil war, and as between tyranny and civil war the options were quite inadequate.

As we have seen, even at the time the Framers were inscribing this myth into the Second Amendment, it may have been on its way to obsolescence. The universal militia was less and less of a real-world reality, its existence mostly a matter of empty legal prescription. On the issue of the use of violence, whatever cultural unity Americans might have enjoyed during the War of Independence was dissolving as low-level insurrection erupted across the backcountry. Yet however ephemeral the myth might have been, the Framers of the amendment deemed it critical to the health of their constitutional system.

Today, celebrating diversity more than commonality, Americans find it much more difficult to accept a myth of unity. This trend is vast, familiar, and ongoing. The evidence for it is so substantial that an extended description is both unnecessary and incomplete, so a quick tour must suffice. Historians now generally agree that around the end of the eighteenth century and the beginning of the nineteenth, American political culture shifted away from civic republicanism, with its emphasis on the common good, and toward liberalism, with its emphasis on individual rights. There is disagreement on exactly when the shift occurred and how substantial it was. Clearly, the shift was not total: even before the end of the eighteenth century, Americans placed great store by individual rights, and even after the beginning of the nineteenth, they celebrated the common good. Nonetheless, it is plain that a real change occurred. As the decades wore on, nostalgic republicans feared that in their pursuit of self-interest, Americans would wreak harm to the future of their country.[1]

With respect to the Second Amendment itself, Justice Joseph Story wrote a classic description of the trend toward individualism and away from collective organization. He opined that the right to arms "offers a strong moral check against the usurpation and arbitrary power of rulers." He worried, however, that Americans had become too self-regarding to devote themselves to the militia service critical to checking government: "Though . . . the importance of a well regulated militia would seem so undeniable, it cannot be disguised, that among the American people there is a growing indifference to any system of militia discipline, and a strong disposition, from a sense of its burthens, to be rid of all regulations. How it is practicable to keep the people duly armed without some organization, it is difficult to see. There is certainly no small danger, that indifference may lead to disgust, and disgust to contempt; and thus gradually undermine all the protection intended by this clause of our national bill of rights."[2]

Over the course of the nineteenth and twentieth centuries, the American social landscape became increasingly complicated and individualistic. Massive immigration has brought values, cultures, languages, and religions that have enriched the country by making it less homogeneous.[3] As civic republicans feared, the economy has become more complex, bringing pronounced specialization.[4] In the popular imagination and in some schools of political science, politics has become no more than the pursuit of advantage by interest groups and individuals.[5] Finally, to an extent unimaginable in the eighteenth century, Americans have embraced the ideology of personal autonomy above all: the individual has the right to chart his or her own life-course, free of pressure to conform to a communal identity that might form the basis for peoplehood.[6]

This trend has only accelerated in recent years. Indeed, a growing body of social science scholarship, almost a movement, is devoted to documenting and bewailing the transition from relatively greater communitarianism to more radical individualism. In their classic work *Habits of the Heart*, Robert Bellah and his colleagues explore modern Americans' difficulty in articulating moral frameworks that rest on anything more than personal preferences.[7] In the introduction to the updated edition, they argue that we face a "crisis of civic membership," which "at every level of American life and in every significant group" creates "temptations and pressures to disengage from the larger society."[8] As a result, "we are facing trends that threaten our basic sense of solidarity with others."[9] In the same vein, the celebrated, controversial book *Bowling Alone* by Robert Putnam argues that American community-mindedness has gone through a serious decline in the past few decades.[10] He argues that the generation now in its senior years exhibits much greater civic devotion than the generations that have followed it.[11] Sounding like a nineteenth-century civic republican, he worries for the future of the country as self-absorption becomes the norm. And as more Americans "bowl alone" rather than in leagues, so presumably would fewer be willing to serve in the militia or anything like it, and less holds Americans together as a people capable of united revolution.

The shift from solidaristic concerns to individualistic ones has also manifested itself in American law. Indeed, through amendments and judicial interpretation, the Constitution itself has become a vastly different document, placing individual autonomy as its center of concern. As we have seen, Akhil Amar explores the way that Americans' understanding of the Bill of Rights changed from the late eighteenth century to the middle of the nineteenth. At its adoption, its authors saw the Bill of Rights largely as a populist document safeguarding the rights of the people as a body.[12] By the 1860s, however, the Framers of the Civil War amendments had reimagined the Bill of Rights as protections for the rights of individuals, and they incorporated that view into the Fourteenth Amendment itself.[13] In particular, they had come to understand the Second Amendment as a protection for individual self-defense rather than for popular resistance to government.[14] In popular mythography, the lone gunman had replaced the militia member tightly integrated into a functioning *communitas*.

This shift in focus set off reverberations all across the domain of constitutional law. In the 1780s, for example, the states generally limited the franchise to a relatively homogeneous group: white men with a certain amount of property. Then, Jacksonian democracy eliminated most property requirements; the Fifteenth Amendment enfranchised men of color; and the Nineteenth Amendment gave the vote to women. Eventually, many came to see voting as a right guaranteed to the individual so that he or she could defend his or her individual interests through the political process.[15]

That view of voting dominates the Supreme Court's work in this area. In the 1960s, the Court insisted on the principle of "one person, one vote." In this view, the electoral process must give everyone's vote the same weight because legislators must represent individuals as such, not as members of larger groups: "Legislators represent people, not trees or acres. Legislators are elected by voters, not farms or cities or economic interests."[16] The right to vote is fundamental because it allows these individuals to protect their interests in a competitive electoral system: "Undoubtedly, the right of suffrage is a fundamental matter in a free and democratic society. Especially since the right to exercise the franchise in a free and unimpaired manner is preservative of other basic civil and political rights, any alleged infringement of the right of citizens to vote must be carefully and meticulously scrutinized."[17] As a result, "full and effective participation . . . requires, therefore, that each citizen have an equally effective voice in the election of members of his state legislatures. Modern and viable state government needs, and the Constitution demands, no less."[18]

Recently, this individualistic view of the right to vote decided a presidential election. In *Bush v. Gore*,[19] drawing on the one person, one vote cases, the Supreme Court held Florida's vote-counting procedures unconstitutional. In the recount, individual counties developed different standards for what counted as a legal vote, including hanging chads, dimpled chads, completely detached chads, ballots through which light could be seen, and so on.[20] Because some Florida counties used a more permissive vote-counting method than others, some voters had a greater chance of having their vote counted than others simply because of where they lived. According to the Court, this want of uniform rules "has led to unequal evaluation of ballots in various respects."[21] The Court opined that because of the inconsistent standards, Broward County voters effectively had more power than Palm Beach County voters: "Broward County used a more forgiving standard than Palm Beach County, and uncovered almost three times as many votes, a result markedly disproportionate to the difference in population between the counties." Florida's recount therefore violated the Constitution because the "idea that one group can be granted greater voting strength than another is hostile to the one man, one vote basis of our government."[22]

The United States Senate offers another example of the shift to more individualistic views of voting. Each state elects two senators, regardless of population. The Senate therefore patently contradicts the one person, one vote principle: voters in Wyoming have more power than voters in California because even though each group elects the same number of senators, there are many fewer voters in Wyoming than in California. Originally, this disproportionality did not seem especially troublesome. The Framers imagined the states as distinct communities, not assemblies of individual voters with disparate interests. The point in the Senate was to protect the smaller states against the larger ones by deliberately granting them disproportionate power.[23] Once voting has been reconceived simply as a way for individuals to protect their interests, however, the structure of the Senate comes to seem absurd or oppressive, as it allows some individuals more power than others. The leading casebook in the field refers to the "now anomalous position of the U.S. Senate as the one major elected institution in our political order that remains exempt from the constraints of equal representation."[24] Because of its deep individualistic commitments, the Supreme Court has not been able to muster a principled defense of the Senate's structure. Instead, it has argued that the Senate is simply the product of arbitrary events and pressures: it "aris[es] from unique historical circumstances" and was "conceived out of compromise and concession indispensable to the establishment of our federal republic."[25]

The Establishment Clause is still another illuminating example of the movement to a radically individualistic Constitution. The clause provides that "Congress shall make no law respecting an establishment of religion."[26] Originally, the purpose of the clause was to ensure only that the central government did not establish a state religion. The states, by contrast, were free to do so, and indeed, one purpose of the clause was to guarantee that Congress could not interfere with those state establishments. As supporters saw them, established religions were important to ensure a general devotion to the common good and to community solidarity. They feared that in the absence of an established religion, citizens might simply follow their own appetites, without regard for their effect on others, and the republic would disintegrate.[27] In recent decades, however, the Supreme Court has incorporated the Establishment Clause against the states through the Fourteenth Amendment.[28] In this new regime, the point in the clause is not to block central control of religion; it is, rather, to block all establishments of religion, local or central. And at least one reason for this development is that state religions interfere with the rights of the individual to pursue her or his view of the good. Once again, we see the shift: the original Constitution was concerned to protect community solidarity, but the current Constitution is concerned to protect individual autonomy against community solidarity.[29]

Perhaps the most telling evidence of the people's dissolution is the mythic landscape of the Second Amendment itself. Once, the people strode that landscape like a rhetorical colossus. Today, it has vanished, leaving behind giant footprints that are impossible to fill. As we have seen, the conventional debate between states' rights and individual rights theorists divides our social world into the government and individuals. One side in the debate trusts the government; the other side trusts individuals. No one entertains the idea of vesting rights in the people as an organic entity, apparently because it is so plain to everyone concerned that no such entity exists. Indeed, the absence of the people in our political vocabulary is so complete it has been difficult for modern commentators even to grasp that the Framers presupposed its existence.

In fact, until recently, the debate over the amendment focused on the issue of individual self-defense, rather than on resistance to government, the subject that so dominated discussion in the late eighteenth century. The modern debate about personal protection revolves around two sets of private concerns: the right of some individuals to be safe (or feel safe) by having guns, and the right of others to be safe (or feel safe) from those who should not have guns. By contrast, the central concern of supporters of the Second Amendment was the allocation of public power through the distribution of arms to the people as a political actor.

Further, modern Second Amendment myths do not merely omit the people from their accounts; they also affirmatively delineate a social fabric torn asunder. As we have seen, for every one of these myths, the reason for the Second Amendment is that in a divided social world the right people must be able to arm themselves against the wrong ones. In some cases, this mythic premise is obvious. For populists, especially the militia movement, the true people need to take up arms against auslanders. For outgroup theorists, the members of their groups need to take up arms against violent bigots. In some cases, the mythic premise is less salient but equally central. States' rights theorists contend that the state must have a monopoly on violence because those in government are more trustworthy than private gun owners. Indeed, these theorists generally identify the set of governmental officials with the Constitution itself, so that resistance to a current government is treason to the Constitution and its people. Libertarians, on the other hand, would give rights only to abstract individuals, not to groups. As a result, they paint no portrait — indeed, they strenuously avoid painting a portrait — of intergroup conflict or of the people punishing outsiders. Yet because they assiduously refuse to think in collective terms, their theory of revolution becomes untenable. They rhetorically promise that the people will rise up against a tyrannical government when conditions are right. They never explain, however, how all those individuals will cohere into a single entity. Indeed, to talk in such collective terms would deny the very individualism that is the point in the theory: each individual must decide, as a matter of conscience, when the time is right to revolt. As we look across this libertarian landscape, we see millions of points of light, each with a gun, who may or may not find that they have much in common. And so we are left again with a myth of ultimate division.

As a result of these social, demographic, ideological, legal, and mythic changes, the Second Amendment simply cannot, under modern conditions, mean what it meant under eighteenth-century conditions. In proposing that change has rendered the amendment's original meaning null, I wish to stress that this subject presents a very particular type of change. This type of change is somewhat unusual, although it may not be unique to the Second Amendment. And because it is unusual, I especially wish to distinguish my claim from other (and quite divergent) types of common assertions about constitutionally relevant change. First, I do not predicate my argument on changes in values, that is, the Framers took one view of the constitutional organization of violence, but we should take another because we now understand better. Second, I do not predicate my argument on changes in technology, that is, in the Framers' day, lightly armed citizens could effectively resist a professional army, but such resistance is no longer possible because of advances in military weaponry. Third, I do not predicate my argument on changes in policy calculations, that is, the Framers believed a popular right to arms secured more liberty than crime, but now it produces more crime than liberty.

What I mean is that the Framers sought to give the right to arms to an entity that simply no longer exists: the Body of the People, united in a common culture and in the militia. The universal militia is now a thing of the past, and there is not even a remote chance modern legislatures will revive it. In addition, to whatever extent we once had a common culture on the use of political violence, it is dissolving. And as we have seen, neither the National Guard nor the universe of individual gun owners constitutes an acceptable analogue to a people. Yet if the Body of the People no longer exists, then it is no longer possible to protect its rights. It is as though the Framers commanded us to give rights to the extinct Carolina parakeet or the ancient kingdom of Mercia. Even if our values, technology, and policy calculations were identical to those of the Framers, we could not comply. No matter how devoted to our Founding Fathers we may be, we cannot follow their intent because they were living in a world different from ours. As a result, the current debate over the meaning of the Second Amendment is fundamentally misconceived. Each side claims to speak the true will of the Framers, seeking to use that claim as a trump card to silence dissent. In fact, neither speaks for the Framers because neither could; the true will of the Framers cannot have meaning today. As a starting point, therefore, we must concede that we cannot have what they wanted for us. Only after making this concession can we begin to consider what we might have and how close it might be to what they intended.

The Barren Landscape Today

The Framers' old myth of unity will not work for us because it does not suit our circumstances. The new myths of disunity will not serve either, however, because, although they may accurately describe our condition, they do not answer our constitutional needs. Because these myths do not accurately recapitulate the Framers' view, those who care about the Framers' intent may object to them as a matter of constitutional interpretation. The deeper problem with the myths, however, is that they will not perform the function we need the Second Amendment and the military provisions of Article I to perform, namely, organizing political violence so it is yoked to constitutional ends. In fact, the Framers' thinking sheds light on the shortcomings in these modern accounts. Indeed, with adjustment for modern circumstances, the Framers' view may even show the way toward a mythos appropriate to the new millennium. In that sense, the current mythic landscape fails either to capture the Framers' intent or to serve modern needs for the same reason: the Framers' version of the constitutional organization of violence glimpsed important truths that might still be relevant today.

The Framers' mythic scheme for the organization of violence differs from modern myths in two essential ways. First, it is institutionally complex in that it reposes perfect trust in no one institution, seeking instead a system of checks and balances. Like modern myths, the Framers' goal was to seek a distribution of the means of violence that would maximize the chance that political violence would be used to serve constitutional ends. Unlike modern myths, however, the Framers understood that corruption could lurk anywhere. There is danger in both popular and governmental violence, and any adequate model for constitutionally organizing violence must acknowledge that uncomfortable truth. It is therefore unbalanced and ill-advised simply to choose one as the ultimate guarantor of the people's safety, the final backstop in the system. What is needed is a myth that incorporates both views into a larger whole. American political thinking has not yet produced a more promising proposal than the Framers' own insight: when various political actors are all susceptible to corruption, the wisest course is to allow them to check each other within a careful balance of powers, in the hope that the common good will emerge. Unlike modern myths, this account does not offer an unreal security by reserving ultimate power to a single entity that is allegedly perfectly trustworthy. As a result, it cannot promise safety, and it may feel messy or unsatisfactory for that reason. But the Constitution promises no more than this uncertainty because, unless we launch ourselves into illusion, the human condition offers no more.

The second truth that the Framers grasped is that underlying both sides of this balance must be a certain base level of popular unity on the appropriate use of political violence. As we have seen, the Framers emphasized the importance of solidarity among the people-in-militia, as they contemplated an uprising

against a sitting government. Wearing a different hat, however, the same people voted for their representatives, presumably in the expectation that the
legislators would act on the same consensus view about the appropriate use of
political violence. We are so accustomed to tolerating and celebrating difference that insisting on the importance of consensus may seem illiberal or even
oppressive. We can celebrate difference, however, only because we exist within
a social contract that allows for the expression of difference. When we experience profound and ultimate disagreement on the appropriate use of violence,
that social contract will itself have been dissolved. For the moment, the government may constrain us or powerful private groups may overawe us into peace,
but we will have entered a state of incipient civil war.

In fact, the modern mythic landscape of the Second Amendment helps us see
that the alternative to the Framers' hope of unity is unlivable. For modern
mythography, the point in the Second Amendment is no longer the importance
of social unity. Instead, it takes social disunity as a given. It empowers people
to respond to that disunity not by building new consensus, but by shooting
those who would threaten them. In other words, the new mythic landscape
fundamentally assumes that a world of violence and fragmentation is inevitable. As a result, instead of trying to change the unchangeable, it allows people
to survive in that world by arming themselves and perpetuating the division
because, in this terrain, there is no reasonable alternative. If the good people
do not shoot at the villains — the government, the gun culture, the auslanders,
the bigots — then the villains will shoot at them. We have only two options: kill
or be killed.

At this point in the analysis, however, the prospect of any healthy political
future for America has disappeared from the horizon. If we embrace this set of
myths, we will have accepted a radically circumscribed set of political choices.
And if we remain long in this dark, crabbed cave, in which we start at every
shadow, we will eventually become alienated from the better angels of our
nature. Arming the right people against the wrong people will not in the long
run domesticate political violence. A nation deeply divided against itself on
this subject will ultimately collapse into chaos, incapable of either steady
government or a united revolution against a corrupt one. Indeed, a nation that
does not share a social contract on the use of political violence could scarcely
be called a constituted nation at all because the creation of that contract is the
first job of a constitution. Those who would tame political violence, then,
should worry less about who has the guns and more about how to create a
political culture that brings us together on this subject. Paradoxically, these
new myths accomplish just the opposite: by emphasizing our perennial hos-

tility, they encourage the rise of distrust and hostility as constitutionally sanctioned attitudes.

We need, then, new myths that recognize our modern circumstances and celebrate our diversity but also foster the necessary unity. Without such myths, we are in crisis: the genie of violence is loose among us, but we have no prevailing story by which to command it. And so, we must consider how we might create new myths for a new millennium.

Planting for the Future

When the Framers' vision and contemporary needs conflict, we face a classic issue in constitutional interpretation: whether to follow the Framers' "original intent" or to update the meaning of the Constitution for modern times. Happily, when it comes to the constitutional organization of violence, this conflict does not really exist. On the one hand, it is true that we cannot reproduce the Framers' exact scheme because they gave rights to the Body of the People, an entity that does not exist today. As a result, whether we would like to or not, we cannot give the Second Amendment its precise original meaning—not because we believe it inappropriate for modern needs, but simply because it is not possible to do so. To the extent, therefore, that we leave the Framers in the eighteenth century, we may plead necessity.

On the other hand, as the preceding section has argued, the Framers' fundamental conviction about the constitutional organization of violence—the importance of social unity underlying a system of checks and balances between the government and the citizenry—still recommends itself to us today. This conviction must be applied with care, honesty, and rigor to modern circumstances. In that sense, we are adapting and updating the Framers' intent; we are crafting new myths out of the material of old ones. In particular, the Framers built their structure on the cornerstone of the people-in-militia, unified in a common culture. As a structural element in the Framers' design of government, this people provided an essential check on government by threatening revolution. In addition, it presumptively provided the legislature, when it chose to listen, with consensual norms about which uprisings were illegitimate rebellions and which were signs that something was wrong with the practice of government.

As that element in the Framers' design has disappeared, we cannot simply reproduce the Framers' projected institutional structure. If we look to an armed citizenry to perform the tasks that the Framers assigned to it, we will be disappointed. When it comes time for a united citizenry to threaten and overawe the government, we will instead hear a cacophony of discordant voices. Some will praise the government, and some will threaten it with reprisal—just as they are doing today. When it comes time for a united citizenry to give the government clear-cut instructions about which uprisings are legitimate, we will encounter similar dissonance—just as we are encountering today. And when it comes time for a united citizenry to rise in revolution, we will instead face civil war and anarchy—as we may discover to our lasting misfortune.

As a result, in the twenty-first century, the Second Amendment may necessarily function more as a regulative ideal than a doctrine of law. The courts simply cannot enforce the amendment "as written." Nonetheless, the amendment can function as an icon, a reminder of certain ideas about the constitutional organization of violence. That icon can help guide all Americans—courts, legislatures, and the whole citizenry—as they adapt the Framers' convictions to modern circumstances. Finding a meaning for the amendment that is both faithful to the Framers and responsive to modern circumstances therefore requires us to address two questions.

First, we must consider our goal, where we are going. To that end, we will have to imagine a better constitutional organization of violence, one that would more effectively tame illegitimate force and that would also (and for the same reason) be more consistent with the Framers' vision. That organization will include a system of checks and balances and a widespread social contract on the appropriate use of political violence. The social contract, the basis for our unity, will have to live in the hearts and minds of citizens, not only in the pages of Supreme Court opinions and the written provisions of the Constitution. As a result, in this process of imagining, we will have to keep honestly in mind our current circumstances, especially our diversity and individualism, rather than presuming conditions contrary to fact.

Second, we must consider our path, how we will get to where we are going. As we have explored, our mythic landscape is far from the Framers' vision, with their emphasis on unity, on the one hand, and checks and balances, on the other. As a result, under current circumstances, we cannot simply adopt ideas or practices that would be appropriate for a people who dwelt in the landscape to which we wish to go but do not now inhabit. Instead, we need transitional measures to help us get from here to there. For example, if we exhibited the necessary unity, it might be appropriate to constitute the people as a revolutionary body, with universal arming, militia organization, and a jealous readiness to protect their rights against government intrusion. When the people do not exhibit that revolutionary unity, by contrast, the pressing question is how to create it, how to get there from here, instead of assuming that we are already there. And under current circumstances, the practice of universal arming, popular resentment of government, and even militia organization might actually be counterproductive to general unity, plunging us into a chaos of mutual threat.

The law is particularly relevant to these transitional questions because the law, in its nature, is a transitional discipline between the real and the ideal. On the one hand, unlike utopian visioning, the law must deal with social life as it finds it: the law is meant to apply in the here and now, not in the end-time. On the other hand, the law projects a normative vision of how life should be, rather than merely ratifying a current fallen reality, with all its hurts and injustices. In that sense, the law is inherently transformative: although it works on the present world, it is constantly changing it. The late Robert Cover powerfully described this essential nature of law:

> Law may be viewed as a system of tension or a bridge linking a concept of reality to an imagined alternative. . . . A *nomos*, as a world of law, entails the application of human will to an extant state of affairs as well as toward our visions of alternative futures. A *nomos* is a present world constituted by a system of tension between reality and vision. . . Our visions hold up reality to us as unredeemed. By themselves the alternative world of our visions — the lion lying down with the lamb, the creditor forgiving debts each seventh year, the state all shriveled and withered away — dictate no particular set of transformations or efforts at transformation. But law gives a vision depth of field, by placing one part of it in the highlight of insistent and immediate demand while casting another part in the shadow of the millennium.[30]

To answer the questions of where we are going and how we might get there, we must examine both our practice and our myths, for in our constitutional tradition myth and practice have been synthetically related. On the one hand, we frequently derive our constitutional myths from our practices: once we engage in a practice long enough, it attains a mythic status in our constitutional consciousness. On the other hand, we frequently bring our practices into accordance with our myths, so that our mythic vision then controls future practice, which in turn influences the formulation of our myths, and so on. Constitutional myth functions both as a crystallization and a summary of our practices and as a warrant for further practice.

For example, in *Zorach v. Clauson*,[31] the Supreme Court decided that a released-time program in which schoolchildren were given time off from classes in order to attend religious classes in church buildings did not violate the Establishment Clause. In the Court's view, the country had long accepted practices similar to the school program in that they acknowledged the importance of religion. Justice Douglas's opinion offers a long list of such practices as a source of constitutional meaning: "Prayers in our legislative halls; the appeals to the Almighty in the messages of the Chief Executive; the proclamations making Thanksgiving Day a holiday; 'so help me God' in our courtroom oaths... the supplication with which the [Supreme] Court opens each session: 'God save the United States and this Honorable Court.'... A Catholic student applies to his teacher for permission to leave the school during hours on a Holy Day of Obligation to attend a mass. A Jewish student asks his teacher for permission to be excused for Yom Kippur. A Protestant wants the afternoon off for a family baptismal ceremony."[32] On the basis of this list, Justice Douglas offered a famous mythic vision of the nation: "We are a religious people whose institutions presuppose a Supreme Being."[33] That mythic vision served as constitutional warrant for the released-time program at issue in the case, and for similar practices across the nation: "When the state encourages religious instruction or cooperates with religious authorities by adjusting the schedule of public events to sectarian needs, it follows the best of our traditions. For it then respects the religious nature of our people and accommodates the public service to their spiritual needs."[34]

In *Zorach*, the interdependence of myth and practice led the Court to adopt a conservative stance, but it can also lead in the direction of reform, as it did in the development of the Supreme Court's treatment of gender discrimination under the Fourteenth Amendment. In the notorious case of *Bradwell v. Illinois*,[35] the Supreme Court upheld a state law denying women the right to practice law. In his concurring opinion, Justice Bradley stressed that American practice did not include the participation of women in the legal profession: "It certainly cannot be affirmed, as an historical fact, that this has ever been established as one of the fundamental privileges and immunities of the sex." From this practice, he derives a mythic, even religious, view: "The paramount destiny and mission of woman are to fulfill the noble and benign offices of wife and mother. This is the law of the Creator."[36] As late as 1961, despite some changes in our practice, the Court could still offer a similar vision in *Hoyt v. Florida*. In upholding a law excluding women from the jury list unless they specifically requested to be put on it, the Court explained, "Despite the enlightened emancipation of women from the restrictions and protections of bygone years, and their entry into many parts of community life formerly considered to be reserved to men. woman is still regarded as the center of home and family life."[37]

By 1973, however, after a decade that saw a vast change in American practice, a plurality of the Court had come to believe that "classifications based upon sex . . . are inherently suspect and must therefore be subjected to close judicial scrutiny."[38] Justice Brennan's opinion observed that, "over the past decade, Congress has itself manifested an increasing sensitivity to sex-based classifications."[39] And in light of this changed practice, Brennan offered a very different mythic vision of the nation's history. Instead of women being confined to the home in accord with their true nature, Brennan offered the image of women struggling against oppression: "There can be no doubt that our Nation has had a long and unfortunate history of sex discrimination." He criticized Justice Bradley's view of women as " 'romantic paternalism' which, in practical effect, put women, not on a pedestal, but in a cage."[40] And he even compared the historical treatment of women and African Americans: "As a result of notions such as these, our statute books gradually became laden with gross, stereotyped distinctions between the sexes, and indeed, throughout much of the 19th century the position of women in our society was, in many respects, comparable to that of blacks under the pre–Civil War slave codes."[41]

Such discrimination, in Justice Brennan's view, was illegitimate because "the sex characteristic frequently bears no relation to ability to perform or contribute to society."[42] This question — whether women can contribute to the public sphere in the same way as men — had been fiercely controverted for many decades. Yet Justice Brennan merely asserted his answer to that question without citation to any evidence, apparently because he just knew it to be so from his personal experience.[43] Justice Bradley, familiar with one set of gender practices that confined women to the home, would have emphatically denied that women were suited to participation in the public sphere. Justice Brennan, drawing on a changing set of gender practices, reaches the opposite conclusion and a different mythic vision of the nation. That vision has since entered deeply into the Supreme Court's jurisprudence, and it has led to further changes in the nation's practices, such as the invalidation of all-male, public military academies.[44]

The debate over the Second Amendment itself also illustrates this interdependence of myth and practice. Many Americans believe that the Second Amendment protects an individual right to arms because in their view the practice of general arming has always been central to the American character. As we have seen, these people have formulated a powerful mythic account around this individual right to arms, derived from the perceived practice. As a result, Americans who subscribe to this myth come to see gun owning as central to American identity. We may surmise that they then further govern their practice according to this mythic account, as gun owning and gun use become central to their identity. Indeed, the gun culture has largely organized itself in just this way. As we have seen, in recent years states' rights theorists have contested this account of our practices, in hopes that a change in our perception of our practices will correlatively change our mythic vision, which may in turn influence our practices, and so on.

Because myth and practice are interdependent, we must seek to change both simultaneously in order to produce a better constitutional organization of violence. Before we will adopt the right myths, we will need practices in place to convince us of the power of those myths. And before we will adopt the right practices, we will need the right myths in place to convince us of the propriety of those practices. As in any hermeneutic circle, therefore, the place to begin is everywhere at the same time.

9

Redeeming the People

In constructing a constitutional organization of violence that is truer to the Framers' view and more serviceable to modern needs, we must attend to two elements: popular unity and checks and balances. Of the two, the more difficult challenge will likely be popular unity. We are still familiar with checks and balances in our government. Indeed, we presently have a certain set of checks and balances in the organization of political violence itself: private persons and groups, a variety of law enforcement organizations, and the military all hold arms and the capacity to wreak political violence, even in stark opposition to one another. Perhaps that balance should be altered; certainly, it might be consciously systematized with constitutional ends in view. But the general idea and practice of organizing political violence around multiple bodies is familiar.

By contrast, popular unity—Americans' status as a people unified on the use of political violence—is much less familiar. Politicians sometimes invoke the idea, but many Americans view it with distrust. In its place, we have put individuals who stay respectfully out of each other's way. The primary work involved in reconstructing the Second Amendment, then, is redeeming the people. I use this phrase, "redeeming the people," in two senses. First, it refers to creating sufficient popular unity, "constitutional patriotism," among actual Americans that we can speak of the Second Amendment's people as having been redeemed. Second, however, we cannot restore the actual people until we restore the concept of the people, which has fallen into such disfavor. Reconstructing the Second Amendment will therefore also involve redeeming the idea of peoplehood to a position of centrality, in recognition that disciplining political violence cannot be done by governments or individuals alone, but only by united communities.

For that reason, popular unity is more fundamental than checks and balances: in fact, popular unity is the reason for checks and balances. That claim may seem counterintuitive, as the two elements may seem to be in tension. Popular unity calls for binding the people into a single entity, but checks and balances calls for dividing them into multiple power centers. Indeed, if the people are united, it is unclear why we should not just vest them with all power, freeing them to do as they will, rather than subdividing their power.

In this as in other matters, however, the Framers did not settle for simple answers because identification of the popular will is not simple. In the separation of powers, the Framers gave the legislature a preeminent role because that branch was most democratic. Because the legislature cannot be trusted always to speak for the people, however, the Framers surrounded it with checks. And so it is here, because identifying popular will in the minefield of political violence is even more difficult. Because popular unity will never be perfect, there will always be disagreement. The point in checks and balances is to facilitate identification of the popular will. Any particular resistance movement may be a revolution for the people or a rebellion for a faction. In the former case, the people should have power to overcome a tyrannical government, but in the latter, more common case, the government must have power to suppress the insurrection.

The system, therefore, is institutionally divided, but the reason for this division is the apprehension of unity. The constitutional organization of violence assumes that there is a will of the people, and the trick is devising a scheme to uncover it. Without the necessary popular connection, the whole system fails. At this point, in seeking to reconstruct a meaning for the Second Amendment, any commentator, analyst, court, or legislator must face a humbling truth: only the people can generate popular unity, so any scheme for generating it can be worked out only in practice, learning from experience, and grappling with the messy details of our collective lives. As a result, no book, judicial opinion, or legislative agenda can offer more than a sketchy suggestion for change; the people will have to carry out the rest. In that sense, the method and substance of this Second Amendment work are closely interrelated: because the substantive goal is unity among the people, the procedural path to that goal must be action by the people. There are limits on what can be said in advance.

These limits apply to the work of judges as well as to the work of analysts. By themselves, courts cannot effect the work of reconstruction, and they can contribute to it only in limited ways. The courts, as noted, cannot enforce the original meaning of the Second Amendment under modern circumstances. To effectuate Second Amendment values, to construct a modern analogy to the amendment's scheme, we will need to change both our myths and practices. Courts, however, are generally loathe to take up the task of broad social change. And at least in this area, that reluctance has good constitutional warrant: the organization of political violence must be an activity of the people, by the people, and for the people. For the courts to monopolize this field, to turn it into a scheme of arcane doctrine with rules, subrules, and exceptions to the subrules, would be to undercut the whole purpose of the amendment. Unlike, say, the Fourth Amendment's prohibition on searches and seizures, this provision cannot be interpreted and enforced by the judicial system as the ultimate custodian of constitutional values.

Nonetheless, the Supreme Court might still have an important, if limited, leadership role in the reconstruction of the Second Amendment. Most centrally, the Court might assist the country precisely by insisting that the judiciary cannot accomplish this task on its own. To that end, it might explain the original meaning of the amendment, its reliance on checks and balances and popular unity for contextual meaning, the changes that have left it without that contextual meaning, and the resulting judicial inability to enforce the amendment "as written." Such an opinion would clear the way for, and perhaps even inspire, popular action. But responsibility for the ultimate effectuation of this amendment would still lie with the people in their diverse roles — voters, legislators, activists, commentators, journalists, workers, and leaders of every sort. Under this amendment, the best thing that the Court can do is to encourage the people to look to themselves, rather than to the Court, for their safety — because, in the end, the constitutional organization of violence depends on their decency and mutual commitment.

For that reason, it seems appropriate that interest in the amendment has been skewed: courts and the legal establishment have paid it little attention, but popular interest has been intense. Although the popular press has spilled vats of ink on its meaning, the Supreme Court has never offered a definitive interpretation and for decades has not even commented on it. In the work that began the so-called Second Amendment Renaissance, Sanford Levinson summarizes:

To put it mildly, the Second Amendment is not at the forefront of constitutional discussion, at least as registered in what the academy regards as the venues for such discussion. . . . [By contrast,] it is not at all unusual for the Second Amendment to show up in letters to the editors of newspapers and magazines. That judges and academic lawyers, including the ones who write casebooks, ignore it is most certainly not evidence for the proposition that no one cares about it. . . . Campaigns for Congress in both political parties, and even presidential campaigns, may turn on the apparent commitment of the candidates to a particular view of the Second Amendment. This reality of the political process reflects the fact that millions of Americans, even if (or perhaps *especially* if) they are not academics, can quote the Amendment and would disdain any presentation of the Bill of Rights that did not give it a place of pride.[1]

Indeed, the primary purpose of Levinson's influential article was not to offer a "correct" interpretation of the amendment but to broaden the discussion, to convince his fellow elite lawyers that "millions of Americans" might know something they did not.[2] Thanks largely to Levinson's work, some academics have begun to write about the amendment, but outside this group academic interest remains small, and the Supreme Court has yet to make its view known.

The new academic interest may help to legitimate the amendment as a serious intellectual subject, bring light to its background, and lend rigor to its discussion. A definitive Supreme Court decision could do the same. Neither, however, can make the amendment a living reality in the modern world. Indeed, there is even a risk of academic and judicial overinvolvement in the amendment's exposition, as both judges and law professors sometimes claim the Constitution as their exclusive property. In this view, the role of the people is simply to listen to the experts, as the passive recipients of elite wisdom. That course, however, would defeat the whole project of reconstructing the Second Amendment. Happily, that situation does not presently obtain: the people are very much engaged in constructing their own Second Amendment mythography. Even when they do a bad job, they are at least engaged in the right task, with will and energy. If the Second Amendment should become the exclusive province of elites, that popular engagement might vanish. As a result, although measured elite involvement in exposition of the amendment is beneficial, it would be possible to tip the balance too far in that direction.

By contrast, many commentators have urged the Supreme Court to discard its reticence about the Second Amendment and precisely define the relative rights and powers that it creates. Indeed, some writers have accused the Court of being derelict in its duty to enforce the Constitution. In this view, held by people on both sides of the debate, the Court should pronounce the opposing side wrong and settle the debate once and for all. The goal for these writers, in other words, is to enlist the Court as an authoritative ally, so as to place the amendment off-limits to the people.

These analysts thus seek to judicialize the amendment to protect it from popular pressure. Individual rights theorists insist that the Court must announce that the amendment invalidates at least some gun control legislation. As for other rights, the Court's role is to insulate a sphere of individual autonomy from draconian majorities. For example, Michael Quinlan declaims, "There is no excuse for the Court's failure to address the Second Amendment. After all, it is a member of the Bill of Rights family, and it deserves better treatment. . . . The evisceration of the Second Amendment through judicial indifference would be a deep constitutional wound and a blight on the Court's prestige and legitimacy."[3] In response, states' rights theorists insist that the Court should deliver a stinging rebuke to the individual rights camp by announcing that the amendment protects only a power of state governments. The fanciful right to arms will disappear from constitutional discourse, and the matter will have been settled through judicial courage. For either camp, therefore, judicial resolution should help to remove the people from their role in interpreting the amendment's modern significance.

The error in this desire for a final judicial settlement grows out of these writers' views of the amendment's original meaning. If the provision created a simple individual right or governmental power, then the Court might enforce that meaning today by creating a normal body of doctrine comparable to its rulings under the First Amendment or the Commerce Clause. As we have seen, however, the provision does not create individual rights or governmental powers. Instead, it empowers the people if, but only if, they are a people on the organization of violence. To reconstruct the amendment, to reengage the people in this task, is not ultimately a project for normal legal doctrine. Instead, it can be accomplished only through popular action, with the amendment as a regulative ideal, rather than a precise legal rule. For the Court to claim ultimate authority in giving meaning to the amendment, therefore, would accomplish more harm than good. Whatever decision the Court reaches, it should be a charter for the people, not a prison.

Despite all these cautions and limits, it is still possible in a general way to describe the elements involved in reconstructing the Second Amendment. As noted earlier, the project will necessarily involve interdependent change in both myths and practices. On the level of practice, we might reconstruct our distribution of arms in accord with the regulative ideals of popular unity underlying checks and balances. We might also reconstruct our distribution of political power, so that the need for legitimate violence — either popular revolution or governmental suppression of rebellion — might be less likely. On the level of myth, we must confront what may be the most pressing political problem of America's last century. We must find a way not only to preserve the individual freedoms that Americans cherish, but also to ensure sufficient unity to provide a basis for collective action. These two goals are not really in tension with one another because without the unity to tame political violence, individual freedoms cannot exist. When we surrender freedom, therefore, we do so on behalf of freedom.

Because this claim is subject to misconstruction in the current climate, let me be quite clear about the nature of my argument. I am not arguing that individualism is generally bad, or that cultural orthodoxy is generally good, or that we should return to the good old days of the eighteenth century, or that we have degenerated in the twentieth century, or that we are currently primed to kill each other. I am arguing that in a free society, political violence cannot be successfully tamed by only a slice of the population — the government, the militia movement, private gun owners, outgroups, or anyone else. We can tame political violence only through broad popular action. To that end, we need a common account of the appropriate ends and processes of political violence. We do not have such an account. Instead, those who write about the Second Amendment advocate myths of disunity and hostility. Americans who are inclined to moderation may find little in these myths that resembles them, but the present landscape offers them no better story. They deserve one, and we should be engaged in its composition.

The task of reconstructing the Second Amendment is thus vast. Because of the size of the project and because its success ultimately depends on popular action, I will only sketch the outlines of a satisfactory answer. Indeed, rather than present a concrete plan, my chief goal here is to advance two general claims. First, however the reader thinks that we might best secure popular unity expressed through checks and balances (and even if she disagrees with every proposal in this chapter to that end), that is the question we should be addressing, and I seek to open that conversation. Second, my central contention here is precisely that the reconstruction of the Second Amendment does place before us a vast task, one that reaches to the very base of our existence as a people. The main lesson to be learned is that the challenge of the Second Amendment is much bigger than its current theorists generally propose. On its face, the amendment seems to pose a fairly narrow, almost technical question: who gets the guns? In fact, however, that question arises from a much deeper question: how do we collectively organize to tame political violence? In good conscience, with fidelity to the Framers and our own needs, we cannot answer the former question while ignoring the latter.

We would therefore do well to worry less about such minutiae as armor-piercing bullets, Saturday night specials, and high capacity magazines because the true scope of the Second Amendment makes the gun control debate seem fairly small. For many people, the right to arms is fraught with emotion because guns carry symbolic freight. In our national dialogue, it is time to address the issues for which guns are a symbol, rather than focusing myopically on the symbol itself. To illuminate that point, I will concentrate primarily on two elements in the following analysis, each from a different end of the causal relation between myths and practices. When considering checks and balances, I will reflect principally on the practices of arms bearing that might be entailed in a reconstructed Second Amendment; when considering the popular unity that must underlie that system, I will reflect principally on our cultural myths, especially our myths of violence, which make such unity difficult to realize.

Checks and Balances

PRACTICES

In modern America, we already live under a condition of checks and balances for the distribution of arms. Millions of guns rest in private hands. In addition, the federal government maintains an extensive, if shrinking, military force: army, navy, air force, Marine Corps, Coast Guard. Although many troops are located abroad, many are based within U.S. boundaries and have extensive armories containing much more than small arms. With some assistance from the states, the federal government also maintains the National Guard, composed of citizen-soldiers with access to extensive stockpiles of arms. The states support a plethora of law enforcement agencies — state troopers, investigative bodies, special units, county and municipal police — with a bewildering array of de jure and de facto relations. And the federal government has its own byzantine complex of law enforcement agencies, including the FBI, DEA, ATF, U.S. marshals, Secret Service and other Treasury agents, immigration agents, and many others.

All of these groups have the capacity to take up arms for political purposes. Sometimes they use their arms for purposes that are contradictory or in tension: in effect, they check each other. Such incidents have occurred with great frequency, from Shays' Rebellion through the Civil War, the labor unrest of the nineteenth century and its suppression by the National Guard, the mobilization of the Black Panther militia in the 1960s, right up through the conflagration at Waco and the militia eruptions of the nineties. Most often, these incidents involve the suppression of private political violence by public political violence; the people-in-government checked the people-not-in-government. In every case, however, the relation also runs the other way: when faced with civil unrest, the government must decide how to react. Its calculation will be different when faced with an armed, angry citizenry than when faced with a disarmed, passive one. For example, nineteenth-century labor activism, including violent strikes, may have helped secure the great labor laws of this century. In that sense, the citizenry often checks the government. And this dynamic is not confined to a two-way relation between the people and the government. It also occurs between various sectors of the people (as, for example, when white supremacist groups broke off their attacks in the face of armed resistance from the Deacons for Defense and Justice) or of the government (as, for example, when southern police reduced their harassment of civil rights groups after the Justice Department sent in federal agents).

Although we live in a *condition* of checks and balances, however, it would be wrong to call it a *system* of checks and balances: there is nothing systematic about it. Our distribution of arms grew up haphazardly, for a wide variety of reasons, and through an enormous number of decentralized decisions. Private individuals acquired arms for their own purposes, hunting or self-defense or target shooting, probably only rarely with the thought of resisting the government. Law enforcement acquired its arsenals in order to combat crime, and the military built its to fight the nation's wars. The resulting distribution of arms, then, does not represent a self-conscious plan for constitutionally balancing power against power, so as to tame political violence. In the event of rebellion or tyranny, no one ever considered how many and what kind of arms each of these groups should have, or what their likely motivations would be, or how their motivations would interact with one another. It is difficult to predict how the present distribution might work in time of serious unrest because it was not designed with that end in mind.

Our present condition therefore stands in sharp contrast to the Framers' concerns in the late eighteenth century. They worried intensely about the appropriate balance between the states, federal government, and people in the distribution of arms. They gave Congress the power to raise a military, supervise the militia, and suppress rebellion because they thought the states and the people had too much relative power. Then, they worried that Congress might abuse its power by underarming the militia, so they passed the Second Amendment to give the states and people more power. In other words, they developed these constitutional provisions from a self-conscious theory about how we might distribute the capacity for political violence so as to tame it, based on the likely motivations of the various actors. We have nothing like a comparable theory today.

It is understandable that we flinch from talking about such matters. It is unsettling to contemplate that our safety could be based on nothing more solid than a shifting tension between multiple actors, each with independent purposes and violent capacities. In fact, however, Americans have always organized political violence in this way, and ignoring that fact will not make it go away. For our own sakes, we should grasp the nettle, acknowledge the truth, and self-consciously imagine how we could construct a more carefully balanced pattern.

The Military

Again, any such pattern must be worked out in practice, but a few general observations are possible. First, the balance of which I speak is one that lies between two differing manifestations of the people's will: the people speaking indirectly through the legislature and directly through popular action. The professional military and law enforcement agencies as such have no status in this balance; they are merely instruments of the people in the legislature. For virtually all the Framers, the greatest malformation that could befall a constitutional organization of violence was the rise of a standing army as an independent force, a separate caste of men, holding the whip hand for the Republic. For our system of checks and balances, then, the democratization and "civilianization" of the military are important goals. By democratization, I mean that the military and law enforcement agencies must be subject to strict civil control. By civilianization, I mean that the military and law enforcement agencies must have deep connections to the civilian world, mirroring and intermingling with it to the extent practicable.

The subordination of the military to civilian control has long been a part of American political tradition and military culture. As Elaine Scarry has explained, the Framers of the Constitution fervently announced the overriding importance of legislative control of the military in pamphlets, proclamations, and constitutional provisions.[4] An object lesson in this aspect of military culture occurred several years ago: early in the Clinton presidency, Sen. Jesse Helms hinted that the president might be in jeopardy if he visited North Carolina military bases, as some soldiers might object to having a "draft-dodger" as their commander in chief. Breaking their customary silence, military commanders publicly repudiated Senator Helms, explaining that the military's fundamental commitment was to civilian control.[5]

And yet, the military must use some independent judgment in honoring this commitment because to remain subordinate to civilian control, the military must first determine who exercises legitimate civilian authority. Under ordinary circumstances, this process is not difficult: soldiers follow the orders of their commander in chief, the president, as stipulated in the Constitution. Imagine, however, any number of extraordinary circumstances in which a particular president's legitimacy has been cast into deep doubt. For example, a sitting president refuses to leave office after losing the election; or he suffers from a psychotic disorder and refuses to step aside; or, after massive vote fraud, two presidential candidates claim to be the legitimate officeholder; or the president orders the military to commit atrocities against American civilians or to perform acts that Congress and the Supreme Court have forbidden.

Under revolutionary conditions, circumstances might prove even more confusing. Imagine that after a long train of presidential abuses, Congress has impeached the president, but he refuses to leave. His entire administration supports him, so that the vice president and secretary of state refuse to assume the office of president. A group of congressional representatives then declare themselves the legitimate executive body for the Union. They organize a shadow executive — or is it the real executive? — and overwhelmingly the other members of Congress vote to support them. They organize a people's militia to depose the tyrant/president, and in response the president orders the military to bomb them. The situation could become even worse. Imagine that the president has committed his long train of abuses, but the members of his party in Congress support him. The congressional members of the other party resign and go home to organize opposition, leaving only a rump legislature in Washington. At this point, something like true revolution sweeps the country. A people's committee tries the president in absentia and credibly documents that for years he has been using murder, mayhem, and fraud to destroy the opposition and stay in office. The president then orders the military to execute (assassinate?) the members of the people's committee.

In all of these situations, the military has no option but to decide who constitutes the legitimate civil authority. To that end, they must engage in a sophisticated constitutional analysis. Vesting the military with that sort of task is troubling; it raises the specter of a standing army choosing and anointing the civil leader of the country. The whole point in subjecting the military to civil authority was precisely to avoid giving it that sort of king-making power. Yet there is no alternative. Before the military can subject itself to legitimate civil authority, it must identify that authority. Under conditions of turbulence, that identification can become difficult.

In other words, in reconstructing a constitutional organization of violence, we must begin by realizing that military leaders are not mere technicians of war, tasked only with narrow goals. They are civic actors invested with a public trust, occupying a role in the balance of power, part of the nation's constitutional structure. As a result, it is vitally important that those leaders hold a culture of loyalty to the common good, rather than narrow devotion to a particular political creed or a particular person or their own war-making proficiency.

In short, because it will not always be clear who constitutes the civil authority, democratization will not always suffice to keep the military subordinate to the popular will. The external check of democratization, therefore, must be supplemented by the internal check of civilianization: military culture must never become divorced from the culture surrounding it. This counsel grows directly out of eighteenth-century worries about a standing army. Because the military enjoys de facto power, it must never become a separate estate with its own interests and values. If there is to be a standing army, it must resemble the militia as much as possible in being a group of citizen-soldiers devoted to general American values rather than to separatist warrior codes.

One implication is that the military must pursue goals beyond just the ability to wreak injury on the enemy; as a civic actor, it must also serve civic values. When those values and war-making ability come into conflict, we must balance them, rather than insisting that military effectiveness always win. Unfortunately, even the Supreme Court has failed to realize that war-making proficiency is not the be-all and end-all of a republican army. Frequently, the justices have supinely deferred to the military's judgment that constitutional values must be sacrificed to military efficiency. And the Court has based these opinions on the view that the military is a society apart, radically different from the culture around it and governed by different norms.

For example, in *Goldman v. Weinberger*,[6] the Court allowed the air force to forbid a rabbi from wearing his yarmulke while on duty. The Court observed, "The military is, by necessity, a specialized society separate from civilian society."[7] In particular, it must "insist upon a respect for duty and a discipline without counterpart in civilian life." Because courts do not understand this separate military society, they must "give great deference to the professional judgment of military authorities concerning the relative importance of a particular military interest."[8] As a result, the Court accepted without proof the air force's assertion of the overwhelming importance of war-making proficiency in this case. In this view, standardized uniforms are vital to "the necessary habits of discipline and unity," "as vital during peacetime as during war because its personnel must be ready to provide an effective defense on a moment's notice."[9] Rabbi Goldman's yarmulke would have disrupted those habits. If the rabbi found this strange military society too uncongenial, he should apparently consider leaving: "Quite obviously, to the extent the regulations do not permit the wearing of religious apparel such as a yarmulke, a practice described by petitioner as silent devotion akin to prayer, military life may be more objectionable for petitioner and probably others. But the First Amendment does not require the military to accommodate such practices in the face of its view that they would detract from the uniformity sought by dress regulations."[10]

Another implication of this analysis is that the more the military mirrors America, the better. If the military is overwhelmingly composed of or led by heterosexual white male Republicans, it has departed from this representational ideal. That fact has direct relevance to the current furors over women and gays in the military. Some have portrayed these issues as a simple contest between, on one side, military personnel who fear that integration will disrupt military efficiency or morale and, on the other side, women and gays who would like to pursue a career in the armed forces. Predictably for the modern world, this characterization boils the analysis down to a balance between national might and individual rights. The civic dimension of the issue rarely makes an appearance: because the military is a civic association and part of the constitutional balance of power, we all have a deep interest in ensuring that it reflects America. If women or gays — or, for that matter, yarmulke-wearing rabbis or Democrats or environmentalists — reasonably find military culture alien, then the Republic has basis for concern.

Unhappily, the military has often seen itself as a culture not only different from but superior to the American civilization around it. This perceived distance may be increasing. In *Making the Corps*,[11] a firsthand account of Marine basic training at Parris Island, *Wall Street Journal* reporter Thomas E. Ricks offers a compelling account of this cultural gap. As Ricks explains, the military has long seen itself, in Samuel Huntington's words, as "an estranged minority."[12] In fact, Adm. Stanley Arthur, the commander of naval forces during the Gulf War, has observed, "The armed forces are no longer representative of the people they serve. More and more, enlisted as well as officers are beginning to feel that they are special, better than the society they serve." He tellingly concludes, "This is not healthy in an armed forces serving democracy."[13]

Even more worryingly, the military has become much more politically partisan: "Open identification with the Republican party is becoming the norm — even . . . part of the implicit definition of being a member of the officer corps." Moreover, this partisan identification is most extreme among the junior officer corps, which "appears overwhelmingly to be hard-right Republican" and which will someday occupy the highest positions of military power.[14] This more partisan military is also becoming more activist. After generally refraining from voting for many decades, military personnel are now voting at greater than the civilian average.[15] Indeed, for a time it appeared that the military vote might decide the presidential election of 2000. As the Florida electoral votes hung in the balance, the nation waited for the overseas ballots to arrive, and all expected overseas military personnel to vote predominantly Republican.[16] In addition, some claim these changes in the military have affected its subordination to civilian authorities, as "civilians are now less able to get the military to do what they want them to do compared with previous periods in recent U.S. history."[17]

Most disturbing of all, however, is the fact that a minority of military personnel is now openly contemplating that it may soon have to intervene in domestic unrest on behalf of its distinctive values. Some have called for giving the military greater power and freedom from legal restrictions when engaged in "domestic peacekeeping."[18] In an extraordinary essay in the *Marine Corps Gazette,* the military analyst William S. Lind and two Marine reservists offer a prophecy of America's future that resembles a fantasy of the militia movement, except that the saviors will be the Marines rather than private militias. The authors decry recent changes in American culture: "Starting in the mid-1960s, we have thrown away the values, morals, and standards that define traditional Western culture." The familiar villains are "cultural radicals, people who hate our Judeo-Christian culture." These radicals, who are "dominant in the elite, especially in the universities, the media, and the entertainment industries," have "successfully pushed an agenda of moral relativism, militant secularism, and sexual and social 'liberation.'"[19] The authors conclude that the military may need to suppress these cultural radicals now running the nation: "The point is not merely that America's Armed Forces will find themselves facing nonnation-state conflicts and forces overseas. The point is that the same conflicts are coming here." Frighteningly, they warn, "The next real war we fight is likely to be on American soil."[20] In another *Gazette* article, retired colonel Michael Wyly echoed, "We must be willing to realize that our real enemy is as likely to appear within our own borders as without." He warns his readers to face this sad truth, and "if our laws and our self-image of our role do not allow for this, we need to change them." And he urges Marines to refuse to enforce gun control laws because "enforcing such a restriction could quickly make us the enemy of constitutional freedom."[21]

These views may be extreme and atypical among the military, but they appeared in the *Marine Corps Gazette,* not in an obscure, self-published pamphlet of the militia movement. As Ricks concludes, "When the military is politically active, when it believes it is uniquely aware of certain dangers, when it discusses responding to domestic threats of cherished values, then it edges toward becoming an independent actor in domestic politics."[22] As I have discussed, an independent military would prove disastrous for a constitutional organization of violence. In our tradition, the military can be only an instrument of the people-in-government, not its antagonist.

We must look, therefore, for ways to close this culture gap. In point of fact, the military seems to be suffering from the same crisis of mythic absence as everyone else. Ricks summarizes the military's critique of American society, a critique most intense among the Marine Corps: "Over the last thirty years, as American culture has grown more fragmented, individualistic, and consumerist, the Marines have become more withdrawn; they feel they simply cannot afford to reflect the broader society. Today's Marines give off a strong sense of disdain for the very society they protect. They view it, in much the same way the Japanese do, as decadent."[23] In the plight of the Marines, we see the nation's current situation in microcosm. To discipline violence, radical individualism will not work; we need some frame of popular unity around which to organize ourselves. As much as any group in the United States, the Marines have accepted the task of disciplining violence. And as much as any group in the United States, they eschew individualism and cherish their frame of unity—the distinctive Marine Corps culture.

Yet the ultimate goal of the Marine Corps is to protect not the corps or its culture, but a different, larger entity: the United States of America. The Marines believe, however, that the values of American society, "fragmented, individualist, and consumerist," are inconsistent with the values necessary to defend that society through disciplined violence. As a result, they feel that they must withdraw and become less representative of America as a whole. Yet, as the Second Amendment tradition warns us, such withdrawal creates its own risk: as the military becomes more separate, it becomes only a faction in a larger swirl of factions. And because it holds the capacity for violence, it is a dangerous faction. When military commentators begin to contemplate waging war on the American people in the name of conservative values, they have defeated the whole purpose of the armed forces. Like the militia movement, they have come to believe their subculture is the true American people. If we have no prevailing myth of unity, Americans will inevitably create myths of disunity, in which their own group becomes the only standard-bearer for the authentic people.

As long as society remains profoundly fragmented, the military is in a no-win situation, and for that reason so are the rest of us. The military should certainly not become more like American society in becoming fragmented and consumerist, but it should also not withdraw into its own separate culture, convinced of its own superior righteousness. For the military to retain the virtues necessary for taming violence and still remain connected to the rest of

America, the citizenry must itself exhibit the very same virtues necessary to disciplining violence. Reform, therefore, must occur at both ends of the relation, as both the military and civilian society move toward the middle. In a democracy, the military must prize individual freedom, diversity, and toleration, and the citizenry must prize self-sacrifice, devotion to the common good, and a willingness to shoulder the responsibility of taming violence. Again, these goals grow out of an old Second Amendment insight: when a people is unwilling to participate in its own defense and instead relies entirely on a professional military, it creates a monster that will soon devour it.

Once again, then, a relatively narrow challenge — civilizing the military — emerges as inseparable from the larger challenge of redeeming the people. To be sure, even if the citizenry does not change at all, the military should become more representative. Recruiting, integrating, and promoting more women, minorities, and gays might significantly change the culture; it would surely diversify the military's political outlook.[24] In Ricks's view, the military's increasing isolation arises largely because the draft was ended. As an all-volunteer force, the military now draws from a narrow slice of the citizenry, and as a professional force, it sees itself as a society apart, rather than citizens spending a temporary period under arms.[25] Although he acknowledges that it would not be politically feasible, Ricks urges the resumption of the draft: "Consideration should be given to somehow reinstating a draft. Along the line of the current German system, this could be combined with National Service under which youths could perform, say, eighteen months of military service, or two years of alternative work."[26]

As long as the civilian culture remains fragmented, however, making the military more representative can do only so much to close the culture gap. No matter how diverse it might be, the military cannot embrace a culture basically oriented toward self-gratification. And so in reconstructing the Second Amendment, we must still consider how to recreate the conditions for popular unity. In point of fact, if Ricks's proposed draft were broad enough, it might affect not only military but civilian culture as well by reminding citizens of their connection to the whole. When the draft becomes that broad and the military has become a group of citizen-soldiers, then we are no longer talking simply about civilizing the military; instead, we are talking about giving the people a role akin to their old function as the citizen militia.

The People

However much they are democratized and civilized, the military and law enforcement will never be identical with the Body of the People. They will always be only a segment of the whole, and they will retain a certain characteristic culture by virtue of their distinctive work. As a result, even if the arms-bearing parts of government are as good as they can be, it will be important to involve the people directly in the organization of violence. We must search, in other words, for a modern analogue to the old universal militia, to give the people form, virtue, and unity, so they may act as a balance to the people-speaking-in-the-legislature.

One possibility would be to recreate an actual militia and vest it with the power to resist government. In a provocative recent book, *The Minuteman: Restoring an Army of the People*,[27] Gary Hart illuminates, albeit sometimes inadvertently, the difficulties in pondering such a proposal. Hart calls for reviving the militia ideal by expanding the role of the National Guard. In his view, military policy should wean itself from reliance on a large standing army and move instead to a two-tiered system: a small, rapid deployment professional army and a larger National Guard of citizen-soldiers that would deploy more slowly but could add mass to an action.[28] In Hart's view, such a system has several advantages. For one thing, it would save money.[29] For another, it makes military sense. Because large set battles are a thing of the past, replaced by guerrilla conflict, America needs a professional army primarily for small, rapid deployment missions. In larger actions, the military does not have the lift capacity quickly to move a large standing army to a combat arena, so the slower-deploying National Guard will be ready as soon as the transport is.[30]

For Hart, however, the primary advantage of an army of the people is neither economic nor military but civic: "It is a political issue in the classic sense and thus an issue of civic values. It is an issue of the kind of country we are and what kind of people we want ourselves to be."[31] In espousing the civic benefits of an army of citizen-soldiers, Hart self-consciously positions himself within the civic republican tradition.[32] He believes, for example, that service in such an army might help to inculcate civic virtue among a broad slice of the citizenry.[33] He also hopes that reliance on a National Guard may persuade the nation to rely less on a standing army, with its proclivity to get involved in foreign wars and raid the public fisc.[34] Most of all, however, an army of citizen-soldiers could act as a check on the government and on the regular military by involving citizens in the making of military policy and civilianizing a greater part of our fighting forces.

Hart hopes that giving the guard a greater role would tie the military more closely to society, reducing the culture gap. He warns, "The military is neither a separate creature from nor a professional adjunct to the nation as a whole. It has become too much so in post–Cold War America. . . . [I]solation of the military from society is unhealthy at best and dangerous at worst."[35] Greater reliance on the National Guard would help to reduce such isolation because citizen-soldiers would form a larger part of the nation's armed forces, and contact with guard members might connect regular military personnel more closely to the nation: "Throughout the country's history the citizen-solider has served the professional well, not least by linking him, even in spite of himself, to the nation at large."[36]

Even more important in Hart's view, relying on an army of citizen-soldiers would reengage citizens in the national debate on military and foreign policy because they would be directly affected. Hart returns to this idea again and again as the central plank in his proposal: "Requiring political leadership to explain the national interest that requires a reserve call-up in a conflict or crisis is an important constraint on leadership's otherwise unilateral authority and is a vivid means of engaging citizens in decisions that affect their, and their sons' and daughters', lives";[37] "A citizen army — an army of the people — participates in the debate as to why it exists, what threat it must repel, and how and where it might be used";[38] "Drawing the bulk of national defense forces directly from the people would greatly strengthen citizen awareness of and involvement in issues of national security";[39] "The central objective of a citizen defense is to engage the public in decisions regarding deployment of expeditionary forces to take part in overseas military ventures."[40] In short, the principal advantage of an army of the people is that it will check the government and its standing army: being directly affected by military decisions, the citizenry will not stand idly by and let the authorities have their way.

And yet, having defended this new militia as a check on government, Hart is ambiguous about how that check will operate. He contemplates that, when aroused, the people will use their electoral power to control the government: "With an army of the people, the people would hold their representatives in Congress more accountable for their performance, or nonperformance, in defense matters."[41] But he waffles on whether the guard should also use some kind of direct action — as by refusing to go to war or even resisting the government by force of arms. He fundamentally distinguishes his expanded National Guard from private antigovernment militias by insisting that the guard would strictly obey the state's commands. Sounding like a states' rights theorist of the Second Amendment, he explains, "The difference — and it is fundamental — is that the former [the National Guard] is the instrument of the state and the latter are not. The national militia is organized, armed, clothed, trained, and — most important — paid by the state. . . . Throughout history, soldiers have tended to obey the orders of those who paid them."[42]

Yet Hart also sometimes suggests that his army of the people should exercise much more independence. Flatly contradicting the previous passage, Hart insists that his ideal Minuteman, with "heroic qualities that eventually assumed mythic proportions," "is never an instrument of the state, but rather he is the guarantor of his own freedom."[43] Indeed, he condemns the standing army precisely for its unthinking subservience to governmental commands.[44] He projects that guard leaders should resign when ordered to conduct overly dangerous missions: "Military commanders must not permit these forces to be misused by eager or ambitious politicians, being prepared to resign their commissions in visible protest rather than lead troops into unjustified danger." With a reduced standing army, the president would have to call up guard units for any extensive commitment. As a result, "both citizen-soldiers and their communities" would engage in "a public debate regarding the wisdom of the enterprise"—apparently deciding whether they will serve or resign.[45] And at one point, sounding very like an individual rights theorist of the Second Amendment, Hart argues that, because it holds the "ultimate military power," a popular militia can restrain a tyrannical president bent on military adventuring: "The surest check on such power is direct citizen participation in those decisions. The surest way to guarantee citizen involvement is to place the ultimate military power in the hands of the people. The surest way to transfer this ultimate power is to re-create the army of the people."[46]

In classic American fashion, Hart wants to have the matter both ways without noting the resulting tension. He remembers both Oklahoma City and Lexington and Concord. When contemplating the threat of factional insurrection, he emphasizes the obedient quality of the militia; when contemplating the threat of government abuse, he emphasizes its independence. He promises that militia officers might resign in an act of symbolic protest, but he avoids discussing whether whole units might lay down their arms, as that prospect apparently seems disturbingly subversive to him. The ambivalence is understandable. From the Framers on, honest Americans have understood that no institution can promise perfect safety, so tension and oscillation, checks and balances, are a rational response to the problem of domesticating violence. Hart distrusts the government, but he realizes that his expanded National Guard could abuse its military power as well. Even at its larger size, the guard is still only a part of American society. And even if it included every American citizen, it would still reflect the lines of hostility and division that beset American society. Resistance to government by the National Guard would rapidly become internecine warfare.

Hart's ambivalence raises the question of whether any modern "army of the people" should have the right, within an appropriate constitutional organization of violence, to resist the government by force of arms. Hart's uncertainty about that question highlights the difficulty in answering it: on the one hand, to deny the right would be to leave the government with a troubling monopoly on violence; on the other hand, to recognize the right under conditions of fragmentation would be to invite civil war and anarchy. In other words, as long as the citizenry is not unified on the appropriate use of political violence, it is only prudent to hesitate before making the armed people a direct check on the government. On the other hand, having dissolved the people as a check, we face a burning need for something to take its place.

As a result, we must shift the question. Instead of asking whether the people should have the right to check the government by force of arms, we should ask, *Under what conditions* would it be appropriate for the people to have the right to resist the government by force of arms? and how do we secure those conditions? Answering those questions will take us away from the narrow, technical issue of who should get the guns to the broad, political issue of how we invigorate the basis of our unity. I will explore paths to that end in later sections.

Hart's work itself tenders one proposal: arms bearing in the service of the common good has traditionally been regarded as one of the best schools of civic virtue. As a result, perhaps vesting the people with some responsibility for their own safety will create the conditions necessary for vesting them with more, in a virtuous spiral. If so, the general distribution of arms could self-generate the conditions necessary for its own justification. Quoting the great military analyst John McAuley Palmer, Hart expounds the republican insight that citizens can learn the *habits* of responsibility for their own safety only through the *practice* of such responsibility: "Standing armies threaten government by the people, not because they consciously seek to pervert liberty, but because they relieve the people themselves of the duty of self-defense. A people accustomed to let a special class defend them must sooner or later become unfit for liberty."[47] Hart concludes, "An army *of* the people must be among the vital institutions of a government *by* the people."[48]

Hart therefore calls for a "system of brief universal military training and longer voluntary national service, both military and non-military." In his view, such a system would lead to "restoration of citizen involvement in the nation's life, abatement of alienation, [and] revival of a sense of national community"; further, it would provide the "socializing advantages of young and mature men and women interacting across class and racial boundaries."[49] He traces this prediction to the civic republican tradition that underlies the Second Amendment: "The republican ideal is dependent upon civic virtue. . . . Nothing is as central to a republic as its defense and security. Nothing would more likely reawaken a dormant sense of patriotism in American young people than a universal training requirement." In the end, he believes that the challenges facing America are not primarily military but cultural, and they can be answered only by "national unity, which itself will be strengthened by citizen-soldiers and restoration of an army of the people."[50]

There is no way to know in advance whether Hart's proposal would achieve all that he promises. It seems unlikely that a period of "brief universal military training" would significantly change civilian culture, and his voluntary service option would likely attract few takers. A universal service requirement of one or two years might go much further toward creating a sense of common citizenship and identity, but, like Ricks, Hart apparently believes that such a requirement would be politically unpalatable. So it may be necessary to start small and piecemeal: instead of adopting a single national program of service, states and communities might multiply the opportunities for citizens to assume responsibility for taming the political violence in their midst. Neighborhood watch and patrol groups, auxiliary police units, and the like may play an important part in a reconstruction of the Second Amendment.

Contrary to Hart's claim, the difference between such groups and private militia units is not that they would always obey the orders of the state. If the state should ever turn truly tyrannical, it might be desirable for them to resist. Instead, the difference is that to the extent they are legitimate, the former identify themselves with the good of the American people as a whole, not with a narrow and regressive slice of it. In fact, part of the raison d'etre for these groups is to foster a sense of broad identification. If they do not do so, then they have proved themselves a failed experiment. To secure that end, the state (even the federal government) will likely have to play a central role in the organization and training of such groups — just as it did in the eighteenth century. The state might raise some of these groups, and it might govern the behavior of private groups for the public good. In so doing, it should strive to yoke both types into some kind of common frame and inculcate a sense of common identity.

Part of the point in restoring "an army of the people" is to give the citizenry a forum in which to create popular unity on the use of political violence. It may be that the citizenry will find their unity without state involvement. If so, state supervision of these militialike groups will be much less important, perhaps unnecessary. Our citizenry, however, is not at that point, and it is pointless to pretend it is. An arrangement appropriate for a unified populace may not be appropriate for a populace deeply divided on itself. We may become a unified type of citizenry through collective arms bearing, but that transformation will likely require the participation of the government, the only public body accountable to the whole. Ironically, the government will have to enter this task in the awareness that it is creating a system of armed bodies charged with keeping the government itself in line. As we have seen, however, that odd cycle is at the heart of republican democracy, in which rulers and ruled are not sharply distinguishable. And so the Second Amendment has always embraced this tension: the state may be necessary to the creation of a militialike citizenry that can effectively check the state.

Disciplining Violence without Guns

The balance proposed here is likely to please neither side in the debate on the meaning of the Second Amendment. Individual rights theorists will worry that the state's involvement in organizing the armed people will hopelessly compromise the people's independence; the only solution, in their view, is to arm individuals unconnected to the state. States' rights theorists will worry that the arming of multiple popular groups will produce a seething morass of tension and conflict; the only solution, in their view, is to give the state a monopoly of violence to discipline the country.

The answer to both these worries is severalfold. First, any organization of violence may be assessed only relatively: a system of checks and balances poses undoubted danger, but it would be even more dangerous to repose perfect trust in either the state or the mass of private individuals. Second, any organization of violence must be worked out in practice: although a system of checks and balances might give rise to the projected dangers, it must then be corrected through trial and error. Third, no system of checks and balances could work well without an underlying popular unity, the subject of the next section. With such unity, the worries of both sets of theorists should be reduced: acting as a bloc, the people would pose a greater check on the government, and their unity would make widespread unrest much less likely.

Finally, for a system of checks and balances in the distribution of arms to work well, it must be supplemented with a system of checks and balances in ordinary politics. For Second Amendment purposes, the point in such a system is that peaceful politics should make legitimate recourse to violence, whether revolution or repression of rebellion, uncommon because unnecessary. Proponents of the Second Amendment were as concerned about avoiding violence as about readying themselves to use it if it became unavoidable. Reconstructing the Second Amendment, therefore, cannot be a flight from politics into a romance about blood and glory; instead, it must begin with a resilient hope for peaceful politics, to be abandoned only in desperation for the more treacherous politics of violent action. We must seek, in other words, to discipline violence through mechanisms other than guns.

To that end, two paths are important. First, to obviate the need for revolution, the ordinary political system must keep the government closely tied to the popular will and the common good. That goal is the perennial aim of the

American political tradition, as old as the Republic itself. It is the primary purpose of the Constitution itself and the subject of endless theorizing and planning ever since. In recent decades, Americans have proposed many new devices for keeping the government honest and representative: campaign finance reform, electoral law reform, government "sunshine" laws, term limits, electronic town halls, and the like. A review of such proposals is far outside the scope of this book. The present point, however, is that the Second Amendment cannot be comprehensively considered apart from such proposals. The best way to tame political violence is to make it unnecessary. In fact, as the people have become a less effective check on the government through arms, it is important that they become a more effective check through politics.

Second, to obviate the need for governmental suppression of rebellion, the government must seek to bring angry groups, self-styled Second Amendment patriots, back into the political mainstream. Whether their cause for resentment is just, the very existence of these groups creates difficulties for realizing Second Amendment ideals. In the end, the government may have to suppress such groups by force of arms, but such suppression tends to breed further resentment and violence, as the reaction to Ruby Ridge and Waco attests. And that resulting social division further undermines the possibility of popular unity. As a result, the government must proactively identify such groups and, to the extent consistent with the common good, address their alienation. When subgroups start to craft Second Amendment myths of resistance, there is reason to believe that ordinary electoral competition will not alleviate their anger.

The government has generally avoided such proactive engagement because American individualism has militated a laissez-faire style of government: the state informs individuals of the rules, and then they sink or swim through their own decisions. If a person fails at the market, he has only himself to blame — and he will be poor. If a person fails at politics, she has only herself to blame — and she will be powerless. And if a person commits a crime of rebellion, he has only himself to blame — and he will be punished. The answer to crime, including political crime, is more jails. The Second Amendment highlights the limits of this kind of individualism by focusing attention on the unity that must underlie our political system. If rebellious groups contribute to the disintegration of the political fabric, they are not hurting only themselves; they are subverting the constitutional organization of violence. If suppression of these groups contributes to that disintegration, the government has further subverted the constitutional organization of violence, whether those groups deserve suppression or not. Under the Second Amendment, we are not insulated from one another, and we cannot tame violence without one another. Individuals cannot pursue their individual goods without a collective frame protecting the collective good.

Globalism and Secession

The system of checks and balances contemplated by our constitutional organization of violence occurs at the national level, and it rests on the unity of a nation. The United States Constitution is a charter for the country as a whole, and it describes the appropriate relation between the citizenry of that country and the national government. When we seek a social contract for the use of violence, therefore, we seek at the level of the nation, not at the level of individual states or international associations. For better or worse, our constitutional organization of political violence is therefore not a charter for secession or globalism. In that sense, the Constitution presupposes a political unit with stable boundaries because it insists that force must flow from the will of the American people, not from the peoples of the various states or the peoples of foreign countries. In fact, the Framers would condemn uprisings on behalf of states or international bodies, to the extent that they departed from the national good, as factious violence. As a practical matter, this insistence on stable units may be necessary to organize violence: to develop the necessary unity, we must know who "we" are.

This claim, that our constitution disciplines political violence at the national level, does not deny that state and international actors may play an important part in constitutionally organizing violence. The Framers contemplated that state governments might prove to be rallying points for a people in revolution. Under the right circumstances, even international organizations might be a focus of organization for legitimate resistance. And the people of the nation may even decide that state and global interests form an important part of the nation's common good. In all these cases, however, the states and international bodies are channels for the will of a national people; they are not acting on their own interests. In other words, although states and global organizations may influence the system of checks and balances by way of the popular will, they are not constitutive elements of that system in their own right. Armed secession and global peacekeeping are thus not part of the constitutional organization of violence. Second Amendment "patriots" therefore appear to be on solid ground when resisting an international organization of violence, but in deep error when asserting a right to secession.

Yet even though our written Constitution does not endorse secession or globalism, our broader constitutional tradition does not categorically deny their legitimacy. In the Constitution's purview, a secessionist movement is a rebellion because it is made by a portion of the population against the whole.

If the rest of the country should agree to let the secessionists go as in their common interest, the movement would not be a rebellion, but then the issue of armed force would never arise. Secessionist movements cannot therefore plausibly claim the sanction of the Second Amendment. Yet it does not follow that such movements are always illegitimate in the broader tradition of which the Second Amendment is a part because although the amendment refers to the people of a stable nation, our general constitutional tradition regards political boundaries as somewhat more fluid. For example, the American War of Independence began as a secessionist movement, to separate the colonies from the British Empire. To remain consistent with their legal tradition, the revolutionaries first redefined the relevant political unit from the empire to the new people of the thirteen colonies. From the perspective of that new unit, they could argue that the war was a revolution by the Body of the People against an alien government, rather than a rebellion by the periphery against the center.

As this example shows, when we are assessing whether an uprising is a revolution or rebellion, we must first define the relevant political unit: what might seem a revolution from the perspective of South Carolina might seem a rebellion from the perspective of the United States of America. For that reason, early backcountry rebels could see themselves as the heirs of 1776: because they defined the people locally, they were the Body of the People resisting a foreign government. But at the same time, state and national authorities could also claim the mantle of 1776: because they defined the people nationally, they were the people's agents in squashing these local rebellions. Without having predefined the relevant set of boundaries, one cannot make sense of the distinction between rebellion and revolution.

The American doctrine of revolution does not offer an exact theory of how one ought to draw such boundaries. The War of Independence suggests that political boundaries should roughly group those of similar lifeways together, so that peoplehood becomes possible. Yet virtually all nations contain substantial political, ethnic, religious, and linguistic diversity, and the thirteen colonies were no exception. All that peoplehood requires for the constitutional organization of violence is commitment to a common social contract on the use of political violence. It is not simple diversity but divergence from that contract that makes peoplehood impossible. Because our Constitution undertakes to implement that contract at the national level, the distinction between revolution and rebellion is to be drawn at the level of the nation. Therefore, secession is rebellion. And yet, although our particular Constitution rejects secession, our general constitutional tradition does not categorically repudiate it. The way has always lain open for would-be secessionists to claim the legacy of the War of Independence: in the name of a "higher constitutionalism," they may argue that the relevant boundaries should be redefined, so that their rebellion becomes a revolution. They may not claim the Second Amendment as warrant, but neither are they wholly outside the realm of constitutional discourse. In America, secession has a bad name, and appropriately so because it has been embraced by those with regressive goals. Secession, however, is not categorically regressive, as witness the struggles for liberation of countless colonized peoples in the twentieth century.

Similarly, the Constitution mandates that we yoke force to the common good of the American citizenry, not to the world's population. If either the people or the government were to lend armed support to a foreign movement opposed to American interests, they could claim no support from the Constitution. Indeed, complicity in such a movement is virtually the definition of treason. If the government were to deploy troops at home as part of that action, it would be making real what has so far been only a fantasy of the paranoid fringe. Yet although the Constitution rejects organizing violence at the international level, it does not follow that the Constitution brands international peacekeeping efforts as categorically illegitimate. First, the constitutional organization of violence rejects only those international uses of force actually in conflict with the national good. In the past century, many Americans have come to believe that the American good is bound up in global peace, which can best be secured by international efforts. Sometimes, indeed, those efforts may require America to surrender some control over military intervention to units broader than the nation, like the United Nations. So long as that surrender is in the national good, it does not offend the constitutional organization of violence. In effect, international organizations have become part of our system of checks and balances, in service to the popular will. The patriot movement is thus mistaken in thinking that whenever the United States enters international arrangements for the global domestication of violence, it necessarily departs from the national interest.

On the other hand, if the United States surrendered authority to international peacekeepers in derogation of the American common good, such action would offend this Constitution. And yet, as for secession, even such a surrender would not necessarily be illegitimate in the constitutional system broadly considered. Again, whether an uprising is a revolution or a rebellion depends on where one draws the relevant boundaries. Our current constitution draws them at the level of the nation; therefore, a movement that serves the global good, considered as a whole, but hurts the American good, considered separately, would be a rebellion. Considered from the perspective of a hypothesized global legal order, however, that movement would be entirely legitimate. As for secession, the path remains open for globalizers to claim that, just as the War of Independence scaled down the boundaries in the interest of constitutional values, so today we should scale them up, for the same reason. In this view, a higher American constitutionalism would militate for the broadest possible political order — the One World Government of the militia movement's nightmares — so that the globe can be governed according to principles of justice and democracy, instead of the factional squabbling of self-interested nations.

MYTHS

Mythically, reliance on a system of checks and balances rejects an un-critical trust in any single entity as the pure voice of the people. Government can depart from the popular will and the common good, but so can any group of private gun owners. The best we can do is to create a distribution of arms among multiple groups, each capable of either trustworthiness or perfidy de-pending on the circumstances. In other words, we must wean ourselves of the hope for a savior waiting in the wings to dispense an ultimate safety. In the end, the government and private gun owners cannot be better than the Ameri-can people itself. If the people are divided and hateful, there is no route to a promised land of peace and plenty. If politics goes sour, a gun in the right hands will not be a solution because there will be no right hands. Moving to a myth of checks and balances therefore requires us to give up the hope of an apolitical Eden without sin to which we can escape when government or the people become hopelessly corrupt. Even after revolution has commenced or the government has cracked down on insurrection, those who have the means of force will still be embroiled in politics, with all its temptation to venality.

Yet although a system of checks and balances encourages us to abandon the myth that any single entity can speak for the American people, it does not reject the idea that Americans must possess a single framework for organizing political violence. In other words, on this subject the point in checks and balances is not that each component in the system should articulate its own separate interests; instead, the point is that each unit should articulate its best assessment of the common good, in the hope that through such multiple in-puts violence might best be yoked to constitutional ideals. In short, beneath multiplicity must lie unity.

Popular Unity

To some modern sensibilities, talk of mythic unity may seem disturbing or even dangerous. Let me therefore be clear about what I am not proposing before suggesting the nature of a healthy unity. I am not proposing that we create a myth of ethnic, cultural, religious, or linguistic unity, or one of ecstatic and mystical oneness in the volk, or one of profound self-sacrifice in service of the greater good, or one of boundless merger into a greater and aboriginal whole, or one that demonizes individual rights or suggests we have devolved from a prelapsarian state of unconscious solidarity. I am suggesting rather that to domesticate political violence, we need a widely shared set of norms—a social contract—on its appropriate use. Our constitutional tradition supports this course; prudence counsels it because without such a social contract we will disintegrate into warring cells; and even the idea of constitutionalism argues for it because without such a social contract we are outside a single constituted legal order. Within that legal order, diversity and individualism may prevail, but not so far as to deny the common frame for taming violence. The Second Amendment tradition does not eschew difference as such; instead, it rejects a particular attitude toward difference, holding that some differences justifiably give rise to hostility and detachment. Within a shared legal order, whatever our differences, we bear obligations to each other for the common domestication of violence.

In theory, then, the Second Amendment tradition insists only that we share a body of norms for the organization of violence; on everything else, we may differ. In practice, however, for a people to share norms on violence, they may need to share norms on other matters as well. The Second Amendment itself does not prescribe a set of specific rules for when the people should rebel or when the government should suppress an uprising; it merely directs in a general way that violence should be yoked to the common good, as perceived by the Body of the People, on the assumption (or hope) that more particular specifications will be part of our shared parlance. At any given point, those rules may be quite extensive. For example, Americans have traditionally believed that they have a right to revolt when government departs from the ends for which it has been created. To know when the right to revolution exists, then, we must agree on the ends of government, a goal that may require agreement on a broad range of matters. Conceptually, therefore, the organization of violence may swell to influence a good bit of our political life, but it all depends on the instant body of common norms for taming coercion.

In addition, the organization of violence may swell to influence much of our common life in a way that is more practical and less conceptual: to tame violence, citizens must be highly motivated to engage with one another in the development of shared norms and in their defense, even by armed action if necessary. In other words, the Second Amendment depends on a certain kind of patriotism: active devotion not only to one's narrow interests but also to the common enterprise. That devotion must be real, widespread, and actually experienced in Americans' lives — a rhetorical construct or an abstract assertion will not do. To secure the conditions of life that will produce such patriotism, we might have to modify the way we currently live our lives. Many Americans, for example, spend all day in economic competition according to a market culture that values only personal advancement; imbued with those beliefs, they may find it difficult to perceive, let alone serve, a larger whole.[51] Again, the answer can be worked out only in practice, and it is difficult to specify in advance how pervasive the changes would have to be.

In short, although in principle the constitutional organization of violence requires agreement only on a limited subject, it may in practice require much more commonality. Nonetheless, it is important to stress that the Second Amendment tradition is not hostile to diversity or individualism as such. To the extent that reconstructing the amendment might limit personal autonomy, those restrictions constitute a reluctant concession to the necessity of taming violence, rather than a celebration of orthodoxy or cultural discipline or sublime merger.

In addition, it bears repeating that consensus on the organization of violence is only a regulative ideal, always in process and never realized, rather than a static nirvana of perfect agreement. Indeed, if the Constitution could secure complete and stable agreement, violence would never occur, and we would not need to worry about organizing it. Yet though contestation and disagreement are normal and inevitable, even with regard to the norms governing violence, still the Second Amendment urges us to strive for peoplehood on this subject. In the Constitution's scheme, there is a difference between a citizenry that has agreed ultimately to disagree on the uses of violence and a citizenry that seeks agreement despite present fissures. The former group is more a set of civic strangers than a true citizenry, whereas the latter is a citizenry always in the process of realizing itself.

In reconstructing the Second Amendment, therefore, we should look not for norms that are held with complete unanimity or stability, but for a common commitment to develop norms, however shifting they might be. Drawing on the work of Jürgen Habermas, Frank Michelman has called this quality "constitutional patriotism."[52] In Michelman's account, to believe in the constitution as a modern social contract, legitimately binding on all, one must believe that "specific exercises of coercive political power are justified when . . . they are validated by a set of constitutional essentials . . . that everyone can see that everyone affected has reason to accept in light of his or her interests."[53] The problem with staking legitimacy to universal acceptance in this way is that in practice, there will be no "settled agreement among a country's people on a description of the actual thing [the 'constitutional essentials'] in all its concrete specificity." So, in the absence of agreement on the exact meaning of the constitution in application, a contracted group of citizens must share a commitment to work out their identity as a people, in community. Michelman dubs this commitment "constitutional patriotism": "Consider, now, that 'constitutional patriotism' surely seems to name some sort of motivational disposition. It names, I believe, a disposition of attachment to one's country, specifically in view of a certain spirit sustained by the country's people and their leaders in debating and deciding agreements of essential constitutional import."[54] That "spirit" involves the citizens' mutual dedication, even in the face of intense disagreement, to construct their joint identity as a people: " 'Constitutional Patriotism,' it appears, is the morally necessitated readiness of a country's people to accept disagreement over the *application* of core constitutional principles of respect for everyone as free and equal, without loss of confidence in the univocal content of the principles, because and as long as they can understand the disagreement as strictly tied to struggles over constitutional identity."[55] Constitutional patriotism thus connects citizens through a common set of unifying principles (the common good, constitutional ends), even though persons may not agree on their application at any given moment. In other words, constitutional patriotism calls for that same search for ultimate if hypothetical unity, through a system of conflicting perspectives (checks and balances), that underlies the Second Amendment's scheme for the domestication of political violence.

In the end, both the Second Amendment and constitutional patriotism must find a root for this mutual commitment to construct a collective identity, even in the face of intense disagreement over that identity. The amendment, as noted, traces the origin of this disposition to a felt sense of peoplehood, a historically specific experience of being bound together, the popular contract that came into being before the rectoral contract and that survives even when the government dissolves. Michelman traces constitutional patriotism to the same basic idea: "And what explains *that* readiness, when and where it is found? The answer to that must be that conditions then and there warrant a level of confidence that the struggle *over* corporate identity occurs *within* a corporate identity that is already incompletely, but to a significant degree, known and fixed. The answer is, in other words, a cultural contingency."[56]

Yet because this sense of constitutional patriotism is contingent — the experience of a historically situated people, not the hypothetical thoughts of abstract reasonable persons — it can disappear. If it disappears, the Second Amendment's scheme for taming violence will disappear as well. And, as Michelman reminds us, so will the constitutional contractarian basis for legitimating coercive legal power. We must attend, therefore, to the lived myths and practices that will sustain this emotional disposition in an actual people, rather than merely develop theoretical accounts of the origin of political power.

PRACTICES

As observed in the last chapter, myths and practices tend to change in tandem: myths of unity make commensurate practices seem desirable, and practices of unity make commensurate myths seem realistic. To promote myths of unity, therefore, we must also promote corresponding practices. The breakdown of common life in America has been the subject of extensive recent commentary, and practical proposals for its remedy are various and inventive. Summarizing and evaluating these many ideas or offering some alternative blueprint is outside the scope of this work. Instead, I offer two observations to help frame the task in Second Amendment terms.

First, the reconstruction of the Second Amendment cannot be conceived in isolation from the rest of American culture. Regardless of the distribution of arms, we cannot realize Second Amendment ideals without generating popular consensus on the appropriate organization of political violence. At its root, the amendment is not about who gets to pull the trigger but about how we imagine the basis of our constitutional connection. As a result, we must understand the amendment as part of the broader debate on the revival of a common life: that debate should include discussion of the right to arms, and discussion of the right to arms must rely on that debate. If we keep our focus narrowly limited to the possession of firearms, we will never break out of the current impasse on the amendment's meaning.

Second, the Second Amendment tradition has especially relied on universal service in the militia for the generation of unity. Right-to-arms proponents imagined the militia as a forum in which citizens of every sort would mix, become civic friends, and be trained to virtue. As a result, in reconstructing the amendment, we might pay particular attention to service schemes of various sorts. The most obvious possibility would be the recreation of something like the eighteenth-century militia updated to reflect broader notions of citizenship. This militia would include in its ranks as large a slice of the citizenry as practicable, be trained to virtue, and bear the responsibility of resisting the government should it become corrupt. Ideally, the militia should encourage a self-revisory political dialogue in which each citizen comes to understand her own interests in light of the interests of the whole. Such a possibility is not unthinkable. The Swiss, for example, maintain a popular militia that is an important symbol of unity and might provide a focus for resistance in the event of foreign aggression.[57] American folklore depicts the military as a melting pot in which young men from varying backgrounds come to understand one another.[58] And military history suggests that the primary source of combat bravery is intense commitment to fellow soldiers — a promising basis for dialogic self-revision.[59]

Yet while it may not be unthinkable, the universal militia as an engine of popular unity seems unpromising under modern circumstances. For one thing, it may be politically impossible to launch such a plan, as liberty-loving Americans would not tolerate the imposition on their lives. Perhaps that reluctance to serve reflects the very sort of self-absorption that frustrates the realization of unity, but it is still a powerful impediment to a militia scheme. For all his celebration of universal service, Hart, as noted, stops short of calling for mandatory enrollment in his Army of the People because it would be politically unpalatable. He offers instead a system of incentives for citizens to serve their country. A volunteer militia, however, might draw only on certain demographic sectors, much the way the volunteer regular military does. As a result, the new militia might imagine itself as a separate caste, after the style of the Marine Corps, rather than as a melting pot.

In addition, in times of disunity, a militia ready and able to resist the government poses a plain risk of rebellion and disorder. A select militia especially poses that risk, but the danger is present even when a universal but divided militia decides to take up arms. To worry about this kind of disorder is not to be faithless to the Second Amendment, whose proponents equally worried that a slice of the population might use arms to advance its own narrow aims. As I proposed in the last section, it might therefore be appropriate to arm the people for resistance to government — but only as part of a careful, incremental, and pragmatic strategy. It would certainly be unwise to arm Americans in the expectation that they will spontaneously form a united people when they might more likely become a series of mobs. The Second Amendment requires hope; it does not require naïveté.

Universal militia service may therefore be a relatively late step in reconstructing the Second Amendment. By contrast, public service in the military or civic aid efforts may be a relatively early step because it does not involve encouraging the mass of individuals to ponder overthrowing the government. For that reason, service plans might serve poorly as a direct check on government, but they might generate popular unity, which could then indirectly help to check the government. Of late, a number of commentators and politicians have championed service plans, especially for a term of years in youth.[60] The promised benefits mirror some of those anticipated for a militia. Service would bring together people from different classes, occupations, and ways of life into a common experience that would offer a basis for self-revisory dialogue.[61] And service to others and the state, through feeding the elderly, working in disadvantaged areas, rebuilding the nation's infrastructure, and the like, would promote self-sacrifice, reduce self-absorption, and expose one to people of different backgrounds.[62]

Unfortunately, service plans also suffer from some of the drawbacks of proposals for a militia. In the first place, it would not be politically acceptable to require service; for that reason, virtually all of the current proposals would offer incentives like college aid, salaried jobs, or tax benefits.[63] Such incentive mechanisms, however, might greatly reduce class-mixing in service because they would primarily attract the less affluent.[64] If the citizenry ever comes to see public service as rewarding in its own right, the more affluent might choose to join, but that change in attitudes will likely have to come about through measures other than a service plan itself.

In short, although a popular militia or a public service scheme may be critically important to reconstructing the Second Amendment, they may in the short run be either impossible, ill-advised, or of limited effect. Reconstructing popular unity for the sake of the Second Amendment will thus have to draw on ideas from outside the Second Amendment tradition narrowly defined. Re-imagining the amendment probably cannot proceed from a single great plan — such as a grand judicial interpretation or a sweeping legislative scheme — but from the incremental, piecemeal, and multitudinous actions of the citizenry as a whole. Ultimately, the amendment's well-being will likely depend on the health of our national political life. Only through such collective activity can we generate genuinely popular debate about and devotion to a common understanding of the uses of political violence. Michelman has suggested that a republican politics (and, he might have added, a Second Amendment politics) could occur "in the encounters and conflicts, interactions and debates that arise in and around town meetings and local government agencies; civic and voluntary organizations; social and recreational clubs, schools public and private; managements, directorates, and leadership groups of organizations of all kinds; workplaces and shop floors; public events and street life; and so on."[65]

In the end, a reconstructed Second Amendment and a vital social contract are mutually dependent; we cannot have the one without the other. Our constitution tries to tame political violence through broad popular engagement; it rests on the conviction that political violence should occur only with the assent of the Body of the People. Yet without a lived social contract, no Body of the People can exist because it is defined by its consensual commitments. Without a social contract, we are all, in effect, either tyrants or rebels because without general agreement on the frame we can pursue only our own separate good. Second Amendment patriots, therefore, should worry less about arming themselves against the dark forces that they see in their fellow Americans and more about invigorating our mutual commitment.

At the same time, a vital social contract may not be possible without popular engagement in the domestication of political violence. Most centrally, the Second Amendment insists that as disciplining violence is the first task of constitutional order, it is also the first duty of citizenship. A citizenry that has surrendered the taming of violence to governmental specialists has, in effect, surrendered part of self-government into the bargain. As the citizenry becomes passive consumers of government protection services, public discussion of the appropriate use of political violence will begin to wither, until we awake one morning to find that we no longer possess a lived social contract on this most important of constitutional issues. Political violence will have become the domain of experts and government insiders, and the rest of us will become spectators, pressure groups, or victims — but not self-governing citizens. Weberians would therefore do well to worry less about forcing government to discipline the gun culture and more about creating a common life in which the gun culture's members can play a welcome and important part.

MYTHS

Resources

Because they must enjoy broad popular support, our norms for organizing violence commonly take the form of constitutional myths, rather than a prolix and technical legal code. In fact, the history of the Second Amendment is the best evidence of the provision's affinity for popular myth: the amendment has always been embraced more eagerly by the people than by the courts. The people have always seen in it deep significance about the meaning of America, and they have always expressed that significance in the form of myth. In fact, Americans have tended to render the whole Constitution into myth. In the absence of a shared language, race, ethnicity, or religion, we have been united in large part by our great public professions of faith,[66] and the Constitution has been central among them.[67] We have looked to our constitutional tradition for stories that unite us as a people and provide for a common culture of inclusion and decency.

Although the Constitution is generally mythogenic, however, the Second Amendment may be the best examplar of this quality. Although their range of interpretations is wide, Americans still approach the Second Amendment as myth. With its complex brew of violence, peoplehood, and law, the amendment holds this mythic status because it deeply moves us. When fellow citizens tell us stories about the right to arms, we may glimpse in those accounts their deepest hopes and fears, ideals and doubts, about what it means to be American. By couching their stories in constitutional terms, Second Amendment mythographers signal the centrality of these stories to their perception of the sociopolitical world; they believe that the ideas in the stories are so significant to our common life that they must be enshrined in our fundamental law.

As a result, when people tell Second Amendment tales, they implicitly make a claim of connection to the rest of us: these are your stories, too, they are saying. We share a common body of myths that makes us fellow Americans, and you are therefore obliged to respond to my narrative. In fact, because we share a constitution, we must come to a shared understanding of when political violence is appropriate. Hidden within the welter of discordant stories about the Second Amendment is this flickering light: as long as people are telling constitutional myths in form (even if the substance of those myths is deeply divisive), they are expressing a hope for the very unity that the Second Amendment demands, a hope that people will pursue not just their diversity and autonomy but also their obligations to develop a common frame and to bear arms in its defense.

America has important cultural resources for this reconstruction of the mythic Second Amendment. Indeed, the recovery of more solidaristic traditions has become a cottage industry among academics in the past several decades. *Habits of the Heart* is the seminal work from which much of this writing springs.[68] In this now-classic volume, Robert Bellah and his colleagues explain that virtually all Americans speak a "first language" of individualism, but they also have available "second languages" in the biblical and republican traditions.[69] The first language frees us to do as we will, but it tells us little about what is worth doing; it therefore grants few resources to construct a coherent life or society.[70] By contrast, the biblical and republican traditions have insisted that "the American experiment is a project of common moral purpose, one which places upon citizens a responsibility for the welfare of their fellows and for the common good."[71] In language that directly tracks Second Amendment thinking, they maintain, "It is solidarity, trust, mutual responsibility that allows human communities to deal with threats and take advantage of opportunities."[72] And so they call for a kind of conversion, "a turning away from preoccupation with the self and toward some larger identity." In their view, this conversion can occur only through mythic revival: "Conversion cannot come from willpower alone, but if it is to be enabled we must recover the stories and symbols in whose terms it made sense."[73]

More recently, Michael Sandel has amplified the central argument of *Habits of the Heart*. In *Democracy's Discontent,* he offers a historical account of the rise of liberal individualism to the status of an American orthodoxy, along with the dogged persistence of republican thinking as a secondary world-view.[74] He too calls for the revival of the republican strand in American think-ing to answer a "discontent that besets American public life today":[75] "The hope of our time rests instead with those who can summon the conviction and restraint to make sense of our condition and repair the civic life upon which democracy depends."[76]

In both of these books, the writers divide the American political tradition into a liberalism that has little concern for the common good and a republican/biblical tradition that has more. This bifurcation may accurately describe the state of American culture today. At its inception, however, even liberalism in-sisted that individuals should heed more than their own interests. The founder of modern liberalism, John Locke himself, argued that entry into the social contract entailed commitment to a certain people and to a resolving of differ-ences from within that identity. Even after the government has been dissolved, the society endures and must find a way to act collectively so as to constitute a new government. In short, although these Lockean individuals prize their autonomy, they are not loose political atoms, not minirepublics of one. In-stead, they are firmly yoked into an entity to which they owe civic obligations and which is the framework for their lives and freedoms.

Hope

In other words, both historical liberalism and republicanism insist on a concern for the common good, at least when it comes to the constitutional organization of violence. To many readers, in fact, it may seem clichéd to claim that we need agreement on the use of political violence and bear obligations to the common enterprise. Perhaps few Americans would self-consciously deny these concepts in principle. Yet many commentators deny them in practice by leaving no room for them in their tales of division, strife, and self-interest. Virtually all Second Amendment mythographers imagine a landscape of ulti-mately contending, mutually hostile groups; looking to the government or to a gun in the hand for protection even when the social frame is cracked, they hold out no hope for a better world. More broadly, many commentators perceive in American culture a general valorization of the pursuit of personal preference without reference to any larger structures.[77] From an overinsistent concern to protect the individual, this outlook concludes that individuals, having no re-sponsibility to one another, rise and fall through their own efforts. At least for the organization of violence, this outlook is mistaken: we can rise and fall only as a people.

The most telling example of the inability to find a path to redemption may be the writing of Robert Cover, who was America's most profound commentator on the relation between myth, violence, and law. Cover stressed the importance of legal stories for domesticating violence, but he never raised the hope that Americans might develop common myths to this end. His work is keenly insightful about the importance of myth and community. If even he could find no place for common myths, we may infer that hope for them has largely fled.

In his classic article *Nomos and Narrative*,[78] Cover maintained that "we inhabit a nomos — a normative universe," a world that "we constantly create and maintain" through legal narratives. Professional lawyers may identify law only with legal precepts — the law on the books. In fact, however, law takes its primary meaning from the narratives that "locate it and give it meaning. For every constitution there is an epic, for each decalogue a scripture. Once understood in the context of the narratives that give it meaning, law becomes not merely a system of rules to be observed, but a world in which we live." Thus, because law and narrative are inseparably related, every rule finds its meaning in myth: "Every prescription is insistent in its demand to be located in discourse — to be supplied with history and destiny, beginning and end, explanation and purpose."[79] A legal tradition includes not only a set of legal precepts "but also a language and a mythos" that provide "paradigms for behavior"[80] and is in turn sustained by the "force of interpretive commitments" of those affected.[81] And the creation of a nomos occurs not primarily through formal law but through popular culture: "The nomos that I have described requires no state. And, indeed, it is the thesis of this [article] that the creation of legal meaning — 'jurisgenesis' — takes place always through an essentially cultural medium."[82]

To this point, Cover's analysis acutely describes the history and theory of the Second Amendment: as we have seen, the amendment has functioned as a mythic account, popularly developed and embraced, to explain the use of political violence. And indeed, Cover especially applies his theory of the mythic function of law to the special problem of violence. In his view, our interpretive commitments sometimes require us to inflict or suffer violence. As a result, communities must develop "texts of resistance," which explain to members when violence is appropriate in defense of their ideals:

> For a group to live its law in the face of predictable employment of violence against it requires a new elaboration of "law" — the development of an understanding of what is right and just in the violent contexts that the group will encounter. . . . In interpreting a text of resistance, any community must come to grips with violence. It must think through the implications of living as a victim or perpetrator of violence in the contexts in which violence is likely to

arise. . . . And we commonly believe situations of violent interaction to be dominated by special principles and values. The invocation of these special principles, values, and even myths is a part of the hermeneutic of the texts of resistance.[83]

Yet Cover departs from the Second Amendment tradition in a fundamental way: he suggests that meaningful texts of resistance can exist only in subcommunities that sharply distinguish themselves from the rest of the citizenry. He denies, in other words, the possibility of a unified Second Amendment people. Early in his article, Cover distinguishes between "paideic" and "imperial" patterns of nomoi. The former creates a "normative world in which law is predominantly a system of meaning rather than an imposition of force." In paideic communities, members are committed to "(1) a common body of precept and narrative, (2) a common and personal way of being educated into this corpus, and (3) a sense of direction and growth that is constituted as the individual and his community work out their law." Paideic communities thus rest on a "vision of a strong community of common obligations."[84]

Rich and nourishing as these communities are, however, they produce myths that are sometimes incommensurate with and hostile to the myths of other paideic communities. As a result, the state must enforce an "imperial" pattern of law by creating the conditions of peace. Unlike the paideic pattern, the imperial function does not create normative worlds; instead, it is "world maintaining"[85] in that it maintains the "minimum conditions for the creation of legal meaning in autonomous interpretive communities."[86] In this conception, norms provide no meaning for citizens' lives, and indeed, they "need not be taught at all." Instead, they need only be "effective" by being "*enforced* by institutions."[87] As a result, "interpersonal commitments are weak, premised only upon a minimalist obligation to refrain from . . . coercion and violence."[88] To keep the peace when communities come into conflict, judges must resolutely suppress the normative world of one or the other group: "Judges are people of violence. Because of the violence they command, judges characteristically do not create law, but kill it. Theirs is the jurispathic office. Confronting the luxuriant growth of a hundred legal traditions, they assert that *this one* is law and destroy or try to destroy the rest. . . . But judges are also people of peace. Among warring sects, each of which wraps itself in the mantle of a law of its own, they assert a regulative function that permits a life of law rather than violence."[89]

On the constitutional organization of violence, then, Cover's map of the legal landscape depicts multiple warring groups, each trying to preserve its own law against the others and against the state, which must kill some in the interests of the whole. In this vision, the only actor responsible to the whole is the state, but the state can engage only in the imperial pattern. It can create among its citizens no sense of strong obligation, and it can create no normative meaning or powerful myths.

Cover describes only two varieties of paideic communities, both of which constitute discrete, insular minorities; neither holds out any hope of embracing the American citizenry as a whole. First, insular communities such as the Amish have a strong sense of themselves as a separate people with a separate law; they are intent on securing the boundary that divides them from the rest of the population, so that they can maintain their distinctive ways. Second, redemptive constitutionalists such as the nineteenth-century antislavery movement seek to transform the world by converting it to their law.[90] Yet although these communities are oriented outward, they still must be distinct peoples within a larger whole: "Despite the interactive quality that characterizes transformational association, however, such groups necessarily have an inner life and some social boundary; otherwise it would make no sense to think of them as distinct entities."[91] Redemptive constitutionalists presumably wish to convert the whole society, and if they ever were to succeed, this "social boundary" between the part and the whole would disappear. Yet Cover never considers this possibility. Instead, he peremptorily rules it out of consideration: "American political life no longer occurs within a public space dominated by common mythologies and rites and ooccupied by neighbors and kin. Other bases are necessary to support the common life that generates legal traditions."[92]

In short, then, Cover offers no vision of an American people organized around common myths and norms, not even on the organization of violence. Instead, in Cover's vision, America is and must be a hodgepodge of multiple contending nomoi on the use of violence. The state, which in Cover's vision seems disconnected to any actual human beings except judges and other officeholders, kills worlds in the interests of peace, but only according to a desiccated imperial morality, as it cannot aspire to any shared vision, strong mutual commitment, or meaning-giving narrative. The paideic communities can provide meaning, but they must contend with the state through their texts of resistance. Cover starkly draws the conclusion of this grim portrait, which he calls "simple and very disturbing": "There is a radical dichotomy between the social organization of power and the organization of law as meaning."[93] The state must exercise power to kill, but it cannot do so according to any scheme of meaning, and the communities can provide meaning but possess only limited power. We are therefore doomed to struggle.

Cover's reason for this stark vision seems clear: he wants to decenter state law, removing it from its privileged position. He emphatically rejects the state's claim to an "exclusive or supreme jurisgenerative capacity"[94] and instead insists on "the destruction of any pretense of superiority of one *nomos* over another."[95] Of necessity, the state may have to exercise "superior brute force," but it cannot claim normative primacy. As a result, the courts should exercise only that power necessary to allow for the "creation of legal meaning in autonomous interpretive communities,"[96] and they should always be open to the legal tales that resisters have to tell. Cover concludes, "Legal meaning is a challenging enrichment of social life, a potential restraint on arbitrary power and violence. We ought to stop circumscribing the *nomos;* we ought to invite new worlds."[97]

Yet one must wonder whether, in rejecting the state's claim to privilege, Cover has thrown the baby out with the bathwater, for he has also rejected the possibility of popular solidarity that might exist above or outside the state. One might speculate that he rejects this possibility for the same reason he decenters state law: he worries that paideic communities might face pressure to merge into the alleged American people. And, to be sure, Second Amendment mythographers sometimes use restrictive talk of peoplehood to attaint those different from themselves. Yet if we entirely reject the concept of peoplehood, even when defined expansively, we may face equally oppressive results: with nothing to hold us together, we revert to the primordial loyalties of race, ethnicity, and religion. Rightly conceived, the claim that we must be one people on fundamentals points to Michelman's "constitutional patriotism": a shared disposition to work out struggles over a corporate identity from within a "corporate identity that is already incompletely, but to a sufficient degree, known and fixed."[98]

Talk of constitutional patriotism creates a real risk of forced assimilation, but one must consider the alternative. Cover leaves his paideic communities in this situation: they have their own autonomous nomoi, and they can only hope that the state will respect that nomoi because of its concern for imperial virtues. Yet how reasonable is that hope? The state does not share a world of meaning with these communities, nor do the various communities share meaning with each other. Judges must either come from within some normative community — in which case they may not sympathize with rival communities — or they must exist outside of all such communities — in which case they presumably have no sense of the importance of mythic meaning to ordinary people. And if the state does not respond in a way that respects these paideic communities, what is to be done? Cover has ex ante ruled out any popular solidarity even on the appropriate use of violence, so we are left only with contending, mutually unintelligible forces. Cover becomes a lonely voice crying in the wilderness of the law journals: "We ought to invite new worlds."

In the end, Cover's analysis promises a certain realism, but it is the realism promised by most Second Amendment mythographers: it is a jungle out there. We can hope the state will listen, but we will probably have to turn to our text of resistance. By ruling that the American people cannot be paideic, Cover has managed to preserve the independence of his paideic subcommunities, but only by giving up hope for a nation with common myths and norms on the use of violence. As we saw when we considered the situation of Second Amendment outgroups, surrendering that hope may prove threatening to the continued existence of those very groups. Particular communities may find in their sacred texts a mandate for resistance, even if that resistance will destroy the larger community and imperil their own survival. Celebrating that resistance may prove satisfactory to those whose overriding priority is the purity of local traditions. That course, however, is not a plausible rendition of our Second Amendment tradition, and it will not prove effective in taming political violence. Participation in a common venture of organizing force is the minimum cost of membership in a constitutional community. Cover describes a situation that may generate a "challenging enrichment of social life," but it will almost surely not provide a "restraint on arbitrary power and violence."[99]

In all likelihood, Cover eschews common myths because he has given up hope that the American people could ever create them. In fact, the current fractured landscape of the Second Amendment gives one little confidence in such a project. Yet if the alternative is to plead for state protection in the absence of common myths, the only sane course may be to strive for a more unified nomos. As Cover himself describes, "One constitutive element of a *nomos* is the phenomenon George Steiner has labeled 'alternity': 'the "other than the case," the counterfactual propositions, images, shapes of will and evasion with which we charge our mental being and by means of which we build the changing, largely fictive milieu for our somatic and our social existence.' "[100] If it is in the nature of nomoi to believe in alternity, they ultimately rest on hope. And Second Amendment hopes look toward common myths.

Trust and Love

While we are yearning for alternity, we should recognize that in addition to hope, a reconstructed Second Amendment will rely on trust. The right kind of trust among citizens is necessary to set outside limits on our disagreements, so that we can tame political violence. That point bears emphasis because the current dialogue on the amendment is saturated with insistence on the need for distrust.

Trust and distrust become relevant only when the risks are uncertain. When the threat is clear, we need not either trust or distrust anyone: we simply act in accord with the relevant information. As Claus Offe explains, "The truster is *unable to make sure* or *know for certain* that the trusted person(s) will actually act in the way that the truster expects them to act. . . . The key problem here is that of coping with opaqueness, ignorance, and social contingency."[101] Under our constitutional organization of violence, therefore, trust never becomes an issue when the facts are clearly known: the government has or has not become corrupt, the gun culture is or is not malignant, a particular uprising is or is not a rebellion.

Most of the time, however, we will not have that kind of crystal clear information. At that point, we will have to decide whether to trust people on the basis of what we know about their character. It may be relatively easy to feel a particularized trust in our family, kin, ethnic, racial, or religious group because we share with them an identity, strong commitment, and clear set of norms.[102] By contrast, it is much more difficult to develop generalized trust in the citizenry at large. As Offe explains, we cannot simply exclude the untrustworthy from the citizenry: "One thing that 'the people' cannot decide upon in a democracy is who actually belongs to the people — which is exactly the point of a democracy."[103] Among such strangers, it is problematic to see how civic trust could be possible. When we trust, we become vulnerable, and when we trust with regard to political violence, we become painfully vulnerable.

Because it is aware of this vulnerability, much of the Second Amendment tradition counsels a healthy mistrust, so we should hold our guns close. Because it is right to mistrust popular insurrection, Article I gives Congress the power to suppress rebellion; and because it is right to mistrust the government, the Second Amendment gives the people the ability to make a revolution. And because it is never exactly clear who is most (or least) trustworthy, the Constitution poses the people-in-militia and the people-in-legislature as checks and balances against one another. The Constitution grows out of a culture saturated in suspicion of those who hold any kind of power.

And yet . . . for collective action ever to be possible, for political violence ever to be yoked to the common good, those involved must find a way to trust one another. Without being counterweighted by trust, Second Amendment mistrust turns on itself, making the domestication of political violence unimaginable. The Second Amendment rests on this complicated balance: we must hold onto a realistic distrust, but we cannot allow it to poison us. Second Amendment suspicion was never an end in itself but a means to good government. When it has become so acute that it makes good government unrealizable, then it has defeated itself. Because the Second Amendment is about violence, it is tempting mythically to fill it with all our unresolved hostility. But the amendment is about taming violence, not celebrating it, and so its proclivity to force must be balanced by a yearning for peace through connection. Otherwise, the provision becomes a charter for survival of the fittest, an assertion that might makes right. In that sense, the Second Amendment must simultaneously insist upon and decenter its counsel of mistrust, so that it lurks in waiting at the edge of our constitutional landscape but does not dominate our vision.

In recent years, a growing body of scholarship has argued that civic trust can produce great benefits for a democracy. One commentator glowingly proclaims, "Trust promotes cooperation. . . . It leads people to take active roles in their community, to behave morally, and to compromise. People who trust others aren't quite so ready to dismiss ideas they disagree with. When they can't get what they want, they are willing to listen to the other side. Communities with civic activism and moral behavior, where people give others their due, are more prosperous."[104] Whether or not trust will secure all these benefits, we may add a further argument: without it, we will be unable to tame violence. If citizens followed the Second Amendment counsel of distrust without check, they would presume, in the absence of firm information to the contrary, that government and private parties were always engaged in subversion of the common good. For one who holds that belief, the only sane course might be a survivalist retreat into the mountains or a preemptive attack. Either way, such extreme mistrust will increase, not tame violence, as it sunders our connections.

As necessary as generalized trust may be, we must wonder nevertheless whether it is achievable among a nation of strangers. The face-to-face interactions that generate local trust will not serve, nor will a particularized trust rooted in kin identity or the like. Again, the only apparent alternative is a shared body of norms, customs, and myths. As Mark Warren observes, "Ultimately, collective action depends upon the good will of the participants, their shared understanding, their common interests, and their skilled attention to contingencies. . . . Trust is a way of describing the way groups of individuals presume the good will of others with respect to [these matters]."[105] Similarly, in explaining how people can trust institutions, Offe argues that one trusts the people staffing the institutions to act in accord with shared norms: " 'Trusting institutions' means . . . *knowing* and recognizing as valid the values and forms of life incorporated in an institution and deriving from this recognition the assumption that this idea makes sufficient sense to a sufficient number of people to motivate their ongoing active support for the institution and the compliance with its rules."[106] One can therefore imagine that a reconstructed Second Amendment could grow out of institutional practices — the militia, the military, even the "American nation" — that facilitate the development of the norms necessary for trust.

Still, even having a rich set of norms for the organization of violence, we will never know for sure that our fellow citizens will act in accord with them. As many Second Amendment theorists would insist, there is hazard in overtrusting. These writers tell us how good it is to hold a gun in your hand against public oppression or to take guns from those who would work private oppression. Yet there is also hazard in undertrusting: unless someone first puts himself at the risk of disappointment and loss, people will never interact sufficiently to develop a common fabric of norms, obligations, and expectations. As Yul Brynner ponders in *The King and I*, "It's a danger to be trusting one another. . . . But unless someday somebody trusts somebody, there'll be nothing left on Earth excepting fishes!"

For that reason, Jane Mansbridge argues that trust is sometimes altruistic behavior. This sort of trust "commits one to making . . . a leap of faith beyond (perhaps only slightly beyond) that warranted by pure prediction." For the good of others, one might make that leap for three reasons: first, "trusting expresses positive concern for the other"; second, "trusting expresses positive concern for the relationship between self and other" in hope of "turning a potentially hostile interaction into a potentially cooperative one"; and third, "trusting may serve as a model to others, making them more likely to trust in similar circumstances."[107] Because this kind of trust is concerned with the good of the other and one's relationship to the other, we might call it a species of civic love. Such civic love, concerned to build connection so as to make possible coordinated action for the common good, is the necessary counterbalance to civic suspicion, concerned to detect attacks on the common good before it is too late. In other words, at the heart of the Second Amendment is not only violence but love. When necessary, we are willing to do violence, not because we worship violence, but because we love. Under the right conditions, that love can keep us from becoming creatures of the night, consumed by violence, reduced by the need for self-protection to the very thing that we were protecting ourselves against.

How might we create citizens who will give each other the benefit of the doubt in this way, so that the Second Amendment's hopes can be realized? Again, that question is far beyond the scope of this work. Possible answers might include certain styles of child rearing, certain religious traditions, easily discernible markers of trustworthiness, democratic governance, high levels of optimism, participation in certain associational activities, and general economic prosperity, so that risks do not seem potentially catastrophic.[108]

The story of the Second Amendment offers two insights relevant to the question of how we generate a culture of appropriate trust. First, the amendment insists that this question is the central issue in the organization of violence, and so we should devote most of our attention to it rather than to the distribution of arms. If we get this right, the distribution of arms will not much matter, and if we get this wrong, the distribution of arms will not much help. Second, the current mythic landscape of the Second Amendment suggests that we make trust possible (or not) through the stories we tell about political violence. Through these myths, we learn, communicate, and pass on our wisdom about law, coercion, identity, democracy, and the future. If we tell unbalanced myths about the inevitability of hatred and fear, they may come true. But we can tell a different Second Amendment myth, truer to its history and more serviceable to our needs: the world may hurt us, and so we need to take care. Yet if the need to take care ever anneals our hearts, so that we see in the other only a threat rather than a hopeful, hurting, and precious soul, then we will always live in a world of hurt. So we need always to be looking not only for threat but also for the promise of redemption.

The Future

Our constitutional organization of violence rests on the conviction that we belong to each other in hope, trust, and love, as members of a shared social covenant. The separate pursuit of personal desire may be appropriate in many walks of life, but not in this one. For this purpose, solidarity and connection are necessary components of a healthy social life, as no individual, group, or institution can safely domesticate political violence for the community as a whole. It may be important that we arm ourselves, but it is even more important that we form the social affiliations that will allow us to use those arms in good ways. In the discordant din of voices today, this part of the Second Amendment's meaning is surely the most neglected.

Any form of sociopolitical organization must rest at least on one hope: People can develop the commonality and care for one another that will allow them to modulate the violence that is in them. To be effective, those qualities must extend broadly across the citizenry, so that most Americans are yoked into a shared enterprise. Yet as necessary as this hope may be, it runs counter to the trajectory of much contemporary American thinking. Talk of hope, trust, love, intimacy, solidarity, commonality, and connection seems to many naive at best, oppressive at worst. Some right-wing analysts decry it as creeping corporatism; some left-wing analysts decry it as creeping authoritarianism. Some market ideologists insist that social organization exists only to serve the preferences of individuals. Some multiculturalists insist that America is composed of mutually unintelligible cultures. Some conservative pundits insist that "minority" cultures should be disciplined into conformity, and some radical pundits insist that the "majority" culture should be dismantled. Many liberals and libertarians insist that individuals, from the privacy of their own autonomous spheres, should simply leave each other alone. And perhaps most Americans just want to get on with their private lives without taking up arms against anyone. To be sure, almost all these people would agree that Americans should have a common frame for taming violence, but they are content to let that frame take care of itself. Yet in the absence of citizens habitually devoted to maintaining the frame, it will eventually crumble — when the economy turns sour, or foreign nations threaten, or citizens lose a common language to discuss where we go from here.

Reconstructing a Second Amendment based on commonly held norms may seem unrealistic, especially given the provision's current mythic landscape. Virtually all major schools of Second Amendment theory insist that we should fear someone, and they urge the appropriate actors to arm themselves to get control of the situation. The dialectic between myths and practices makes unity seem even more unreachable: we will not change our practices until we embrace more hopeful myths, but we will not embrace those myths until they seem affirmed by our experience of social practices. Under these circumstances, it may make sense to give up on connection and to adopt a myth of disunion: because the social world is a sea of anger, the best we can do is to rely on mutual deterrence. Such a scheme could be called a constitutional organization of violence, but it amounts only to a domestic arms race. It does little to tame the beast, and in the long run it courts disaster. To purge this land with blood, we will have more Wacos and more Oklahoma Cities.

We are at the nub here of what may be America's most pressing, perennial, and unanswerable question: Can a society that celebrates freedom and difference maintain enough commonality to preserve the conditions necessary for freedom and difference? In the Constitution, the Framers insisted that if the government ever turned against "us," then "we" could revolt, and if rebels ever threatened "our" political fabric, then "we" could suppress them. In this scheme, they presumed that there would always be a we — a Body of the People. In the decades since, America has continually defined and redefined that we — most commonly in ways that are restrictive, bigoted, and oppressive.[109] In light of that past, it is tempting to abandon the people and insist that only individuals and subcultures are real or important.

In the end, however, if there is no we left, then who has his/her/their/its finger on the trigger? Once again, the current landscape of the Second Amendment leaves us with an unacceptable dichotomy between connection and autonomy. As is so often the case, introducing violence into the equation may shift our calculations. In theory, we can best preserve autonomy if we minimize the demands of peoplehood, so long as everyone amicably decides to go along with that system of autonomy. In practice, however, if we exist only as competitive individuals or groups, with no sense of shared commitment, it is unlikely (if not downright inconceivable) that we will respect each other's rights when the guns come out. By contrast, we do not kill people for whom we hold civic love, people with whom we form a body, and neither do we demand that they surrender their distinctive identity. The lesson of the Second Amendment, therefore, is that even autonomy depends on a sense of mutual devotion among the citizenry, rather than just an abstract belief in a system of rights. And this devotion must be the right sort: the sort that prizes the concrete well-being of the other, rather than the sort that subordinates the other to a scheme for cultural purity.

It is a lot to hope for that sort of mutual devotion in a large, multicultural democracy. In the scheme of history, it may seem a miracle that humans ever tame political violence long enough to plan their lives in peace and promise, drinking up the good things that life can offer. It seems even more of a miracle that we could tame violence through connection while still respecting freedom and diversity. And yet miracles happen because people believe they can happen. In 1776, few would have believed that women and people of color would ever enjoy formal—if not yet truly substantive—equality. Yet they do, because a few people found the courage to hope and, by hoping, made it possible for others to share their conviction. In 1976, few would have believed that democracy was about to sweep the world, bringing down one totalitarian government after another. And yet it did, because citizens of those governments found a way to believe that they could change the world in solidarity. As hope grows on hope, trust grows on trust, and love grows on love, and they all grow on the resources that our myths offer us. If we live out our stories, then, we need to be sure we tell the right ones, as they set the limits of our future. And to heal the violence that scars us, even as we recognize the fears and threats on every side, we must incorrigibly insist on believing in stories of endless possibility.

Notes

Introduction to Part 1

1. For an overview of the current debate on the meaning of the Second Amendment, see David C. Williams, *Civic Republicanism and the Citizen Militia,* 101 Yale L.J. 551, 556–59 (1991). Significant contributions from the individual rights school include Don Kates, *Handgun Prohibition and the Original Meaning of the Second Amendment,* 82 Mich. L.Rev. 204 (1983); Sanford Levinson, *The Embarrassing Second Amendment,* 99 Yale L.J. 637 (1989); L. A. Powe, *Guns, Words, and Constitutional Interpretation,* 38 Wm. & Mary L.Rev. 1311 (1997); Glenn Harlan Reynolds, *A Critical Guide to the Second Amendment,* 62 Tenn. L.Rev. 461 (1995); William Van Alstyne, *The Second Amendment and the Personal Right to Arms,* 43 Duke L.J. 1236 (1994); Eugene Volokh, *The Commonplace Second Amendment,* 73 NYU L.Rev. 793 (1998). In recent years, the states' rights camp has garnered less support from law professors and lawyers, but important contributions include Carl T. Bogus, *Race, Riots, and Guns,* 66 S. Cal. L.Rev. 1365 (1993); Keith A. Ehrman and Dennis A. Henigan, *The Second Amendment in the Twentieth Century: Haw You seen Your Militia Lately?* 15 U. Dayton L.Rev. 5 (1989); Dennis A. Henigan, *Arms, Anarchy and the Second Amendment,* 26 Val. U. L.Rev. 107 (1991); and the articles by law professors in a symposium issue of the Chicago-Kent Law Review,

Symposium on the Second Amendment: Fresh Looks, 76 Chi.-Kent L.Rev. 1–716 (2000). In addition, a group of historians have self-consciously organized to denounce the individual rights view. *See, e.g.,* Michael A. Bellesiles, *Suicide Pact: New Readings of the Second Amendment,* 16 Const. Comm. 247 (1999); Saul Cornell, *Commonplace or Anachronism: The Standard Model, the Second Amendment, and the Problem of History in Contemporary Constitutional Theory,* 16 Const. Comm. 221 (1999); Don Higginbotham, *The Second Amendment in Historical Context,* 16 Const. Comm. 263 (1999).

2. For individual rights theorists, see Levinson, *supra* note 1, at 646–47; Reynolds, *supra* note 1, at 466. For states' rights theorists, see Carl T. Bogus, *The Hidden History of the Second Amendment,* 31 U.C. Davis L.Rev. 309, 369 (1997); Ehrman and Henigan, *supra* note 1, at 39–40. Historians opposed to the individual rights view are especially prone to accuse lawyers in that camp of selective citation — sometimes in rancorous tones. *See* Garry Wills, A Necessary Evil: A History of American Distrust of Government 214–16 (1999); Bellesiles, *supra* note 1, at 247–50; Cornell, *supra* note 1, at 222–25; Higginbotham, *supra* note 1, at 263–64. Unfortunately, as we will see, these historians are sometimes not immune from the disease they discern in others.

3. *See* Michael Bellesiles, *The Origins of the Gun Culture in the United States, 1760–1865,* in Guns in America: A Reader 17–18 (Jan E. Dizard et al. eds., 1999). More recently, Bellesiles has compiled much of his historical research in a book that has also achieved widespread attention, Michael A. Bellesiles, Arming America: The Origins of a National Gun Culture (2000).

4. In a symposium issue of the Tennessee Law Review, Glenn Harlan Reynolds claimed that modern legal scholarship has cohered on a "standard model" of the Second Amendment that understands it as a protection for an individual right to arms. *See* Reynolds, *supra* note 1, at 463. More recently, a group of historians have objected to the idea that American history can ever produce a standard model of anything. Thus, Saul Cornell comments, "The notion that American political thought might be understood in terms of a single ideological paradigm has collapsed under the accumulating weight of evidence demonstrating the incredible vitality and diversity of American political culture in the Revolutionary era." Cornell, *supra* note 1, at 222. Bellesiles goes even further: "The vast majority of historians have rejected the idea that any aspect of American history can be understood 'in terms of a single ideological paradigm.'" Bellesiles, *supra* note 1, at 249.

5. "'Too much orderliness . . . makes historians suspicious.' . . . Put another way, professional historians immediately doubt any case for which all the evidence falls completely on one side. Historians know that history is full of ambiguities and paradoxes, and expect to find them." Bellesiles, *supra* note 1, at 248–49 (citation omitted).

6. Ronald Dworkin has offered perhaps the most elaborate, elegant, and exhaustive exposition of this view of judging in Law's Empire (1986).

7. *See, e.g.,* Akhil R. Amar, *Second Thoughts: What the Right to Bear Arms Really Means,* The New Republic, July 12, 1999, at 24, 26–27.

8. For example, Justice John Marshall Harlan explained that due process refers to a balance between order and liberty that is "struck by this country, having regard to what history teaches are the traditions from which it developed as well as the traditions from which it broke. That tradition is a living thing." Poe v. Ullman, 367 U.S. 497, 542–43 (1961)(dissenting opinion of J. Harlan).

Chapter 1. The Background of the Framers' Thinking

1. The historical works discussing this debate are legion. Louis Hartz's classic work is The Liberal Tradition in America (1955). Pocock's most famous book is The Machiavellian Moment (1975); Wood's is The Creation of the American Republic 1776–1787 (1969); and Bailyn's is The Ideological Origins of the American Revolution (1976). Isaac Kramnick provides an excellent overview of the debate as well as his own syncretistic reading of the time, in Republicanism and Bourgeois Radicalism (1990).

2. J. G. A. Pocock, *Civic Humanism and Its Role in Anglo-American Thought,* in Politics, Language and Time: Essays on Political Thought and History 80, 86 (J. G. A. Pocock ed., 1973). *See* Pocock, *supra* note 1, at 68, 71, 75; Wood, *supra* note 1, at 53–57. The classic exposition of these ideas, and the inspiration for later republicans, is Aristotle's Politics. *See* Pocock, *supra* note 1, at 66–68. For republicans, the common good did not necessarily stand in opposition to individual freedoms. Republicans typically believed that part of the common good was liberty for all, *see* Wood, *supra* note 1, at 18–28, and, as I will explain, liberty was instrumentally necessary to the commonweal. Indeed, Machiavelli may even have valued a politics of the common good chiefly as an instrument to secure negative liberty against government. The common good, however, did not include the pursuit of self-interest as such, as an end in itself; liberty must always be justified in terms of the common good, rather than the other way around. *See* Quentin Skinner, *The Idea of Negative Liberty: Philosophical and Historical Perspectives,* in Philosophy in History 193, 204–19 (Richard Rorty et al. eds., 1984).

3. *See* Pocock, *supra* note 1, at 74–75, 204–05; Wood, *supra* note 1, at 118–19. By the same token, state and society can be mutually reinforcing if both are virtuous. For American republicans, "the relationship between government and society, in America as in England, was reciprocal, and America's healthy republican society presented the proper framework for a government that would in turn sustain the integrity of a republican society and economy." Drew R. McCoy, The Elusive Republic 62 (1980).

4. I speak of this tension as a paradox because at its strongest it involves logically inconsistent propositions: citizens must be simultaneously the creatures and creators of the state; a republic can come into being only through a citizenry that can come into being only through a republic; rights are both the precondition and product of deliberative politics. The paradox might be only apparent; indeed, for republics to exist, it would have to be. In a less stark form, the tension might more closely resemble a dialectic: a somewhat virtuous state may act on a citizenry, which would then react on the state to make it more virtuous, and so forth. I express this tension, however, in its strong, paradoxical form to stress the anxiety it caused, anxiety that entered into the formulation of the Second Amendment: as militia members, citizens are a product of the state but must also be independent.

5. *See* McCoy, *supra* note 3, at 5. Unlike republicanism, which insists that healthy government depends on highly contingent virtue, some types of classical liberalism presume people to be self-interested, construct a scheme of government to temper even their worst excesses, and so claim to be right for most times and places. Martha Nussbaum has argued that an awareness of vulnerability to conditions is a central difference between the Aristotelian (republican) tradition and the liberal tradition associated with Plato and Kant. *See* Martha C. Nussbaum, The Fragility of Goodness 3–7, 329–30 (1986).

6. *See, e.g.,* Wood, *supra* note 1, at 66, 91–93, 123–24. Some republicans imagined another path out of this paradox: a glorious and virtuous leader might mold the people to virtue. In Hannah Pitkin's view, this idea explains the protofascist elements of Machiavelli's thought. In desperation at Florentine corruption, he conceived the mythical figure of the Founder — infinitely good, powerful, and self-originating — who could shape the Florentines to virtue. *See* Hannah Pitkin, Fortune Is a Woman 54–56, 75–79 (1984). By definition, the Founder is unlike ordinary mortals in that he can be virtuous even outside a republican state and thus escape the paradox of origins. To hope for a Founder, therefore, is to hope for a miracle.

7. *See* McCoy, *supra* note 3, at 7. John Adams, for example, ultimately concluded that virtue was the effect, not the cause, of good government. *See* John P. Diggins, The Lost Soul of American Politics 69–71 (1984). In the view of such republicans, one could therefore secure virtue by changing the form of government. *See* Wood, supra note 1, at 120–22.

8. *See, e.g.,* Lance Banning, The Jeffersonian Persuasion 61 (1978); Pocock, *supra* note 1, at 205, 506–07.

9. For other descriptions of this tangled attitude, see Frank Michelman, *Law's Republic,* 97 Yale L.J. 1493 (1988) [hereinafter cited as Michelman, *Republic*]; Frank Michelman, *The Supreme Court, 1985 Term — Foreword: Traces of Self-Government,* 100 Harv. L.Rev. 4, 42–43 (1986) [hereinafter cited as Michelman, *Traces*]. For an example of a modern writer stuggling with this same tension, see Jennifer Nedelsky, *Reconceiving Autonomy: Sources, Thoughts, and Possibilities,* 1 Yale J.L. & Feminism 7, 20–36 (1989).

10. *See* Michelman, *Traces, supra* note 9, at 43. On this side of the Atlantic, the denunciation of slavish subservience reached its greatest pitch just before and during the War for Independence. *See* Charles Royster, A Revolutionary People at War: The Continental Army and American Character, 1775–1783, at 6–10 (1979); Wood, *supra* note 1, at 37–38, 52–53.

11. *See* Michelman, *Traces, supra* note 9, at 27; Cass R. Sunstein, *Beyond the Republican Revival,* 97 Yale L.J. 1539, 1548–49 (1988); Wood, *supra* note 1, at 61–64; Michelman, *Republic, supra* note 9, at 1505. This paradox may be most acute in republican ideas about property rights. On the one hand, along with arms possession, private property was a critical guarantee of citizen independence from the government. *See* Pocock, *supra* note 1, at 386–89; Gregory S. Alexander, *Time and Property in the American Republican Legal Culture,* 66 N.Y.U. L.Rev. 273, 294–95 (1991); McCoy, *supra* note 3, at 62–68. On the other hand, republicans recognized that property rights were a product of collective decisions and depended on collective protection. They also knew that severe inequalities of property would bring their own form of subjection, that of some citizens to the wealth and power of others. *See* Michelman, *Traces, supra* note 9, at 40–41; Pocock, *supra* note 1, at 386–91; Alexander, *supra,* at 293–94. So what if a system of strong property rights resulted in severe inequalities of wealth through the normal operation of the market? For the state to intervene would be to acknowledge the social construction of property rights and the ephemerality of citizen independence. But for the state not to intervene would be to tolerate the very subjection — of some citizens on others — that property rights were supposed to eliminate in the first place. *See* McCoy, *supra* note 3, at 72; Alexander, *supra,* at 294–302; Wood, *supra* note 1, at 64–65. In the face of this

tension, republican reponses differed: some recommended redistribution of property, *see* Pocock, *supra* note 1, at 387; Michelman, *Traces, supra* note 9, at 41 n.214; Alexander, *supra,* at 290; Wood, *supra* note 1, at 64; some recommended a bar to redistribution, *see* Alexander, *supra,* at 291; and perhaps most conveniently ignored the problem.

12. *See* Pocock, *supra* note 1, at 71–80, 99–100; Banning, *supra* note 8, at 22–28, 33–34, 40–41; Wood, *supra* note 1, at 197–202; Michelman, *Traces, supra* note 9, at 43–46.

13. The classic formulation of this problem, sometimes recited in the eighteenth century, was the Polybian cycle. A republic might achieve equilibrium among the three estates, but never for long. As it became more prosperous and powerful, it would become impossible to maintain the balance. It would then begin to degenerate into less healthy forms of government in a predictable sequence. *See* Pocock, *supra* note 1, at 79–80; Banning, *supra* note 8, at 42, 47–48.

14. *See* Banning, *supra* note 8, at 42–43, 54, 65–66; Wood, *supra* note 1, at 32–34; Pocock, *supra* note 1, at 406–08.

15. *See* Banning, *supra* note 8, at 78–82, 84–87; Edmund S. Morgan, Inventing the People 245–47 (1988); Pocock, *supra* note 1, at 514–17; Wood, *supra* note 1, at 32–34, 111–30, 200–02, 208–09.

16. *See* Wood, *supra* note 1, at 70–73, 205–07, 237–55; Pocock, *supra* note 1, at 515.

17. *See* Banning, *supra* note 8, at 67; McCoy, *supra* note 3, at 23, 37–38; Pocock, *supra* note 1, at 430–31, 444–45, 462–66. For example, Members of Parliament looked to their own income rather than to the public welfare when they took monarchical bribes, *see* McCoy, *supra* note 3, at 57–58; Banning, *supra* note 8, at 52, 59; Kramnick, *supra* note 1, at 178. Also, the standing army looked to ensure its own continued employment by fomenting standing wars. *See* Pocock, *supra* note 1, at 409–10, 412–14; Kramnick, *supra* note 1, at 178. The monied interest, too, encouraged war because war gave rise to public debt, which made money for men of wealth. *See* Banning, *supra* note 8, at 65–67; Pocock, *supra* note 1, at 409–10; Kramnick, *supra* note 1, at 178. Deeply complicit in this vast conspiracy was the Crown, which now possessed both money and military might, so if anyone were inclined to protest, the resistance could not last long. *See* Banning, *supra* note 8, at 52–59, 65–67.

18. The Court Party and its intellectual backers defended specialization as progress because it created prosperity and culture. *See* Pocock, *supra* note 1, at 459–60; McCoy, *supra* note 3, at 25–32. The Country Party, the self-conscious expositors of republican ideas, responded that if prosperity and culture could come only with specialization, it was better to accept some coarseness and still retain political morality. *See* McCoy, *supra* note 3, at 32–33; Pocock, *supra* note 1, at 430–31, 499–505. In the context of eighteenth-century Britain, one might describe the Country Party itself as a special interest: the party of rural, backward-looking landed wealth. *See* Kramnick, *supra* note 1, at 165, 177; Isaac Kramnick, Bolingbroke and His Circle: The Politics of Nostalgia in the Age of Walpole (1968). They did not perceive themselves as such, however, because they believed that if all citizens remained like themselves, Britons could share a common good. By contrast, in a specialized economy, soldiers, administrators, stockjobbers, farmers, lacemakers, and factory owners could never coalesce into a shared interest. *See* Banning, *supra* note 8, at 68–69. Later American republicans would exhibit a similar tendency to identify the middle class with the people as a whole. *See* Kramnick, *supra* note 1, at 277.

19. *See* Banning, *supra* note 8, at 75–80; Kramnick, *supra* note 1, at 268–69; McCoy, *supra* note 3, at 57–58, 62–70; Wood, *supra* note 1, at 34–37, 52–53, 57–60, 98–101, 113–14.

20. *See* Banning, *supra* note 8, at 63–64; Wood, *supra* note 1, at 20. Because republicans often conflated the good of the Many with the good of the whole, it was presumably easy for American republicans to reimagine themselves, from being champions of the Many to champions of the unspecialized republic. *See* Wood, *supra* note 1, at 20.

21. For example, James Burgh, the great transmitter of republican ideas to the colonies, *see* Banning, *supra* note 8, at 60–62, made the connection between power and arms: "Those, who have the command of arms in a country, says Aristotle, are masters of the state, and have it in their power to make what revolutions they please." 2 James Burgh, Political Disquisitions: Or, An Enquiry Into Public Errors, Defects, and Abuses 345 (London, 1775). On power following property, the classic republican source is James Harrington, who made that claim the center of his theory of government. *See* Pocock, *supra* note 1, at 385–91.

22. *See* Lawrence D. Cress, Citizens in Arms: The Army and the Militia in American Society to the War of 1812, at 20, 23–25 (1982); Andrew Fletcher, *A Discourse of Government with Relation to Militias,* in Selected Political Writings and Speeches 1, 4, 6, 10, 15 (David Daiches ed., 1979); Pocock, *supra* note 1, at 409–10, 412–13; W. A. Speck, Reluctant Revolutionaries 145–46, 154–56 (1988); John Trenchard and Thomas Gordon, *Cato's Letters No. 94,* reprinted in The English Libertarian Heritage 222–23 (David L. Jacobson ed., 1965).

23. *See generally* Douglas E. Leach, Roots of Conflict: British Armed Forces and Colonial Americans, 1677–1763 (1986). The colonies never raised a standing army; they defended themselves against attack first by militia and later by expeditionary forces of volunteers or impressed paupers, sometimes commanded by British officers. *See* Cress, *supra* note 22, at 4–8; Wayne Carp, *The Problem of National Defense in the Early National Period,* in The American Revolution: Its Character and Limits 19–20 (Jack P. Greene ed., 1987). Colonial militias served, moreover, with British regulars in various conflicts and came away with sour recollections. Through the century, there was also constant tension between colonists and regulars over quartering troops and impressment. *See* Cress, *supra* note 22, at 10–11; Leach, *supra,* at 10–11, 87–92; Pauline Maier, From Resistance to Revolution 6–7, 9–12, 20, 124–25 (1974).

24. *See* Jack P. Greene, Peripheries and Center 8–82 (1986).

25. *See* Cress, *supra* note 22, at 11, 36–39; Carp, *supra* note 23, at 21–22; Royster, *supra* note 10, at 36. Famously, the Declaration of Independence condemns George III for sending "large Armies of foreign mercenaries to compleat the work of death, destruction, and tyranny." The Declaration of Independence, para. 27 (U.S. 1776).

26. *See* Maier, *supra* note 23, at 200–203, 208–211, 234–238.

27. *See* Cress, *supra* note 22, at 8–9, 11, 36–38, 47, 60–61; Greene, *supra* note 24, at 83–84; Royster, *supra* note 10, at 51–53.

28. *See* Cress, *supra* note 22, at 19; Fletcher, *supra* note 22, at 6, 9, 12; Pocock, *supra* note 1, at 409–13, 430–32.

29. Joel Barlow, Advice to the Privileged Orders in the Several States of Europe 44 (1956).

30. *See* Fletcher, *supra* note 22, at 4, 6, 9; Cress, *supra* note 22, at 19; Pocock, *supra* note 1, at 199–200, 203–04. Barlow claimed that when the people lay down their arms, they "lose at once the power of protecting themselves, and of discerning the cause of their oppression" because disarmament "palsies the hand and brutalizes the mind." Barlow, *supra* note 29, at 45.

31. Many republicans believed that the militia offered another advantage: it would be more effective against foreign enemies than would a professional army because it fought for home and hearth rather than for lucre. *See* Morgan, *supra* note 15, at 154–56; Fletcher, *supra* note 22, at 9, 17; Cress, *supra* note 22, at 43–44. In fact, however, militias were never very effective, especially against trained bands and especially given the increasing sophistication of warfare in the eighteenth century. *See* Morgan, *supra* note 15, at 160–62. By the 1780s, most Americans had come to perceive the militia's shortcomings. *See* Royster, *supra* note 10, at 37; Cress, *supra* note 22, at 58–59. Americans still quarreled over the appropriate role of an army, but the basis of the disagreement had shifted. Opponents now argued not that an army was less effective than a militia, but that it was more and thus posed a threat to liberty. The militia was perhaps less proficient but at least it was virtuous. *See* Cress, *supra* note 22, at 75–93.

32. *See, e.g.,* Morgan, *supra* note 15, at 153–73.

33. *See, e.g.,* Fletcher, *supra* note 22, at 16; Pocock, *supra* note 1, at 87–91 (Leonardo Bruni), 196–99, 202–03, 210–11 (Machiavelli), 389–91 (Harrington).

34. *See* Cress, *supra* note 22, at 29; Fletcher, *supra* note 22, at 9; Pocock, *supra* note 1, at 414; John Trenchard and Walter Moyle, An Argument Shewing, That a Standing Army Is Inconsistent with a Free Government, and Absolutely Destructive to the Constitution of the English Monarchy 7 (London, 1697); Cress, *supra* note 22, at 19. One of the best examples of this view was the creation of the utopian Georgia colony by English philanthropists. They sought to prevent the development of self-interest and to promote virtue by restricting the market in land and labor. Instead of economic activity, "the chief form of group participation would be military service, which was required of all adult male inhabitants." J. E. Crowley, This Sheba, Self: The Conceptualization of Economic Life in Eighteenth Century America 20–21 (1974).

35. All citations to Locke's work in this section are to John Locke, *The Second Treatise of Government,* in Two Treatises of Government (Peter Laslett ed., 1960). In the text, I cite to this work by paragraph number. For clarity, I omit all italics in the original.

36. *See, e.g.,* Nicholas Johnson, *Beyond the Second Amendment: An Individual Right to Arms Viewed Through the Ninth Amendment,* 24 Rutgers L.J. 1, 12–16 (1992); Don B. Kates, Jr., *The Second Amendment and the Ideology of Self-Protection,* 9 Const. Comm. 87, 89–93 (1992); Nelson Lund, *The Second Amendment, Political Liberty, and the Right to Self-Preservation,* 39 Ala. L.Rev. 103, 117–20 (1987).

Chapter 2. The History of the Second Amendment

1. This story has been told many times, from a number of perspectives. For accounts written within a states' rights framework, see Michael A. Bellesiles, Arming America: The Origins of a National Gun Culture 208–18 (2000); Garry Wills, *To Keep and Bear Arms,* N.Y. Rev. Books, Sept. 21, 1995, 62. For accounts written within an individual rights

framework, see Joyce Lee Malcolm, To Keep and Bear Arms: The Origins of an Anglo-American Right 135–64 (1994); Stephen P. Halbrook, That Every Man Be Armed: The Evolution of a Constitutional Right 55–88 (1984).

2. U.S. Const., art. I, sections 12, 13, 14.

3. *Id.* at art. I, section 16.

4. *Id.* at art. III, section 3.

5. *Id.* at art. I, section 8.

6. *Id.* at art. IV, section 4.

7. David P. Szatmary, Shays' Rebellion: The Making of an Agrarian Insurrection (1980), is a full-length account of Shays' Rebellion and its aftereffects. For shorter accounts, see Thomas P. Slaughter, The Whiskey Rebellion: Frontier Epilogue to the American Revolution 46–60 (1986); Bellesiles, *supra* note 1, at 210–12; Richard D. Brown, *Shays's Rebellion and the Ratification of the Federal Constitution in Massachusetts,* in Beyond Confederation: Origins of the Constitution and American National Identity 113 (1987); Don Higginbotham, *The Federalized Militia Debate: A Neglected Aspect of Second Amendment Scholarship,* reprinted in Whose Right to Bear Arms Did the Second Amendment Protect? 97, 103 (Saul Cornell ed., 2000).

8. Szatmary, *supra* note 7, at 123. *See also* Bellesiles, *supra* note 1, at 212; Brown, *supra* note 7, at 113; Higginbotham, *supra* note 7, at 103; Szatmary, *supra* note 7, at 120–34.

9. *See* The Federalist No. 6, at 105, 108 (Alexander Hamilton), No. 25, at 195 (Alexander Hamilton), No. 28, at 205 (Alexander Hamilton) (Isaac Kramnick ed., 1987).

10. *See* The Federalist Nos. 2, 3, 4, 5 (John Jay); The Federalist Nos. 6, 7, 8 (Alexander Hamilton).

11. The Federalist No. 9 (Alexander Hamilton), *supra* note 9, at 118, 121.

12. James Madison, Notes of Debates in the Federal Convention of 1787 Reported by James Madison 478 (1969).

13. The Federalist No. 23 (Alexander Hamilton), *supra* note 9, at 186.

14. The Federalist No. 4 (John Jay), *supra* note 9, at 99.

15. *See* The Federalist Nos. 6, 7 (Alexander Hamilton); No. 8 (Alexander Hamilton), *supra* note 9, at 115; No. 25 (Alexander Hamilton), *supra* note 9, at 193.

16. Madison, Notes of Debates, *supra* note 12, at 515.

17. The Federalist No. 27 (Alexander Hamilton), *supra* note 9, at 202.

18. The Federalist No. 28 (Alexander Hamilton), *supra* note 9, at 204, 205.

19. The Federalist No. 29 (Alexander Hamilton), *supra* note 9, at 208, 212.

20. The Federalist No. 28, *supra* note 9, at 206.

21. *Essay by a Farmer and Planter,* in 5 The Complete Anti-Federalist 2.3 (Herbert J. Storing ed. 1981).

22. For further discussion of this reform movement, see Higginbotham, *supra* note 7, at 103–07; Stephen P. Halbrook, *The Right of the People or the Power of the State: Bearing Arms, Arming Militias, and the Second Amendment,* 26 Valparaiso L.Rev. 131, 186–89 (1991).

23. 9 The Documentary History of the Ratification of the Constitution 957 (John P. Kaminski and Gaspare J. Saladino eds., 1976–).

24. 3 Jonathan Elliott, The Debates in the Several State Conventions on the Adoption of the Federal Constitution, as Recommended by the General Convention at Philadelphia in 1787, at 379 (2d ed. 1836).

25. *See* Bellesiles, *supra* note 1, at 216–17; Higginbotham, *supra* note 7, at 106; Keith A. Ehrman and Dennis A. Henigan, *The Second Amendment in the Twentieth Century: Have You Seen Your Militia Lately?* 15 U. Dayton L.Rev. 1, 28–29 (1989).

26. *See* Bellesiles, *supra* note 1, at 216.

27. *United States v. Miller,* 307 U.S. 174, 179–81 (1938).

28. Additional Letters from the Federal Farmer 169 (New York, 1788).

29. 3 The Debates in the Several State Conventions, *supra* note 24, at 425–26.

30. 1 American Archives 1022 (P. Force ed., 1837–53).

31. 1 George Mason, Papers 215 (R. Rutland ed. 1970).

32. Quoted in R. Meade, Patrick Henry 28 (1969).

33. 1 B. Schwartz, The Bill of Rights: A Documentary History 239 (1971).

34. 9 Documentary History of the Ratification of the Constitution, *supra* note 23, at 440.

35. *See* 1 The Debates in the Several State Conventions, *supra* note 24, at 244, 327–28; Halbrook, *supra* note 1, at 83.

36. 1 Annals of Congress 434 (8 June 1789).

37. *See id.* at 750 (1789).

38. *See* Journal of the First Session of the Senate 71, 77 (Washington, D.C., 1820).

39. *See* Lawrence D. Cress, *An Armed Community: The Origins and Meaning of the Right to Bear Arms,* 71 J. Am. Hist. 22, 25, 29 (1984).

40. *See* Malcolm, *supra* note 1, at 140–41; Carl T. Bogus, *The Hidden History of the Second Amendment,* 31 U.C. Davis L.Rev. 309, 335–58 (1997). Robert Cottrol and Ray Diamond have, however, argued that in practice colonial militias often included Blacks. *See* Robert Cottrol and Ray Diamond, *The Second Amendment: Toward an Afro-Americanist Reconsideration,* 80 Geo. L.J. 309, 331–332 (1991).

41. *See* Lawrence D. Cress, Citizens in Arms: The Army and the Militia in American Society to the War of 1812, at 5–7 (1982); E. Wayne Carp, *The Problem of National Defense in the Early American Republic,* in The American Revolution: Its Character and Limits 14, 19–20 (Jack P. Greene ed., 1987).

42. In earlier decades, some republicans may have believed that the universal militia possessed only a right of resistance, rather than a true right of revolution. Under the right of resistance, the people had the right only to frustrate unpopular governmental programs, like the Stamp Act, and perhaps to replace tyrants or suppress demagogues. *See* Gordon S. Wood, The Creation of the American Republic 1776–1787, at 20–23 (1969). A right of revolution, by contrast, goes further: it gives the people the right to reorder society from top to bottom, "to institute new Government, laying its foundation on such principles and organizing its powers in such form, as to them shall seem most likely to effect their Safety and Happiness." The Declaration of Independence, para. 2 (U.S. 1776). In practice, however, the line between resistance and revolution was not sharp; once the American revolutionaries had rejected British rule, they were compelled to put a new government in its place, and accordingly they rewrote their state constitutions to provide for more democratic government. *See* Wood, *supra,* at 282–91.

43. *See* Edmund S. Morgan, Inventing the People 164 (1988); Pauline Maier, From Resistance to Revolution 16–26 (1974); Carp, *supra* note 41, at 20.

44. The study of legitimate popular disturbances in colonial and Revolutionary society has generated a substantial and growing body of historical scholarship. *See, e.g.,* Edward Countryman, A People in Revolution (1981); Paul A. Gilje, The Road to Mobocracy (1987); Maier, *supra* note 43; Alan Taylor, Liberty Men and Great Proprietors (1990).

45. Thomas Jefferson, *Letter to William S. Smith (Nov. 13, 1787),* in Jefferson: Writings 910, 911 (Merrill D. Peterson ed., 1984).

46. 3 John Adams, A Defense of the Constitutions of Government of the United States of America 475 (1787–88).

47. *Id.* at 471–72.

48. The Antifederalist Papers 75 (Morton Borden ed., 1965).

49. *Id.* at 19.

50. Federal Farmer, *supra* note 28, at 170.

51. 4 The Debates in the Several State Conventions, *supra* note 24, at 203.

52. 3 The Debates in the Several State Conventions, *supra* note 24, at 45, 48.

53. *Id.* at 380.

54. The Federalist No. 46 (James Madison), *supra* note 9, at 301.

55. The Federalist No. 28 (Alexander Hamilton), *supra* note 9, at 206.

56. Noah Webster, *An Examination into the Leading Principles of the Federal Constitution (1787),* in Pamphlets on the Constitution of the United States 56 (P. Ford ed., 1888).

57. Federalist No. 8 (Alexander Hamilton), *supra* note 9, at 116.

58. The Federalist No. 29 (Alexander Hamilton), *supra* note 9, at 211.

59. 3 The Debates in the Several State Conventions, *supra* note 24, at 382–83, 419.

60. *See* Garry Wills, A Necessary Evil: A History of American Distrust of Government 121 (1999).

61. Don Higginbotham and Carl Bogus have adopted the same basic approach in deemphasizing the Anti-Federalists and emphasizing the Federalists, and especially in examining Madison's psyche as the touchstone of the amendment's meaning. *See* Higginbotham, *supra* note 7, at 108; Bogus, *supra* note 40, at 359–69. *See also* Michael A. Bellesiles, *The Origins of Gun Culture in the United States, 1760–1865,* in Guns in America: A Reader 17, 46 n.70 (describing Wills's work as "the finest critique" of the individual rights school).

62. Wills, *supra* note 60, at 121.

63. *Id.* at 114, 122.

64. Wills, *supra* note 1, at 72.

65. *See* Robert E. Shalhope, *To Keep and Bear Arms in the Early Republic,* 16 Const. Comm. 269, 275–80 (1999); Sanford Levinson, David C. Williams, Glenn Harlan Reynolds, John K. Lattimer, and Garry Wills, *To Keep and Bear Arms: An Exchange,* N.Y. Rev. Books, Nov. 16, 1995, 61–64.

66. Wills, *supra* note 60, at 121.

67. *Id.* at 122.

68. Robert H. Bork, The Tempting of America 144 (1990).

69. 1 Annals of Congress 749–50 (1789).

70. *Id.*

71. 3 Samuel Adams, Writings 251 (Henry A. Cushing ed., 1906).

72. *A Pennsylvanian,* Pennsylvania Gazette, Feb. 20, 1788, reprinted in 2 Documentary History of the Ratification of the Constitution (Microfilm supp.), *supra* note 23. For other examples of this line of thought, see Federal Farmer, *supra* note 28, at 169; Algernon Sidney, Discourses Concerning Government 155–57 (London, 1698); Cress, *supra* note 41, at 3, 43–45, 100; Cress, *supra* note 39, at 31–32; Joel Barlow, Advice to the Privileged Orders in the Several States of Europe 46 (1956); Andrew Fletcher, *A Discourse of Government with Respect to Militias,* in Selected Political Writings and Speeches 18–21 (David Daiches ed., 1979); J. G. A. Pocock, The Machiavellian Moment 410 (1975).

73. *See* Federal Farmer, *supra* note 28, at 169; Cress, *supra* note 41, at 100; Cress, *supra* note 39, at 31–32.

74. 3 The Debates in the Several State Conventions, *supra* note 24, at 659.

75. Charleston State Gazette, 8 Sept. 1788.

76. Federal Farmer, *supra* note 28, at 169.

77. *See* Barlow, *supra* note 72, at 46; Cress, *supra* note 39, at 31–32; Malcolm, *supra* note 1, at 148–50.

78. Federal Farmer, *supra* note 28, at 169.

79. John Smiley, *Pennsylvania Convention, December 6, 1787,* in 2 Documentary History of the Ratification of the Constitution, *supra* note 23, at 509.

80. The most famous exposition of this idea is Jefferson's: "What country can preserve its liberties, if their rulers are not warned from time to time that their people preserve the spirit of resistance?" Jefferson, *supra* note 45, at 911.

81. *See* Charles Royster, A Revolutionary People at War: The Continental Army and American Character 1775–1783, at 5–7, 16 (1979).

82. *See* Maier, *supra* note 43, at 36–39; Reginald C. Stuart, War and American Thought 19–21 (1982).

83. *See, e.g.,* Carp, *supra* note 41, at 32; Slaughter, *supra* note 7; Michael A. Bellesiles, Revolutionary Outlaws: Ethan Allen and the Struggle for Independence on the Early American Frontier (1993); Szatmary, *supra* note 7; Taylor, *supra* note 44.

84. *See* Slaughter, *supra* note 7, at 31–34, 39, 47–48, 54, 127–30; Szatmary, *supra* note 7, at 46–47, 67, 69.

85. Quoted in Szatmary, *supra* note 7, at 76.

86. Madison, Notes of Debates, *supra* note 12, at 515.

87. The Federalist No. 46 (James Madison), *supra* note 9, at 300.

88. *Proclamation of President Washington on the Whiskey Rebellion (Aug. 7, 1794),* in The Tree of Liberty: A Documentary History of Rebellion and Political Crime in America (Nicholas N. Kittrie and Eldon D. Wedlock, Jr. eds., rev. ed. 1998).

89. The Federalist No. 29 (Alexander Hamilton), *supra* note 9, at 212.

90. The Federalist No. 8 (Alexander Hamilton), *supra* note 9, at 116.

91. *See* Szatmary, *supra* note 7, at 97, 101.

92. The Federalist No. 6 (Alexander Hamilton), *supra* note 9, at 105–06. *See* Szatmary, *supra* note 7, at 71–73, 128–34.

93. *See, e.g.,* Slaughter, *supra* note 7, at 44–45.

94. *See* Cress, *supra* note 39, at 23; Cress, *supra* note 41, at 9, 111; Morgan, *supra* note 43, at 156; Pocock, *supra* note 72, at 203–04, 210–11.

95. Maier, *supra* note 43, at 87–88.

96. Richard M. Brown, Strain of Violence 61–62 (1975).

97. Quoted in Maier, *supra* note 43, at 64.

98. Declaration of Independence, para. 1 (U.S. 1776).

99. Adams, *supra* note 46, at 251.

100. A Pennsylvanian, *supra* note 72, at 1778–80.

101. *See* Federalist No. 10 (James Madison), *supra* note 9, at 123–25, 127–28.

102. The Federalist No. 46 (James Madison), *supra* note 9, at 300–01.

103. The Federalist No. 2 (John Jay), *supra* note 9, at 91.

104. The Federalist No. 29 (Alexander Hamilton), *supra* note 9, at 210, 211.

105. *See* Royster, *supra* note 81, at 25, 31. For accounts of the Loyalists, see Janice Potter, The Liberty We Seek: Loyalist Ideology in Colonial New York and Massachusetts (1983); Christopher Moore, The Loyalists: Revolution, Exile, Settlement (1984).

106. *See, e.g.,* Robert M. Calhoon, *The Reintegration of the Loyalists and the Disaffected,* in The American Revolution: Its Character and Limits, *supra* note 7, at 51–74; Countryman, *supra* note 44, at 170–75, 186, 214–15, 235–36, 284–85.

107. For example, Henry Knox, the first secretary of war, presented to Congress a militia plan which emphasized that the conditions of service should be dreadful in order to accustom members to self-sacrifice. *See* Henry Knox, *General Knox's Militia Plan,* 2 Annals of Congress 2088, 2100–01 (1790). *See also* Fletcher, *supra* note 72, at 20–24; Pocock, *supra* note 72, at 201–02.

108. *See* Knox, *supra* note 107, at 2090, 2099–2101; Fletcher, *supra* note 72, at 20–24.

109. *See* Royster, *supra* note 81, at 25, 31.

110. *See* Pocock, *supra* note 72, at 203–04, 210–11, 385–86; Cress, *supra* note 41, at 16–17, 23–24, 49.

111. Barlow, *supra* note 72, at 47.

112. *See* Barlow, *supra* note 72, at 45, 47; Fletcher, *supra* note 72, at 5–6; Royster, *supra* note 81, at 28; Robert E. Shalhope, *The Ideological Origins of the Second Amendment,* 69 J. Am. Hist. 599, 604–07 (1982).

113. *See* Carp, *supra* note 41, at 19–20; Cress, *supra* note 41, at 4–6.

114. Higginbotham, *supra* note 7, at 104.

115. For example, Garry Wills, who has emerged as a leader of the states' rights theory, and Robert Shalhope, whose work has formed the historical basis for much individual rights theorizing, agree that protection of the state militia was one purpose of the amendment. *Compare* Wills, *supra* note 60, at 121, with Shalhope, *supra* note 65, at 280.

116. *See, e.g.,* Wills, *supra* note 60, at 116–22; Michael Bellesiles, *Suicide Pact: New Readings of the Second Amendment,* 16 Const. Comm. 247, 258 (1999); Bogus, *supra* note 40, at 344–58.

117. *See, e.g.,* Wills, *supra* note 60, at 121; Don Higginbotham, *The Second Amendment in Historical Context,* 16 Const. Comm. 263, 268 (1999).

118. The Federalist No. 46 (James Madison), *supra* note 9, at 301.

119. The Federalist No. 28 (Alexander Hamilton), *supra* note 9, at 207.

120. The Federalist No. 28 (Alexander Hamilton), *supra* note 9, at 206.

121. *See* Malcolm, *supra* note 1, at 146–50.

122. *See* Cress, *supra* note 39, at 29–37.

123. The Federalist No. 28 (Alexander Hamilton), *supra* note 9, at 206.

Chapter 3. The Original Legal Meaning of the Second Amendment

1. *See, e.g.,* John H. Ely, Democracy and Distrust 95, 227 n.76 (1980); John Levin, *The Right to Bear Arms: The Development of the American Experience,* 48 Chi.-Kent L.Rev. 148, 158–59 (1971); Roy G. Weatherup, *Standing Armies and Armed Citizens: An Historical Analysis of the Second Amendment,* 2 Hastings Const. L.Q. 961, 999 (1975).

2. *See* 10 U.S.C. section 101(c)(2)(B)-(D) and 4(B)-(D)(2000).

3. *See id.* at 12002(a) (2000).

4. *See generally* Martha Derthick, The National Guard in Politics (1965).

5. *See* Nell I. Painter, Standing at Armageddon 15, 21–22 (1987).

6. *See* James D. Wright et al., Under the Gun 116–17 and n.9 (1983); James D. Wright and Linda L. Marston, *The Ownership of the Means of Destruction: Weapons in the United States,* 23 Soc. Probs. 93, 99–103 (1975).

7. *See* U.S. Dep't of Justice, Sourcebook of Criminal Justice Statistics — 1987, at 169 tbl. 2.50 (Timothy J. Flanagan and Katherine M. Jamieson eds., 1988) [hereinafter cited as Sourcebook]; Wright et al., *supra* note 6, at 104–09; Wright and Marston, *supra* note 6, at 95–98; American Firearms Industry Dealer Survey (1988) (unpublished survey, on file with the author) [hereinafter cited as Industry Survey]. Although white gun owners outnumber African American owners in absolute terms, the relative rates of ownership may be roughly comparable between the two groups. See Wright et al., *supra* note 6, at 108–09. But absolute number, not the percentage rate, would be the critical fact in a revolution: more white gun owners mean more white power.

8. Similarly, Akhil Amar has argued that the function of the jury was to create popular control over the administration of justice. The beneficiary of the jury was thus not just the individual defendant but the whole community. Accordingly, in a republican scheme, the defendant may not have the right to waive a jury trial. *See* Akhil Amar, *The Bill of Rights as a Constitution,* 100 Yale L.J. 1131, 1196–99 (1991).

9. *See, e.g.,* Stephen P. Halbrook, *The Right of the People or the Power of the State: Bearing Arms, Arming Militias, and the Second Amendment,* 26 Valp. L.Rev. 131, 131–32 (1991).

10. *See* Osha Gray Davidson, Under Fire: The NRA and the Battle for Gun Control 134–36 (1993).

11. Eugene Volokh, *The Commonplace Second Amendment,* 73 N.Y.U. L.Rev. 793, 805–06 (1998). Volokh does add that the purpose clause may have one function: it "may *aid* construction of the operative clause but may not *trump* the meaning of the operative clause: To the extent the operative clause is ambiguous, the justification clause may inform our interpretation of it, but the justification clause can't take away what the operative clause provides." *Id.* at 807. He goes on to argue that because the meaning of

the operative clause is "rather unambiguous" in protecting a right of individuals, then we should not consult the purpose clause in its interpretation at all; otherwise, we would be using the purpose clause to trump the operative language. *Id.* at 810. As a result, Volokh believes that the purpose clause should play no role in our interpretation of the Second Amendment. Whether the operative clause really is unambiguous in referring to individuals is, however, exactly the question, and consulting the purpose clause in a process of unitary interpretation may help us understand that the *people* does not necessarily refer to individuals.

12. *See* Sutherland Statutory Construction, sections 46.05, 46.06 (5th ed. 1992).

13. Volokh, *supra* note 11, at 802.

14. U.S. Const., art. II, section 3.

15. *Id.* at art. I, section 8.

16. 1 Annals of Congress 750–51 (1789).

17. Centinel, Revived, Independent Gazeteer, No. 29, Sept. 9, 1789, at 2.

18. *See* Robert E. Shalhope, *The Ideological Origins of the Second Amendment,* 69 J. Am. Hist. 599, 608–10 (1982); Lawrence D. Cress, *An Armed Community: The Origins and Meaning of the Right to Bear Arms,* 71 J. Am. Hist. 22, 29–31 (1984).

19. *See* E. Wayne Carp, *The Problem of National Defense in the Early American Republic,* in The American Revolution: Its Characters and Limits 19 (Jack P. Greene ed., 1987); *United States v. Miller,* 307 U.S. 174, 179–82 (1939).

20. *See* Lawrence D. Cress, Citizens in Arms: The Army and the Militia in American Society to the War of 1812, at 5–7, 59–60 (1982); Carp, *supra* note 19, at 19–20; Carl T. Bogus, *The Hidden History of the Second Amendment,* 31 U.C. Davis L.Rev. 309, 335–37 (1997).

21. *See* Cress, *supra* note 20, at 80–81, 90–91. One congressman insisted, "As far as the whole body of the people are necessary to the general defence, they ought to be armed, but the law ought not to require more than is necessary, for that would be just cause of complaint." 1 Annals of Congress 1806 (1791). Perhaps because of this anxiety, congressional debates over allowing exemptions from militia service tended to be interminable and unfocused. *See, e.g.,* 2 Annals of Congress 1804–12 (1790).

22. *See* Remarks of Rep. Smilie, 18 Annals of Congress 2177, 2191–92 (1808); 3 Joseph Story, Commentaries on the Constitution of the United States 746–47 (Boston, 3d ed. 1858).

23. *See* 10 U.S.C. section 311(2) (2000).

24. *United States v. Miller,* 307 U.S. 174, 180–81 (1939).

25. *Id.* at 179.

26. *See* Robert D. Shalhope, *The Armed Citizen in the Early Republic,* in Whose Right to Bear Arms Did the Second Amendment Protect? at 27, 39 (Saul Cornell ed., 2000).

27. Fed. Gazette and Philadelphia Evening Post, June 18, 1789, at 2, col. 1.

28. Pennsylvania Gazette (Philadelphia), May 7, 1788, at 3, col. 2.

29. *See* Michael A. Bellesiles, Arming America: The Origins of a National Gun Culture 173, 183 (2000); Keith A. Ehrman and Dennis A. Henigan, *The Second Amendment in the Twentieth Century: Have You Seen Your Militia Lately?* 15 U. Dayton L.Rev. 5, 29 (1989).

30. *See* David B. Kopel, The Samurai, the Mountie, and the Cowboy: Should America Adopt the Gun Controls of Other Democracies? 282–86 (1992).

31. *See* Akhil Amar, The Bill of Rights: Creation and Reconstruction 140–45 (1998).

32. U.S. Const., amend. XIV.

33. *See, e.g., Planned Parenthood v. Casey,* 505 U.S. 833, 848–49 (1992); *Griswold v. Connecticut,* 381 U.S. 479, 500 (1965)(concurring opinion of J. Harlan).

34. *See, e.g., Malloy v. Hogan,* 378 U.S. 1 (1964); *Duncan v. Louisiana,* 391 U.S. 145 (1968).

35. *See Miller v. Texas,* 153 U.S. 535, 536 (1894); *Presser v. Illinois,* 116 U.S. 252, 264 (1886).

36. *See* Don B. Kates, *Handgun Prohibition and the Original Meaning of the Second Amendment,* 82 Mich. L.Rev. 204, 252–57 (1983); Nelson Lund, *The Second Amendment, Political Liberty, and the Right to Self-Preservation,* 39 Ala. L.Rev. 103, 103–04 (1987).

37. *See* Amar, *supra* note 31, at 216–18, 257–68.

38. *Cf. Planned Parenthood v. Casey,* 505 U.S. 833, 848–51 (1992)(holding that the living tradition standard protects rights of reproductive autonomy).

39. Saul Cornell has been especially forceful in making this point. See Saul Cornell, *Commonplace or Anachronism: The Standard Model, the Second Amendment, and the Problem of History in Contemporary Constitutional Theory,* 16 Const. Comm. 221, 237–45 (1999).

40. Michael A. Bellesiles, *Suicide Pact: New Readings of the Second Amendment,* 16 Const. Comm. 247, 255 (1999).

41. *Id.* at 251, 252, 253.

42. *See* Cornell, *supra* note 39, at 237–38; Bellesiles, *supra* note 40, at 255–56; Garry Wills, A Necessary Evil: A History of American Distrust of Government 215–18 (1999); Dennis Henigan, *Arms, Anarchy, and the Second Amendment,* 26 Valp. U. L.Rev. 107, 127–29 (1991).

43. For illustration of this process, the reader may consult any good constitutional law casebook, for example, Paul Brest et al., Processes of Constitutional Decisionmaking: Cases and Materials (4th ed. 2000); Jesse H. Choper et al., The American Constitution: Cases — Comments — Questions (9th ed. 2001); Geoffrey R. Stone et al., Constitutional Law (4th ed. 2001).

44. For example, Don Kates, who believes the amendment guarantees an individual right, nonetheless emphasizes that the right would be subject to reasonable regulation. *See* Kates, *supra* note 36, at 258–67. Akhil Amar, who believes that the amendment guarantees a popular right, also believes that "realistic gun control" would be constitutional. Akhil Reed Amar, *Second Thoughts,* The New Republic, July 12, 1991, at 24, 27.

45. Robert Shalhope places heavy reliance on this fact in arguing that the amendment protects an individual right to arms. *See* Robert D. Shalhope, *The Armed Citizen in the Early Republic,* in Whose Right to Arms Did the Second Amendment Protect? at 27, 39 (Saul Cornell ed., 2000).

46. Again, Shalhope relies on this evidence for his individual rights interpretation. *See id.* at 39.

47. *See, e.g.,* Kates, *supra* note 36, at 222.

48. Pennsylvania Convention, *Declaration of Rights, August 21, 1776,* in Declaring Rights: A Brief History with Documents 86–87 (Jack N. Rakove ed., 1998).

49. *The Address and Reasons of Dissent of the Minority,* in 2 The Documentary History of the Ratification of the Constitution 623–24 (Merrill Jensen ed., 1976).

50. *See Tennessee Gas Pipeline Co. v. Federal Energy Regulatory Comm'n,* 626 F.2d 1020, 1022 (D.C. Cir. 1980).

51. *Posadas v. National City Bank,* 296 U.S. 497, 503 (1936).

52. The Federalist No. 10, at 127 (James Madison) (Isaac Kramnick ed., 1987).

53. *Id.* at 125.

54. *Id.* at 127.

55. *Garcia v. SAMTA,* 469 U.S. 528, 571 (1985)(dissenting opinion of Powell, J.) (citation omitted).

56. Federalist No. 47, *supra* note 52, at 303 (James Madison).

57. Federalist No. 48, *supra* note 52, at 311 (James Madison).

58. Federalist No. 51, *supra* note 52, at 320 (James Madison).

59. *Id.* at 319.

60. *Id.* at 321.

Chapter 4. Antirevolutionists

1. *See United States v. Cruikshank,* 92 U.S. 542 (1875). At one point, somewhat confusingly, this case maintains that the right to arms "is not a right granted by the Constitution." That fact does not, however, mean that the Constitution does not protect the right. Instead, the right existed before the Constitution: it is not "in any manner dependent upon that instrument for its existence." Instead, of originating the right, therefore, the Constitution merely declares that "it shall not be infringed by Congress." *Id.* at 553.

2. *See Miller v. Texas,* 153 U.S. 535, 536 (1894); *Presser v. Illinois,* 116 U.S. 252, 264 (1886).

3. 307 U.S. 174 (1939).

4. As I explain in the text, this case is ambiguous about whether it recognizes an individual right to arms. In addition, it is deeply confused on another point: the relation of the right to federal power. The Court first pointed out that Article I gives Congress power over the militias. It then held that the Second Amendment was designed to help effectuate this federal power: "With obvious purpose to assure the continuation and render possible the effectiveness of such forces the declaration and guarantee of the Second Amendment were made." 307 U.S. at 178. The Court here seems to be saying the Second Amendment guarantees a right to arms, so that the militia will be ready for Congress's call. The provision thus protects a federal interest in the readiness of the militia. That reading of the amendment, however, makes little sense. Even without the Second Amendment, Congress already had power under Article I to keep the militia armed. Instead, the point in the amendment must have been to limit Congress's power, so as to protect some other entity — individuals, states, or the people.

5. Ch. 757, 48 Stat. 1236 (1934).

6. 307 U.S. at 178.

7. For an example of this reading, see Don B. Kates, Jr., *Handgun Prohibition and the Original Meaning of the Second Amendment,* 82 Mich. L.Rev. 204, 247–50 (1983).

8. 307 U.S. at 179.

9. 131 F. 2d 916 (1st Cir. 1942).

10. *Id.* at 922.

11. *Id.* at 923.

12. 530 F.2d 103 (6th Cir. 103).

13. *See* 26 U.S.C. sections 5861(d), 5871 (1970).

14. 530 F.2d at 106.

15. *Id.* at 105.

16. *Id.* at 106 (quoting *United States v. Miller,* 307 U.S. 174, 178 (1939).

17. 564 F.2d 384 (10th Cir. 1984).

18. *Id.* at 387.

19. 978 F.2d 1016 (8th Cir. 1992).

20. Keith A. Ehrman and Dennis A. Henigan, *The Second Amendment in the Twentieth Century: Have You Seen Your Militia Lately?* 15 U. Dayton L.Rev. 5 (1989).

21. 978 F.2d at 1019.

22. *See* Ehrman and Henigan, *supra* note 20, at 23–34.

23. 978 F.2d at 1019.

24. *See id.* at 1020.

25. *Id.* at 1019 (citations omitted).

26. Ehrman and Henigan, *supra* note 20.

27. *Id.* at 7.

28. *Id.* at 24.

29. *Id.* at 23.

30. *See id.* at 34–38.

31. *Id.* at 38.

32. *Id.* at 39.

33. *Id.* at 40. In this same general discussion, Ehrman and Henigan merge two sets of their critics: some object that the National Guard is dominated by the federal government, unlike the old state militias; and some object that the National Guard is a governmental unit, unlike the old "unorganized" militia. Most of Ehrman's and Henigan's responses go to the latter set of critics. Thus, they argue that the amendment does not protect an individual right to arms for revolutionary purposes: the amendment protects only a "state-organized, state-trained unit," not "an anonymous 'armed citizenry at large.'" *Id.* at 40. Similarly, they maintain, "It should also be remembered that at the time the second amendment was drafted, the states discussed using their militias to put down insurrections. This is certainly not consistent with the idea of encouraging an armed 'revolution' by the populace." *Id.* at 40 n.255. In the text, I focus on the former objection because, given their view of the history, Ehrman and Henigan ought to take this concern seriously. The fact they do not helps us see the mythic structure lying behind and conditioning their use of history.

34. *New York v. United States,* 505 U.S. 144, 181 (1992)(citation omitted).

35. *Id.* at 182.

36. Denis Henigan, *Arms, Anarchy, and the Second Amendment*, 26 Valp. L.Rev. 107 (1991).

37. *Id.* at 110.

38. *Id.* at 115.

39. *Id.* at 129 (quoting Roscoe Pound, The Development of Constitutional Guarantees of Liberty 91 (1957).

40. *Id.*

41. *Id.* at 110.

42. *Id.* at 117 (quoting 3 Records of the Federal Convention 208–09 (Max Farrand ed., 1974)).

43. *Id.* at 120 (quoting The Federalist No. 46, at 299 (James Madison) (Clinton Rossiter ed., 1961) (emphasis added by Henigan)).

44. *Id.* at 112.

45. *Id.* at 117 (emphasis added).

46. *See id.* at 108–09.

47. *Id.* at 115.

48. *See* Glenn Harlan Reynolds, *A Critical Guide to the Second Amendment*, 62 Tenn. L.Rev. 461–71 (1995).

49. *See* Garry Wills, A Necessary Evil: A History of American Distrust of Government (1999) [hereinafter cited as A Necessary Evil]; Garry Wills, *To Keep and Bear Arms*, N.Y. Rev. Books, Sept. 21, 1995, at 62; Michael A. Bellesiles, Arming America: The Origins of a National Gun Culture (2000) [hereinafter cited as Arming America]; Michael A. Bellesiles, *Suicide Pact: New Readings of the Second Amendment*, 16 Const. Comm. 247 (1999); Saul Cornell, *Commonplace or Anachronism: The Standard Model, the Second Amendment, and the Problem of History in Contemporary Constitutional Theory*, 16 Const. Comm. 221 (1999).

50. *See* Bellesiles, *supra* note 49, at 255; Arming America, *supra* note 49, at 218; A Necessary Evil, *supra* note 49, at 116–21.

51. *See* Bellesiles, *supra* note 49, at 257–58; Arming America, *supra* note 49, at 246; A Necessary Evil, *supra* note 49, at 117–18.

52. *See* Cornell, *supra* note 49, at 238–45; Bellesiles, *supra* note 49, at 250–55; A Necessary Evil, *supra* note 49, at 209–14, 218.

53. Bellesiles, *supra* note 49, at 250.

54. *Id.* at 252.

55. *Id.* at 254.

56. *Id.* at 255.

57. *Id.* at 256.

58. *Id.* at 259.

59. Arming America, *supra* note 49, at 218.

60. *Id.*

61. Cornell, *supra* note 49.

62. Pennsylvania Convention, *Declaration of Rights, Aug. 21, 1776*, in Declaring Rights: A Brief History with Documents 86–87 (Jack N. Rakove ed., 1998).

63. *The Address and Reasons of Dissent of the Minority*, in 2 The Documentary History of the Ratification of the Constitution 623–24 (Merrill Jensen ed., 1976).

64. Cornell, *supra* note 49, at 232 (quoting An Old Whig, *Essays of An Old Whig,* in 3 The Complete Anti-Federalist 17, 49 (Herbert J. Storing ed., 1981)).

65. Cornell, *supra* note 49, at 228.

66. *Id.* at 233.

67. *See id.* at 230–31, 237. Actually, Cornell's analysis of the Test Act is not dispositive of the meaning of the Pennsylvania Constitution. In passing the Test Acts, Pennsylvanians may simply have been acting unconstitutionally; they set themselves a constitutional ideal but then failed to meet it. Legislatures do this sort of thing all the time, even shortly after adopting constitutions.

68. *Id.* at 229.

69. *Id.* at 235.

70. *Id.* at 228.

71. *Id.* at 232.

72. Abraham Lincoln, *First Inaugural Address,* in Abraham Lincoln: Speeches and Writings 1859–1865, at 215, 222 (Don E. Fehrenbacher ed., 1989).

73. *Id.* at 217.

74. *Id.* at 223.

75. *Id.* at 220.

76. *See Texas v. White,* 74 U.S. (7 Wall.) 700, 726 (1869); Bernard Schwartz, From Confederation to Nation: The American Constitution 1835–1877, at 133–34 (1973).

77. *See Dennis v. United States,* 341 U.S. 494, 497–98 (1951).

78. *Id.* at 501.

79. Wills, *supra* note 49, at 69. In the interest of full disclosure, I should reveal that Wills names me as one of the "wacky scholars" who embrace constitutional absurdity. *See id.* Actually, I have never argued that the Constitution protects a right to revolution. I have argued that once upon a time, the Constitution protected a right to own arms so the people might be ready to make a revolution. As I have tried to demonstrate, those two contentions are jurisprudentially quite different.

80. Cornell, *supra* note 49, at 238.

81. Bellesiles, *supra* note 49, at 255–56.

82. Henigan, *supra* note 36, at 128.

83. *See* Hannah Arendt, On Revolution 35–36, 50–52 (1963).

84. *Cf.* Wills, *supra* note 49, at 69.

85. *See* Richard Ashcraft, Revolutionary Politics and Locke's Two Treatises of Government 293–94 (1986).

86. A Necessary Evil, *supra* note 49, at 217.

87. 5 U.S. (1 Cranch) 137 (1803).

88. *See, e.g.,* Jesse H. Choper, Richard H. Fallon, Jr., Yale Kamisar, and Steven H. Shiffrin, Constitutional Law: Cases — Comments — Questions 13–14 (9th ed. 2001).

89. *Cooper v. Aaron,* 358 U.S. 1, 17 (1958).

90. Lincoln, *supra* note 72, at 221. For an account of the controversy over judicial supremacy, see Sanford Levinson, Constitutional Faith 37–53 (1988).

91. *See* Robert Cover, *The Folktales of Justice: Tales of Jurisdiction,* in Narrative, Violence, and the Law: The Essays of Robert Cover 173, 186, 178–201 (1995).

92. *See* A. E. Dick Howard, The Road from Runnymede 18–19, 118–24 (1968);

William F. Swindler, Magna Carta: Legend and Legacy 166–207 (1965); Barbara Black, *The Constitution of Empire: The Case for the Colonists,* 124 U. Pa. L.Rev. 1157, 1174–1210 (1976).

93. *See Colegrove v. Green,* 328 U.S. 549 (1946). In Colegrove, the Court decided it could not decide a claim that a state's apportionment scheme was unconstitutional because some districts had more voters than others. Several years later, the Court decided it could pass on that question, but under the Equal Protection Clause rather than the Guaranty Clause. *See Baker v. Carr,* 369 U.S. 186 (1962). The Court still believes that the Guaranty Clause is nonjusticiable and that protecting the republican nature of state government is not a judicial responsibility.

94. John Locke, *The Second Treatise of Government,* in Two Treatises of Government, paras. 226, 227 (Peter Laslett ed., 1960).

95. *See* Edmund S. Morgan, Inventing the People: The Rise of Popular Sovereignty in England and America 108–10, 119–20 (1988).

96. *See* Arendt, *supra* note 83, at 165–72.

97. David Hackett Fischer, Albion's Seed: Four British Folkways in America 193, 193 n.15 (1989).

98. *See* Jack Rakove, The Beginnings of National Politics: An Interpretive History of the Continental Congress 81 (1979); Gordon S. Wood, The Creation of the American Republic, 1776–1787, at 268–71 (1969). There is disagreement about whether the revolutionaries were right about their constitutional claim, but there is no serious dispute about the fact they portrayed themselves as faithful to the constitution. *See* Bernard Bailyn, The Ideological Origins of the American Revolution (1967); Jack P. Greene, Peripheries and Center (1986); Wood, *supra,* at 10–13; Black, supra note 92.

99. Whether to invoke natural law or constitutional law was one of the first debates entertained by the First Continental Congress. *See, e.g.,* Rakove, *supra* note 98, at 54.

100. *See* Bailyn, *supra* note 98, at 77–79; Greene, *supra* note 98, at 23–28.

101. *See* Bailyn, *supra* note 98, at 202–29; Black, *supra* note 98, at 1157–1211. *See also* Rakove, *supra* note 98, at 58–59.

102. *See* Bailyn, *supra* note 98, at 124–25, 131–33.

103. *See* Wood, *supra* note 98, at 271, 197–214. That transposition followed an old pattern for the colonists. They had sought to model their governments on England's, claiming the imperial constitution sanctioned this home-rule arrangement. *See* Greene, *supra* note 98, at 31–32. Independence from Great Britain may therefore have changed the form of the constitution, as the revolutionaries sensed, *see* Rakove, *supra* note 98, at 81–83, 139–41, but perhaps not its basic principles.

104. *See* Bailyn, *supra* note 98, at 272–301, 184–89.

105. *See, e.g., Youngstown Sheet and Tube Co. v. Sawyer,* 343 U.S. 579, 637 (1952) (Jackson, J., concurring) ("Congressional inertia, indifference, or quiescence may sometimes, at least as a practical matter, enable, if not invite, measures of independent presidential responsibility. In this area, any actual test of power is likely to depend on the imperatives of events and contemporary imponderables rather than on abstract theories of law").

106. *See* Levinson, *supra* note 90, at 37.

107. For a description of the remarkable early authority of the Continental Congresses, see Rakove, *supra* note 98, at 32–41, 66–69, 71, 108–09.

108. *Compare* Charles McIlwain, The American Revolution: A Constitutional Interpretation (1923); Black, *supra* note 98, at 1207–11; Greene, *supra* note 98 (all sympathetic to the Americans' case), *with* Julius Goebel, *Book Review,* 30 Colum. L.Rev. 273 (1930); Robert Schuyler, Parliament and the British Empire (1927) (unsympathetic to the Americans' case).

109. *See* Bailyn, *supra* note 98, at 175–84, 189–91, 200–02; Wood, *supra* note 98, at 259–69; Black, *supra* note 92, at 1172–75.

110. *See* Black, *supra* note 92, at 1203–07.

111. *See id.* at 1200–03.

112. *See* Charles Fried, *The Supreme Court, 1994 Term, Foreword: Revolutions?* 109 Harv. L.Rev. 13, 19–27 (1995).

113. *See* Bailyn, *supra* note 98, at 272–301, 184–89.

114. *Dennis v. United States,* 341 U.S. 494, 501 (1951).

115. *See* Wood, *supra* note 98, at 596–97 (1969); Gordon S. Wood, The Radicalism of the American Revolution 6–8 (1992). Wood's subtitle sums up his thesis: "How a Revolution Transformed a Monarchical Society into a Democratic One Unlike Any That Had Ever Existed."

116. *See* Eric Foner, Reconstruction: America's Unfinished Revolution 1863–1977, at 1–11 (1988).

117. *See* Samuel Issacharoff, Pamela S. Karlan, and Richard H. Pildes, The Law of Democracy: Legal Structure of the Political Process 68–107, 264–66 (1988); *Giles v. Harris,* 189 U.S. 475 (1903).

118. *See* Issacharoff et al., *supra* note 117, at 71–107, 264–366.

119. *See id.* at 367–68, 441.

120. *See id.* at 410–40; *Thornburg v. Gingles,* 478 U.S. 30 (1986).

121. *See* Issacharoff et al., *supra* note 117, at 411, 431–34; *Johnson v. DeGrandy,* 512 U.S. 997 (1994).

122. *See, e.g, Holder v. Hall,* 512 U.S. 874, 905 (1994) (concurring opinion of J. Thomas).

123. *See Shaw v. Reno,* 509 U.S. 630, 649 (1993); *Miller v. Johnson,* 515 U.S. 900, 914–15 (1995); *Bush v. Vera,* 517 U.S. 952, 957 (1996); *Bush,* 517 U.S. at 999–1003 (concurring opinion of J. Scalia).

124. *See Holder,* 512 U.S. at 905 (concurring opinion of J. Thomas).

125. *See* Issacharoff et al., *supra* note 117, at 122; *Colegrove v. Green,* 328 U.S. 549 (1946).

126. *See Reynolds v. Sims,* 377 U.S. 533 (1964).

127. *See Davis v. Bandemer,* 478 U.S. 109, 144 (1986) (concurring opinion of J. O'Connor).

128. *Id.* at 132 (controlling opinion of J. White).

129. *Id.* at 140.

130. *Id.* at 177–78 (opinion of J. Powell, concurring in part and dissenting in part) (quoting an Indiana state legislator).

131. *See* Issacharoff et al., *supra* note 117, at 244–63.

132. *See Timmons v. Twin Cities Area New Party,* 520 U.S. 351, 367 (1997).

133. *See Igartua De La Rosa v. US,* 229 F.3d 80 (1st Cir. 2000) (per curiam) (upholding denial of right to vote for president and vice president to citizens of Puerto Rico); *Adams*

v. Clinton, 90 F. Supp. 2d 35 (D.D.C. 2000) (per curiam) (upholding denial of right to vote for congressional representatives to citizens of the District of Columbia).

134. *See* Wood, *supra* note 98, at 173–76.

135. *See, e.g.,* Francis Fukuyama, Trust: The Social Virtues and the Creation of Prosperity 19–21 (1995); Mark Granovetter, *Economic Action and Social Structure: The Problem of Embeddedness,* 91 Am. J. Soc. 481 (1985); Amartya Sen, *Rational Fools: A Critique of the Behavioral Foundations of Economic Theory,* 6 Phil. and Pub. Affairs 317 (1977).

136. *See, e.g.,* E. J. Dionne, Jr., They Only Look Dead: Why Progessives Will Dominate the Next Political Era 295–99 (1996); Fukuyama, *supra* note 135, at 4–5; The Reemergence of Civil Society in Eastern Europe and the Soviet Union (Zbigniew Rau ed., 1991); Robert D. Putnam, Bowling Alone: The Collapse and Revival of American Community (2000); Michael J. Sandel, Democracy's Discontent: America in Search of a Public Philosophy (1996).

137. *See* Arendt, *supra* note 83, at 166–74; Stephen A. Conrad, *The Rhetorical Constitution of 'Civil Society' at the Founding: One Lawyer's Anxious Vision,* 72 Ind. L.J. 335 (1997); *Jack P. Greene, Response — Civil Society and the American Founding,* 72 Ind. L.J. 375 (1997).

138. Cornell, *supra* note 49, at 223.

139. Wills, *supra* note 49, at 62.

140. *Id.* at 69.

141. *Id.* at 71.

142. *Id.* at 72.

143. Bellesiles, *supra* note 49, at 259.

144. *See* Randy F. Barnett and Don B. Kates, *Under Fire: The New Consensus on the Second Amendment,* 45 Emory L.J. 1139, 1179–92 (1996).

145. *See* Arming America, *supra* note 49, at 3–9.

146. *Id.* at 4.

147. *See id.* at 6–8.

148. Wendy Brown, *Guns, Cowboys, Philadelphia Mayors, and Civic Republicanism: On Sanford Levinson's The Embarrassing Second Amendment,* 99 Yale L.J. 661 (1989).

149. *Id.* at 666.

150. *See* Carl T. Bogus, *The Hidden History of the Second Amendment,* 31 U.C. Davis L.Rev. 309 (1997).

151. A Necessary Evil, *supra* note 9, at 15.

152. Arming America, *supra* note 49, at 15.

153. Perhaps the most famous example of such an approach is the French Revolution. *See* Arendt, *supra* note 83, at 148–49.

154. *Id.* at 18–19.

155. At times, this veneration seems to become a civil religion. See Thomas C. Grey, *The Constitution as Scripture,* 37 Stan. L.Rev. 1, 21–25 (1984); Sanford Levinson, "The Constitution" in American Civil Religion, 1979 Sup. Ct. Rev. 123, 123–25 (1979).

156. *See* David C. Williams, *Legitimation and Statutory Interpretation: Conquest, Consent, and Community in Federal Indian Law,* 80 Va. L.Rev. 403, 416–29 (1994).

157. Arendt, *supra* note 83, at 18–19.

158. Glenn Harlan Reynolds alone has sought to introduce into Second Amendment scholarship some discussion of when a revolution might be justified. In particular, he has argued that revolution would never be justified as long as democratic redress at the polls is possible. *See* Reynolds, *supra* note 48, 505–07. Most remarkable about Reynolds's work, however, is that his call for a discussion of standards has not been answered by others working in the field.

159. *See* Rakove, *supra* note 98, at 54, 71–72, 141.

Chapter 5. Libertarians and Populists

1. Sanford Levinson, *The Embarrassing Second Amendment,* 99 Yale L.J. 637 (1989).

2. *See* Levinson, *supra* note 1; Nelson Lund, *The Second Amendment, Political Liberty, and the Right of Self-Preservation,* 39 Ala. L.Rev. 103 (1987); Glenn Harlan Reynolds, *A Critical Guide to the Second Amendment,* 62 Tenn. L.Rev. 461 (1995); Don B. Kates, Jr., *Handgun Prohibition and the Original Meaning of the Second Amendment,* 82 Mich. L.Rev. 204 (1983); *United States v. Emerson,* 270 F.3d 203 (5th Cir. 2001).

3. *See* Kates, *supra* note 2, at 267–68; Levinson, *supra* note 1, at 646–51; Lund, *supra* note 2, at 111–16.

4. *See, e.g.,* Stephen Halbrook, That Every Man Be Armed 84–87 (1984); Kates, *supra* note 2, at 218; William Van Alstyne, *The Second Amendment and the Personal Right to Arms,* 43 Duke L.J. 1236, 1236–37 (1994).

5. *See, e.g.,* Kates, *supra* note 2, at 223–25.

6. Kates, *supra* note 2.

7. *Id.* at 267–68.

8. *Id.* at 270.

9. *Id.* at 270–71.

10. *See* Lund, *supra* note 2. Like the other articles I discuss in this section, Lund's article has attracted widespread, respectful attention from other individual rights theorists, perhaps because it is uncommonly sophisticated and careful. Unfortunately, most writers have ignored what may be the most interesting and original part of the piece: a proposal to control gun ownership through mandatory insurance requirements. *Id.* at 127–30.

11. *Id.* at 111.

12. *Id.* at 111, 113–14.

13. *See id.* at 116.

14. *Id.* at 115.

15. Levinson, *supra* note 1.

16. *See, e.g.,* George F. Will, *America's Crisis of Gunfire,* Wash. Post, Mar. 21, 1991, at A21; Stephen Hunter, Point of Impact 9 (1993).

17. Levinson, *supra* note 1, at 642.

18. *Id.* at 645.

19. *Id.* at 650–51.

20. *Id.* at 648 (emphasis added).

21. *Id.* at 650.

22. Reynolds, *supra* note 2.

23. *Id.* at 461.

24. *Id.* at 463.

25. *Id.* at 466.

26. *Id.* at 504.

27. *Id.* at 510.

28. *Id.* at 511.

29. *Id.* at 506.

30. *Id.* at 509.

31. *Id.* at 487.

32. *Id.* at 488.

33. *Id.* at 505–06.

34. *Id.* at 506–07.

35. *Id.* at 507.

36. *United States v. Emerson,* 270 F.3d 203 (5th Cir. 2001).

37. *Id.* at 211.

38. *See Emerson v. United States,* 46 F. Supp.2d 598 (N.D. Tex. 1999).

39. *Emerson,* 270 F.3d at 220.

40. *Id.* at 220 n.12.

41. *Id.* at 227.

42. *Id.* at 273 (concurring opinion of Judge Parker).

43. *See id.* at 221–27 (opinion of the majority).

44. *See id.* at 227–29, 233–36.

45. *See id.* at 236–51.

46. *See id.* at 251–59.

47. *Id.* at 260.

48. *Id.* at 259–60.

49. *Id.* at 257 (quoting Joseph Story, Commentaries on the Constitution 708–09 (1987) (1833)).

50. *Id.* at 258 (quoting Thomas M. Cooley, The General Principles of Constitutional Law in the United States of America 270–72 (1981) (1880)).

51. *Id.* at 240 n.53.

52. *Id.* at 261.

53. *Id.* at 262.

54. *Id.* at 260–64. For this reason, in his separate concurrence, Judge Parker argued that the court should not have decided whether the amendment protects an individual right at all, since either way it is subject to reasonable regulation—as the majority itself agrees. In Judge Parker's view, therefore, the majority was simply stirring the pot of Second Amendment controversy. *See id.* at 272–74 (concurring opinion of Judge Parker).

55. *See* B. Bruce-Briggs, *The Great American Gun War,* reprinted in The Gun Control Debate: You Decide 63, 84 (Lee Nisbett ed., 1990) [hereinafter cited as The Gun Control Debate].

56. Lee Kennett and James LaVerne Anderson, The Gun in America: The Origins of a National Dilemma 254–55 (1975).

57. Eugene H. Balof, *Popular and Media Images of Firearms in American Culture,* in The Gun Culture and Its Enemies 153, 158–160 (W. Tonso ed., 1990) [hereinafter cited as The Gun Culture].

58. James D. Wright et al., Under the Gun: Weapons, Crime, and Violence in America 113 (1983).

59. Perhaps the most prominent academic partisan is William R. Tonso, a sociologist at the University of Evansville. *See, e.g.,* William R. Tonso, A View from Inside the Gun Culture, in The Gun Culture, *supra* note 57, at 7. Perhaps the most prominent opponent was the late historian Richard Hofstadter. *See, e.g.,* Richard Hofstadter, America as a Gun Culture, in The Gun Control Debate, *supra* note 55, at 25.

60. Statistics bear out this observation: many more people per capita own arms in rural areas than in cities. *See* Wright et al., *supra* note 58, at 104–05; James D. Wright and Linda L. Marston, *The Ownership of the Means of Destruction: Weapons in the United States,* 23 Soc. Probs. 93, 95 (1975).

61. Some sociologists have argued that the South exhibits a distinctive subculture of violence—a set of family-transmitted values that glorifies violence. *See* Raymond D. Gastil, *Homicide and a Regional Culture of Violence,* 36 Am. Soc. Rev. 412 (1971); Sheldon Hackney, *Southern Violence,* in The History of Violence in America 505 (H. Graham and T. Gurr eds., 1969). Others have contested this claim, arguing that the South's rural geography, rather than any distinctive culture, accounts for its gun-loving ways. *See* Wright et al., *supra* note 58, at 109–12. In either event, the South is plainly a particular center of the gun culture. Per capita, southerners own more arms, *see* Wright et al., *supra* note 58, at 106–07; Wright and Marston, *supra* note 60, at 95; U.S. Dep't. of Justice, Sourcebook of Criminal Justice Statistics—1987, at 169 tbl. 2.50 (Timothy J. Flanagan and Katherine M. Jamieson eds., 1988) [hereinafter cited as Sourcebook], and commit more violent crimes than other Americans, *see* Bruce-Briggs, *supra* note 55, at 80; David B. Kopel, The Samurai, the Mountie, and the Cowboy 159 (1992), and southern politicians vote against gun control in greater percentages, *see* Balof, *supra* note 57, at 153–54; Hofstadter, *supra* note 59, at 33.

62. In fact, while the gun culture may be concentrated in the working class, gun ownership is concentrated in the middle and upper middle classes, no doubt because they have the means to purchase guns. *See* Wright et al., *supra* note 58, at 107–08; Wright and Marston, *supra* note 60, at 95–97; Sourcebook, *supra* note 61, at 169 tbl. 2.50.

63. Levinson, *supra* note 1, at 658–59.

64. Wright et al., *supra* note 58, at 323–24. Other writers, clearly partisans of the gun culture, argue even more emphatically that gun owners are an embattled, victimized class and that the urban elite, especially the media elite, view them with disdain, ignorance, and bigotry. See Brendan F. J. Furnish, *The New Class and the California Handgun Initiative: Elitist Developed Law as Gun Control,* in The Gun Culture, *supra* note 57, at 127; Richard Hummel, *Firearms' Stereotypes in American T.V. and Films: "Truth" and Consequences,* in The Gun Culture, *supra* note 57, at 143; William R. Tonso, *Social Problems and Sagecraft: Gun Control as a Case in Point,* in The Gun Control Debate, *supra* note 55, at 35; William R. Tonso, *The Media and Gun Control: A Case Study of World-View Pushing,* in The Gun Culture, *supra* note 57, at 185.

65. Kennett and Anderson, *supra* note 56, at 163–64.

66. *Id.* at 251–52.

67. Hofstadter, *supra* note 59, at 33. As I will later elaborate, many right-to-arms proponents do not deny these attempts by the dominant elements in society to disarm

outgroups and to arm themselves; indeed, they emphasize them, arguing that the Second Amendment right to arms is important precisely because gun control has so often been a means to disarm "deviant" elements. They generally fail to note, however, that such attempts to disarm outgroups are as often a product of the gun culture itself as they are of the urban elite.

68. See Richard Slotkin, Gunfighter Nation: The Myth of the Frontier in Twentieth-Century America (1992) [hereinafter cited as Gunfighter Nation]; The Fatal Environment: The Myth of the Frontier in the Age of Industrialization, 1800–1890 (1985); Regeneration Through Violence: The Mythology of the American Frontier, 1600–1860 (1973).

69. Gunfighter Nation, *supra* note 68, at 10.

70. *Id.* at 12.

71. *See id.* at 14, 18–19, 42–49, 549–54, 544–47, 649–52.

72. *Id.* at 655.

73. Balof, *supra* note 57, at 158.

74. Nicholas Johnson, *Beyond the Second Amendment: An Individual Right to Arms Viewed Through the Ninth Amendment,* 24 Rutgers L.J. 1, 24 (1992).

75. *Id.* at 25–26 (footnote omitted).

76. Kates, *supra* note 2, at 227.

77. *See* Kopel, *supra* note 61, at 431.

78. *See id.* at 45–46, 96–97.

79. *See id.* at 392–93, 422, 431–32.

80. *Id.* at 419, 432.

81. Wright et al., *supra* note 58, at 114. *See* Kennett and Anderson, *supra* note 56, at 250. Again, statistics bear out this observation: many more men than women own guns. *See* Wright et al., *supra* note 58, at 109; Sourcebook, *supra* note 61, at 169 tbl. 2.50.

82. *See* Wright et al., *supra* note 58, at 108.

83. Bruce-Briggs, *supra* note 55, at 66.

84. *See, e.g.,* David H. Bennett, The Party of Fear: The American Far Right from Nativism to the Militia Movement (1995).

85. *See generally* Bennett, *supra* note 84.

86. *See, e.g.,* Wright et al., *supra* note 58, at 108–09; Nathan McCall, Makes Me Wanna Holler: A Young Black Man in America 60–61 (1994).

87. *See* Ted Ownby, Subduing Satan: Religion, Recreation, and Manhood in the Rural South 1865–1920, at 16–17, 26 (1990).

88. *See* Wright and Marston, *supra* note 60, at 98 and n.8.

89. *See, e.g.,* Catherine McNicol Stock, Rural Radicals: Righteous Rage in the American Grain 148 (1996).

90. *See* Kennett and Anderson, *supra* note 56, at 250. I am suggesting only that men and women associate guns with penises and therefore with masculinity. I am not arguing for the broader "priapic" theory of gun ownership—that male gun owners are sexually insecure and buy guns to assuage that insecurity. *See* Don B. Kates and Nicole Varzos, *Aspects of the Priapic Theory of Gun Ownership,* in The Gun Culture, *supra* note 57, at 93, 93–95.

91. Ann Scales, *Militarism, Male Dominance, and Law: Feminist Jurisprudence as*

Oxymoron? 12 Harv. Women's L.J. 25, 42–43 (1989). Militarism is not the same thing as the gun culture. In objecting to militarism, however, these feminists are fundamentally objecting to force as the basis for social relations. Their objection therefore runs to any culture organized around the use of force.

92. *See* Sara Ruddick, Maternal Thinking: Toward a Politics of Peace 219–51 (1990).

93. *See id.* at 141–45.

94. *See id.* at 151–56, 221.

95. *See id.* at 130–34, 156–84, 205–21.

96. *See id.* at 185–205.

97. Wendy Brown, *Guns, Cowboys, Philadelphia Mayors, and Civic Republicanism: On Sanford Levinson's The Embarrassing Second Amendment,* 99 Yale L.J. 661, 665 (1989). The reference is to Levinson, *supra* note 1.

98. *Id.* at 663–64.

99. *Id.* at 666–67.

100. *See* David Biale, Power and Powerlessness in Jewish History, at ix, 4–5 (1986); Paul Breines, Tough Jews: Political Fantasies and the Moral Dilemma of American Jewry 3, 26–27, 29 (1990).

101. *See* Biale, *supra* note 100, at 198; Robert Cover, *The Folktales of Justice: Tales of Jurisdiction,* in Narrative, Violence, and the Law: The Essays of Robert Cover 173, 179–86 (Martha Minow et al. eds., 1995) [hereinafter cited as Cover Essays]; Charles E. Silberman, A Certain People: American Jews and Their Lives Today 360–66 (1985).

102. Michael Selzer, Zionism Reconsidered: The Rejection of Jewish Normalcy, at x (1970).

103. David S. Ariel, What Do Jews Believe?: The Spiritual Foundations of Judaism 126 (1995).

104. Mark Zborowski and Elizabeth Herzog, Life Is with People: The Culture of the Shtetl 149 (1952), quoted in Breines, *supra* note 100, at 108 (internal quotations omitted).

105. Jean-Paul Sartre, Anti-Semite and Jew 117–18 (George J. Becker trans., 1965). Similarly, Philip Roth recalls, "Our worth as human beings, even perhaps our distinction as a people, was embodied in the incapacity to perpetuate the sort of bloodletting loosed upon our ancestors." Philip Roth, The Facts: A Novelist's Autobiography 28 (1988).

106. Breines, *supra* note 100, at 3.

107. *See* Wright et al., *supra* note 58, at 108 n.5.

108. *See* Ownby, *supra* note 87, at 179.

109. *See* Wright et al., *supra* note 58, at 108–09; McCall, *supra* note 86, at 60–69, 72–73; Hofstadter, *supra* note 59, at 33.

110. *See* Michael Eric Dyson, Making Malcolm: The Myth and Meaning of Malcolm X, at xi–xiii (1995).

111. *See, e.g.,* Hugh Pearson, The Shadow of the Panther: Huey Newton and the Price of Black Power in America 20–21, 28–31 (1994).

112. *See* Carl T. Rowan, The Coming Race War in America: A Wake-up Call 186–90, 283 (1996); Carl Bogus, *Race, Riots, and Guns,* 66 So. Cal. L.Rev. 1365, 1383–87 (1993).

113. *See* Pearson, *supra* note 111, at 96, 101, 109–11, 131–32.

114. *See* Rowan, *supra* note 112, at viii, 282–83.

115. *See* Bogus, *supra* note 112, at 1367.

116. *Id.* at 1373–74 (footnote omitted).

117. Quoted in Osha Gray Davidson, Under Fire: The NRA and the Battle for Gun Control 44 (expanded ed. 1998).

118. All three of these writers, especially Metaska and LaPierre, have published a number of expositions of the Second Amendment. Because these expositions do not differ very much, I will confine my attention in this section to one illustrative text for each. *See* Charlton Heston, *The Second Amendment: America's First Freedom,* in Guns in America: A Reader 199 (1999); Wayne LaPierre, Guns, Crime, and Freedom (1994); Tanya K. Metaska, *Self-Defense: A Primary Civil Right,* in Guns in America, *supra,* at 194.

119. Metaska, *supra* note 118, at 195.

120. LaPierre, *supra* note 118, at 3 (emphasis in the original).

121. Metaska, *supra* note 118, at 194.

122. *Id.* at 196.

123. LaPierre, *supra* note 118, at 8.

124. Metaska, *supra* note 118, at 195.

125. LaPierre, *supra* note 118, at 20.

126. *Id.* at 86.

127. Metaska, *supra* note 118, at 198.

128. LaPierre, *supra* note 118, at 10.

129. *See* Metaska *supra* note 118, at 196–97.

130. LaPierre, *supra* note 118, at 28.

131. *Id.* at 32–33.

132. *See id.* at 201–19.

133. *Id.* at 204.

134. *See id.* at 210–19.

135. *Id.* at 170.

136. *See id.* at 159–61.

137. *See id.* at 156–57.

138. *Id.* at 157–58 (internal quotation marks omitted).

139. *Id.* at 159–60.

140. *Id.* at 161.

141. *Id.* at 161–62.

142. *Id.* at 163.

143. *Id.* at 165.

144. *See id.* at 160–61.

145. *Id.* at 72.

146. *Id.* at 78.

147. *Id.* at 106.

148. *Id.* at 194.

149. *See* Susan Faludi, Stiffed: The Betrayal of the American Man 436 (1999).

150. For example, the Militia of Montana markets a video entitled "Janet (Butch) Reno, by Jack Thompson," the blurb for which announces, "Reno is a flaming lesbian!" *See* The Militia of Montana (Sanders County, Unit Alpha), New Materials Update 2. Some even allege that Attorney General Reno once was a man. *See* Faludi, *supra* note 149, at 415–16.

151. Heston, *supra* note 118, at 199.
152. *Id.* at 200.
153. *Id.*
154. *Id.* at 204.
155. *Id.* at 200.
156. *Id.*
157. *Id.* at 201.
158. *Id.* at 201–02.
159. *Id.* at 202.
160. *Id.* at 204.
161. *Id.* at 199.
162. *Id.* at 203.
163. *Id.*
164. *Id.* at 204.
165. *Id.* at 203.
166. *Id.* at 200.
167. *Id.* at 201.

Chapter 6. The Militia Movement's Theory of the Second Amendment

1. M. Samuel Sherwood, The Guarantee of the Second Amendment, at dedication page (1994) (self-copied photocopied book, on file with the author).

2. *See* Militia of Montana Declaration (flyer) (on file with the author); Linda Thompson, American Justice Foundation, *Declaration of Independence of 1994,* at 1–3 (on file with the author), reprinted in Kenneth Stern, The American Jewish Committee, Militias: A Growing Danger, vol. 5, pub. no. 1, app. 102 (1995).

3. Militia of Montana Declaration, *supra* note 2, at 5.

4. Militia of Montana, Militia of Montana Catalogue, Nov. 21, 1994, at 11 (Noxon, Mont.)(on file with the author).

5. *Declaration of Independence of 1994, supra* note 2, at 2.

6. Militia of Montana, The Militia 8 (pamphlet from MOM in Noxon, Mont.) (on file with the author).

7. Jim Faulkner, *Martial Law and Emergency Powers,* Federal Lands Update, Nov. 1994, at 5. As its title suggests, Federal Lands Update sees the threat of tyranny particularly in federal land policy and environmental regulation.

8. The Free Militia, Field Manual Section 1, at 47 (1994) (on file with the author). A particularly malignant expression of this idea comes from the National Alliance, a neo-Nazi group. A flyer explains that "Free Money can be yours — if you are an 80-IQ welfare mother," an illegal alien, a "member of Jewish organized crime gangs," or a "homosexual 'performance artist.'" On the other hand, "all this free money is *not* available to you if you are an ordinary straight White American, a descendant of the men and women of Europe who discovered, pioneered, and built America." Instead, "*your* job is to work hard to provide all the free money and free goodies that the criminals — uh, I mean the politicians — like to give away to buy the votes of the minority and the special interest voting blocs." Free Money (flyer distributed by the National Alliance) (on file with the author).

9. *Declaration of Independence of 1994, supra* note 2, at 2.

10. For example, "U.S. Marines were asked if they would be willing to KILL American civilians who resisted confiscation of privately owned firearms. The sad commentary on that question was that the U.S. Marine Corp [*sic*]; in which we all have a son, daughter, grandchild, relative, or an acquaintance just down the street, in that tightly regimented organization; the overwhelming answer was YES! Sad, but true." Faulkner, *supra* note 7, at 6.

11. John Grady, *U.S. Government Initiates Open Warfare Against American People,* Militia News, Collector's Edition 1994, at 2, reprinted in Stern, *supra* note 2, app. 104.

12. *See, e.g.,* Beth Hawkins, *Patriot Games,* Detroit Metro Times, Oct. 12–18, 1994, at 14; *Hate Movement Shifts Tactics in 1994,* Klanwatch Intelligence Report (Southern Poverty Law Center, Montgomery, Ala.), Mar. 1995, at 9, 11; Philip Weiss, *Off the Grid,* N.Y. Times, Jan. 8, 1995, Section 6 (Magazine), at 24, 29–30, 44–52.

13. *See* Evan Thomas et al., *The Manhunt: Cleverness and Luck,* Newsweek, May 1, 1995, at 32–34.

14. *Richard Snell Update,* Taking Aim (MOM, Noxon, Mont.), Mar. 1995, at 7. References to Waco and Ruby Ridge abound in the militia materials. The Militia News, for example, opines: "The recent 51 day siege and massacre of nearly one hundred men, women and children in Waco, Texas, was a crime of the greatest magnitude. It was a cruel, sadistic, brutal crime. It was a crime which violated nearly every article of the Bill of Rights. . . . It resembled the burning and obliteration of Christian cities and the annihilation of their inhabitants by Mogul hordes." Grady, *supra* note 11, at 3. About Ruby Ridge, the Free Militia recounts, "The BATF attempted to entrap Randy Weaver in Idaho. When he refused to become one of their henchmen, his cabin was put under 24-hour BATF surveillance, leading to a surprise confrontation that left Weaver's son and wife dead and Weaver acquitted of any wrongdoing." The Free Militia, *supra* note 8, at 43.

15. *Richard Snell Update, supra* note 14, at 7. *See Richard Snell Update, supra* note 14, at 8; Jo Thomas and Ronald Smothers, *Oklahoma City Bombing Was Target of Plot As Early as '83, Official Says,* N.Y. Times, May 20, 1995, at A6.

16. Chris Bouneff, *Leader: Militia Misunderstood,* Idaho Press-Trib., Apr. 9, 1995, at 4A. Sherwood has denied the statement. *See id.*

17. *See Declaration of Independence of 1994, supra,* note 2, at 2.

18. *See* James Corcoran, Bitter Harvest 27 (1990).

19. *See* Bouneff, *supra* note 16, at 4A.

20. *Six O'Clock Newscast* (Indianapolis Eyewitness News, May 1, 1995).

21. The Militia, *supra* note 6, at 3.

22. Militia of Montana Declaration, *supra* note 2, at 5.

23. The Militia, *supra* note 6, at 8.

24. The Free Militia, *supra* note 8, at 47.

25. Jim Faulkner, *Why There is a Need for the Militia in America,* Federal Lands Update, Oct. 1994, at 6.

26. The Free Militia, *supra* note 8, at 39.

27. Second Amendment Militia Application (Second Amendment Committee, Hanford, Calif.) (on file with the author) [hereinafter cited as Application].

28. Grady, *supra* note 11, at 4. Other militia writers rely on another familiar im-

precation by Henry: "Guard with jealous attention the public liberty. Suspect everyone who approaches that jewel! Unfortunately, nothing will preserve it but downright force. Whenever you give up that force, you are ruined." Sherwood, *supra* note 1, at 60.

29. Faulkner, *supra* note 7, at 3.

30. John Grady, *The Right to Bear Arms*, Militia News, Collector's Edition 1994, at 3, reprinted in Stern, *supra* note 2, app. 104.

31. McAlvany Intelligence Advisor, March 1994, at 20.

32. The Militia, *supra* note 6, at 3.

33. Faulkner, *supra* note 7, at 1; Faulkner, *supra* note 25, at 2; The Militia, *supra* note 6, at 7. A single-page flyer distributed at militia meetings also bears the quoted language and an attribution to Sarah Brady ("in HER OWN WORDS"), in letters large enough to fill the whole page. *See* Brady Flyer (on file with the author).

34. The Free Militia, *supra* note 8, at 47. According to the Detroit Metro Times, Michigan militia leaders agree: they "say semi-automatic weapons are militia-style arms. Therefore, the only reason to ban them is to lay the groundwork for enslaving the populace." Beth Hawkins, *Guns and Glory*, Detroit Metro Times, Oct. 12–18, 1994, at 12.

35. The Free Militia, *supra* note 8, at 42a. The description of these bills as "subversive" seems ironic, coming from a group committed to subversion and regarding bills that enjoyed popular support. As I will later argue, however, this usage is consistent with militia ideology: they see themselves as the true American people and those who oppose them as traitors or foreigners. The bills are therefore subversive of the real America.

36. The Militia, *supra* note 6, at 7–8.

37. Faulkner, *supra* note 25, at 2.

38. Faulkner, *supra* note 7, at 5.

39. The Free Militia, *supra* note 8, at 42.

40. Hitler Flyer (on file with the author). To reinforce the message, the document goes on as follows: "Political prisoners and Death Camps can't exist without 'Gun Control'. Some Americans still feel 'Gun Control' is a good idea. To save America from these Nazi-lovers, we must destroy 'Gun Control'!!" *Id.*

41. The Militia, *supra* note 6, at 6–7.

42. *See, e.g.,* Stephen Dresch, *Local Militia Starts Up*, The Peninsula News, Dec. 11, 1994; Hawkins, *supra* note 12, at 13–14.

43. *See* Grady, *supra* note 30, at 6; Application, *supra* note 27; The Free Militia, *supra* note 8, at 47; Sherwood, *supra* note 1, at xv.

44. Grady, *supra* note 30, at 5.

45. Sherwood, *supra* note 1, at 58.

46. Faulkner, *supra* note 25, at 6.

47. The Militia, *supra* note 6, at 7. The Second Amendment Committee purports to derive this conclusion from a linguistic analysis of the amendment itself: according to "A. C. Brocki, teacher of Advanced English, a foremost expert in grammar, former Senior Editor for Houghton Mifflin," "the sentence means that *the people* are the militia." Bernadine Smith, Interpreting the Meaning and Purpose of the Second Amendment (Second Amendment Committee, Hanford, Calif.) (on file with the author).

48. Exact definitions of the unorganized militia vary. Federal Lands Update asserts that

the unorganized militia consists of every "able bodied male between 18 and 65." This definition is "a true vestige of the intent of the Founding Fathers and a heritage of the Guarantee of the Second Amendment." Faulkner, *supra* note 25, at 6. MOM explains that the unorganized militia includes "all able-bodied citizen's [*sic*] of this state" and "therefor [*sic*], the unorganized militia conforms with 'Militia' as provided for in the second amendment." The Militia, *supra* note 6, at 6. In fact, current law defines the unorganized militia as all males between the ages of seventeen and forty-five and all female officers of the National Guard. *See* 10 U.S.C. section 311 (2000). At present, that definition has no functional significance: the U.S. Code does not provide for the arming, equipping, organizing, training, or funding of the unorganized militia. In fact, section 311 seems to do only one thing: it allows those who fit the statutory definition to proclaim that they are members of the militia, as militia writers are eager to do. For example, Linda Thompson has proclaimed herself "Acting Adjutant General" of the Unorganized Militia of the United States "pursuant to 10 U.S.C. Section 311 and Articles I and II of the Bill of Rights." Linda Thompson, Ultimatum to Each Member of the United States House of Representatives and United States Senate (Apr. 19, 1994) (on file with author).

49. Ray Southwell, cofounder of the Michigan Militia, explained the appeal: "What I've found is that people are so angry they're loose cannons. . . . They come into the militia and their anger level drops. Now we have a common goal, a common good. He's realized he's not alone." Beth Hawkins, *Conspiratorial Views,* Detroit Metro-Times, Oct. 12–18, 1994, at 13.

50. The Militia, *supra* note 6, at 7.

51. Faulkner, *supra* note 25, at 6.

52. The Free Militia, *supra* note 8, at 47.

53. Smith, *supra* note 47.

54. *See* Osha Gray Davidson, Under Fire: The NRA and the Battle for Gun Control 134–35 (expanded edition 1998).

55. Faulkner, *supra* note 25, at 6.

56. Grady, *supra* note 11, at 3.

57. Faulkner, *supra* note 25, at 4 (emphasis added).

58. United States Militia Assoc., Official Policy and Announcement, Member Behavior Toward Law Enforcement Personnel 7 (1995) [hereinafter cited as USMA pamphlet].

59. The Militia, *supra* note 6, at 8.

60. Letter from North American Volunteer Militia to Judge Jeff Langton (Dec. 30, 1994) (copy on file with the author).

61. Ultimatum by Linda Thompson, *supra* note 48.

62. *See* James A. Aho, The Politics of Righteousness 93 (1990); Corcoran, *supra* note 18, at 29, 238.

63. *See* James William Gibson, Warrior Dreams 220–30 (1994). One further example: members of the Covenant, the Sword, and the Arm of the Lord firebombed a Jewish community center near my home in Bloomington, Indiana. *See* Laura Lane, *Neo-Nazis admit setting '83 fire at Jewish Center,* Bloomington Herald-Telephone, July 18, 1985, at 1; *United States v. Ellison,* 793 F.2d 942 (8th Cir.), *cert. denied,* 479 U.S. 937 (1986).

64. Shortly before the bombing, McVeigh telephoned Elohim City, a Christian Identity

compound. Furthermore, the timing of the bombing may be significant: aside from being the anniversary of the assault at Waco, it coincided with the scheduled execution date for Richard Snell, a white supremacist who held Christian Identity beliefs and who plotted a similar bombing against the same building in 1983. *See* Thomas and Smothers, *supra* note 15, at A6.

65. *See, e.g.,* Aho, *supra* note 62, at 83–113; James Coates, Armed and Dangerous 77–103 (1987).

66. *See* Aho, *supra* note 62, at 93–94.

67. I draw this summary from, inter alia, Gibson, *supra* note 63, at 216–17 and Aho, *supra* note 62, at 92–104.

68. *See* Chip Berlet, Political Research Associates, Armed Militias, Right Wing Populism, and Scapegoating 4 (Apr. 27, 1995) (copy on file with the author); *Hate Movement Shifts Tactics in 1994, supra* note 12, at 9, 10–11; Montana Human Rights Network, A Season of Discontent: Militias, Constitutionalists, and the Far Right in Montana 2, 8 (May 1994); Hawkins, *supra* note 12, at 13.

69. *See, e.g.,* Hawkins, *supra* note 12, at 13. For example, the Texas Constitutional Militia urges, "Open your militia to all races, creeds, religions. This is what America is really all about. This is why they came." Johnny Johnson, *Texas Militia — Statement* 3 (Feb. 11, 1995), reprinted in Stern, *supra* note 2, app. 15. Similarly, the USMA does not "participate, sanction, or support" racist groups such as "the Nazis, Skin-heads, fascists, KKK," and it "allow[s] all men the full freedom and exercise of their conscience to worship." USMA pamphlet, *supra* note 58, at 3.

70. For example, some militia members believe that eight Jewish families control the Federal Reserve System. *See, e.g.,* Hawkins, *supra* note 49, at 13; Roger Tatarian, *Rationale for Citizen Militias is Frightening,* Fresno Bee, Nov. 20, 1994, at B7.

71. Grady, *supra* note 11, at 1.

72. Aho, *supra* note 62, at 246 (quoting Gordon Kahl).

73. *Id.* at 247–49 (quoting Robert Matthews).

74. *The Militia,* Calling Our Nation, no. 73, at 30.

75. *Id.* at 31.

76. *Id.* at 30.

77. *See* Corcoran, *supra* note 18, at 28.

78. *See* Gun Rights Were Meant to Be Beyond the Reach of Government Officials (distribution of the Second Amendment Committee) (on file with the author); Season of Discontent, *supra* note 68, at 11.

79. *Which Constitution,* The Patriot, Jan. 1990, at 1.

80. *See* Aho, *supra* note 62, at 261.

81. Pace Amendment, Art. of Amend. XXVII section 1 (on file with the author).

82. *See* David C. Williams, *Civic Republicanism and the Citizen Militia: The Terrifying Second Amendment,* 101 Yale L.J. 551, 602–03 (1991).

83. *See* Jost Delbruck, *Global Migration — Immigration — Multiethnicity: Challenges to the Concept of the Nation-State,* 2 Ind. J. of Global L. Stud. 45, 48–51, 57–58 (1994); David Williams, *European and U.S. Perspectives on Civic Republicanism,* 2 Ind. J. of Global L. Stud. 71, 74–75 (1994).

84. *See, e.g.,* John Rawls, Political Liberalism 18–19 (1993).

85. *See* Kenneth Karst, Belonging to America (1989); Delbruck, *supra* note 83, at 51–53.

86. *See, e.g.,* Herbert J. Gans, Middle American Individualism: The Future of Liberal Democracy (1988).

87. *See, e.g., Police/Military Alert: United Nations Treachery Exposed,* Aid & Abet Police Newsletter 1, 1 (Special Edition No. 12). One uncommonly complete list includes not only the predictable members of the Clinton administration — Bruce Babbitt, Henry Cisneros, and Donna Shalala — but some less likely candidates as well: Newt Gingrich, Larry Pressler, Sandra Day O'Connor, and Laurence Silberman. *See* Fund to Restore an Educated Electorate, *The CFR/Trilateral/New World Order Connection* (paid advertisement), Prescott Sun, Dec. 1, 1993, at 11.

88. "Though not realized at the time, the UN Charter, ratified as a *treaty* by the Senate and signed by the President, was an instrument of surrender." Louis Stradling, *The Constitution vs. the UN Charter,* Aid & Abet Police Newsletter 2, 2 (Special Issue Number 12). By the 1950s, "the plans for the dissolution of the nation, the surrender of our sovereignty, and the merger of the U.S. into a one world government under the United Nations was well underway." Grady, *supra* note 11, at 1.

89. The plot seeks "the emasculation of our national security and the transfer of all our military forces to a United Nations command in preparation for the New World government." Grady, *supra* note 11, at 2. The conspirators will "establish an International Army under the United Nations to control the people of the world. . . . All independent national military forces will be dissolved." Central Yavapai Center for Action, *The Hidden Agenda* (paid advertisement), Prescott Sun, Dec. 1, 1993, at 11. They will "disarm citizens; transfer US military to the UN." Stradling, *supra* note 88, at 2.

90. "There are presently over one million (1,000,000) foreign troops in these United States." Faulkner, *supra* note 7, at 6. "The federal government, at this Time, is transporting large Armies of foreign Mercenaries to complete the work of Death, Desolation, and Tyranny, already begun, often under the color of the law of the United Nations." *Declaration of Independence of 1994, supra* note 2, at 3.

91. For those with the interest, MOM's publication *Taking Aim* offers the most detailed and complete conspiracy theories. *See especially* Militia of Montana, Taking Aim (February 1995); Militia of Montana, Taking Aim (Special Edition 1994).

92. "Mysterious military operations with 'black helicopters' [are] being conducted all across the United States." Faulkner, *supra* note 7, at 6.

93. "All people will be required to maintain a federal identity card, ultimately a computer chip under the skin of your hand will be the technique used to identify you and all pertinent information about you." *The Hidden Agenda, supra* note 89, at 11.

94. "Why are tons of barbed wire and over 5,000 mattresses being off-loaded at Ft. Chaffee, Arkansas?" Faulkner, *supra* note 7, at 6.

95. "Troop movement markers (bright colored reflective stickers on the backs of road signs) and U.N. Troops are already in place in this country." *Declaration of Independence of 1994, supra* note 2, at 5.

96. *See* Charles Zeps, ALERT! Militias Targeted 24/03/95, *posted* Talk.Politics.Guns, Mar. 24, 1995.

97. "When the federal government decides to enact martial law; and they will; the director of FEMA becomes a virtual DICTATOR." Faulkner, *supra* note 7, at 5.

98. *See* Alex Heard, *The Road to Oklahoma City,* New Republic, May 15, 1995, at 15.

99. The Militia of Montana Catalogue, for example, lists the following videotapes, among others: "America in Peril," "Equipping for the New World Order," "New World Order Land and Farm Confiscation," "New World Order Seminar," "New World Order—Take Over of America," "Enroute to Global Occupation." Militia of Montana Catalogue, *supra* note 4, at 2–5.

100. Stradling, *supra* note 88, at 2.

101. Grady, *supra* note 11, at 3.

102. Step 3 in the Hidden Agenda is to "establish a national propaganda machine. . . All national T.V. networks, national newspapers, and radio networks are currently controlled by those that would destroy us." *The Hidden Agenda, supra* note 89, at 11. "Our national media has become nothing but the official mouthpiece of the government, putting forth false 'polls' and outright propaganda to sway the public opinion." *Declaration of Independence of 1994, supra* note 2, at 5. "The majority of the 240 million residents of the U.S. are non-thinking sheep, easily led and programmed." Grady, *supra* note 11, at 3. "To trusting Americans, it is unbelievable, but veteran readers know that the NEW WORLD ORDER is to be a socialist dictatorship. That popular media and high officials ignore or deny and ridicule it, confuses people and thwarts organized opposition." Stradling, *supra* note 88, at 2. "The trust people put in the media is beyond reason. As babes at the breast of Mother Media, they suck their daily sustenance of managed 'news.' " *Id.* at 9.

103. "There are millions who have not fallen for the conditioning, and of these millions, hundreds of thousands will physically resist. . . . These are our hope." Grady, *supra* note 11, at 3.

104. *See* Richard Ashcraft, Revolutionary Politics and Locke's Two Treatises of Government 22–28 (1986); Pauline Maier, From Resistance to Revolution 42, 183–97 (1972); Williams, *supra* note 82, at 565, 581–86.

105. *See* Maier, *supra* note 104, at 224–27. The Militia News relies on Patrick Henry for its inspiration: "It is natural to man to indulge in the illusions of hope. We are apt to shut our eyes against a painful truth. Is this the part of wise men, engaged in a great and arduous struggle for liberty? . . . For my part, whatever anguish of spirit it may cost, I am willing to know the whole truth; to know the worst and to provide for it." Grady, *supra* note 11, at 3. "What is needed is millions of Paul Reveres, shouting the message, 'The enemy is here.' " Stradling, *supra* note 88, at 9.

106. *See* Maier, *supra* note 104, at 224–27.

107. *See, e.g.,* Susan Williams, *Feminist Legal Epistemology,* 8 Berk. Women's L.J. 63, 68–72 (1993). *See generally* Richard Rorty, Philosophy and the Mirror of Nature (1979) (describing traditional epistemology as holding that human knowledge reflects such an objective reality and criticizing that approach).

108. For criticisms of the possibility of such a "universal" perspective, see generally Sandra Harding, Whose Science? Whose Knowledge? (1991); Naomi Scheman, *Individualism and the Objects of Psychology,* in Discovering Reality: Feminist Perspectives on Epistemology and Metaphysics 255 (Sandra Harding and Merrill B. Hintikka eds., 1983).

109. *The Hidden Agenda, supra* note 89, at 11.

110. *See* Corcoran, *supra* note 18, at 14–29.

111. *See* Richard Hofstadter, *The Paranoid Style in American Politics,* in The Paranoid Style in American Politics and Other Essays 23–40 (1965); Eli Sagan, The Honey and the Hemlock: Democracy and Paranoia in Ancient Athens and Modern America 13–34 (1991).

112. *See* Berlet, *supra* note 68, at 6.

113. *See* Aho, *supra* note 62, at 162–63, 185–211.

114. *See* Aho, *supra* note 62, at 135–63, 185–211; Hawkins, *supra* note 12, at 13–14.

115. *Texas Militia — Statement, supra* note 69, at 6.

116. Letter from North American Volunteer Militia to Judge Jeff Langton, *supra* note 60.

117. Faulkner, *supra* note 7, at 2.

118. The Militia, *supra* note 6, at 8.

119. *See, e.g.,* Aho, *supra* note 62, at 37–42.

120. The Free Militia, *supra* note 8, at 44. *See* Corcoran, *supra* note 18, at 51. Linda Thompson further explains, "The Federal Government, under the Constitution, never had the legal authority to pass a national tax on income and the 16th Amendment (the law that enacted the income tax) was never ratified, as required by law." *Declaration of Independence of 1994, supra* note 2, at 5.

121. *See* Aho, *supra* note 62, at 39.

122. The Free Militia, *supra* note 8, at 45.

123. *See, e.g.,* Elizabeth Larson, *Secessionism in the West,* The Defender, Nov. 1994, at 1, 9.

124. The Free Militia, *supra* note 8, at 44.

125. *See* Larson, *supra* note 123, at 1.

126. For example, the North American Militia warns state officeholders, "You have state agents who are threatening to take wildlife from an individual. The individual is not a corporation and has certain unalienable rights. The state of Montana does not own the wildlife. The regulations do not pertain to the human being inhabitants of Montana." Letter from North American Volunteer Militia to Judge Jeff Langton, *supra* note 60.

127. For example: "The bad news is that the Clintonistas want your property and are serious about stealing it." McAlvany Intelligence Advisor, *supra* note 31, at 18.

128. James Catron, *Watch Out!,* Federal Lands Update, Oct. 1994, at 3.

129. USMA Pamphlet, *supra* note 58, at 3.

130. Jill Smolowe, *Enemies of the State,* Time, May 8, 1995, at 58, 68.

131. Grady, *supra* note 30, at 5–6.

132. The Militia, *supra* note 6, at 3–4.

133. *See* Laurence H. Tribe, American Constitutional Law 301 (2d ed. 1988).

134. *See, e.g.,* John H. Ely, Democracy and Distrust 13–41 (1980); Laurence H. Tribe, God Save This Honorable Court 42–43 (1985); Geoffrey R. Stone et al., Constitutional Law 38–39 (2d ed. 1991).

135. *See, e.g.,* Ronald Dworkin, Law's Empire, (1986); Stanley Fish, Is There a Text in This Class? (1980); Owen M. Fiss, *Objectivity and Interpretation,* 34 Stan. L.Rev. 739 (1982); William M. Eskridge, Jr., *Gadamer/Statutory Interpretation,* 90 Colum. L.Rev.

609 (1990); William D. Popkin, *The Collaborative Model of Statutory Interpretation,* 61 S. Cal. L.Rev. 541 (1988).

136. *See, e.g., Planned Parenthood of Southeastern Pennsylvania v. Casey,* 505 U.S. 833 (1992) (five opinions); *Board of Education of Kiryas Joel Village School District v. Grumet,* 512 U.S. 687 (1994) (six opinions); *United States v. Lopez,* 514 U.S. 549 (1995) (six opinions).

137. Grady, *supra* note 30, at 5–6. Sadly, such accusations of bad faith are also common in the scholarly debate over the Second Amendment. *See* Andrew Jay McClurg, *The Rhetoric of Gun Control,* 42 Am. U. L.Rev. 53 (1992).

138. *Declaration of Independence of 1994, supra* note 2, at 3. Similarly, Calvin Greenup and others published an open letter in a local newspaper declaring: "I . . . solemnly Publish and Declare my American National Status and Rights to emancipate absolute my 'res' in trust from the foreign jurisdiction known as the municipal corporation of the District of Columbia. . . . By this emancipation I return to an estate of primary sovereignty and freedom that pre-exists all government(s)." *Letter to the Editor,* Ravalli Republic, Sept. 28, 1993, reprinted in Stern, *supra* note 2, app. 7.

139. *Texas Militia—Statement, supra* note 69, at 3.

140. How to Activate the Constitutional Militia in Your Area, *posted* Talk.Politics. Guns, March 24, 1995. Similarly, another posting urges, "The [recruiting] team should visit likely places and persons who might refer them to prospective recruits. Gun shops, American Legion and VFW halls, civic organizations, sheriff and fire departments." Jon Roland, Militia Organizing—Advance Teams, *posted* Talk.Politics.Guns, March 24, 1995.

141. The Militia of Montana, Sanders County, Unit Alpha, Rules and Regulations 2 (copy on file with the author).

142. *Id.* at 3.

143. *Id.* at 1.

144. An interview with Norman Olson, a cofounder of the Michigan Militia, brings the interpretive and political problems together. The interviewer asked Olson, "If you establish 83 militias in every county in the state, who's to say that they'll all agree?" Olson responded, "You have to listen to our mission: defend the Constitution and see that all men remain free." The interviewer then pointed out the interpretive problem: "But hundreds of courts interpret the Constitution differently. . . . Who would decide if there were dozens of militias?" Olson's answer to that difficulty raised the political difficulty instead: "What happens if a person doesn't like the philosophy of the brigade? He just walks away—that's it." Robert Downes, *On the Front Lines with Northern Michigan's Militia,* Northern Express, Aug. 22, 1994, at 4. This ultimate solution—the exit option—may allay worries about the rights of the individual, but it practically guarantees the disintegration of a revolutionary people.

145. *See generally* Stanley B. Greenberg, Middle Class Dreams (1995).

146. Grady, *supra* note 30, at 2.

147. *The Hidden Agenda, supra* note 89, at 11.

148. The Texas Constitutional Militia urges each of its chapters to "educate its members in . . . the Bible, which has been the greatest single guiding influence for all great nations desiring to be free. . . . [and to] [s]eek the protection, wisdom, and leadership of

Almighty God as we submit to Him to do His will in protecting the liberty and freedom He has given to all Americans." *Texas Militia — Statement, supra* note 69, at 7.

149. Gordon Kahl raged in his last letter, "These enemies of Christ have . . . thrown our Constitution and our Christian Common Law (which is nothing other than the Laws of God as set forth in the Scriptures) into the garbage can." Aho, *supra* note 62, at 246. One publication explains that our constitutional rights are "the divine endowment of the Creator to each person. . . . Note that there is no mention of HUMAN or CIVIL rights." Stradling, *supra* note 88, at 3. Under the Constitution, "our system of justice is founded in the wisdom of God based on Bible laws preserved through the centuries by Anglo-Saxons." *Id.* at 4.

150. "God intends the government to do you good by maintaining law, order, and justice. When the government systematically punishes the upright citizen and commends wrongdoing, it is no longer serving God's purpose. . . . If we are submitted to Jesus Christ and committed to Constitutional liberties, then our conscience demands the resistance of unconstitutional authority, which is no authority at all." The Free Militia, *supra* note 8, at 11. In short, "WHEN ELECTED OFFICIALS BREAK THEIR OATH TO UPHOLD THE CONSTITUTION, IT IS NOT THE PATRIOTIC CITIZEN WHO IS IN REBELLION, BUT THE GOVERNING OFFICIAL." *Id.*

151. For example, the Free Militia lists the following as examples of "violated civil rights": "For a generation we have had legalized abortion which denies the right of the unborn child to live. . . . Attempts have recently been made to require state certification of private school teachers and homeschoolers. . . . The America 2000 education program is designed to standardize the curriculum in and centralize control of all public schools by imposing 'outcome based' education." The Free Militia, *supra* note 8, at 40–41.

152. One distribution is overt about the battle lines: in the New World Order, "all congregations affiliated with the National Council of Churches and liberal Jewish councils, may continue to function. These groups are not incompatible with the aims and designs of the Alliance. However, all other fundamental, independent, Bible-centered congregations; all conservative Greek and Russian orthodox churches; Orthodox Hebrew synagogues and Roman Catholic parishes with large Eastern European ethnic constituencies, will cease operation at once." John Grady, When Will It Happen? (one-page handout on file with the author).

153. *See Planned Parenthood of Southeastern Pa. v. Casey,* 505 U.S. 833 (1992); *Wallace v. Jaffree,* 472 U.S. 38 (1985); *Stone v. Graham,* 449 U.S. 39 (1980).

154. *See* Barry A. Kosmin and Seymour P. Lachman, One Nation Under God 10–11, 230–31 (1993).

155. *See id.* at 157–251.

Chapter 7. Outgroups and the Second Amendment

1. At least one gay organization in New York City, the Pink Panthers, has embraced the right to arms as a response to gay bashing. *See* Alisa Solomon, *Fired Up: Should Gays Carry Guns?* Village Voice, Nov. 27, 1990, at 43–44. Doubtless members of other outgroups have generated similar theories as well.

2. *See generally* David Biale, Power and Powerlessness in Jewish History (1986); Paul

Breines, Tough Jews: Political Fantasies and the Moral Dilemma of American Jewry (1990).

3. *See* Biale, *supra* note 2, at 72–77; Breines, *supra* note 2, at 81, 83, 88–90, 97–101, 105–20, 132–35.

4. *See* Breines, *supra* note 2, at 139–49.

5. *See id.* at 30–31, 49, 149–67.

6. *See id.* at 56–73.

7. *See id.* at 3–4, 17–18, 61, 70, 79, 83–84.

8. See Leslie Camhi, *Imaginary Jews: America Develops a Masada Complex,* Village Voice, July 11, 1995, at 29.

9. The copyright notice for *Lethal Laws* requires the following citation: Lethal Laws, Jay Simkin, Aaron Zelman, and Alan M. Rice, Jews for the Preservation of Firearms Ownership, Inc., 2872 South Wentworth Avenue, Milwaukee, Wis. 53207, (414) 769–0760 [hereinafter cited as Lethal Laws]. They seem to be trolling for members. The citation for *"Gun Control"* is simpler: Jay Simkin and Aaron Zelman, "Gun Control": Gateway to Tyranny (1992).

10. For reviews by individual rights theorists, see Don B. Kates, Jr., and Daniel D. Polsby, *Of Genocide and Disarmament,* 86 J. Crim.L. and Criminology 247 (1995); David B. Kopel, *Book Review: Lethal Laws,* 15 N.Y.L.Sch. J. Int'l and Comp. L. 355 (1995). For media accounts, see Camhi, *supra* note 8, at 29; Erik Eckholm, *Owners Say Mild Limit Would Lead to Handgun Ban,* N.Y. Times, Mar. 12, 1992, at D21; Keith Epstein, *Militias Aim for Better Image,* Plain Dealer (Cleveland), June 19, 1995, at 1A; Charles Holmes, *Pro-Gun Ad Targeting Jews Is Denounced,* Atlanta Constitution, Apr. 30, 1991, at A2; Jody McPhillips, *No-More-Hate Message Replaces Hitler Billboard that Caused Fury,* Providence Journal-Bulletin, Nov. 5, 1994, at 3A; *New York: Schumer Shot Down by Jewish Gun Group,* Hotlne, Apr. 25, 1991, *available in* LEXIS, Cmpgn Library, Hotline File [hereinafter cited as *Schumer Shot Down*]; Charley Reese, *The Best Protection Against Tyranny Is the Right to Bear Arms,* Orlando Sentinel, Oct. 12, 1993, at A8; Frank Smyth, *Crossfire: Wounded by Congress, the NRA's Regime Bullies its Own Board and Launches a New Offensive on America,* Village Voice, June 21, 1994, at 26; Jim Strang, *Hitler's Influence on U.S. Gun Law,* Plain Dealer (Cleveland), April 18, 1993, at 1B; Ed Vulliamy, *Cults 2,* Observer (London), May 21, 1995, at 20, *available in* LEXIS, News Library, Obsrvr File.

11. Lethal Laws, *supra* note 9, at 1.

12. *Id.* at 12 (emphasis omitted).

13. *Id.* at 4 (emphasis added). In a letter to the Atlantic Monthly, Jay Simkin denies that JPFO has argued that gun control causes genocide; rather, "murderous politicians and government bureaucrats plan and carry out genocides." Jay Edward Simkin, *Letter to the Editor,* Atlantic Monthly, June 1996, at 12. This denial, however, is either disingenuous or a quibble: certainly, some set of human beings must carry out genocide, but Lethal Laws claims that the existence of gun control, all by itself, "promotes genocide" by such people.

14. Lethal Laws, *supra* note 9, at 9–10 (emphasis omitted) (internal quotations omitted).

15. These examples include the persecution of Armenians in Turkey (1911–17),

political dissidents in China (1948–52), Mayans in Guatemala (1964–81), Christians in Uganda (1971–79), and opponents of Pol Pot in Cambodia (1975–79). *See id.* at 14. JPFO's definition of genocide includes the extermination of a group defined by its "political beliefs," *id.* at 9, hence the inclusion of Chinese and Cambodian dissidents.

16. *See id.* at 151–52.

17. *Id.* at 11.

18. *Id.* at 153.

19. *Id.* at 11, 156–58.

20. *Id.* at 27.

21. Vulliamy, *supra* note 10, at 23 (internal quotations omitted) (quoting Jay Simkin). *See* Strang, *supra* note 10, at 1B.

22. Camhi, *supra* note 8, at 29 (quoting JPFO literature).

23. Vulliamy, *supra* note 10, at 20 (internal quotations omitted) (quoting Jay Simkin).

24. McPhillips, *supra* note 10, at 3A (providing a photograph of the advertisement); Reese, *supra* note 10, at A8 (describing the advertisement).

25. *See* Kathleen Best, *Senate Panel OK's Major Gun Control Bill,* St. Louis Post-Dispatch, May 8, 1991, at 4A; Joanne Haas, *Loftus Calls NRA "Bullies,"* UPI, Nov. 7, 1989, *available in* LEXIS, News Library, Upstat file.

26. Strang, *supra* note 10, at 1B (internal quotations omitted) (quoting JPFO advertisement).

27. Eckholm, *supra* note 10, at D21 (internal quotations omitted) (quoting JPFO advertisement).

28. Vulliamy, *supra* note 10, at 20 (internal quotations omitted) (quoting Jay Simkin).

29. Reese, *supra* note 10, at A8 (internal quotations omitted) (omissions in original) (quoting JPFO member Theodore Haas).

30. Abraham H. Foxman, *Jewish Pro-Gun Group,* N.Y. Times, May 21, 1995, section 4, at 14 (letter to the editor) (internal quotations omitted) (quoting JPFO materials).

31. Lethal Laws, *supra* note 9, at 159 (emphasis omitted). JPFO has reserved its harshest criticism for Rep. Charles Schumer: "Most Jews are not stupid or pro-criminal, but Charles Schumer is both!" *Schumer Shot Down, supra* note 10 (internal quotations omitted) (quoting a JPFO advertisement). Even more pointedly, Zelman told an NRA board meeting: "Charlie Schumer, who claims to be a Jew, should crawl back to the rock he came from." Smyth, *supra* note 10, at 30 (internal quotations omitted) (quoting Aaron Zelman).

32. Epstein, *supra* note 10, at D21 (internal quotations omitted) (quoting Aaron Zelman).

33. *New York: Liberals to Endorse Abrams Today,* Hotline, May 2, 1991, *available in* LEXIS, Cmpgn Library, Hotlne File (internal quotations omitted) (omissions in original) (quoting a JPFO advertisement) [hereinafter cited as *Liberals*]. Similarly, the New York Times has attributed to Bruce R. Chesley, JPFO's field representative in New England, the belief that "some Jewish members of Congress who favor tighter gun control measures were feeding anti-Semitism in the United States." Michael Janofsky, *Two States, Two Gatherings and a Lot of Anti-Government Sentiment,* N.Y. Times, May 15, 1995, at A10.

34. Lethal Laws, *supra* note 9, at 4. Pro–gun control Jewish leaders have, in turn,

accused JPFO of promoting anti-Semitism by these attacks. Rabbi David Saperstein, director of the Religious Action Center of Reform Judaism, charges, "The injection of religious bigotry into public debate is unacceptable in America. The fact that the attack is launched by Jews does not make it any less anti-Semitic." Holmes, *supra* note 10, at A2 (internal quotations omitted) (quoting Rabbi David Saperstein). Similarly, Abraham Foxman wrote to the New York Times, "Anti-Semitism has a long and painful history, and the linkage to gun control is a tactic by JPFO to manipulate the fear of anti-Semitism toward their own end. . . . It is a campaign that has been viewed with concern by many in the Jewish community." Foxman, *supra* note 30, section 4, at 14.

35. Lethal Laws, *supra* note 9, at 2.

36. *Id.* at 3–4.

37. *Id.* at 159 (emphasis omitted).

38. *See* Breines, *supra* note 2, at 47–48.

39. *Cf. id.* at 114–15 (explaining that in the early twentieth century, some Jews regarded Jewish gangsters with pride, as a symbol that Jews were becoming normalized into American culture).

40. Camhi, *supra* note 2, at 29.

41. JPFO's leaders have spoken to the NRA, *see* Smyth, *supra* note 10, at 58, and to Radio Free World, an outlet for the militia movement and other fringe right-wing crusades, *see* Vulliamy, supra note 10, at 20. Some parts of the gun culture have been open to such alliance with JPFO, often as a response to charges of anti-Semitism. The leader of the Militia of Montana claimed, "We have good credentials with people who aren't white folks [*sic*]," citing "support from JPFO." William Petroski, *Soviet Threat Lives On, Militia Leaders Believe,* Des Moines Register, Nov. 30. 1995, at 5M (internal quotations omitted) (quoting John Trochman). Similarly, Larry Pratt, President of Gun Owners of America and Chair of the 1996 Buchanan for President Campaign, repudiated charges of anti-Semitism thus: "I am a member of Jews for the Preservation of Firearms Ownership, [which] . . . recently issued a statement saying that JPFO and Gun Owners of America have worked hand-in-hand to restore the Second Amendment rights of all Americans and will continue to do so." Larry Pratt, *Allegations are "Outrageously False,"* Post and Courier (Charleston, S.C.), Feb. 26, 1996, at A9. JPFO has warmly welcomed such overtures: according to Aaron Zelman, "JPFO considers Larry Pratt to be cut of exactly the same cloth as the many righteous gentiles who risked their lives during the Holocaust to rescue Jews from the hands of Nazi murderers." *Id.* (internal quotations omitted) (quoting Aaron Zelman).

42. For example, the Hitler flyer appears at militia gatherings, and the Free Militia reiterates the claim that the 1968 Gun Control Act was copied from the Nazi Weapons Law. See David C. Williams, *The Militia Movement and Second Amendment Revolution: Conjuring with the People,* 81 Cornell L.Rev. 879, 903 (1996). More generally, militia members rely on JPFO to buttress their claim that the federal government is preparing a Nazi-like Holocaust for gun owners. See Camhi, *supra* note 8, at 29.

43. Lethal Laws, *supra* note 9, at 10.

44. *Id.* at 12.

45. *Id.* at 69.

46. *Id.* at 71.

47. *See generally* Daniel Jonah Goldhagen, Hitler's Willing Executioners: Ordinary Germans and the Holocaust (1997); Omer Bartov, Hitler's Army: Soldiers, Nazis, and War in the Third Reich (1991).

48. Lethal Laws, *supra* note 9, at 158–59.

49. *See* James D. Wright et al., Under the Gun: Weapons, Crime, and Violence in America 113–14 (1983).

50. *See* M. Elizabeth Blair and Eva M. Hyatt, *The Marketing of Guns to Women: Factors Influencing Gun-Related Attitudes and Gun Ownership by Women,* 14 J. Pub. Pol. and Marketing 117, 118 (1995).

51. This program is entitled "Refuse To Be a Victim." Advertisements for the program (running in women's magazines like Cosmopolitan and Family Circle) feature a frightened mother holding a small child and walking through an unlit garage. Those who call a toll free number receive a safety tips brochure that includes advice on owning a gun. Interested persons can take an NRA safety course that includes discussion of guns as one option among others. See Ellen Neuborne, *Cashing In on Fear: The NRA Targets Women,* Ms. Magazine, May/June 1994, at 46, 47–49.

52. For example, a Smith and Wesson advertisement features a "serious, thirtyish woman poised at a shooting range, with the headline 'What Would Mom Think Now?'" Blair and Hyatt, *supra* note 50, at 118 (quoting Smith and Wesson advertisment). Another S&W advertisement asserts, "Independence. . . As more women have entered the job market, become heads of households, purchased their own homes, they've taken on a whole new set of responsibilities. For their own decisions. For their own lives. For their own — and their families' — security." Letty Cottin Pogrebin, *Neither Pink nor Cute: Pistols for the Women of America,* The Nation, May 15, 1989, at 658, 668 (internal quotations omitted) (quoting a Smith and Wesson brochure). Colt Firearms' advertisement "pictures a young woman tucking her child into bed. Under this blissful domestic scene are two models of Colt semiautomatic pistols with the headline: 'Self-protection is more than your right. . . it's your responsibility.'" Carrie Goerne, *Gun Companies Target Women; Foes Call It "Marketing to Fear,"* Marketing News, Aug. 31, 1992, at 1. Significantly, the Colt advertisement appeared not in a gun magazine but in Ladies' Home Journal. *See id.*

53. Specifically, the poll found that gun ownership among women had increased 53 percent between 1983 and 1986, to an estimated 12 million women. As Smith and Wesson interprets the poll results, it also found 15.6 million "potential female gun purchasers" in 1989, twice the number for 1983. *See* Tom W. Smith and Robert J. Smith, *Changes in Firearms Ownership Among Women, 1980–1994,* 86 J. Crim. L. and Criminology 133, 136 (1995). Unfortunately, Smith and Wesson has refused to release the poll data for study by independent analysts. *See id.* at 141. Gallup itself has criticized Smith and Wesson for misusing the data by claiming that 15.6 million women are potential buyers. Instead, Gallup explains, the 15.6 million figure refers to women who said that there was "at least some chance" they will buy a gun. In reality, "only 900,000 women could be considered potential purchasers." *Id.* (quoting Gallup response).

54. Relying on data from the National Opinion Research Center at the University of Chicago, two researchers conclude, "According to the best available data, the ownership of firearms among women is not increasing, the gender gap is not closing, and the level of ownership is much lower than commonly stated, with about 11 to 12 percent of women

owning a gun and 4.5 to 8 percent owning a handgun." Smith and Smith, *supra* note 53, at 145. A study conducted by the Indiana University School of Law in 1994 found that gun ownership increased only 2.2 percent from 1980 to 1994. *See* Kelly Shermach, *Gun Advocates Decry Study on Firearms Sales to Women,* Marketing News, Jan. 16, 1994, at 14. The National Science Foundation "says there's been no increase in female gun ownership in the last decade." Colleen O'Connor, *Women's Self-Defense: Big Business,* Dallas Morning News, Oct. 24, 1993, at 1F.

55. *See* Smith and Smith, *supra* note 53, at 144.

56. *See* Smith and Smith, *supra* note 53, at 134–40.

57. *See* Reggie Nadelson, *Magnum Force in High Heels,* Independent (London), May 5, 1992, at 14. The Second Amendment Foundation purchased the magazine in 1989. *See* Peggy Tartaro, *Evolution,* Women and Guns, Mar. 1993, at 50, 50.

58. *See* Lisa M. Bowman, *Aim at Self-Defense, Urges Author of 'Armed and Female',* L.A. Times, Aug. 18, 1995, at B1; Jeanne Beach Eigner, *Women and Guns: They're Aiming at Personal Protection and a Sense of Empowerment,* San Diego Union-Tribune, Nov. 8, 1992, at D1; Sonny Jones, *NRA Launches New Women's Instructor Development Program,* Women and Guns, May 1993, at 39, 39–42; O'Connor, *supra* note 54, at 1F; Paxton Quigley, *An Essay on Revolvers: A Good Choice for Beginners,* Women and Guns, July 1995, at 26, 26–28.

59. *See* Kathryn Casey, *Up in Arms,* Ladies' Home J., Aug. 1995, at 89, 98; Tony Semerad, *Utah Women for Gun Control? Not This Group,* Salt Lake Tribune, Sept. 5, 1994, at A1; Dave Shiflett, *Lock and Load, Ladies: Shooting for Some Common Sense to Gun Ownership Laws,* Rocky Mtn. News (Denver), Feb. 19, 1995, at 58A.

60. *See* Paxton Quigley, Armed and Female, at xvii (1989) [hereinafter cited as Armed and Female]; Paxton Quigley, Not An Easy Target 14 (1995).

61. *See* Armed and Female, *supra* note 60, at 131–38, 171–77.

62. See Bowman, *supra* note 58, at B1; *A Call to Arms,* People, Jan. 10, 1994, at 60, 63.

63. *See, e.g.,* Naomi Wolf, Fire with Fire: The New Female Power and How It Will Change the 21st Century, at xv–xix (1993) [hereinafter cited as Fire with Fire].

64. *Id.* at 53.

65. *Id.* at 54.

66. *Id.* at 216.

67. *Id.* at 217.

68. *Id.* at 219–20.

69. On feminism's desire to empower women, see, e.g., Catharine A. MacKinnon, Toward a Feminist Theory of the State 242 (1989).

70. Mitchell Landsberg, *More Women Turning to Firearms Out of Fear,* L.A. Times, Feb. 21, 1993, at A18 (internal quotations omitted) (quoting a female gun owner).

71. Julianne Versnel Gottlieb, *Dear Self-Reliant Reader,* Women and Guns, Sept. 1994, at 58. I offer the quoted language as just one example of Gottlieb's position; virtually every column of "Dear Self-Reliant Reader" includes similar language about empowerment.

72. Neuborne, *supra* note 51, at 46.

73. Eigner, *supra* note 58, at D1 (internal quotations omitted) (quoting Paxton Quigley).

74. In a survey of the readership of Women and Guns, 68 percent responded that self-

defense was their reason for owning a gun. *See* Peggy Tartaro, *A Picture of Women Gunowners,* Women and Guns, Mar. 1994, at 30, 31.

75. Julianne Versnel Gottlieb explains, "Ironically, perhaps to some, it is the fact that I have small children that has made me more vehement in my stand to be able to defend them and myself." Julianne Versnel Gottlieb, *Dear Self-Reliant Reader,* Women and Guns, April 1993, at 50. Women and Guns declaims, "If [women] are to compete successfully in the business world, they must be free to travel without fear. . . . For too long women have accepted the roll [*sic*] of natural victim. This must stop." Karen McNutt, *Perpetuating the Victim Status of Women,* Women and Guns, Dec. 1991, at 7.

76. Fire with Fire, *supra* note 63, at 220.

77. Katherine Seligman, *Women Taking Up Firearms,* San Francisco Examiner, Jan. 16, 1994, at A1 (internal quotations omitted) (quoting Nancy Bittle, founder of the group Arming Women Against Rape and Endangerment).

78. McNutt, *supra* note 75, at 7.

79. Peggy Tartaro, *From the Editor,* Women and Guns, Aug. 1995, at 6, 7.

80. *See* Katharine T. Bartlett, *Feminist Legal Methods,* 103 Harv. L.Rev. 829, 837–49 (1990).

81. Carol Ruth Silver and Don B. Kates, Jr., *Self-Defense, Handgun Ownership, and the Independence of Women in a Violent, Sexist Society,* in Restricting Handguns: The Liberal Skeptics Speak Out 139, 139 (Don B. Kates ed., 1979).

82. *Id.* at 169.

83. Blair and Hyatt, *supra* note 50, at 123 (internal quotations omitted).

84. Semerad, *supra* note 59, at A1 (paraphrasing the head of Women Against Gun Control).

85. Peggy Tartaro, *From the Editor,* Women and Guns, May 1993, at 6, 6.

86. *New Colorado Group Will SWARM Concealed Carry Reform,* Women and Guns, Feb. 1995, at 8, 8.

87. For a mainstream feminist expression of this idea, see Susan Muller Okin, Justice, Gender, and the Family 124 (1989).

88. Armed and Female, *supra* note 60, at 44–45.

89. Karen McNutt, *Legally Speaking: Comus,* Women and Guns, Feb. 1996, at 48.

90. Ann Jones, *Living with Guns, Playing with Fear,* Ms., May/June 1994, at 38, 42–43.

91. Kathleen Kernicky, *Women and Guns: Shooting Away the Stereotypes,* Buffalo News, Aug. 15, 1995, at C1 (quoting a gun dealer).

92. Ann Japenga, *Would I Be Safer with a Gun?,* Health, Mar./Apr. 1994, at 52, 57 (internal quotations omitted) (quoting Paxton Quigley).

93. Pogrebin, *supra* note 52, at 668.

94. Julianne Versnel Gottlieb, *Dear Self-Reliant Reader,* Women and Guns, June 1993, at 50, 50.

95. Julianne Versnel Gottlieb, *Dear Self-Reliant Reader,* Women and Guns, Oct. 1994, at 58, 58.

96. Fire with Fire, *supra* note 63, at 220.

97. Julianne Versnel Gottlieb, *Dear Self-Reliant Reader,* Women and Guns, Mar. 1994, at 58, 58.

98. *Glamour Asks Why?*, Women and Guns, July 1993, at 8, 9 (internal quotations omitted) (quoting a letter from a reader).

99. Julianne Versnel Gottlieb, *Dear Self-Reliant Reader*, Women and Guns, Sept. 1993, at 50, 50.

100. *Id.*

101. Gottlieb, *supra* note 94, at 50.

102. *Glamour Asks Why, supra* note 98, at 9.

103. *See* Armed and Female, *supra* note 60, at 71–77.

104. *Id.* at 108.

105. Inge Anna Larish, *Why Annie Can't Get Her Gun: A Feminist Perspective on the Second Amendment*, 1996 U. Ill. L.Rev. 467, 473.

106. *Id.* at 504.

107. *See id.*

108. *Id.* at 505.

109. *Id.* at 472, 503.

110. *Id.* at 503.

111. *See* Eugene D. Genovese, Roll, Jordan, Roll: The World the Slaves Made 587–98 (1976).

112. *See* David B. Kopel, The Samurai, the Mountie, and the Cowboy: Should America Adopt the Gun Controls of Other Democracies? 332–35 (1992); Robert J. Cottrol and Raymond T. Diamond, *The Second Amendment: Toward an Afro-Americanist Reconsideration*, 80 Georgetown L.J. 309, 339–342 (1991) [hereinafter cited as *Afro-Americanist Reconsideration*].

113. *See* Hugh Pearson, The Shadow of the Panther: Huey Newton and the Price of Black Power in America 25–28, 35–39 (1994); Robert F. Williams, Negroes with Guns (Marc Schliefer ed., 1962).

114. *See Afro-Americanist Reconsideration, supra* note 112, at 357–58.

115. *See* Kopel, *supra* note 112, at 338–40.

116. Pearson, *supra* note 113, at 110–11.

117. Don B. Kates, Jr., *The Necessity of Access to Firearms by Dissenters and Minorities Whom Government is Unwilling or Unable to Protect,* in Restricting Handguns: The Liberal Skeptics Speak Out 185, 186 (Don B. Kates, Jr. ed., 1979). Similarly, John Salter reflects on his own experience: "There is no question but that the known existence of pervasive firearms ownership in Southern Black communities prevented much (though not all) massively violent racist retaliation." John R. Salter, Jr., *Social Justice Community Organizing and the Necessity for Protecting Firearms,* in The Gun Culture and Its Enemies 19, 20 (William R. Tonso ed., 1990).

118. *See* Kopel, *supra* note 112, at 336–38; Don B. Kates, Jr., *Toward a History of Handgun Prohibition in the United States,* in Restricting Handguns: The Liberal Skeptics Speak Out, *supra* note 117, at 7, 14–20.

119. *See* Kates, *Toward a History of Handgun Prohibition, supra* note 118, at 25.

120. *Id.* at 20 (quoting B. Bruce-Briggs, *The Great American Gun War,* in The Gun Control Debate: You Decide 63, 76 (Lee Nisbett ed., 1990).

121. The primary work is *The Second Amendment: Toward an Afro-Americanist Reconsideration, supra* note 112. More recently, Cottrol and Diamond completed a

second chapter in what they describe as "our ongoing effort to explore the connections between racial conflict in American history and the evolution of the right to bear arms in American constitutionalism." Robert J. Cottrol and Raymond T. Diamond, *"Never Intended to Be Applied to the White Population": Firearms Regulation and Racial Disparity—The Redeemed South's Legacy to a National Jurisprudence,* 70 Chi.-Kent L.Rev. 1307 (1995).

122. *Toward an Afro-Americanist Reconsideration* has appeared, inter alia, in Guns: Who Should Have Them? 127 (David B. Kopel ed.,1995); Safeguarding Liberty: The Constitution and Citizen Militias 135 (Larry Pratt ed.,1995). In a concurring opinion, Justice Thomas also cited the same article in *Printz v. United States,* 521 U.S. 898, 938 n.2 (1997).

123. *Afro-Americanist Reconsideration, supra* note 112, at 319.

124. *See id.* at 321–27.

125. *Id.* at 327.

126. *Id.* at 328.

127. *Id.* at 330.

128. *Id.* at 331 (footnote omitted).

129. *See* Carl Bogus, *Race, Riots, and Guns,* 66 S. Cal. L.Rev. 1365, 1367–74 (1993).

130. *Afro-Americanist Reconsideration, supra* note 112, at 332.

131. *See id.* at 331–32.

132. *Id.* at 332.

133. *See id.* at 339–42.

134. *Id.*

135. *See id.* at 332–35, 342–45.

136. *Id.* at 349.

137. *Id.* at 358.

138. *Id.* at 360.

139. *Id.* at 359.

140. *Id.* at 361.

141. *Id.* at 359.

142. Pearson, *supra* note 113, at 210 (internal quotations omitted) (quoting Saul Alinsky).

143. *See* Epstein, *supra* note 10, at 1A.

144. Michael Walzer, On Toleration 18–19 (1997).

145. *See* Walter Laqueur, Black Hundred: The Rise of the Extreme Right in Russia 119–296 (1993); David Remnick, Resurrection: The Struggle for a New Russia 49 (1997).

146. *See, e.g.,* Misha Glenny, The Fall of Yugoslavia: The Third Balkan War 12–14 (1992);. Robert D. Kaplan, Balkan Ghosts: A Journey Through History 39–40 (1993).

147. For non-European examples of ethnic hatred displacing or arising in the stead of strong state authority, see Robert D. Kaplan, The Ends of the Earth: A Journey at the Dawn of the 21st Century (1996).

148. *See* Lethal Laws, *supra* note 9, at vi (discussing Robert Melson, Revolution and Genocide: On the Origins of the Armenian Genocide and the Holocaust (1992)).

149. *See* Melson, *supra* note 148, at 18, 278.

150. *Id.* at 267.

151. *Id.* at 268–69.

152. Ted Robert Gurr, *The History of Protest, Rebellion, and Reform in America: An Overview,* in 2 Violence in America: Protest, Rebellion, Reform 11, 14–15 (Ted Robert Gurr ed., 1989).

153. Hugh Davis Graham, *Violence, Social Theory, and the Historians: The Debate Over Consensus and Culture in America,* in 2 Violence in America, *supra* note 152, at 329, 342. Graham is paraphrasing the analysis of Richard Hofstadter, one of America's great historians albeit a partisan in the gun culture debate, in his introduction to American Violence: A Documentary History 3, 10–12 (Richard Hofstadter and Michael Wallace eds., 1970). A generation of historians has rediscovered the prevalence of ethnic and racial violence in this country's story. A partial bibliography would include David H. Bennett, The Party of Fear: The American Far Right from Nativism to the Militia Movement (1995); T. J. Davis, A Rumor of Revolt: The 'Great Negro Plot' in Colonial New York (1985); Michael Feldberg, The Turbulent Era: Riot and Disoder in Jacksonian America (1980); Paul A. Gilje, The Road to Mobocracy: Popular Disorder in New York City, 1763–1834 (1987); Thomas P. Slaughter, Bloody Dawn: The Christiana Riot and Racial Violence in the Antebellum North (1991); Catherine McNicol Stock, Rural Radicals: Righteous Rage in the American Grain (1996).

154. Gurr, *supra* note 152, at 18.

155. *See* James Button, *The Outcomes of Contemporary Black Protest and Violence,* in 2 Violence in America: Protest, Rebellion, Reform, *supra* note 152, at 286, 288–91; Doug McAdam and Kelly Moore, *The Politics of Black Insurgency, 1930–1975,* in 2 Violence in America, *supra* note 152, at 255, 271–74.

156. *See* McAdam and Moore, *supra* note 155, at 280–82; Button, *supra* note 155, at 293–94, 297–99, 302–03.

157. *See, e.g.,* Michael Kazin, The Populist Persuasion: An American History 34–42, 52–77 (1995).

158. *See, e.g., id.* at 1–2; Stock, *supra* note 153, at 3–5, 8.

159. *See, e.g.,* Kazin, *supra* note 157, at 2, 7, 14–15, 34–36, 40–41; Stock, *supra* note 153, at 5–7, 10–13, 128–31, 139–42, 148–49.

160. *See, e.g.,* Kazin, *supra* note 157, at 21–22.

161. *See, e.g.,* Kazin, *supra* note 157, at 40–41; Stock, *supra* note 153, at 6, 128–30.

162. *See, e.g.,* Kazin, *supra* note 157, at 4–5, 222–86; Stock, *supra* note 153, at 152–53.

163. *See* Kazin, *supra* note 157, at 34–36; Stock, *supra* note 153, at 110–11, 131–35, 142.

164. Catherine McNicol Stock powerfully describes this fusion of promise and threat in rural populism: "The roots of violence, racism, and hatred can be and have been nourished in the same soil and from the same experiences that generated rural movements for democracy and equality. In many places and at many times in the American past, the best and worst, the most forgiving and most vengeful, the most egalitarian and most authoritarian, the brightest and darkest visions of American life were alive in the same men's souls, nurtured at the same dinner tables, learned in the same schools, and preached from the same pulpits. Not two sets of beliefs, then, but two expressions of the

same beliefs and circumstances bound left and right together in an unwavering, desperate, synthetic embrace." Stock, *supra* note 153, at 148.

165. *See* Kazin, *supra* note 157, at 34–36.

166. *See, e.g.,* Alison M. Jaggar, Feminist Politics and Human Nature 28–34; (1983) Patricia J. Williams, The Alchemy of Race and Rights 146–56 (1991); Richard A. Epstein, *The Interior Diaspora,* N.Y. Times, Aug. 10, 1997, section 7, at 26 (book review). Recently, this dislike of populist ideologies has manifested itself in the lukewarm reception that civic republicanism has received among outgroup thinkers. *See, e.g.,* Derrick Bell and Preeta Bansal, *The Republican Revival and Racial Politics,* 97 Yale L.J. 1609 (1988); Linda K. Kerber, *Making Republicanism Useful,* 97 Yale L.J. 1663 (1988).

167. *See, e.g.,* Stock, *supra* note 153, at 89–91, 109–42, 163–76.

168. *See id.* at 124, 128, 131, 140–42, 163, 171.

169. For that reason, I do not believe that my position is necessarily inconsistent with the view of many Critical Race theorists that racism will never cease and the struggle against it must therefore be perpetual. *See, e.g.,* Derrick Bell, *Racial Realism,* 24 Conn. L.Rev. 363, 378 (1992). It may, however, require a belief that racial conditions can be meaningfully improved—a belief that some Critical Race theorists may not share. *See id.* at 373–74.

170. *See, e.g.,* Karl P. Adler et al., *Firearms Violence and Public Health: Limiting the Availability of Guns,* 271 JAMA 1281 (1994); Don B. Kates, et al., *Guns and Public Health: Epidemic of Violence or Pandemic of Propaganda,* 62 Tenn. L.Rev. 513 (1995).

171. *See, e.g.,* Susan H. Williams, *Feminist Legal Epistemology,* 8 Berkeley Women's L.J. 63, 68–72, 72 n.28 (1993).

172. *See, e.g.,* Walzer, *supra* note 144, at 87–90.

173. In claiming that a shared culture on the organization of violence is necessary for the safety of outgroups, I do not wish to claim that the culture must or should be controlled, produced, and limited by the state. In that sense, following Robert Cover, *see* Robert Cover, *Nomos and Narrative,* in Narrative, Violence, and the Law: The Essays of Robert Cover 95, 141–44 (Martha Minow, Michael Ryan, Austin Sarat eds. 1995), I do not wish to privilege state tales of violence over others. Also, it bears noting that outgroups might reject a protective shared culture for reasons other than safety, such as fidelity to a distinct religious tradition. *See* Cover, *supra,* at 121–31, 144–55. In that case, however, they have chosen fidelity over safety, in contrast to what these outgroup theories claim to do.

174. *See, e.g.,* Thomas Hobbes, Leviathan 228 (C. B. MacPherson ed., 1985) (a commonwealth is "One Person, of whose Acts a great Multitude, by mutuall Covenants one with another, have made themselves every one the Author, to the end he may use the strength and means of them all, as he shall think expedient, for their Peace and Common Defence"); John Locke, *Second Treatise,* in Two Treatises of Government 344 (Peter Laslett ed., 1960) ("The end of Civil Society, being to avoid, and remedy those inconveniencies of the State of Nature, which necessarily follow from every man being Judge in his own Case, by setting a known Authority, to which every one of the Society may Appeal"); John Rawls, A Theory of Justice 5 (1971) ("If men's inclination to self-interest makes their vigilance against one another necessary, their public sense of justice makes their secure association together possible").

175. Alternatively, the outgroup theorists might argue that we ought to privilege the Framers' perspective, which, in the view of these theorists, reads the amendment as a personal right to arms. Again, this rendition of the outgroups' argument seems untrue to their intent: if the Framers' perspective really does control, then the perspective of outgroups is simply irrelevant in interpreting the Second Amendment — at best an interesting digression, rather than a reason to read the provision in a certain way. Both JPFO and the women and guns movement, moreover, seem largely uninterested in examining the Framers' intent. And Cottrol and Diamond expressly acknowledge that the Framers valued the amendment as a protection for a revolutionary majority, rather than as a protection for hated minorities.

176. *See, e.g.*, Cass Sunstein, *Beyond the Republican Revival,* 97 Yale L.J. 1539, 1542–45, 1549–50 (1988).

177. *See, e.g.*, Francis Fukuyama, Trust: The Social Virtues and the Creation of Prosperity 3–57 (1995); Robert D. Putnam, Making Democracy Work: Civic Traditions in Modern Italy 167–80 (1993); Adam Seligman, The Idea of Civil Society 169–96 (1992).

178. *See generally* Kevin Toolis, Rebel Hearts: Journey Within the IRA's Soul (1995); Glenny, *supra* note 146.

179. *See, e.g.*, Carl T. Rowan, The Coming Race War in America: A Wake-up Call 29–35 (1996).

180. *Afro-Americanist Reconsideration, supra* note 112, at 357 n.273 (citations omitted).

181. *See, e.g.*, Robert H. Wiebe, Self-Rule: A Cultural History of American Democracy 15, 72–75 (1995).

182. *See* Eric Foner, Reconstruction: America's Unfinished Revolution 1863–1877, at 454–59, 569–75, 582–83, 587–88, 593–95 (1988).

183. *See, e.g.*, Okin, *supra* note 87, at 124.

184. *See, e.g.*, Robert J. Cottrol and Raymond T. Diamond, *The Fifth Auxiliary Right,* 104 Yale L.J. 991, 1011 (1995) (book review) ("Far from being inferior rights, in the practical constitutional sense, Blackstone understood these auxiliary rights [such as the right to arms] as the mechanisms that protected the subjects' natural or inherent rights."); Miguel A. Faria, *Women, Guns, and the Medical Literature — A Raging Debate,* Women and Guns, Oct. 1994, at 14, 15 (asserting that the "Second Amendment is the right that secures all others").

185. For an example of such a vision, see Cover, *supra* note 173, at 101–03.

Chapter 8. The Silent Crisis

1. *See, e.g.*, Thomas L, Pangle, The Spirit of Modern Republicanism: The Moral Vision of the American Founders and the Philosophy of Locke (1988); J. G. A. Pocock, The Machiavellian Moment (1975); Steven Watts, The Republic Reborn: War and the Making of Liberal America, 1790–1820 (1987); Gordon S. Wood, The Creation of the American Republic 1776–1787 (1969).

2. Joseph Story, 3 Commentaries on the Constitution of the United States 746–47 (1833).

3. *See, e.g.,* John Higham, Strangers in the Land: Patterns of American Nativism, 1860–1925 (1988); Kenneth L. Karst, Belonging to America (1989).

4. *See, e.g.,* The Countryside in the Age of Capitalist Transformation: Essays in the Social History of Rural America (Steven Hahn and Jonathan Prude eds., 1985).

5. *See* E. J. Dionne, Why Americans Hate Politics (1991); James Buchanan and Gordon Tullock, The Calculus of Consent: Logical Foundations of Constitutional Democracy (1962); George J. Stigler, *The Theory of Economic Regulation*, 2 Bell J. Econ. and Mgmt. Sci. 3 (1971).

6. *See, e.g.,* David C. Williams and Susan H. Williams, *Volitionalism and Religious Liberty*, 76 Cornell L.Rev. 769, 776–89, 880–81 (1991).

7. *See* Robert N. Bellah et al., Habits of the Heart: Individualism and Commitment in American Life 75–81 (updated edition 1996).

8. *Id.* at xi.

9. *Id.* at xxx.

10. *See* Robert D. Putnam, Bowling Alone: The Collapse and Revival of American Community 27 (2000).

11. *See id.* at 33–36, 247–76.

12. *See* Akhil Reed Amar, The Bill of Rights: Creation and Reconstruction 3–133 (1998).

13. *See id.* at 137–294.

14. *See id.* at 261–66.

15. *See* Gordon S. Wood, The Radicalism of the American Revolution 294 (1992); U.S. Const., amends. XV, XIX.

16. *Reynolds v. Sims,* 377 U.S. 533, 562 (1963).

17. *Id.* at 561–62.

18. *Id.* at 565.

19. *Bush v. Gore,* 531 U.S. 98 (2000).

20. *See id.* at 106–07.

21. *Id.* at 106.

22. *Id.* at 107 (internal citation omitted).

23. *See* Wood, *supra* note 1, at 562.

24. Samuel Issacharoff, Pamela S. Karlan, and Richard H. Pildes, The Law of Democracy: Legal Structure of the Political Process 177 (1998).

25. *Reynolds v. Sims,* 377 U.S. 533, 574 (1963).

26. U.S. Const., amend. I.

27. *See, e.g.,* Amar, *supra* note 12, at 32–33, 246–48; Thomas J. Curry, The First Freedoms: Church and State in America to the Passage of the First Amendment 217–21 (1986).

28. *See Everson v. Board of Education,* 330 U.S. 1, 15 (1947).

29. *See id.* at 15, 34, 246–54.

30. Robert Cover, *Nomos and Narrative,* in Narrative, Violence, and the Law: The Essays of Robert Cover 95, 101–02 (Martha Minow, Michael Ryan, Austin Sarat eds., 1995).

31. *Zorach v. Clauson,* 343 U.S. 306 (1952).

32. *Id.* at 312–13.

33. *Id.* at 313.

34. *Id.* at 314.

35. *Bradwell v. Illinois,* 83 U.S. (16 Wall.) 130 (1873).

36. *Id.* at 141 (concurring opinion of J. Bradley, joined by JJ. Swayne and Field).

37. *Id.* at 61–62.

38. *Frontiero v. Richardson,* 411 U.S. 677, 682 (1973).

39. *Id.* at 687.

40. *Id.* at 684.

41. *Id.* at 685.

42. *Id.* at 686.

43. Justice Brennan cites only to a law journal article describing recent changes in Equal Protection doctrine, rather than to any empirical evidence. See *id.* at 686 n.18 (citing *Developments in the Law—Equal Protection,* 82 Harv. L.Rev. 1065, 1173–74 (1969)).

44. *See United States v. Virginia,* 518 U.S. 515 (1996).

Chapter 9. Redeeming the People

1. Sanford Levinson, *The Embarrassing Second Amendment,* 99 Yale L.J. 637, 639, 641–42 (1989).

2. *Id.* at 642.

3. Michael J. Quinlan, *Is There a Neutral Justification for Refusing to Implement the Second Amendment or Is the Supreme Court Just "Gun Shy"?* 22 Capital U. L.Rev. 641, 692 (1993).

4. Elaine Scarry, *War and the Social Contract: Nuclear Policy, Distribution, and the Right to Bear Arms,* 139 U. Pa. L.Rev. 1257, 1281–82, 1301–02 (1991).

5. *See* Steven Greenhouse, *Helms Takes New Swipe at Clinton, Then Calls It Mistake,* N.Y. Times, Nov. 23, 1994, at A19.

6. 475 U.S. 503 (1986).

7. *Id.* at 506 (citations omitted).

8. *Id.* at 507 (citations omitted).

9. *Id.* at 508.

10. *Id.* at 510.

11. Thomas E. Ricks, Making the Corps (1997).

12. *Id.* at 274 (quoting Samuel Huntington, The Soldier and the State (1981)).

13. *Id.* at 276 (1997) (quoting Adm. Stanley Arthur).

14. *Id.* at 280.

15. *Id.* at 283.

16. *See Counting the Vote Update: A Hearing in the Florida Supreme Court,* N.Y. Times, Nov. 21, 2000, at A19.

17. Ricks, *supra* note 11, at 275–76 (quoting Harvard political scientist Michael Desch).

18. *Id.* at 292–93.

19. *Id.* at 293–94.

20. *Id.* at 294.

21. *Id.* at 294–95.

22. *Id.* at 295.

23. *Id.* at 22.

24. *Id.* at 280.

25. *Id.* at 276, 278, 285–86.

26. *Id.* at 296.

27. Gary Hart, The Minuteman: Reviving an Army of the People (1998).

28. *See id.* at 5.

29. *See id.* at 164–65.

30. *See id.* at 149–52.

31. *Id.* at 5.

32. *See id.* at 77–115.

33. *See id.* at 21–22, 24, 131–32, 170–71.

34. *See id.* at 7, 60–75.

35. *Id.* at 12.

36. *Id.* at 148.

37. *Id.* at 6.

38. *Id.* at 7.

39. *Id.* at 73.

40. *Id.* at 170.

41. *Id.* at 73.

42. *Id.* at 23.

43. *Id.* at 77.

44. *See id.* at 7, 25, 171.

45. *Id.* at 152.

46. *Id.* at 25.

47. *Id.* at 132 (quoting John McAuley Palmer, Statesmanship or War 74 (1927)).

48. *Id.*

49. *Id.* at 21–22.

50. *Id.* at 170–71.

51. *See, e.g.,* Robert Wuthnow, Poor Richard's Principle: Recovering the American Dream Through the Moral Dimension of Work, Business, and Money 8–10, 12 (1996).

52. *See* Frank I. Michelman, *Morality, Identity, and "Constitutional Patriotism,"* 76 Denver L. Rev. 1009 (1999).

53. *Id.* at 1017.

54. *Id.* at 1022.

55. *Id.* at 1026.

56. *Id.*

57. *See* John McPhee, La Place de la Concorde Suisse (1983).

58. This bit of folklore is especially prominent in novels and movies. For examples, see Philip Caputo, A Rumor of War (1977); Susan F. Schaefer, Buffalo Afternoon (1989); and Neil Simon's film Biloxi Blues (Universal, 1988). Kenneth Karst notes the same phenomenon. Kenneth L. Karst, *The Pursuit of Manhood and the Desegregation of the Armed Forces,* 38 UCLA L.Rev. 499, 501 (1991).

59. *See, e.g.,* Gerald F. Linderman, Embattled Courage 234–36 (1987); Reid Mitchell, Civil War Soldiers 17–18 (1988).

60. *See, e.g.,* William F. Buckley, Jr., Gratitude (1990); Charles Moskos, A Call to Civic Service (1988); National Service (Williamson M. Evers ed., 1990). The roster of those on record supporting the idea includes senators and ex-senators Sam Nunn, Charles Robb, Edward Kennedy, and George Mitchell. *See* National Service, *supra,* at xvii.

61. *See* Amitai Etzioni, An Immodest Agenda: Rebuilding America Before the Twenty-First Century 160 (1983); Buckley, *supra* note 60, at 28–30.

62. *See* Amitai Etzioni, *Comments,* in National Service, *supra* note 60, at 154; Tim W. Ferguson, *Comments,* in National Service, *supra* note 60, at 72–73; Don Wycliff, *Discussion,* in National Service, *supra* note 60, at 260; Moskos, *supra* note 60, at 4–6; Buckley, *supra* note 60, at 8.

63. *See, e.g.,* National Service, *supra* note 60, at xix–xx.

64. *See* Benjamin R. Barber, *Discussion,* in National Service, *supra* note 60, at 80.

65. Frank Michelman, *Law's Republic,* 97 Yale L.J. 1493, 1531 (1988).

66. *See, e.g.,* Seymour Martin Lipset, American Exceptionalism: A Double-Edged Sword 31, 50–51 (1996).

67. The Constitution has thus functioned as a kind of civil religion. *See* Sanford Levinson, Constitutional Faith 9–17 (1988); Robert A. Burt, *Constitutional Law and the Teaching of the Parables,* 93 Yale L.J. 455, 467–489 (1984); Thomas C. Grey, *The Constitution as Scripture,* 37 Stan. L.Rev. 1, 3 (1984).

68. Robert N. Bellah, Richard Madsen, William M. Sullivan, Ann Swidler, and Steven M. Tipton, Habits of the Heart: Individualism and Commitment in American Life (updated ed. 1996).

69. *See id.* at ix, 20, 27–28.

70. *See id.* at 20–26.

71. *Id.* at ix.

72. *Id.* at xxx.

73. *Id.* at xxxi.

74. Michael J. Sandel, Democracy's Discontent: America in Search of a Public Philosophy (1996).

75. *Id.* at 322.

76. *Id.* at 351.

77. *See, e.g.,* Bellah, *supra* note 68; Todd Gitlin, The Twilight of Common Dreams: Why America is Wracked By Culture Wars (1995); Sandel, *supra* note 74.

78. Robert Cover, *Nomos and Narrative,* in Narrative, Violence, and the Law: The Essays of Robert Cover 95 (Martha Minow, Michael Ryan, and Austin Sarat eds., 1995).

79. *Id.* at 95–96.

80. *Id.* at 101.

81. *Id.* at 98–99.

82. *Id.* at 103.

83. *Id.* at 150–52.

84. *Id.* at 105–06.

85. *Id.* at 106.

86. *Id.* at 144.

87. *Id.*

88. *Id.* at 106.

89. *Id.* at 155.

90. *See id.* at 121–31.

91. *Id.* at 131.

92. *Id.* at 149.

93. *Id.* at 112.

94. *Id.* at 142.

95. *Id.* at 144.

96. *Id.*

97. *Id.*

98. Michelman, *supra* note 52, at 1026.

99. Cover, *supra* note 78, at 172.

100. *Id.* at 101 (footnote omitted).

101. Claus Offe, *How Can We Trust Our Fellow Citizens?*, in Democracy and Trust 42, 47–48 (Mark E. Warren ed., 1999).

102. *See* Offe, *supra* note 101, at 55–57; Eric M. Uslaner, *Democracy and Social Capital*, in Democracy and Trust, *supra* note 101, at 121, 123–26.

103. Offe, *supra* note 101, at 57.

104. Uslaner, *supra* note 102, at 122.

105. Mark E. Warren, *Introduction*, in Democracy and Trust, *supra* note 101, at 1, 14.

106. Offe, *supra* note 101, at 70.

107. Jane Mansbridge, *Altruistic Trust*, in Democracy and Trust, *supra* note 101, at 291, 292.

108. *See* Ronald Inglehart, *Trust, Well-Being, and Democracy*, in Democracy and Trust, *supra* note 101, at 88, 96, 103–04; Mansbridge, *supra* note 107, at 303–06; Uslaner, *supra* note 102, at 138–40, 141, 144–47; Warren, *supra* note 105, at 11–12.

109. *See, e.g.*, Rogers M. Smith, Civic Ideals: Conflicting Visions of Citizenship in U.S. History (1997).

Index